INTRODUCTION TO THE PRACTICE OF PSYCHOANALYTIC PSYCHOTHERAPY

INTRODUCTION TO THE PRACTICE OF PSYCHOANALYTIC PSYCHOTHERAPY

by

Alessandra Lemma

WILEY

Published 2003 by John Wiley & Sons Ltd, The Atrium, Southern Gate, Chichester,
West Sussex PO19 8SQ, England

Telephone (+44) 1243 779777

Email (for orders and customer service enquiries): cs-books@wiley.co.uk
Visit our Home Page on www.wileyeurope.com or www.wiley.com

Reprinted January 2006

Other Wiley Editorial Offices

John Wiley & Sons Inc., 111 River Street, Hoboken, NJ 07030, USA

Jossey-Bass, 989 Market Street, San Francisco, CA 94103-1741, USA

Wiley-VCH Verlag GmbH, Boschstr. 12, D-69469 Weinheim, Germany

John Wiley & Sons Australia Ltd, 33 Park Road, Milton, Queensland 4064, Australia

John Wiley & Sons (Asia) Pte Ltd, 2 Clementi Loop #02-01, Jin Xing Distripark, Singapore 129809

John Wiley & Sons Canada Ltd, 22 Worcester Road, Etobicoke, Ontario, Canada M9W 1L1

Wiley also publishes its books in a variety of electronic formats. Some content that appears
in print may not be available in electronic books.

Library of Congress Cataloging-in-Publication Data

Lemma, Alessandra.
  Introduction to the practice of psychoanalytic psychotherapy / by Alessandra Lemma.
    p. cm.
  Includes bibliographical references and index.
  ISBN 0-470-84458-2 (paper : alk. paper)
  1. Psychoanalysis. I. Title.

RC504 .L45 2003
616.89′17–dc21   2002156448

British Library Cataloguing in Publication Data

A catalogue record for this book is available from the British Library

ISBN 10: 0-470-84458-2 (PB)   ISBN 13: 978-0-470-84458-8 (PB)

Typeset in 10/12pt Palatino by Laserwords Private Limited, Chennai, India

In doing psychoanalysis I aim at: keeping alive; keeping well, keeping awake. I aim at being myself and behaving myself. Having begun an analysis, I expect to continue with it, to survive it, and to end it. (Winnicott, 1962: 166)

CONTENTS

ABOUT THE AUTHOR

Alessandra Lemma is a consultant clinical psychologist in the Adolescent Department at the Tavistock Clinic and in the Psychology Treatment & Assessment Service at Camden & Islington Mental Health and Social Care Trust. She is also an honorary senior lecturer in clinical psychology at University College London. She is trained as an adult psychoanalytic psychotherapist.

She is the author of the following books on psychology and psychotherapy: *Starving to Live: The Paradox of Anorexia Nervosa* (Central Publishing, 1994), *Invitation to Psychodynamic Psychology* (Whurr, 1995), *Introduction to Psychopathology* (Sage, 1996), *Humour on the Couch* (Whurr, 2000) and *The Perversion of Loss: Psychoanalytic Perspectives on Trauma* (Ed. with S. Levy: Whurr, in preparation).

PREFACE

This book has been largely inspired by teaching psychoanalysis to trainee clinical psychologists and other clinicians from different mental health backgrounds, who were often approaching psychoanalysis with little knowledge or experience of it. Even so, many were primed to be critical of it on the basis of prior learning or exposure to psychoanalytic interventions that had been experienced as unhelpful. I approach the subject matter in this book largely with this audience in mind, remembering some of the questions my students have put to me over the years and the criticisms they have voiced. The book is intended primarily as a practical, clinical text for workers in the mental health field who are relative newcomers to the practice of psychoanalytic therapy. It does nevertheless assume a core background in one of the mental health professions, clinical experience with patients and a degree of familiarity with the practice of psychotherapy and/or counselling more generally.

Teaching psychoanalysis has helped remind me that when we are trained psychoanalytically it is all too easy to forget that our practice is based on so much that is taken for granted, and on the idiosyncrasies of our own personal analytic experiences with training therapists and supervisors, that it is unsurprising when the newcomer to it finds the ideas confusing and the theories difficult to translate into practice. Teaching is indeed a salutary experience – unless we teach the converted – since it forces us to revisit cherished assumptions. It has taught me to beware the dangers of overvalued ideas, though I am sure that while reading this book you will come across several ideas with which I am all too reluctant to part company.

A word of caution is called for before embarking on this book – I am a synthesiser. In this book, I have traded specificity for generalities and subtle differences in theoretical concepts for common strands between the many psychoanalytic theories that are available. It will thus probably disappoint if you are in search of sophisticated critiques of particular metapsychologies or of the philosophical underpinnings of psychoanalysis. This is not the aim of this book. Rather, my efforts are directed at developing a guiding, yet always provisional, framework for my own clinical work, based as it is on my understanding of theory and on what "works" in my own clinical practice.[1] To this end, I draw on several psychoanalytic theories as I have yet to come across one model or theory that can satisfactorily account for all my analytic work.

In this book I am concerned with articulating my "private" clinical theory (Sandler, 1983) and its implications for technique. In some of the chapters I summarise some of the ideas that guide my work as "practice guidelines". These are not intended to be in any way prescriptive but merely reflect my own attempt to make explicit how I approach my interventions, and to share the technical teachings that my own clinical supervisors have imparted to me over the years. This book pools together these experiences into a working framework that is inevitably personal and evolving. In light of this, I can make no claims that what I do and what I have written about is empirically sound, but I have endeavoured, wherever possible, to anchor my practice in the empirical research that I am familiar with.

Because this is an introductory text at the end of each chapter, I have made some suggestions for further reading which will help extend the study of the concepts and ideas presented. If approaching this book with little prior knowledge of psychoanalytic ideas, it will probably be more helpful to read it sequentially as each chapter relies on an understanding of concepts discussed in the preceding chapter.

In this book I will outline key psychoanalytic concepts as they relate to practice guided by the psychoanalytic model that I espouse, namely, an object relational model. In doing so, I am clear, however, that the interventions that I experience as consonant with this model and that lend some coherence to my clinical work are, for the most part, awaiting empirical validation. I am all too aware too that my interventions could be justified by a diverse range of psychoanalytic theoretical orientations. While I cannot take any credit for the ideas that I shall refer to, I do take responsibility for the way they inform my practice and how I present them in this book.

One of my explicit agendas in writing this book is to encourage psychoanalytic work within public health service contexts by hopefully providing

---

[1] I am mindful here of Sandler's (1983) helpful, if challenging, distinction between public and private theories. Private theories, according to Sandler, are preconscious and relate more directly to clinical work. He suggests that they do not logically follow from the stated public theories that we consciously subscribe to.

an accessible text that will stimulate those who would otherwise be put off by the seeming complexity of psychoanalytic therapy. This book aims to demystify psychoanalytic practice. In so doing, it will strike some psycho-analytic practitioners as oversimplifying concepts and as implying that there are such things as psychoanalytic "skills" that can be taught to those who may not have either the inclination or the funds to undertake lengthy psychoanalytic trainings.

The experience of undertaking one's own personal analysis is a key aspect of what it means to work psychoanalytically. This experience is unique. It is not possible, for example, to teach either through writing or lectures what it means to be vulnerable or dependent on another person, what it means to be in the grip of powerful projections or to long to identify with another person. The kind of self-knowledge that personal analysis fosters is indispensable to all those who wish to understand another person's unconscious. However, to set up psychoanalysis as the only path to self-knowledge is to set it up as an idealised object. In my work as a trainer, I have been repeatedly impressed by the perceptiveness of some of the students who have never even been near a couch. Their reports of work with patients could be easily confused with those of a seasoned therapist in training. This should not surprise us. After all, as Etchegoyen (1991) wryly observes, after a good analysis we are better than previously but not necessarily better than others.

It seems to me that even those practitioners who have not undergone a long personal analysis or training can make good use of psychoanalytic ideas. Moreover, the argument that there are no teachable psychoanalytic skills as such – or certainly not ones that can be safely handled without years of personal analysis to support their use – does not stand up to close scrutiny. Nor does it facilitate the wider dissemination of analytic ideas and practice.

Analytic trainings appear to operate on the implicit assumption that students learn how to work analytically through a process of osmo-sis. It is true that many important aspects of analytic work can only be learnt through experience either in supervision or in our own per-sonal analysis. However, this method of learning does not encourage the articulation of why we do what we do and it does not reach those clinicians who are not undertaking analytic trainings. Making psycho-analytic ideas and their application more accessible requires that we operationalise our terms and make explicit what it is that we think we do rather than eschew this challenge by arguing that it is difficult to teach psychoanalytic skills in less than the requisite minimum four years of analytic training. I am aware that in saying this I may be saying, for some people at least, that psychoanalytic therapy should be more like cognitive behaviour therapy with its skills manuals. Although I do not think that the therapeutic encounter can ever be reduced to a manualised therapy, much can be learnt from those approaches that attempt, however imperfectly, to pin down what it is that we do in therapy so that we may achieve a more sophisticated understanding of those factors that facilitate psychic change.

I wish to make it clear that I am not suggesting that analytic training that prepares people for intensive work with patients can be replaced by a short series of seminars or reading this book. However, I do believe in the importance of once-weekly therapeutic work, which is the mainstay of analytic practice within public health service settings. For the most part, this work is carried out by the least experienced clinicians, many of whom do not have any formal training in psychoanalytic therapy but undertake this work under supervision, for example, doctors and psychologists. This work is very valuable and requires of those who are analytically trained a willingness to approach the teaching of psychoanalytic practice differently, by specifying more clearly the implicit rules that guide practice and by being upfront about the fact that, for the most part, these are not based on research evidence, but mostly reflect therapeutic styles that will appeal more to some and less to others.

If more patients within public health service contexts are to benefit from the rich insights that can be gleaned from psychoanalysis, we have to find ways of making psychoanalysis more accessible to those who work in these settings and who will be at the sharp end of service delivery. Of course, these individuals will not be equipped to carry out an intensive therapy. This is not the goal of teaching them psychoanalytic skills. Rather, the goal is to impart an understanding of the unconscious mind and some of the techniques that help the therapist to translate her understanding into the tools that will help the patient to be relieved of psychic pain. It is my hope that this book will go some small way towards fulfilling this aim.

On a personal note

Over the thirteen years that I have been on my analytic journey, I have travelled through Freudian and Kleinian personal analyses with a few supervisory stopovers in the middle ground of the Independents. My analytic journey has been, and continues to be, enriching. Each experience has taught me many things of value and it has raised many questions, some uncomfortable, not only about myself but also about psychoanalysis as a method of therapy, as an institution and as a profession.

There are several different versions of psychoanalysis. In this book I have approached some chapters at times from different perspectives, pooling together insights gleaned from divergent theoretical orientations within psychoanalysis. Perhaps this makes me a pluralist or an integrationist though I am never sure what these terms really mean. If they mean that I think there are different ways of understanding the human mind and the process of therapy, that is true. If they mean that I have difficulty identifying primarily with only one school of psychoanalysis, that is true too. If they mean that I believe that when I work with a patient what matters is a flexible approach that is guided by what the patient needs at any given moment rather than what a particular theory prescribes, that is also true. Perhaps as someone who had to learn different languages to adapt to the changing cultural landscapes of my childhood, I have an ingrained sense of contingency within me that prevents me from adopting any therapeutic language as final. Whichever model of the mind or of psychotherapy we espouse, it is no more and no less than a metaphor. This would not be a cause for concern were it not for the fact that metaphors have a dangerous habit of being reified into statements of truth. Any beliefs or metaphors that are so reified are usually those that are integral to our identity and their presence or absence serves as a criterion for sorting out "good" from "bad" (Rorty, 1989). But we have to face up to the fact that we are not in possession of criteria for choosing between these different metaphors: we can only compare languages or metaphors with one another. Debate is important. Difference is dynamic and keeps us thinking. The danger lies in using difference to justify the superiority of one theory or approach over another.

On terminology and clinical vignettes

For the sake of clarity, I have chosen to refer to the patient as "he", to the therapist as "she" and to the baby and child as "she" unless otherwise specified. I shall refer to "psychoanalytic psychotherapy" as "therapy" unless I am distinguishing it from other therapeutic modalities or from intensive psychoanalysis as a treatment modality. I also use the terms *psychoanalytic* and *analytic* interchangeably.

In this book, I have made use of case vignettes to illustrate clinical concepts. To preserve confidentiality I have used composite case studies, collapsing two or more patients into one case. This means that the interventions that I report having made in the examples are to varying degrees works of fiction, constrained by my concern when constructing the vignettes to minimise the chances of any patient feeling that the confidentiality of our relationship has been breached. The end result is never as convincing or rich in associative linkages as "real" clinical material but, in my experience, asking the patients' permission to write about them represents all too often an intrusion into the therapy that I wanted to avoid in order to protect the therapy.

In reading the vignettes and my interpretations, it will help if you bear in mind that the examples condense into a few pages the construction of interpretations that in reality can take many hours of analytic work to arrive at. Working analytically involves struggling within oneself and with the patient with periods of time when nothing makes sense and when we are at a loss as to how to intervene. This kind of uncertainty and the painstaking nature of analytic work are hard to reproduce in a textbook such as this one.

ACKNOWLEDGEMENTS

This book would never have been possible without my students' curiosity, criticism and enthusiasm, or without my husband's support and good humour. It is to them that I dedicate this book.

As ever, there are so many people that I would like to thank that were I to do so this would require a book in itself. I am therefore restricting myself to thanking two people in particular who are valued friends and colleagues and who, in different ways, have contributed significantly to this book. I am indebted to Susan Howard for her generous support, feedback and discussions about this book. I would also like to thank Heather Wood with whom I have taught psychoanalysis to trainee clinical psychologists for many years. Although the views expressed in this book are my own, I owe their development to our productive teaching partnership and to the many insights I have gleaned from her teaching. Finally, I would like to thank Gill Crusey who helped with the typing of the manuscript.

INTRODUCTION:
PSYCHOANALYSIS
IN THE TWENTY-FIRST
CENTURY

FREUD IS DEAD

I do not wish to begin this book on an alarmist note, but Freud *is* dead. Of course, this is not news as such, but it is just as well to be reminded of this fact if we are to approach psychoanalysis with a level-headed, critical, yet open attitude. Freud was a great theorist but he made mistakes. And we mustn't forget that there is much more to psychoanalysis than Freud. He helped us get started. It is us who can't let go of him.

Freud arouses strong passions even from the grave so that psychoanalysis is all too often approached from extreme, polarised positions. I was reminded of this some years ago when a colleague asked me to listen to a tape recording of a series of lectures on psychoanalysis. When I asked him why he wanted me to do this, he simply assured me that I would find it interesting. I duly sat and listened. One of the voices on the tape struck me in particular. This was of a young woman, rather fired up in her protestations against Freud and psychoanalysis, accusing those seeking analysis for themselves of self-indulgence. Moreover, she added rather smugly, "There's no evidence that it works".

The advantage of audio tapes is that they defy denial. After many years on the couch, I now find the courage to admit, somewhat sheep-ishly, that this person was actually me. My early "recorded" hostility towards psychoanalysis has since made me curious about why I had felt so strongly about it at that time. Of what personal consequence could the words of an old Viennese man be? Why did it matter to me if the Oedipus complex could not be proven? These were only ideas after all. No one was forcing me to subscribe to them. I shall spare you my own psychopathology, but suffice to say that with the benefit of hindsight, I think that I was afraid. I did not want to think about what psychoanalysis seemed to be pushing me towards. Put more simply, I did not want to think about the less palatable aspects of myself. Instead, I conveniently hid behind facile academic criticisms and allied myself with Freud's fiercest opponents. As a psychologist, this was all too easy to do. I was reared on a diet of behaviourism and empiricism spiced up with the odd rat or mouse finding its way round a labyrinth. Psychoanalysis and the unconscious were anathema. Along with other critics, I simply found myself resurrecting Freud only to then admonish him.

My initial resistance towards psychoanalysis has since given sway to a passionate engagement with it. My interest was first fuelled by an excellent teacher and it grew as a result of my personal experience of being in analysis. Although I have trained in other therapeutic modalities and make use of them, I keep coming back to psychoanalysis as it is what I find sustains me the most in my clinical work. I nevertheless struggle with aspects of psychoanalytic theory and practice. More to the point, my criticisms relate to the inward-looking attitude and the tribal mentality all too prevalent in psychoanalytic institutions. But my aim in this book is not to dwell too much on the problematic aspects of psychoanalysis as a theory or as an institution; rather I want to share those analytic understandings that have enriched my work as a clinician. I feel professionally enriched by the application of psychoanalysis to an understanding of the mind and of psychological problems. This is why I think Freud should be laid to rest in peace. No one can ever get everything right. We treat Freud as if he were a father figure, but we forget that no parent is ever perfect. We expect so much of him that he can only disappoint. Perhaps, the most we can conclude is that even though Freud was wrong about some of his hypotheses, we cannot escape the hallmark of his thinking. It pervades our language and the way we make sense of our emotional life. Whether we consciously acknowledge it or not, we see the world through Freudian lenses.

When Freud is not standing accused, he has been embalmed, hailed as a genius who revolutionised our understanding of ourselves and "... democratised genius by giving everyone a creative unconscious" (Rieff, 1961: 36). Amongst those who are partisan to psychoanalysis, there are the zealots who seem to forget that embalming Freud is not the same as keeping him alive in our minds in a creative way that allows for change and revision (Olivier, 1989). It is the spirit of Freud's endeavour, his willingness to confront our darker side and ask uncomfortable questions, that we need to retain, but not necessarily the answers that he found. The only way that we have of keeping the spirit of Freud alive is to take his observations further with the help of the method of enquiry he developed – analysis – but without the phobic avoidance of other methods of enquiry such as empirical research. If psychoanalysis is to survive external criticism, its supporters also need to approach it critically. Psychoanalysis will withstand our criticism as long as our criticism is not, in fact, an unconscious attack on whatever psychoanalysis represents for us at that moment, in which case, in our minds at least, it will then destroy it.

The schisms that abound within the psychoanalytic world between those who support different schools of psychoanalysis do little to help psychoanalysis retain the strong presence it deserves amongst the sciences of the mind. I want to make it clear that I do not wish to discourage dissenting voices or differences, as these are vital to the evolution of ideas. A difference is not in itself a value judgement; it simply is. What we do in our minds with a perceived difference is another matter. The neglect of attachment theory within psychoanalysis until comparatively recently comes to mind as one of many examples of how prejudices rather than rational argument can exclude a body of theory that is highly relevant to psychoanalysis.

The best scientists are those who are ironic enough in their pursuit of truth to realise that there will be another scientist around the corner who will take their theories further and possibly disprove them. But it is also perhaps necessary that in the pursuit of knowledge, those who seek it do so with passion. Passion is not a crime, though it can lead us down some blind alleys. Indeed, Freud himself pointed out to us the pitfalls of desire. Freud undoubtedly went down a few theoretical alleys that, with the benefit of a hundred years of hindsight, we can now see were unhelpful. But there is only one loser if we throw out the psychoanalytic baby with the bathwater – ourselves. This is because psychoanalysis, more than any other psychological theory, gets the measure of us by focusing squarely both on our desire and our destructiveness.

SEX, DEATH AND LIES

Psychoanalysis touches a raw nerve: you either feel passionate about it or are suspicious of it, but it is rare to feel neutral about it. Psychoanalytic ideas arouse curiosity and interest, but they reliably also attract fierce opposition. There are several reasons for this mixed response. For a start, until comparatively recently, there was a dearth of empirical evidence to support important psychoanalytic assumptions – a fact that, unfortunately, seldom reigned in the enthusiasm with which psychoanalytic practitioners themselves embraced their beliefs and presented them as the truth. This may be because, as Kirsner highlights:

> Like religion, psychoanalysis asks big questions, and, like religion, is easily influenced and seduced by dogmatic answers to these difficult questions (2000: 9).

The core message of psychoanalysis is also hard to digest. Unlike humanistic theories that depict a view of human beings as essentially good but corrupted by the environment, psychoanalysis reflects back to us a rather unflattering picture: we are beings driven by sexual and aggressive urges, we are envious and rivalrous, and we may harbour murderous impulses even towards those whom we consciously say we love. This is a mirror that we would rather not look into.

At its core, psychoanalysis is about the vagaries of desire, our recalcitrant renunciations and the inevitability of loss. It shows us that we can be our own very worst enemy. As a movement, psychoanalysis may be besieged by theoretical splits, but everyone agrees on one thing: conflict is inevitable. Whichever way you look at it, someone somewhere is always missing something in the psychoanalytic drama. Psychoanalysis suggests that disillusionment and frustration are intrinsic to development. Within Freudian theory, renunciation is a necessary evil if society is to survive. Freud, the bearer of bad news, starkly reminded us that we simply cannot have it all our own way. The hard lessons begin at birth. As reality impinges on us, the experiences of frustration, disappointment, loss and longing make their entry into the chronicles of our existence. The reality is that the breast – that archetypal symbol of never-ending nourishment and care – eventually dries up. These very experiences, however painful, are those that have been singled out by psychoanalysis as privileged in our development towards adaptation to the so-called real world. Even if it were possible to create a situation in which our every need could be satisfied, this would not be desirable since it would not equip us with the resilience born of the endurance and survival of moments of frustration and disappointment. Our capacity to delay gratification, to withstand absence and loss, are hard-won lessons that challenge our omnipotent feelings while also reassuring us that we can face reality without being overwhelmed by the enormity of the task.

Psychoanalysis also challenges our preferred belief in conscious thought as the ultimate datum of our experience. Whether we acknowledge it or not, most of us prefer to believe that what we see and experience accounts for all that is important in life. All too often we rely on our sense impressions and make little or no effort to probe deeper. Psychoanalysis, however, suggests that we are driven by conflicting thoughts, feelings and wishes that are beyond our conscious awareness but which nonetheless affect our behaviour – from behind the scenes, as it were. The possibility that we may not know ourselves undermines our wish for self-determination and casts a shadow over our preferred belief that we can control the future.

The notion of the unconscious is hard to digest not only because it suggests that we may not know ourselves but also because, even more provocatively, it proposes that we deceive ourselves and others. From the very start, psychoanalysis questioned the trustworthiness of human beings. It teaches us never to trust what appears obvious; it advocates an ironic, sceptical stance towards life and our conscious intentions. This is because, Freud suggested, we are beings capable of self-deception. Our mind appears to be structured in such a way that it allows for a part to be "in the know" while another part is not "in the know".

The picture of human beings that we see through psychoanalytic lenses is a sobering one. Strive as we might to be in control of ourselves, psychoanalysis tells us that we will never be wholly successful in this endeavour. Strive as we might to be happy and to overcome our conflicts, psychoanalysis tells us that conflict is an inescapable part of life. It reminds us that the best we can hope for is to find ways of managing, not eradicating, the conflict that is an inherent part of what it means to be human – and that will be £50 per session, thank you very much. At a glance, the psychoanalytic sound bites do not make for good PR. Freud's original views and those of his followers indeed continue to arouse passionate debates and schisms. Yet, their influence on our thinking about the mind is very much apparent. The question is whether their influence will endure. To a large extent, this will depend on the willingness of psychoanalytic practitioners to engage in a dialogue with other related fields of enquiry.

RESEARCH AND SCIENCE: FRIEND OR FOE?

Psychoanalytic thinking has vibrancy and depth. It is, in my opinion, the most intellectually satisfying view of the mind. Yet, psychoanalysis is in crisis, which is not to say that this is a fact widely recognised within the psychoanalytic community (see Fonagy *et al.*, 1999). To a lay audience, and even to some well-versed in psychoanalytic assumptions, the psychoanalyst is often seen as the one peddling ideas that are best laid to rest. The continued use of obscure or vague concepts with little or no evidence to back them and psychoanalysis' overall resistance to change do little to improve this image. Attempts to expose analytic ideas and the practice of psychoanalytic approaches to scientific evaluation are sometimes viewed with suspicion by some psychoanalytic clinicians. Psychoanalysis has traditionally adopted an arrogant attitude even towards other therapeutic models. At best, they are tolerated. At worst, they are regarded with a degree of contempt that perhaps masks a fear of the "other". A colleague once humorously captured this fear as she described psychoanalysis' view of cognitive behaviour therapy (CBT) as "Darth Vader's therapeutic arm". To be fair, psychoanalysis too is regarded by some CBT therapists in an equally irrational manner.

The historical insularity of psychoanalysis and its inward-looking attitude have meant that until comparatively recently, it has lacked the kind of perspective that tempers omnipotence. Although research in psychoanalysis is ongoing, it is by no means yet a well-integrated activity within its own field. Psychoanalytic therapy trainings, on the whole, teach psychoanalytic ideas with little more than token reference to research, viewing the latter as largely redundant to an understanding of the mind or the practice of psychotherapy.

Psychoanalytic theory has traditionally evolved around the hearsay evidence of the treating therapist. As each therapist accumulates the so-called evidence, it becomes the grounds for establishing the truthfulness of psychoanalytic assumptions on the basis of a well-known logical error, namely, the argument of past co-occurrence. This refers to the logical fallacy of assuming that if it's happened once before, for example, if a patient expressed his anger by turning it into depression, and if this same pattern is observed again, this means that the theory is correct, that is, depression is anger turned inwards. This argument is compelling but it has little probative value. Generally speaking, as clinicians we find it hardest to identify negative instances when the patient's reaction is *not* as we would have hypothesised it to be on the basis of the specific hypotheses or theories that guide our work.

Psychoanalysis has remained for far too long shrouded in mystery, the province of a privileged few, hermetically sealed-off from other fields of enquiry, which, as the current interest in neuroscience is now proving (e.g. Kaplan-Solms & Solms, 2000), could help support key psychoanalytic assumptions. The response of a significant proportion of the psychoanalytic community has, however, been negative to neuroscience though this perspective is in keeping with the spirit of Freud's original project.

The prevailing attitude to empiricism has been equally questionable as if to invite science into the debate about the validity of analytic theories, or the effectiveness of psychoanalysis, is equivalent to selling its soul to the devil. To argue, as some psychoanalytic clinicians do, that psychoanalysis is not a science and that it is therefore meaningless to evaluate it by the standards of other scientific endeavours merely sidesteps a critical issue: if psychoanalysis and psychoanalytic therapy are treatments for psychological problems, we have a responsibility to ensure that we understand how they work and check if they are effective. I am far from being a diehard experimentalist: if psychoanalysis only claimed to be a philosophy, for example, experimental validation would not be an issue. Heidegger's or Nietzsche's views about human nature are important and help us think about ourselves and our lives. But neither Nietzsche nor Heidegger set themselves up to formally treat psychological problems, though they have a great deal to say about human nature that is enlightening. It is because psychoanalysis claims to be a treatment for psychological problems and it seeks public funding for its provision that we have a responsibility to evaluate its effectiveness notwithstanding the limitations of the methodologies currently available to us.

Having criticised psychoanalysis' ambivalent relationship to science, it is also worth mentioning the somewhat narrow-minded conceptualisation of science espoused by the critics of psychoanalysis. The debate about the scientific status of psychoanalysis is by now well worn and circular. As Fonagy reminds us:

> Many disciplines are accepted as sciences, even if quantification is not instrumental and experiments are not possible to repeat as in palaeontology. Newton's theory is not falsifiable. Moreover, it is evidence that beyond a certain point of generality a theory is not possible to "prove"; it can only be accepted or not as organising a wide array of facts (quoted in Fonagy *et al.*, 1999).

Science is all too often idealised as the only respectable path to knowledge. Yet, scientific endeavour is anything but neutral or dispassionate. Behind the statistics proving one theory and disproving another lie researchers fuelled by deep passions. This should not deter us, however, from exploring what may be helpful in the empirical tradition to the future of psychoanalysis.

Psychoanalysis allows us to make conjectures about the human mind. Many of these are hard to test empirically. Psychoanalytic concepts are

complex, but complexity is not a good enough reason to avoid opera-
tionalising our terms. There is little doubt – in my own mind at least – that
psychoanalysis could try harder to operationalise its terms so that those
gifted enough to find ingenious ways of researching concepts could do
so more productively, and thereby provide an empirical base to psychoanalysis as a theory. In the absence of a more established empirical base,
allegiances to particular theories develop because we are "grabbed" by
an idea or because our psychoanalytic education has been conducted "in
an atmosphere of indoctrination" (Kernberg, 1986: 799). The theories we
subscribe to are then used to justify what we do with our patients.

If we approach psychoanalytic practice more soberly and openly, we have
to confront two uncomfortable facts: what we are practising is based
on cumulative clinical experience that may or may not translate into
effective interventions, and what we are theorising might be a useful
adjunct to clinical practice but it cannot be its epistemic justification. These
problems, although infrequently articulated, become quickly apparent if
you assemble a group of psychoanalytic clinicians, present them with the
same case history and ask them to formulate the case and advise on how to
intervene. What you are likely to get are several different interpretations of
the same behaviour alongside varying degrees of uniformity of approach
at the clinical level. Where there are differences of opinion as to how to
intervene, there is no valid or reliable way of evaluating which intervention
would be the most effective.

Needless to say, adopting a scientific, rigorous approach to one's work
does not necessarily entail personally engaging in research trials. However, I firmly believe that it is incumbent on all therapists, psychoanalytic
or otherwise, to regard being familiar with research as one of the respon-
sibilities inherent in our professional role. If you are in any doubt about
this, ask yourself what your expectations would be of a doctor. Would you
trust his recommendations knowing that he was only well read on a few
doctors who practised a hundred years ago, or if he could not answer you
in an informed manner about why he was opting for one procedure over
another or could not tell you if his chosen intervention had been shown
to be effective? Let us not forget that psychotherapy is a powerful tool, all
the more so because we as yet understand so little about how it works.

Our relative ignorance about therapeutic action is well hidden away in
many texts on psychoanalytic theory and practice. In the analytic literature,
it is not uncommon to find ideas or techniques supported by beliefs presented as facts rather than evidence. This, however, need not be the case.
Although we are still short of evidence, some psychoanalytic ideas have

received empirical support. Moreover, even if we do not yet fully understand which interventions lead to psychic change, there have nevertheless been some helpful indicators emerging from the research literature.

Given the relative paucity of research on the effectiveness of specific psychoanalytic interventions, this book would be on the thin side if I restricted myself to presenting only those techniques supported by research. Incidentally, this would also be the case for a book on other types of psychotherapy. The fact that CBT has received good support from the psychotherapy outcome literature does not imply that we know which key interventions make a difference. If anything, what research suggests is that some of the key interventions associated with good outcome are those techniques that are traditionally associated with psychoanalytic practice. (see Chapter 1).

APPROACHING PSYCHOANALYSIS IN THE CONSULTING ROOM

Teaching a structured and evidence-based therapy often guarantees a happy, and usually grateful, group of students. By the end of the teaching session, they feel they have "something to take away" that will help them when they face their patients the following day. Teaching psychoanalytic therapy is a more uncertain and risky enterprise. Students often feel overwhelmed by this therapeutic approach, which, unlike many others, has the potential to evoke such anxiety that it paralyses otherwise able practitioners. Faced with the lack of structure or agenda for a therapeutic session, they are unsure about what to say to the patient. The anxiety arises not only because the psychoanalytic approach does not have the reassuring structure found in CBT approaches, for example, but also because it is an approach that encourages therapists to address unconscious forces in their patients as well as in themselves – an undertaking that we all at best approach with a measure of dread.

Unlike CBT, the psychoanalytic approach is harder to specify and to teach at the level of skills. Scattered throughout the literature, we find "rules of technique" (especially within the Freudian classical tradition), but these are at best general guidelines that provide little reassurance when faced with a challenging patient who does not do what they are supposed to. Psychoanalytic trainings aim largely at imparting an "attitude" or a mode of thinking and receptivity, which defies the operationalisation of skills that many students anchor for.

As if the ethereal quality of the psychoanalytic attitude were not intangible enough for the fledgling psychoanalytic practitioner, the picture is further complicated by virtue of the sheer diversity of psychoanalytic theories that are often at odds with each other, along with the technical recommendations that are advocated. As we have seen, because psychoanalytic therapists have traditionally been research-shy, rival theories have coexisted without any attempts to establish their respective validity. Likewise, for the techniques that are used. For a newcomer to the field, it becomes difficult to decide in a rational manner which theory to follow and how to apply it in the consulting room. This difficulty is further compounded by the absence, as Fonagy suggests:

> [of] any kind of one-to-one mapping between psychoanalytic therapeutic technique and any major theoretical framework. It is as easy to illustrate how the same theory can generate different techniques as how the same technique may be justified by different theories. (1999a: 20).

Theory does not neatly translate into practice. Freud or Melanie Klein's ideas may be inspiring, but putting them into practice is a tall order. Students, panic-stricken, might well ask, "So, the patient is attacking me because they are envious of me. What do I *say* now?" Knowing what to say and whether to say it is enough to generate such anxiety that an alternative option, say of asking a patient to keep a diary of his negative automatic thoughts, is a welcome oasis of certainty.

Sitting in a room with experienced psychoanalytic therapists might only serve to enhance the students' anxiety: theoretical orientation does not promise uniformity of therapeutic approach. In Britain, Freud's ideas eventually evolved into three divergent theoretical schools, namely, the Contemporary Freudians, the Kleinians and the Independents. Whilst the three groups subscribe to different theoretical perspectives, the within-group differences at the level of practice are sometimes as striking, if not more so, than the between-group differences. Amongst therapists who hold theoretically divergent points of view, the differences at the level of their interventions may also sometimes be hard to gauge. Nowadays, you would be hard pressed to accurately categorise therapists, in terms of their primary theoretical allegiances, on the basis of their reported practice alone. It is possible, for example, to *caricature* Kleinians as working in the "here-and-now" more than Freudians, but in Britain many people who consider themselves to be Contemporary Freudians also focus on the "here-and-now" systematically. Furthermore, at times one could be forgiven for gaining the impression that some therapists operate on the basis of idiosyncrasies that are more reflective of personality variables than any theory that they align themselves with.

It is notoriously the case that therapists' public theories do not always match what they actually do with their patients. I am not suggesting that therapists are consciously preaching one thing and practising another. Rather, this apparent disjunction between theory and practice points to a more endemic problem that is seldom addressed, but has been cogently exposed by Fonagy (1999a). He argues that when it comes to the relationship between theory and practice, we all make a fundamental logical error: we assume that theory has a deductive role. Fonagy suggests, however, that its role is purely inductive, that is, theory helps us to elaborate clinical phenomena at the level of mental states; it does not allow us to deduce what we should be doing clinically. Psychoanalytic technique has arisen largely on the basis of trial and error rather than being driven by theory. Freud arrived at his technical rules on the basis of experience, and sometimes it would appear that his practice never matched the rules he wrote about (see Chapter 3). Currently, clinical theory is independent from any metapsychology. If psychoanalysis as a treatment modality is to develop, we need to be aware that what we do with our patients does not flow logically from the metapsychology we subscribe to.

THE FUTURE: PSYCHOANALYSIS, RESEARCH AND NEUROSCIENCE

For many years, I am ashamed to admit, any word prefixed by "neuro" was enough to turn me into an "anti-brain" demonstrator. Biology and neuropsychology, I then believed, were irrelevant to an understanding of the human mind. I viewed them as reductionistic attempts that neglected the meaning and affective experiences that I was grappling with in my clinical work and within myself. I situated myself comfortably in the hermeneutic tradition, believing that psychoanalysis was, at the core, about finding meaning and that this had nothing to do with scientific testing or brain anatomy. Indeed, psychoanalysis is, amongst other things, about interpreting meaning. But it has never contented itself with this. Psychoanalytic theories are not simply evocative narratives: they expound universal claims about mental events. If psychoanalysis makes universal claims, it has to buttress them with evidence in order to be taken seriously. If, on the other hand, we shy away from this challenge and argue that all that psychoanalysis is about is the creation of more or less helpful narratives, psychoanalysis abandons finding answers to the questions that Freud initially posed. This, to my mind, would be our loss.

I now write this book in the firm belief that to survive, psychoanalysis has to learn from other disciplines and has to engage in a dialogue with them to acquire new methodologies so as to assist us with the testing of some of its ideas. In particular, it needs to engage in a dialogue with biology and cognitive neuroscience (Kandel, 1999). I now appreciate that to focus on the neurobiology of the mind does not mean that we reduce it to something that can ever be fully known objectively, thereby making psychoanalysis redundant. Neurobiology, for example, will never be able to give us another person's experience of an image or an emotion (Damasio, 1999). We may all look at the same picture, but we will each generate the experience according to our own unique developmental histories.

A dialogue between psychoanalysis and the neurosciences is evolving (e.g. Solms & Turnbull, 2002). Nowadays, it is becoming more common-place for discussions about the aetiology of psychopathology to give due consideration to both genetic and experiential factors. This was indeed Freud's own view. In order to keep psychoanalysis firmly on the map, it will increasingly need to examine from a psychoanalytic *and* a neuro-science perspective the range of phenomena that we subsume under the term *unconscious*. Even though we do not currently have an intellectually satisfactory biological understanding of any complex mental processes, Kandel (1999) argues that biology can nonetheless help us to delineate the biological basis of various unconscious processes, of the role of uncon-scious processes in psychopathology and of the therapeutic effects of psychotherapy.[1]

It is true that there is no simple and straightforward relationship between psychoanalysis and neuroscience. Psychoanalysis discusses highly com-plex psychic processes that do not neatly map onto current knowledge in neuroscience. However, the attempts to bridge the gap that has existed for far too long are laudable: it is not about reducing psychoanalytic concepts to neurobiological ones; it is about recognising that "agendas overlap even if they are not identical" (Kandel, 1999).

A FEW WORDS ABOUT PSYCHOANALYTIC KNOWLEDGE AND FACTS

One of the most commonly voiced criticisms of psychoanalytic therapists when viewed from the vantage point of other more explicitly collaborative forms of psychotherapy is that the psychoanalytic therapist approaches her

---

[1] In the long term, it may be possible to track the therapeutic process by imaging the patient's hippocampus and seeing what degree of anatomical changes correlate with an involvement in psychotherapy.

work with unwarranted certainty. In discussions about psychoanalysis, I have often heard students argue that psychoanalytic therapists assume that they can know the mind of a patient better than the patient himself and that this cannot be possible. They caricature the way in which the psychoanalytic therapist always takes the patient's "no" to mean "yes" at an unconscious level. They argue that the notion of a dynamic unconscious is a license for abuse: the therapist can always invoke an unconscious motivation not yet known to the patient to prove the correctness of her interpretation. They condemn psychoanalysis on account of the imbalance of power in the therapeutic relationship. Of course, there is truth in some of these accusations, in some instances. However, behind these well-articulated criticisms often lies our own muddled relationship to so-called truth or knowledge and to our own professional competence. In setting ourselves up to treat those in emotional distress, we both implicitly claim to be in a position to help and, therefore, to presumably know something about the mind, and in one fell swoop, we deny that we can ever *really* know anything.

Whilst some psychoanalytic clinicians all too often err on the side of omnipotence in their claims to knowledge, since the rise in deconstructionist perspectives, many therapists err perhaps too much on the side of a denial of knowledge. I have digested some of the post-modern critiques of psychoanalysis and have found them to offer a salutary reminder of how facts can become overvalued, of how seductive the search for truth is and of how something more elusive, yet vitally important about the nature of psychic pain, can get lost in the search for certainty or truth. I have also found that such accounts foster a degree of denial. Although truth can never be anything but partial and elusive, some facts do exist. Our work is to help patients manage uncertainty, but it is also about helping them to develop the emotional resilience to know some facts about themselves. I have in mind here "facts" such as one's aggression and one's corporeality.

If we deal in nothing other than life narratives that can be re-written, does it follow that any story is potentially useful to the patient? If this is not the case, are we then not saying that some stories are perhaps more adaptive[2] than others? And if we are saying that there are more adaptive stories, then are we not also saying that we know something about what helps people live more fulfilling lives?

---

[2]That a story might be more adaptive does not make it the truth. I am merely wishing to point out that we never approach all stories as equivalent. In our work with patients, whatever our model of therapy, we are burdened by assumptions about what helps create more satisfying relationships.

To be truly responsible practitioners, we need to own what we know and be clear about our own professional competence. We need to be open to what we do not know and bear this without elevating our uncertain knowledge into a virtue that disguises muddled thinking and sometimes sheer incompetence. If we assume the title "psychotherapist", we are taking on a particular responsibility to know something about the mind. My impression is that sometimes we shy away from our own knowledge and competence because we are actually shying away from the inevitable dynamic that exists in any therapeutic encounter, namely, the asymmetry between therapist and patient. This asymmetry or imbalance is uncomfortable. The patient is vulnerable whilst the therapist, at least in the therapeutic situation, is there to help him on account of the knowledge that she has acquired with respect to the functioning of the human mind. It is our responsibility to invite the patient to examine critically the power he wishes to attribute to us rather than taking it at face value, or avoiding an uncomfortable exploration about this by setting up the therapeutic relationship in such a way that it pretends that there are no differences between therapist and patient.

There is a difference, which is often blurred in our minds, between author-itative competence and authoritative dominance (Novick & Novick, 2000). There is an important distinction to be made between having knowledge and the use we make of it. The challenge for us is to find a psychic stance congruent with the knowledge and experience we do possess, and which bestows upon us the onerous task of helping another person make sense of their unconscious whilst not abusing the inevitable asymmetry that all such professional relationships entail. If we know something, we have to bear what our knowing means to the patient and thus be receptive to his potential envy and hostility or to his longing to be passively understood, thus renouncing using his own mind. We can only achieve this if we can own what we know and manage the uncertainty born of what we do not know.

1

AN OVERVIEW OF THE SCHOOLS OF PSYCHOANALYSIS: THEORY AND PRACTICE

I. THEORY

Psychoanalysis in Context

Psychoanalysis is often approached critically by those who are not involved with it. This is partly because it is perceived as an exclusive, precious club whose membership consists of people who regard themselves as having access to truths about human nature and the process of psychotherapy that are lost on the average non-psychoanalytic clinician. There is some truth in this perception but it is not altogether accurate as the psychoanalytic membership includes a broad range of people with different values and attitudes. Its membership is in some respects incontrovertibly privileged: it consists mostly of people who are sufficiently socio-economically advantaged to undertake a lengthy training that requires a second mortgage. There is little doubt too that psychoanalysis has all too often adopted a dismissive – even arrogant – attitude to related fields of enquiry and to other therapeutic modalities. Nowadays, psychoanalytic training institutions are acutely aware of the dwindling numbers in the applications to train psychoanalytically. Keenness to recruit more students into the analytic fold has contributed to a much-needed review of admission procedures and the content and process of training.

Psychoanalysis is currently negotiating a transitional phase. Entrenched theoretical positions, perhaps owing more to political agendas than anything else, are gradually being challenged and opened up for evaluation. Cross-fertilisation of ideas between different schools and between different disciplines is gaining momentum. This change is exciting and unsettling: some practitioners are reaching out for the new while others remain fiercely attached to cherished assumptions, seemingly impervious to what other fields of enquiry might have to offer psychoanalysis.

Despite these efforts, psychoanalytic institutions remain more inaccessible, and more inward looking than is desirable for the growth of the profession. Understanding this predicament requires some appreciation of the inauspicious beginnings of psychoanalysis. From the outset, Freud provoked dissent and criticism. His views were indeed challenging and provocative. They were considered to be all the more so because he was Jewish. Freud was acutely aware of the effect of his Jewish roots on the acclaim of his ideas. When his friend and colleague, the Swiss psychiatrist Carl Jung – the only non-Jew then affiliated to the psychoanalytic movement – left Freud's following in 1914, Freud was concerned that psychoanalysis would be considered as no more than a "Jewish national affair".

Freud may well have wanted to play down the Jewish connection, but this fact was at the forefront of other peoples' minds. In the 1930s, with the rise of the Nazis, psychoanalysis was attacked: Freud's writings, together with those of Einstein, H.G. Wells, Thomas Mann and Proust, were burnt in public bonfires for their "soul disintegrating exaggeration of the instinctual life" (Ferris, 1997). Along with Darwin, Freud was vilified for subverting the high values of the fair-skinned races. His position in Vienna became untenable. On March 12, 1938, German troops moved into Austria. On March 13, 1938, the Board of the Psychoanalytic Society met for the last time. Freud likened their predicament to that of Rabbi Johannan ben Zakkai who fled Jerusalem after the Romans destroyed the temple and he began a religious school in his place of refuge. Freud urged his colleagues to follow this example. In a strong vote of confidence, the Board, before dissolving, agreed that the Society should reconstitute wherever Freud settled.

Freud was reluctant to leave Vienna, but a week later, when the Gestapo took away his daughter, Anna Freud, for questioning, he no longer needed persuading. By the time Anna was released the following day, plans were afoot for Freud to go into exile. Travelling via Paris, Freud fled to London. Many of his colleagues were also forced into exile. They moved to America, Britain, Palestine, Australia and South America. Those analysts who remained in Germany practised but only under strict Nazi requirements: classical Freudian analysis itself was deemed unacceptable.

The very real persecution suffered by the psychoanalytic movement in its infancy left a deep scar. From the outset, Freud saw psychoanalysis as a cause to be defended against attack and the analytic institutes that emerged could be seen to be the "bastions" of this defence (Kirsner, 1990). This had the unfortunate effect of also keeping at bay other perspectives and related fields of enquiry, fearing their evaluation, criticism and attack.

The movement's paranoia has not just been a feature of its relationship with the outside, non-analytic world. It has also been a striking quality of the relationships within the psychoanalytic establishment itself amongst its own rival theoretical offspring. The history of psychoanalysis is one of schisms. Indeed, psychoanalysis is an umbrella term covering a number of theoretical schools which, whilst all originating from and honouring some of Freud's ideas, have since evolved very different theories about personality development and different techniques for achieving the goals of psychoanalysis as a treatment for psychological problems.

The development of psychoanalysis in Britain is a very good example of the difficulties of living in a pluralistic society (Hamilton, 1996). The British Psychoanalytic Society was established by Ernest Jones. Since its inception, three distinct groups – the Contemporary Freudians, the Kleinians and the Independents[1] – have had to live together within one society with the unavoidable tensions associated with living in close proximity to neighbours who do not necessarily share the same point of view. It is to their credit that they have managed to co-exist within one society.

Each group represents a heterogeneous mix of practitioners most of whom have been influenced both by relational and developmental perspectives within psychoanalysis, as well as including those who lean more specifically towards contemporary Kleinian thinking. There are only a small number of older Freudians who were trained by, and remain loyal to, Anna Freud and who would be more appropriately referred to as "Classical Freudians". In North America, ego psychology and self psychology have a stronger presence, whilst Kleinian ideas have been slower on the uptake, though recent publications suggest a greater espousal of these ideas (e.g. Caper, 2000). Overall, heterogeneity dominates psychoanalytic theory, where within-group differences are sometimes as striking as between-group differences. This adds to the richness of analytic thinking

---

[1]To regard oneself as belonging to any one of the three groups usually reflects the training therapist's allegiance, that is, a training therapy with a Freudian makes one, usually, also a Freudian.

but raises the thorny question of which theory, if any, reflects back to us the most valid model of the mind and of development.

The aim of this chapter is to provide an all too brief overview of the development of psychoanalytic ideas from Freud onwards to the present day. Of necessity, only the ideas of a few of the key players in the history of psychoanalysis are presented. To simplify this overview, the two most influential theories have been grouped as Freudian and Kleinian, respectively, with the focus on only a few of the most salient concepts propounded by these two dominant figures. Unfortunately, this is at the cost of glossing over the *many* Freudian and Kleinian theories that exist and those approaches that have grown out of these early beginnings. We will therefore only be covering, in broad terms, some of the most common assumptions of these two main theories and, only cursorily, some of the post-Freudian and Kleinian developments. This overview, by virtue of its attempt to synthesise, glosses over the subtler differences that do exist between the various schools and veers towards simplifying complex concepts. For those interested in metapsychology, it is therefore not a substitute for a careful reading of both Freud's and Klein's original texts.

The Early Years: Freud's Topographical Model of the Mind

Freud proposed two models of the mind to account for the experience of intrapsychic conflict. The first model is known as the *topographical model* consisting of three levels of consciousness. The first level, the *conscious*, corresponds to that which we are immediately aware of, whatever we may be concentrating on at any given moment – for instance, reading this chapter. Beneath the conscious level lies the *preconscious*, consisting of whatever we can voluntarily recall. That is, the preconscious acts as a kind of storage bin for all those memories, ideas and sense impressions that are readily available to us, but to which we are simply not attending all the time. Beneath the preconscious lies the *unconscious*.

Freud used the term unconscious in three different senses. Firstly, he used it descriptively to denote that which is not in our consciousness at any given moment but is nonetheless available to us. This is no longer a controversial notion in contemporary psychology. Cognitive neuroscience has shown that most of the working brain is non-conscious in this sense; for example, memory can be acquired without any conscious awareness and thinking, decision making and problem solving all involve unconscious aspects (Milner *et al.*, 1998). Even our processing of emotional experience has been shown to occur unconsciously in an automatic way (Solms &

Turnbull, 2002). Moreover, this type of processing is qualitatively different from conscious processing at the level of the neuro-mechanisms involved (Milner *et al.*, 1998).

Secondly, Freud used the term unconscious in a systemic sense denoting his understanding of the unconscious, not as a gradation of consciousness, but as a hypothetical system of the mind with particular properties. Finally, he used the term to denote the *dynamic unconscious*, that is, a constant source of motivation that makes things happen. Freud understood the inability to recall the contents of the unconscious voluntarily as the outcome of an active force that attempted to keep the contents of the unconscious from reaching consciousness, that is, *repression*. The unconscious in this sense is said to contain sexual and aggressive drives, defences, memories and feelings that have been repressed.

The preconscious and the conscious systems both obey the usual rules of thinking, namely, logical, reality tested and linear in time and causality. These rules are typical of what is referred to as *secondary process thinking*. The unconscious system obeys a different set of rules typical of *primary process thinking*. In this part of our mind, information is not subject to any kind of reality testing so that mutually exclusive "truths" may coexist and contradictions may abound. Because of these properties, the unconscious has been likened to an infantile and primitive part of our mind.

Towards Ego Psychology: Freud's Structural Model of the Mind

In his paper, *The Ego and the Id*, Freud (1923b) gave an account of his shift away from the topographical model to the *structural hypothesis*.[2] This new model conceptualised the human psyche as an interaction of three forces: the *id, ego and superego*. These are three different agencies of our personalities, each with its own agenda and set of priorities. They were said to have their own separate origins and their own highly specific role in maintaining what might be regarded as "normal" personality functioning. Difficulties arise because of the potential conflict between the demands of the different agencies. Within the structural model, a conflict refers to the opposition of two or more intrapsychic[3] aims. In this model, interaction

---

[2]This enabled Freud to outline an approach to psychic functioning that recognised environmental and biological determinants for his notion of drives and for both the reality principle and the pleasure principle.

[3]This term refers to internal conflict, for example, between the id and superego.

with the external world is given more prominence as Freud argued that conflicts could arise from external pressures as well as from internal ones.

The id

According to Freud, each one of us is endowed with a specific amount of *psychic energy*. In the newborn infant, psychic energy is bound up entirely in the *id*, which refers to the mass of biological drives (sexual and aggressive) with which we are all born. A *drive* is an internally generated biological force that seeks discharge. An accumulation of drive tension is subjectively experienced as a state of unpleasure, whereas its discharge is experienced as pleasurable. All drives possess four core characteristics:

- A source in the body.
- An aim (i.e. a particular mode of gratification).
- A pressure (i.e. a quantitative level of excitement).
- An object (i.e. that which allows the aim to be realised).

The id is pre-verbal, expressing itself in images and symbols. It is pre-logical, having no concept of time or limitations. It is not amenable to reason, logic, reality or morality. It is essentially a primitive kind of cognition, which is not well suited to the exigencies of reality. The id is only concerned with one thing: the reduction of whatever tensions our organism may experience. Our innate tendency to maximise pleasure and minimise pain was referred to as the *pleasure principle* by Freud. He believed that the infant, in the first year of life, was primarily narcissistic, its psychic functioning governed by the pleasure principle, with no differentiation between inner and outer – a view that has since been radically challenged by developmental psychologists who have demonstrated that the baby is from birth actively seeking engagement with others and is aware of other people.

The id is entirely unconscious. Its contents can be considered to be equivalent to the unconscious of Freud's earlier topographical model. Its existence is inferred from *derivatives* such as dreams or slips of the tongue. The energy of the id is divided between two types of instincts: the life and the death instincts. The *life instinct* is aimed at survival and self-propagation. The energy of the life instinct, the *libido*, was considered by Freud to be the driving force permeating our entire personalities and propelling us through life. In his earliest formulations, Freud spoke of our basic drive as being entirely sexual and all other aims and desires as arising from some modification of our sexual drive. Among Freudian therapists nowadays, the term libido has lost a great deal of its original sexual connotations and refers essentially to the idea of drive energy;[4] that is, the energy we may invest in the pursuit of our particular interests in some topic, activity or in a relationship with others. Freud believed that we cathect, that is, we invest, people, objects or ideas with psychic energy. *Cathexis* refers to the amount of psychic energy that becomes attached to the mental representative of a person or object that is, to the memories, thoughts or fantasies about a person. This investment of psychic energy is an indication of the emotional importance of the person or object to the individual in question.

In opposition to the life instinct stands the *death instinct*. Discussions of the death instinct, including Freud's, tend to be rather vague. It is clear, however, that Freud saw the human organism as instinctively drawn back to a state in which all tension would be dissipated – in short, the state of death. This instinctive attraction towards death gives rise to self-directed aggressive tendencies. However, since self-destruction is opposed and tempered by the life-preserving energy of the libido, our aggression, in most instances, is redirected outward against the world. Aggressive instincts are a component of what drives behaviour. Our self-preservative instinct relies on a measure of aggression at its disposal to fulfil its aims. Aggression thus also has a "propelling function" (Perelberg, 1999), which is essential to preserve life.

The death instinct represents Freud's broadest philosophical speculation. Amongst Contemporary Freudians, few still hold on to the notion of a death instinct and find it much more useful to talk about, and to work with, such concepts as guilt, aggression, anger or conflict with the superego. It is the Kleinians who have developed the notion further; they implicitly invoke the notion of a death instinct when discussing self and other destructive behaviours, which are seen to be a derivative of the operation of the death instinct.

The ego

While the id knows what it wants and needs, it is in some respects "blind" – blind to what constitutes safe or ethical ways of getting what it wants since it takes no account of reality. To fulfil this function, Freud suggested that the mind developed a new psychic component, the *ego*, which he believed emerged at about six months of age. The ego is responsible for voluntary thought and action and is in contact with the

---

[4]The notion of psychic energy was used by Freud to understand the workings of our mental life and was characteristic of his tendency to draw analogies between psychological and physical events.

external world via the senses. It is concerned with key mental functions such as perception, reality testing, sense of time, thinking and judgement. Freud's interest in reality becomes clearer in the structural model as he placed more emphasis than hitherto on the strength of the ego in relation to the other agencies of the personality.

The central function of the ego is to serve as a mediator between the id and reality. In contrast to the id's pleasure principle, the ego operates on what is called the *reality principle*. Because the ego's role is to adapt to reality, an important aspect of functioning that psychoanalytic therapists are interested in assessing is the patient's *ego strength*, namely, his capacity to acknowledge reality without falling back on the extensive use of defences, especially the more primitive ones (see Chapters 5 & 7).

The ego has both conscious and unconscious aspects. The conscious ego is closest to what we usually refer to as the "self", whereas the unconscious ego encompasses defensive processes. The terms "ego" and "self" are often used interchangeably and lead to considerable confusion, partly due to Freud's own ambiguous use of the German term "ich". Hartmann (1950) differentiated the ego and the self according to their interactional context. Within this framework, the ego interacted with the other intrapsychic agencies (id and superego) while the "self" was said to interact with objects.[5]

The superego

Freud suggested that as we grow up, we take into ourselves ideas and attitudes held by others around us. The formation of the superego is an instance of what is called *introjection*, that is, as children we absorb our parents' standards and values and these come together to form the *superego*. Parents are thought to play an important role in curbing or inhibiting the id's excesses, helping the child to become attuned to the demands of reality.

The rules, the abstract moral principles and the ideal image of whom we ought to be can be thought of as a person inside us who has strong views and is always ready to criticise, if our behaviour is not up to standard. This person inside us is equivalent to our superego. The superego is divided into two parts: an *ego ideal* representing what the ego aspires to and a conscience that punishes the ego when it fails.

---

[5]Ego psychologists tend to view the "self" as representational rather than as a source of subjective autonomous activity. However, others have taken issue with this suggesting that a concept of the self needs to include subjective experience and personal agency as the self performs a very key role in initiating interaction with the environment.

Like the ego, the superego is partly conscious[6] and partly unconscious. While most of us have some awareness of the moral rules and standards that govern our behaviour, there are other moral, sometimes harsh or persecutory, internal forces that bear on us of which we are unaware.

The psychosexual stages of development

Freud's belief that our sexual life begins at birth led him to describe what are referred to as the *stages of psychosexual development*. He argued that we all progress through a series of stages; at each stage, our psyche directs its sexual energy towards a different *erogenous zone*, that is, a part of our body, which is a source of pleasure. Freud first proposed the *oral* stage (0–1 years) where satisfaction is predominantly derived by the infant via the mouth, for example, from sucking the nipple or the thumb. Second, is the *anal* stage (1–3 years), where gratification is derived from gaining control over withholding or eliminating faeces. Everyday observations of toddlers highlight how, as they negotiate their increasing separateness from their parents, they come to view their faeces as their own possessions, which they want to give up or hold on to in their own good time. The potential for battles and conflict between parent and child, for instance, over toilet training, during this period is great. It is at this stage that defecation is said to symbolise giving and withholding. Metaphorically speaking, conflicts at the anal stage are seen to pose a major dilemma for all children with regard to the need to adapt to, or to resist, parental control.

The third stage (3–5 years), the *phallic* stage, sees the child beginning to be more aware of her genitals with consequent curiosity and anxiety about sexual differences. The phallic stage is thought to be particularly important to our psychological development because it is this stage that provides the backdrop to the Oedipal drama. In Greek mythology, Oedipus unknowingly kills his father and marries his mother. Likewise, according to Freud, all children during the phallic stage long to do away with the parent of the same sex and take sexual possession of the parent of the opposite sex. The notion of an Oedipal phase places desire at the core of our psychology.

The resolution of the *Oedipus Complex* is believed to be especially crucial to our development. Freud hypothesised that at the same time that the little boy harbours his incestuous desires towards his mother, he also experiences *castration anxiety* – the child's fear that his father will punish him for his forbidden wishes by cutting off the guilty organ, his penis.

---

[6]Its conscious aspects refer to the ego ideal.

Lacking penises, girls appear castrated to him and the little boy fears a similar fate. Girls, on the other hand, realising that they have been born unequipped with penises experience the female counterpart to castration anxiety, namely, *penis envy*. They are said to harbour angry feelings towards the mother for having created them without a penis. While the boy's castration anxiety is what causes him to repress his longing for his mother, the girl's penis envy is what impels her towards her father, desiring a child by the father – the desire for a child being merely a substitute for her former desire for a penis.

With time, both the boy's and the girl's Oedipal desires recede; rather than remaining at war with the same-sex parent who is experienced as a rival, both settle for *identification* with the same-sex parent, incorporating their values, standards and sexual orientation. The resolution of the Oedipus complex was therefore linked by Freud to the development of the superego.

Contemporary Oedipal accounts no longer view the conflict of the Oedipal phase as a manifestation of a primary incestuous sexual drive. Both classically and relationally oriented theorists now conceptualise Oedipal development as a complex interplay of triadic object relationships, cognitive development and gender identity consolidation. In this contemporary version, the Oedipal phase is distinguished more by a new level of object relations rather than by an incestuous sexuality (Morehead, 1999).

The Oedipal phase is developmentally crucial because it brings into relief feelings of rivalry and competitiveness and challenges the child with the negotiation of boundaries. Rivalry, which is well managed by the parents, can lead to constructive preoccupations in the child with fairness and justice (Raphael-Leff, 1991). From a developmental point of view, the child's recognition of the parents as sexual partners encourages an essential relinquishment of the idea of their sole and permanent possession. It involves awareness of the differences that exist between the relationship that parents can enjoy with each other as distinct from that which the child can enjoy with them.

Object relationships through the Freudian lens

At the core of the Freudian model, we find drives to be the primary, motivational force. As we have seen, the mind is believed to be driven primarily by instinctual derivatives of the biological body. Human beings are motivated by the pursuit of pleasure contingent upon the discharge of the drive. In this model, object relationships are secondary to tension discharge. A close look at the shift in Freud's theory of anxiety, however, reveals his own recognition of the importance of object relationships.

In Freud's topographical model, anxiety was understood as a triangulation of blocked libido (i.e. undischarged sexual feelings). Anxiety was itself regarded as a discharge phenomenon, which precluded the mental representation of deflected somatic sexual impulses. The id was then thought to be responsible for producing anxiety. Freud later understood this formulation to have been an error. In his second theory, anxiety resulted primarily from conflict between the various demands exerted upon the ego by the id and superego. This new conceptualisation of anxiety had important repercussions. It led Freud to shift from an energetic model to a meaning model, whereby childhood wishes were associated with childhood dangers related to loss (e.g. loss of an object, loss of the object's love, loss of or injury to the genital [castration] and fear of punishment [guilt]). Within this model, a threatening wish-seeking expression in consciousness signals danger to the ego, which, in turn, gives rise to anxiety. Anxiety is thus linked to situations of inner danger as well as external danger.

This shift in theoretical gear highlights the significance that Freud afforded to object relationships both internal and external, real or fantasised. Freud's appreciation of the importance of relationships is more clearly expressed in his 1921 paper *Group Psychology and the Analysis of the Ego* in which he writes:

> In the individual's mental life, someone else is invariably involved, as a model, as an object, as a helper, as an opponent (1921: 69).

Freud's object-relational construction of the ego in which its character is formed by a "precipitate of abandoned object cathexes and a history of object choices" (Freud, 1923b: 29) also strongly suggests a notion of the subjective experience of self that is inextricably bound up with images of other people. Notwithstanding these acknowledgements of the importance of other people to psychic development, it was to be Melanie Klein who most clearly articulated an object-relational perspective in psychoanalysis (see below).

Theory in practice

Classical Freudian therapy focuses on the nature and consequences of conflicts resulting from sexual and aggressive wishes originating in childhood. Pleasure-seeking sexual and aggressive wishes of early childhood are believed to become associated with parental punishment, thus generating conflict and unpleasure (i.e. anxiety, depression). Such states of unpleasure, in turn, trigger defences instituted to reduce unpleasure while allowing as much gratification as possible. This leads to *compromise formations*. Depending on the restrictions that such compromise formations place on the individual, or the degree of destructive behaviour that they may lead to, the compromise formation leads to pathological states (i.e. symptoms). Psychopathology is thus understood to be primarily the result of conflict between impulse and defence and the resultant compromise formations.

A prevalent assumption within this model is that in the course of treatment there will be increasing pressure for drive gratification in the transference. This allows the therapist to examine the patient's conflicts in terms of defences against instinctual drives and the compromise formations reached by the ego in dealing with the id, superego and external reality. Conflict between impulse and defence is therefore the focus of therapy. Because this approach espouses a one-person psychology, the therapist's role is considered to be that of a neutral observer and commentator on the patient's conflicts and the defences used to manage these. Change is said to result through interpretation leading to insight and intrapsychic conflict resolution.

Nowadays, Contemporary Freudians do not reduce everything to drives and defences. Rather, they are more concerned with a variety of motives for the use of defences and for the construction and development of fantasies and transference (Sandler, 1983). In addition to sexual and aggressive drives, consideration is given to motives arising out of threats to feelings of safety, narcissistic injuries, feelings of guilt or shame and other real threats. The technical shift has been towards the earlier interpretation of transference, that is, of those feelings, attitudes or states of mind that are experienced by the patient in relation to the therapist or that are attributed to the therapist by the patient; this change renders many Contemporary Freudian therapists indistinguishable, at the level of technique, from their Kleinian or Independent counterparts.

Beyond Freud: Ego Psychology

Ego psychology took shape in the 1930s. It is rooted in the final phase of Freud's theorising, reflecting the structural hypothesis of id, ego and superego. Its main contributors were Heinz Hartmann, Anna Freud, Rudolf Loewenstein, Ernst Kris, Phyllis Greenacre, Otto Fenichel and

Edith Jacobsen. In related ways, they all extended and modified Freud's structural theory.

The ego-psychological paradigm placed the ego as the central structure emerging, as Freud himself had suggested, out of the perceptual apparatus. The ego functioned as an executive, forging compromises between the id, the superego and external reality. The primary contribution of the post-Freudians was to redress Freud's overemphasis on libido and unconscious motivation. Instead, they emphasised the significance of conscious awareness and the adaptive functions of the ego. The main shift was away from an interest in the contents of the unconscious to the processes that serve the function of keeping those contents out of the consciousness, namely defences.

Hartmann (1950, 1964) was one of the most influential pioneers of ego psychology. His primary contribution was to introduce an account of the relationship between the individual and external reality, that is, other people. The role of external reality and its impact on development was more prominent in his thinking than it ever was in Freud's. This more adaptive point of view placed greater emphasis on the role of the environment in shaping conflicts and introduced an interpersonal dimension to the intrapsychic emphasis that had dominated up until that point. Prima facie, this might appear like the beginnings of object-relational thinking but Hartmann's contribution merely grafted an acknowledgement of the significance of relationships onto Freud's drive model. Nevertheless, the gradual erosion of the primacy of the drives, along with the possibility that reality itself (i.e. the relationship to the external world) might have an impact on the experience of pleasure, paved the way for the object-relations school. Indeed, Hartmann believed that object relations were an important contributing factor in the development of the ego but he did not view them as the central organising feature of development as the later object relation theorists would do.

Within Freud's model, the ego was important in the overall structure of the psyche because of its function in defence. Hartmann took Freud's model one step further by focusing not solely on the defensive aspects of the ego, but also, he insisted, there was a conflict-free sphere of the ego that developed independently of id forces and conflicts. The ego was attributed with certain autonomous functions that were not subject to conflict. As long as a child was born into what Hartmann referred to as *an average expectable environment*, he hypothesised that the primary autonomous ego functions of perception, memory, thought and motility present at birth would flourish without being impeded by conflict.

Hartmann thus focused much more on the adaptive aspects of the ego. Along with Ernst Kris, he understood survival as a primary motivating force and saw adaptation to the environment as essential to this end. Current infant research converges on the view espoused by Hartmann, namely, that the newborn is, from the very outset, actively and adaptively oriented towards external reality and is pre-equipped with sophisticated cognitive and perceptual ego mechanisms (e.g. Stern, 1985).

Anna Freud (1965) was another important analyst who championed Freud's structural hypothesis. She highlighted that the primary function of the ego was to defend the self against anxiety arising from either powerful instinctual strivings, upsetting 'real experiences' or guilt feelings and associated fantasies. Anna Freud was one of the first analysts to adopt a coherent developmental perspective on psychopathology. She argued that psychological disorder could be studied most effectively in its developmental evolution. Her theory was based on the metaphor of developmental lines. Conflicts were understood to be not only intrapsychic but also developmental in nature and therefore transitory. The developmental conflicts were associated with libidinal phases but fixation and regression could occur along all developmental lines.

For the ego psychologists, drives and their assumed location in the system unconscious remain the centre point of their theory and practice. Modern structural theorists retain the essence of the tripartite model with the central premise of the ubiquitous nature of intrapsychic conflict, but they have dispensed with problematic notions such as that of psychic energy. All mental contents, thoughts, actions and fantasies are conceived of as *compromise formations*. The compromise occurs between four elements of the conflict, namely, intense childhood wishes for gratification (i.e. drive derivatives), the anxiety or depressive affect (i.e. unpleasure), the mental operations of varying complexity put in place to minimise unpleasure (i.e. defences) and the resulting guilt, self punishment, remorse and atonement (Brenner, 1994).

Theory in practice

Ego psychology shifted the emphasis in technique from the recovery of the repressed to the modification of the patient's ego. While interpretation was not considered to be the only intervention available to the therapist, it was certainly deemed to be the major intervention that resulted in insight (Kris, 1956).

The aim of the ego psychologist is to extend the patient's autonomous, conflict-free ego functioning. The main technical implications are reflected in the emphasis on strengthening the *observing* ego, through analysis, in order to achieve mastery over the *experiencing* ego. Nowadays, the ego-psychological tradition is best reflected in the work of those therapists who see themselves as adopting a more modern structural theory that includes a greater acknowledgement of object relations. Nonetheless, the analysis of conflict and defence remains the centrepiece of the ego psychologist's clinical practice. A primary focus of interpretations is on intrapsychic conflict and the patient's resistance to awareness of the operation of defences. Interpretation aims to broaden the patient's understanding of how the past remains dynamically integral to current experience (Loewenstein, 1958). Greater adaptation and a capacity for reality testing continue to be the valued goals of therapy.

This approach espouses the belief that traumatic or problematic dynamics/events in early childhood are beyond verbal analysis. This sets them apart from Kleinian and Independent therapists who argue that it is possible to work with pre-verbal experiences as they manifest themselves in the vicissitudes of the therapeutic relationship.

From Ego Psychology to Melanie Klein: The Origins of Object[7] Relations Theory I

Anna Freud's main contribution to psychoanalysis was in the field of child analysis. However, it was another analyst specialising in the treatment of children who ultimately proved to be far more influential on the development of psychoanalytic theory and practice, particularly in Britain and in South America, namely, Melanie Klein.

Melanie Klein arrived in Britain in 1926. By the time the Freuds arrived in 1937, she had already established a loyal following. She believed that therapists could know a lot about the pre-verbal child and that they could work analytically with children using play in lieu of the spoken word. Play was seen to be the equivalent of the adult patient's free associations. In contrast, Anna Freud was wary of what she regarded at best as the surmises and guesses of those who followed Klein. She maintained that a *transference neurosis* (i.e. a re-enactment in therapy of childhood attitudes towards the parental figures) could not develop in children who were only beginning to shape their initial attitudes towards their parents. She emphasised

---

[7]The term "object" originates from instinct theory, referring to the object of the drives. It has been retained within psychoanalysis, somewhat inappropriately, to refer to the people who are significant in our lives (e.g. parents, partners, therapists). However, its use is best restricted to internal objects (i.e. not real people).

the importance of the child's real relationships for development. Klein disagreed: she saw children – even very young ones – as being much like adults: propelled by powerful drives, able to express in their own way the power of their drives and able to respond to the therapist's interpretations. Crucially, she focused on the child's phantasy life.[8]

Anna Freud and Klein argued not only over theoretical matters. They also differed on other levels: in their presentation to audiences, in their manner of expression and, perhaps even more significantly it has been suggested (Coles, 1992), in the connections they made with different aspects of Freud's personality and his interests. They became heated rivals, contributing to significant splits within the British Psychoanalytic Society, resulting in the current groupings that were referred to at the beginning of the chapter. Those who refused to ally themselves either to the Freudians or the Kleinians came to be known as *the Independents*.

Whereas Anna Freud remained loyal to her father's ideas, Melanie Klein built on Freud's ideas and went on to develop her own distinctive theory of the mind. Klein effectively took the object-relations aspect of Freud's libido theory and made it the centrepiece of her theory (Hurvich, 1998). According to Klein, drives are complex psychological phenomena that are closely tied to specific object relations. Drives are directed towards specific objects for specific reasons rather than drives being simply viewed, as Freud had largely suggested, as seeking tension reduction. More specifically, unlike the ego-psychological view of drives as diffuse, undifferentiated tensions, in Kleinian theory, drives are seen as dynamic structures that are innately equipped with knowledge about the characteristics of the objects they seek.

As we have seen, the general trend initiated by Freud and developed further by the ego psychologists was towards a greater appreciation of the conscious mind. Klein, on the contrary, was to focus on the individual's inner life, re-establishing the unconscious as the focal area of interest and interpretation. Her theories reflect a concern with the unconscious mind and take the violent and aggressive world of the id even more seriously than Freud himself had ever done.

Klein's first-hand experience with children enabled her to gain a more sophisticated understanding of psychopathology. Although Freud was revolutionary in suggesting that the origins of mental illness could be traced back to one or two critical years occurring in early childhood,[9]

---

[8]Phantasy is conventionally spelt thus to refer to unconscious phantasies as opposed to conscious ones. This spelling shall be retained throughout the book unless referring specifically to conscious fantasy.
[9]Indeed, the critical period of personality development within classical Freudian theory was thought to be between three and six years, centred around Oedipal conflict and its resolution.

Klein adopted an even more radical view. She believed that the origins of mental illness were historically more remote than Freud had suggested: her emphasis was on the first year of life. Her theories are rooted in a fine-tuned study of early mental processes, which are operative, according to her, from the very beginning of life.

The role of unconscious phantasy

Klein placed great emphasis on the person's subjective experience over the impact of real events. A central tenet of her theory is the notion of unconscious *phantasy*. An unconscious phantasy is the mental represen-tation of an experience or need. Klein maintained that from birth all our bodily impulses and emotional experiences have a mental representation in the form of phantasies, which colour our evolving inner life, that is, our *internal world*, and affect our experience of the external world. For example, one of my patients experienced any physical ill health, however minor, in a very paranoid manner. When she became ill, she often attributed the cause of her colds or flu, for example, to her careless manager who was not monitoring the office water supply or her partner who had prepared food that she believed was past its sell-by date. In other words, whenever she was ill the underlying phantasy that was activated was that she was being poisoned by another person rather than that her body was run down or that she might have picked up a virus at work. Consequently, she became very suspicious of others when physically ill and would not allow anyone to nurse her. This only served to accentuate the internal experience of persecution as she then also felt unsupported and used this as further evidence to back up her internal experience of others as neglect-ful. The origins of this phantasy were rooted in her early experience of growing up with a mother who was psychotic. We later understood this as the patient's experience of her mother "poisoning" her mind with her delusional beliefs.

Subjectively, the experience of phantasy is one of quite concrete objects, which are felt to have particular intentions towards the self – typically either good or bad intentions. For example, for a baby, the state of hunger can be experienced as a bad object inside that is attacking the baby. Klein suggested that infants and young children have a phantasy that they create a world within themselves by taking into themselves parts of the external world. This gives rise to an internal world, which is not an accurate image of the external world but is coloured by the child's phantasised projection of her own emotions into the external world.

To understand how the internal world is built up, we have to understand the function of *projection* and *introjection*. Introjection is based on an unconscious phantasy of incorporation, of taking something into oneself. Projection, on the contrary, is based on an unconscious phantasy of expulsion, of "getting rid of". For example, Klein understood that play provided the child with a means of putting a certain aspect of her mind into the external world through projection, thereby relieving the pressure of a conflict in the child's internal world. Let us take the example of a child in hospital awaiting an operation. This child might play with dolls, pretending that she is the doctor. During the play, she may talk to the doll that is going to be operated upon and tell her that there is nothing to worry about and she cures her. Another child, in a similar predicament, might pretend during play to be the doctor operating on a doll that is made to die. Both children are externalising, that is, projecting their anxieties about their operation into the play with dramatically different outcomes that suggest qualitatively different internal realities at that point: the first child manages to reassure herself through the play that it will be alright whilst the second child reveals in the play his fear that the operation will kill him and no-one will be able to save him. The second child, we might say, reveals through his play a defensive identification with being the doctor whilst his frightened self is split off and projected onto the doll that dies during the operation.

Klein's descriptions of projection and introjection vividly suggest that at a very primitive level the mind acts like "an alimentary tract" (Caper, 2000) taking in and spitting out various feelings or states of mind that would otherwise cause internal conflict. The internal world can be understood as a collection of identifications based on introjections: this is a complex process in so far as when we take in the external world, it is an external world that has already been altered through projection. According to Klein, what exists in the internal world can thus never be considered to be a replica of the external one, but is coloured by the infant's projection of loving and hating impulses onto it.

The internal world is said to be populated by *internal objects*. These are, as Caper (2000) describes them, "versions of those we love and hate". An internal object is a version of an actual person filtered through projective and introjective processes that distort to varying degrees the so-called real person "out there". Klein described the mind as a stage on which an inner drama is played out with the players being phantasised internal objects or *part objects*.[10] Klein assumed that internal objects underwent a developmental progression, at first, being experienced as concrete and physically

---

[10] A part object denotes a rudimentary type of object relating which reduces the "other" to its functions or only parts of the other (e.g. the baby relates to the mother only as the feeding breast).

present, moving on to the representation of an object in the psyche and in the person's memory system, finally to be elaborated as a symbolic representation in words or other symbolic forms (Hinshelwood, 1989).

Our states of mind are a good barometer of what is happening in our internal world. When we feel we are populated, if you like, by benign objects, we feel good about ourselves and safe because we are relating, at that moment, to good internal objects that want the best for us or are there to support us. When we are populated by "bad" objects, we are more prone to feeling suspicious or criticised or unsupported. In the example earlier of the children playing prior to an operation, we might say that the first child appears to have an internal world populated at that point by mostly good objects such that she is able to reassure herself that she is not going to die.

Phantasy was considered by Klein to be an innate capacity. She postulated that the pre-verbal infant was born with innate knowledge about sexual intercourse (in a rudimentary form), the penis and the vagina. She believed that these innate phantasies formed the basis of the baby's rich unconscious phantasy life and interacted with external reality. These ideas often alienate those approaching Kleinian thinking for the first time. However, it is well worthwhile persevering since there are many other aspects of her theorising that are very helpful. More specifically, whilst we might well query the notion of *innate* phantasies, Klein nevertheless offers us a very sophisticated view of phantasy in general, namely, an object-relational view. This perspective suggests that in a phantasy, we are relating in our mind to another person or feel that we are treated by another person in a highly specified way. For example, as we give a talk at work to our colleagues, we think to ourselves: "This is terrible. No one is interested in what I'm saying. They all think I'm inarticulate." We are, in that moment, most probably in the grip of a powerful phantasy, namely, that the "other" in our mind is looking down on us and berating us. According to Klein, our phantasies organise our psyche. This means that if the phantasy of the other as an accusing, critical object who looks down on us as we speak is dominant, our psyche is organised around this phantasy. Unless we manage to talk ourselves through this particular phantasy, it will colour how we interpret other situations. Let us imagine that we might leave work that same day and as we cross the street someone bumps into us and says, irritably: "Look where you're going!" Such a comment is unpleasant but depending on our state of mind at the time, we will either shrug it off or we will recruit the comment into the dominant phantasy in our mind of the object as critical and of ourselves as stupid or incompetent and thereby reinforce the phantasy.

Klein believed that the content of phantasies was not exclusively dependent on the child's experience with external objects. A child might have a phantasy of her mother as "bad" because she has just set down a boundary about bedtime and sent the child to bed whilst the parents stay up watching TV together. As the child's need is frustrated, the mother is no longer a gratifying object: she becomes a "bad" object who rejects her and keeps to herself all the good things, not only television but also a separate, exciting relationship with father which excludes the child.

Although Klein never dismissed the impact of the external environment on the development of the child, the focus of her theory was skewed towards the child's phantasy world. She believed, for example, that it was the representation of the internalised relationship between mother and child that influenced development rather than the actual status of this relationship. Klein has been duly criticised for relying on phantasy and thereby minimising the influence of the environment. It is nevertheless apparent, when reading her original work, that her emphasis on the role of phantasy as a primary factor in psychic development was tempered by a more interpersonal perspective:

> In the young infant's mind every internal experience is interwoven with his phantasies, and on the other hand every phantasy contains elements of actual experience, and it is only by analysing the transference situation to its depths that we are able to discover the past in both its realistic and phantastic aspects (Klein: 1952: 59).

By the 1950s, Klein thus acknowledged explicitly that the constitutional components were also modified by real experience. This interpersonal perspective was developed more extensively by another very influential Kleinian theorist, Wilfred Bion. Bion's (1962a, b) interest was in the mother's role as a "container", as the baby's auxiliary digestive track for emotional events. Bion assumed that the baby, overwhelmed by impressions of the world, required another human mind (i.e. a container) with the capability to accept, absorb and transform these experiences into meaning. Bion's ideas built upon Klein's thinking and afforded a more sophisticated appreciation of the dialectic interplay between external and internal reality.

The paranoid-schizoid position

According to Klein, the newborn is not equipped to deal with the complexities of emotional experience. Klein hypothesised that, at this early stage, the baby manages her emotional experience within a kind of black and white dichotomy. She assumed that all sensations are personified and attributed to either good or bad objects such that in the first few months of life, frustration of the baby's needs is not experienced simply as pain; rather, the subjective experience of frustration is attributed to an active attack from a persecuting, external agent, that is a "bad" object.

The first object that acquires substantial significance in the baby's world is its source of nutrition, namely, the breast. When the baby is fed, the breast provides a plentiful supply of milk, whereas at other times the breast will be empty. These two different states evoke in the baby two corresponding emotional responses: either feelings of being taken care of by an attentive mother (i.e. the good breast/mother), which then contributes to an experience of pleasure and satiation, or the experience of being deprived or neglected (i.e. the bad breast/mother) with the resultant affective experience of anger and perhaps even terror. Klein thus postulated that early on, the object is split into good and bad based on gratifying and frustrating experiences, respectively. The relative preponderance of positive over negative drives and affects was seen as a crucial variable influencing later psychic health.

Klein suggested that, from the very beginning of life, the baby feels a dread of destruction from within and that this has to be somehow channelled away from the self. In the first six months of life, Klein hypothesised that the very early immature ego protects itself from the bad object by a mechanism, which splits the object and the ego.[11] She suggested that the way in which the baby manages this predicament is by projecting its own destructive impulses out into the world, which then becomes bad and persecuting.

In these early months, it is the splitting of the object, which leads the baby to experience the object in a form that magnifies one feature while eclipsing all others. "Bad" objects are experienced as all bad and simply intent on destroying the baby. "Good" ones are, in contrast, all good with solely benign interests in doing good for the baby. The nursing phase thus provides ample opportunities to experience oneself as being taken care of or of being neglected or deprived. This, in turn, provides prototypes of positive and negative relationships that are translated into internalised representations of relationships.

Whilst splitting and projection enable the baby to keep the "good" good by splitting off and projecting what is experienced as "bad", it contributes to an internal state of fear and suspicion of the bad breast/object that might retaliate. This triggers paranoid anxieties, hence Klein called this mental

---

[11]When we use splitting, some aspect of the self is separated and obliterated as if it did not belong to the self. For example, people sometimes deny any aggression or envy in themselves.

state the *paranoid-schizoid position*. This position is marked by extreme lability of mental representations: good is experienced rapidly turning into bad.

The paranoid-schizoid position places human aggression and destructiveness at the core of our psyche. Indeed, Kleinian ideas continue to pivot around the innate destructiveness of the human infant. Klein held that everyone is innately predisposed to develop both libidinal and aggressive phantasies in a relationship with others.[12] Klein's description of the paranoid-schizoid position makes clear her belief that hate and envy are as much a part of the infant's innate emotional repertoire as is its capacity to love.

Klein took Freud's concept of the death instinct further and understood envy to be one of its most important manifestations. Klein (1957) suggests that early primitive envy represents a particularly malignant form of innate aggression. This is because, unlike other forms of destructiveness, which are turned against bad objects already seen as persecutory, envy is hatred directed towards the good object; it arouses a premature expression of depressive anxiety about damage to the good object. Envy may be triggered by frustration or inconsistent parenting. However, according to Klein, envy and other forms of aggression are not inevitably linked to deprivation. The child, for example, may resent the inevitable limitations of maternal care, find it hard to tolerate the mother's control over it and might prefer to destroy it rather than experience the frustration.

Klein has been criticised for attributing to very young infants innate capacities reflecting considerable cognitive complexity. The ability to deal with ego-threatening impulses by splitting them off and projecting them into an external agent presupposes, for example, a degree of differentiation in the cognitive organisation of experience. Moreover, it implies a differentiated sense of self and other, since, if this were not the case, it would be impossible to displace the experienced source of negative affect from the ego to an external object.

Though Klein's developmental claims at first appear to be far fetched, more recent observational evidence is nevertheless consistent with some of them (Gergely, 1991). In sharp contrast to Freud's early depiction of the baby as enveloped in a state of primary narcissism, recent research reveals a very different kind of baby – one who actively perceives and learns, and who is pre-equipped, as it were, with specific expectations about

---

[12]Klein thought that the harsh superego was an early manifestation of the death instinct whereby the death instinct internally directed leads to destructiveness towards the self and others.

the physical and social world. We now know, for example, that babies are capable of relatively complex information processing, organisation and retention (i.e. they have an early functioning short-term memory system) (Stern, 1985; Gergely, 1991), and preferences (e.g. for the human face). Infant research has shown that at birth the baby reveals innate coordination of perception and action, evidenced by imitation of adults' facial gestures based on the availability of a short-term memory system. There is also empirical evidence to suggest that babies assume physical objects have cohesion, boundedness and rigidity.[13] Gergely (1991) and Stern (1985) both argue that the key feature of these early capacities is the baby's sensitivity to abstract properties, not linked to particular sensory modalities; babies are able to detect consistencies across modalities even more than modality specific, physical features. Overall, these various strands of research provide compelling evidence suggesting that babies are equipped, at birth, with the cognitive and perceptual skills that enable them to build internal representational models of the object world.

The depressive position

In the second six months of life, Klein hypothesised that the baby achieves a sufficient level of sophistication to recognise that the loved and hated object are one and the same. This paves the way for "whole object" relating, which rests on an acknowledgement of the object's separateness. This recognition is accompanied by feelings of sadness, guilt and regret for the perceived aggression that was at first directed against the "bad" breast now recognised as being the same as the "good" breast. Klein called this mental state the *depressive position*. The internalisation of objects that attract ambivalent feelings creates a deeply troubling internal world dominated by guilt feelings and attempts to repair the damaged objects. This new-found concern for the other as a whole object is termed *depressive anxiety*.

The depressive position inaugurates a new mode of relating to objects. A fundamental difference between the paranoid-schizoid and the depressive position is that in the former, the concern is that we will be harmed by others whereas in the latter, the anxiety is that we have caused damage to the other. Modern Kleinian theorists (e.g. Steiner, 1992) see the critical aspect of the depressive position as the child's achievement of separateness and the perception of the object's independence. The major developmental challenge, according to Kleinians, is working through the depressive position. This requires that the child learns that love is constant, even in the face of rages and aggressive phantasies. Until the

---

[13]See Gergely (1991) for a very good review of this kind of research.

child learns this, she will interpret all frustrations and separations as a form of retribution because of past destructive phantasies dating back to the paranoid-schizoid position. The child thus has to accept responsibility for the destructive phantasies and therefore experience emotions that reflect mental acts of reparation, such as sorrow and guilt.

It is important to note that Klein spoke of a *position*[14] rather than a stage when writing about the paranoid-schizoid and depressive positions. She used this to mean, in particular, the *position in relation to an object*; a position, or if you like, a state of mind, associated with particular anxieties, defences and phantasies. The paranoid–schizoid position refers to the constellation of anxieties and defences associated with a relatively weak ego that feels threatened from without, whereas the depressive position is associated with a more integrated ego. Klein's theory contains the notion of alternating cycles between the paranoid–schizoid and depressive positions, contrasting with Freud's linear theory of psychosexual stages. There is a dynamic relationship between the two positions and neither is ever resolved once and for all: there may be particular stages in our lives where we might regress to a paranoid–schizoid position and be dominated by paranoid anxieties. Broadly speaking, the more depressive features dominate over paranoid–schizoid features and so if love prevails over hate, the better the prognosis for change. The wish to repair counterbalances destructiveness.

The Oedipus complex

Both Freud and Klein were in agreement about the psychic significance of the Oedipus Complex and its resolution. They disagreed over its timing in developmental terms. Klein believed that the baby had to contend with Oedipal experiences from the first year of life. She suggested that the baby has strong feelings towards her parents that include feelings of being excluded from their relationship. Klein thus proposed that, even at this early developmental stage, the baby experiences the parents as having a relationship with each other. This experience can take on various emotional colourings depending on the baby's state of mind. For example, when loving feelings have the upper hand, the baby experiences the parental union as a productive one that will also benefit the baby. When destructive feelings dominate the baby's mind, she may experience the parents as bad objects who are excluding or attacking her or each other.

---

[14]Klein was clear that she did not want to use the term "phase" as she was not trying to replace the oral, anal and genital phases put forward by Freud, which she maintained within her own model.

According to Klein, the resolution of the Oedipal conflict requires a predominance of loving feelings over hatred for the Oedipal rival, which allows both the loved parent and the hated parent to come together in the child's mind. In other words, successful resolution of the Oedipus complex reflects a capacity for whole object relating. Klein thus effectively reformulated the Oedipus complex as an attempt to resolve depressive anxieties and guilt through reparation.

Contemporary Kleinians have developed her ideas further. They understand that the family triangle provides the child with two links connecting her separately with each parent. Importantly, it also confronts the child with the link between the parents, which excludes her:

> If the link between the parents is perceived in love, and hate can be tolerated in the child's mind, it provides the child with a prototype of an object relationship of a third kind in which he or she is a witness and not a participant. A third position then comes into existence from which object relationships can be observed (Britton, 1998: 42).

How the child negotiates the family triangle[15] is understood to have significant implications for the child's ability to symbolise, that is, to be able to represent her experiences and hence to have perspective. Being able to take the position of an observer allows us to develop perspective, to entertain other points of view and is therefore fundamental to our capacity to communicate with others based on an understanding that they may have different intentions, feelings or desires to our own.

Theory in practice

Contemporary Kleinian thinking has moved on from its early emphasis on the internal world of phantasy (i.e. a one-person psychology) to adopt a more fully interpersonal view (i.e. a two-person psychology), which takes into account the role of real trauma or environmental failure in shaping the contents of the internal world. Kleinian formulations thus encapsulate the complex interplay between phantasy and reality in understanding patients' predicaments. The Kleinian therapist is interested in how external experiences are internalised through the interplay of projection and introjection. At the level of practice, however, the emphasis remains more skewed towards a focus on phantasy and the here-and-now therapeutic situation rather than the patient's past experiences. The

---

[15]This is not to be taken literally. The Oedipus complex does not only occur in families where both parents are present. It is also operative in single parent families. The triangle may relate to an actual threesome or to the idea of a "third" person held in the mind of one of the parents even if the other parent is physically absent.

therapist focuses on the transference relationship and a large proportion of Kleinian interpretations address the complexities of the therapeutic relationship. There is ongoing debate amongst Kleinians as to the role of more reconstructive interpretations that link present behaviour to the past. On the whole, such interpretations are made, but more sparingly than within other approaches, thereby maintaining the focus on the "total transference situation" (Joseph, 1985).

Interpretations typically concern the patient's separation anxiety (e.g. as manifest in reaction to breaks in the therapy) and the defences against it, the projection of aggression and the resultant experience of being persecuted from without, depression and mourning and the patient's efforts at reparation. This emphasis contrasts, for example, with the content of interpretations influenced by an ego-psychological perspective where the focus would more often be on Oedipal triangulation, castration anxiety and the defences against it.

Object-Relations Approaches II: The British Independent School

The psychoanalytic movement in Britain was deeply affected by the schisms that developed between those who followed Anna Freud and those who followed Melanie Klein. The therapists and analysts who were most responsive to Klein's ideas were eventually united under the banner of the object-relations school. The central tenet of the object-relations approach is that we are driven primarily by our attachment needs, that is, we are driven to form relationships with other people. If it is possible to speak of drives, the object-relations theorist would say that drives emerge in the context of relationships and are secondary to relationship needs.

Although Klein's interest lay in the individual's relationships to objects, she was nevertheless primarily focused on primitive instinctual impulses and their phantasised effects upon internal objects. She was less interested in how real people might have contributed to the phantasies and, more generally, to psychopathology. The rise of object-relations theories post-Klein was supported by a shift of interest towards developmental issues and, particularly, a recognition of the impact of the early relationship between the baby and the mother or other primary caregiver.

The term "object relations" made its first appearance in a paper published by Karl Abraham in 1924. It has very strong associations with British analysts such as Ronald Fairburn and Donald Winnicott. Fairbairn (1954) saw object seeking, safety and connection as much more central than pleasure and pain as regulating principles in the psyche. He rejected Freud's biologism and emphasised that it is object relationships that are internalised. Pleasure and anxiety reduction followed the attainment of a desired relationship between self and other. Winnicott (1975) emphasised the key role of the mother's relationship with her baby and is perhaps best-known for coining the phrase the "good enough mother" who cares for her baby but also gradually disillusions her so as to allow the baby to develop her capacity to withstand frustration.

Object-relations theories are diverse and do not have a commonly agreed-upon definition. Many British Independent therapists identify themselves with a broadly object-relational perspective but they do not subscribe to a single coherent framework, hence their collective description as the "Independents". They are united more by a reluctance to be restricted by theoretical constraints, refusing to align themselves exclusively with either the Freudians or the Kleinians.

At the risk of glossing over subtle differences between the Independents, we might say that the Independents abandoned the libidinally driven structural model and emphasised the importance of relationships – especially the earliest relationships – to the developing psyche. These theories reflect a commitment to understanding the development of the individual in interaction with others. The Independents acknowledge the important part played by phantasy in the internal world, but they argue that phantasy has no meaning as an innate capacity; rather, it is understood as arising out of the individual's interaction with real external objects.

Unlike the Kleinians, who view aggression as innate, the Independents see it as reactive to external impingements. Likewise, although most Independents subscribe to the Kleinian notion of psychic positions, the paranoid-schizoid position is understood by many of them as a primarily "reactive development" (Rayner, 1991) consequent upon the child's interaction with the environment and the experience of trauma. Along with most relational theorists, the Independents have de-emphasised the role of the Oedipus complex and sexuality in development. This has been replaced by an interest in the shift from dyadic to triadic relationships associated with fundamental transformations in cognitive and social functioning.

Theory in practice

As with some contemporary Kleinians, many Independent therapists also work with the transference relationship. They are interested in exploring the quality of the patient's earliest relationships that have been internalised and how they manifest themselves in the transference. Through the transference, the therapist can grasp the patient's earliest internalised object relations. This understanding is used to clarify the patient's relationships in the present, because it is assumed that all current relationships are filtered through the highly idiosyncratic lens of these early organised self and object representations. Nevertheless, unlike many Kleinians, the Independents argue that it is important to recognise the reality of the patient's experiences. They understand memories from the past as being elaborations in phantasy of events that actually happened. This emphasis is distinctively different to the primary interest of many Kleinians on the internal world of phantasy.

From a technical point of view many Independents maintain an interest in reconstructive interpretations. The past is explored because of the light it sheds upon the developmental origin of the representations of relationships. The Independents expect that the patient will re-enact in therapy the earliest relationships thus creating an opportunity to re-evaluate these relationships. Outdated maladaptive schemata are worked through and newer, more adaptive relational models are worked towards. Central to this work is countertransference and its use by the therapist to understand the patient's pre-verbal experiences.

Whereas Kleinians tend to approach the interaction between the patient and the therapist with an intrapsychic focus, the Independents approach it more as a mutually constructed interpersonal space. Amongst Independent therapists, there is a recognition that the patient and therapist work in a "transitional space" and that their exchanges ideally contribute to a playful creativity. The approach therefore reflects a greater appreciation of the mutuality inherent in the therapeutic relationship. While sensitive to the patient's negative transference, and in contrast to the Kleinians but in common with the Freudians, many Independent therapists recognise the importance of facilitating a good therapeutic alliance and do so by using the patient's positive feelings about the therapy.

Self Psychology

By the 1960s, clinicians were reporting on challenging patients whose difficulties were insufficiently well captured as problems in managing instinctual urges (i.e. as in drive theory) or the inflexible organisation of defences against anxiety (i.e. as in ego psychology) or the activation of internal objects from which the patient had inadequately differentiated (i.e. as in object-relations theory). Rather, these were patients who reported "feeling empty" and who were in search of constant reassurance even if, on the surface at least, they sometimes appeared self-assured, even arrogant or grandiose. Heinz Kohut's *self psychology* developed in response to this specific group of patients.

Kohut has been one of the most powerful, controversial figures in the American psychoanalytic movement. His ideas grew primarily out of his work with patients with narcissistic disorders. Narcissistic disorders are personality disorders characterised by a weak or unstable sense of self and a corresponding difficulty in regulating self-esteem. Unlike Freud who believed that narcissistic patients were not amenable to psychoanalysis because they were too self-absorbed to engage with the positive transference thought necessary for treatment, Kohut believed that such patients were amenable to treatment but they required some adaptations to standard analytic technique. While Kohut was heavily influenced by his work with narcissistic patients in the development of his theory, over time, his theory and technique have been applied to all forms of psychopathology.

For Kohut, self-cohesion is the primary motivation guiding human behaviour. At the root of anxiety is the self's experience of a defect and a lack of cohesiveness and continuity in the sense of self.[16] In contrast to the object-relations theorists, who emphasise the internalised relationships between representations of self and objects, self psychology is interested in how external relationships help develop and maintain self-esteem. Defences are understood not only as protecting the person from anxiety, but also in helping to sustain a consistent, positively valued sense of self. Accordingly, the focus of Kohut's work has been on understanding the ways in which patients may be in need of particular responses from the environment so as to maintain self-esteem.

Kohut argued that narcissistic needs persist throughout life. He suggested that the development of narcissism has its own developmental path and that caregiving figures (i.e. objects) serve special functions. He emphasised the role of empathy in the development of the self, underscoring his belief that the goal of human maturation involves differentiation within empathic relationships. The term *selfobject* was used to describe the mirroring function that other people perform for the self. Selfobjects can perhaps be best understood as representing functions such as soothing or validating rather than people as such. According to Kohut, we need selfobjects in our environment throughout our life to assist us in our emotional survival.

In his work with narcissistic patients, Kohut noted that they tended to form two particular kinds of transference: the *mirror transference* and

---

[16]Kohut uses the term "self" to denote almost all of the personality.

the *idealising transference*. In the mirror transference, the patient turns to
the therapist to obtain validation. According to Kohut, such approving
responses are essential for normal development. A failure of parental
empathy when the child is in need of a mirroring response was thought
to contribute to a later difficulty in maintaining a sense of wholeness and
positive self-esteem. Without such empathic responses, the child's sense
of self fragments. In Kohutian terms, when we speak of pathology, we are
always speaking of a pathology of the self[17] resulting from a thwarting
or neglect by the parents of the child's early need to be admired and
to admire.

The second form of transference, namely, the idealising transference,
refers to a situation in which the patient experiences the therapist as
an all powerful parental figure whose presence is necessary in order to
feel soothed. Kohut argued that an important aspect of development is
the opportunity for the child to be able to idealise the parental figures
who, in turn, provide a model worthy of idealisation. Empathic responses
from the selfobjects facilitate the unfolding of infantile grandiosity and
encourage feelings of omnipotence that enable the building of an idealised
image of the parent with whom the child wishes to merge. When parents
fail to provide for the child's narcissistic needs, the representation of self
as omnipotent and the representation of the caregiver as perfect become
hardened precluding replacement of omnipotent self-representation with
a realistic sense of self.

Unlike classical Freudian and Kleinian theory, Kohut therefore put forward a theory that placed at its centre the view that the real, and often early,
disturbances of parenting contribute significantly to psychopathology.
Kohut's views can be traced within the British object-relations theories.
There are certainly echoes of his ideas in Winnicott's notion of "good
enough mothering" and Balint's (1968) idea of the "basic fault", that is,
the feeling that something is missing caused, according to Balint, by the
mother's failure to respond to the child's basic needs. Likewise, Fairbairn
(1954) understood his schizoid patient's difficulties as reflecting a failure
by the mother to provide experiences that would reassure him that he was
loved for who he was.

Theory in practice

A major goal of therapy, within this framework, is to strengthen the weak-
ened ego so that it can manage less than optimal self-object experiences

---

[17]The self here is a superordinate structure that encompasses the ego.

without a significant loss of self-cohesion. The focus is on the patient's sense of self as it is empathically grasped by the therapist. Attention is given to the affect-laden configurations of self and other identifications and interactions. The therapist's task is to "correct" the patient's narcissistic defences caused by an assumed lack of empathic caretaking in early life.

Kohutian therapists accentuate the need for an anti-authoritarian attitude. They believe that an objectifying stance towards the patient is inherently traumatising. The approach represents a shift away from the technical neutrality that dominates both Freudian and Kleinian approaches. In this respect, these ideas were precursors to the current wave of interest in the therapist's subjectivity that is at the centre of the preoccupations of the intersubjective and interactional schools of psychoanalysis (see below). Notwithstanding the notable differences between self psychology and Freudian and Kleinian approaches, the view of the mind at the core of self psychology is, as with Freud and Klein, non-intersubjective in that it positions the therapist as an objective, if empathic, observer and interpreter of the true essence of the patient's self.

Postmodernism Meets Psychoanalysis: Intersubjective and Interactional Approaches

At the heart of Freudian and Kleinian psychoanalysis we find the Cartesian doctrine of the isolated mind considered to be an objective entity alongside other objects. The individual is thought capable of accurately perceiving the nature of an object outside his consciousness or frame of reference. From this stance, it is thus possible to sustain a belief in the therapist's neutrality and objectivity, as it suggests that mental life can exist independent of the clinical situation.

The questions of subjectivity and objectivity have long been debated within psychoanalysis.[18] Such debates are at the heart of the development of the intersubjective school reflecting the influence of postmodern thinking on psychoanalysis. Recent psychoanalytic theory and practice – especially in North America – has shifted towards more relational, intersubjective and social-constructionist positions. These present a clinical and epistemological challenge to the classic analytic position. These approaches argue that we cannot approach clinical material as if it were an entity that exists in the patient's mind, conceptually isolated from the relational matrix from which it emerges (Dunn, 1995).

---

[18]See Louw & Pitman (2001) for a good review of these debates.

The literature on intersubjectivity is devoted to a recognition, and exploration, of the subtly complex nature of the mutual influence of therapist and patient on each other and the consequences of this. In many respects, this position seems eminently sensible as it is impossible to argue that the therapist, as a person, has no impact, or that therapists, by virtue of their own training analysis, are beyond being tripped over by their own unconscious. In other words, what transpires in the consulting room is inevitably influenced by the therapist's own psychology. To argue otherwise, in any polarised fashion, is indefensible. The fact that psychoanalysis involves intersubjectivity does not, however, necessarily mean that it lacks objectivity altogether. Subjective and objective aspects of psychoanalysis can be considered to be dialectically related. Objectivity needs to be understood as relative given our subjective limitations and the difficulty of disentangling the influence of the other in self-knowledge. The degree to which this interferes in the therapeutic situation and how such interference needs to be handled are questions worthy of thoughtful debate.

The intersubjectivists are open to multiple theories, which are regarded necessary for reaching the patient's uniqueness and complexity, unlike Freudian or Kleinian therapists who maintain that a single comprehensive theory of mind can be applicable to all patients. Post-modernism has effectively forced psychoanalysis to acknowledge that irrational beliefs lie at the heart of its enterprise, that no one theory holds the truth, as truth is always relative or co-constructed, never fixed. In the therapeutic situation, this means that truth is created by the therapeutic couple.

Levine & Friedman (2000) present intersubjectivity as a "meta theory" that reflects the inherent nature of human relatedness and it is conceptually independent of any theory of mind or school of psychoanalysis. They emphasise that the here-and-now relational experiences shape the expression of the patient's conflicts, not simply as a result of transference, but rather as a result of the co-construction of new contexts by both subjectivities. Hoffman (1992) argues that what takes place between the therapist and the patient will be co-determined by the unconscious desires and the defensive needs of both parties. Ogden (1994) refers to intersubjective reality as the "analytic third". He contends that the therapist's responses are never fully individual events. Rather, the meaning of the therapist's reactions is always a newly created reality by virtue of the original, never-to-be-repeated interactions of the specific therapeutic couple.

The views of those subscribing to this broad school are diverse and there is no definitive intersubjective-relational view. The key ideas of the interpersonal school of psychoanalysis form the foundations of this approach (e.g. Harry Stack Sullivan, Eric Fromm, Frieda Fromm Reichmann). Personality development is linked to the interpersonal field. Past as well as new relationships model psychic life rather than being determined by fixed structures derived from past unconscious conflicts. A lot of importance is accorded to the mother–infant relationship and the difficulties associated with separation-individuation. Neither sexuality nor aggression are seen as driving forces of either development or adaptation. Rather, sexual and aggressive responses are thought to be understandable in the context of the individual's infantile and early childhood experiences that have influenced specific expectations of what happens in relationships. In this approach, we encounter a reluctance to privilege unconscious phantasy over actuality but nowadays most therapists agree that reality is encountered inevitably through imagination and phantasy.

Theory in practice

More than other psychoanalytic therapists, the intersubjectivists have critically challenged the classical positivist view of the therapist's objectivity. The intersubjective schools call for a more open, inclusive and egalitarian dialogue about the nature of the therapeutic relationship. The work of therapy is to explore and interpret the patient's subjectivity within a context that acknowledges that the analytic dialogue and process will reflect, and be constituted from, the mutual and inevitable unconscious emotional interactions between therapist and patient. The core of the psychoanalytic inquiry is therefore not directed at the mind of the patient alone.

The implications for technique are significant. The approach has become associated with the use of less traditional interventions, such as self-disclosure. The intersubjectivists believe in forging intense relationships with their patients rather than maintaining a more aloof stance. Greater fluidity and responsiveness are the hallmarks of the therapeutic stance. The intersubjective tradition firmly believes that the patient's attachment and transference to the therapist cannot optimally occur without an emotional contribution that derives from the humanity and passion of the therapist's engagement with the patient (Levine & Friedman, 2000). The notion of a "real" relationship is implicit in this approach, where the therapist as observer is replaced with a model of the therapist as participant in a shared activity whose own personal psychology shapes the unfolding therapeutic process.

The therapeutic relationship is understood to be co-constructed between therapist and patient with the subjectivity of each contributing to the form and content of the dialogue that emerges.

The work of therapy focuses on an exploration of a new affective relational development. The patient's incorporation of this affective experience is considered to be a major therapeutic factor associated with outcome. What is crucial in therapy is the clarification of the patient's way of handling current anxieties and present experience. Reconstruction of past events is seen as important to clinical work. The concept of transference is regarded more critically as encouraging a fixed view of the patient's unconscious phantasy. This approach is also less concerned with the interpretation of aggression in the transference because aggression is understood to result from a breakdown of the positive relationship with the therapist and the loss of an empathic attitude rather than being primarily linked to intrapsychic conflicts in the patient.

The Significance of Early Relationships: The Contribution of Attachment Theory and Infant Research

An overview of psychoanalysis would be incomplete, and all the poorer, without consideration of the contributions of attachment theory. Early Freudian and Kleinian thinking were dominated by a psychology of absence. Attachment theorists and, more broadly, those psychoanalytically oriented developmental researchers have contributed a much-needed "psychology of presence" (Stern, 2000). Developmental research has devoted close attention to the quality of the child–caregiver bond showing its implications for the child's development of affect regulation, self-esteem, interpersonal functioning and overall mental health.

The views of Bowlby in particular have been deeply influential. Bowlby was a British psychiatrist who trained as a psychoanalyst at a time when object-relations approaches to psychoanalysis were beginning to take hold. Although Bowlby was supervised by Melanie Klein, he clashed with her over the issue of whether to involve the mother in the psychoanalytic treatment of a child – a position he strongly favoured. This difference in emphasis marked the beginning of Bowlby's eventual withdrawal from the mainstream psychoanalytic community. He was ignored within mainstream psychoanalysis for many years. We owe to the work of Fonagy (2001), in particular, the current interest of some psychoanalytic practitioners in Bowlby's ideas.

Unlike many object-relations theorists, for example, Winnicott who retained Freud's emphasis on sexual and aggressive drives and phantasies, Bowlby's attachment theory focused on the affective bond in close interpersonal relationships. He emphasised the baby's need to develop and sustain close relationships, thereby supplanting the importance of aggressive and libidinal drives. He viewed social bonds as primary biological givens. He suggested that the interaction with the caregiver was fundamentally important and provided the child with a secure base for exploration and self development. This was, as we have seen, in contrast to the biological determinism of the times based on the theory of libidinal and aggressive instincts.

Bowlby's work evolved out of his observations during World War II of the consequences of being deprived of contact with the primary caregiver in children who had been separated from them because of the war. Bowlby based his ideas on ethological theory suggesting that the infant attachment bond is an instinctually guided behavioural system that has functioned throughout human evolution to protect the infant from danger and predators. According to Bowlby, attachment behaviours were seen as part of a behavioural system, which involved inherent motivation, in other words, it was not reducible to another drive.

Attachment theory holds that the baby is vitally interested in objects, shows preferences for particular kinds of visual and auditory configurations and enjoys making things happen in the world. There is now a great deal of research supporting the notion that the baby has a biologically determined propensity to sustain his attachment to those who provide vital regulation of physiological, behavioural, neural and affective systems (Slade, 2000).

Bowlby placed great emphasis on the child's real experience, de-emphasising the primacy given by some of his contemporaries to the internal world. He believed that Klein and her followers had overestimated the role of infantile phantasy, thereby neglecting the role of actual experiences in the child's early life. The baby's actual experience with her primary attachment figures is, according to Bowlby, the bedrock of psychic structure.

Despite the historical links with object-relational perspectives, attachment theory has not received as much attention within psychoanalysis as would at first appear likely. It has instead been traditionally of more interest to developmental psychologists concerned with normal development (Fonagy, 2001). The parallel lines along which psychoanalytic theory and attachment theory have developed may be partly accounted for by the fact that Bowlby was very interested in empirically validating his ideas – a practice that was by no means prevalent within psychoanalysis in his

time. He focused on the observable behaviour of babies and their interactions with their caregivers, especially their mothers, and he encouraged
prospective studies of the effects of early attachment relationships on
personality development.

Bowlby's work clearly showed that caregivers varied in their capacity to
provide a secure base for the child with some mothers being more slow
or erratic in responding, for example, to their baby's cries, while others
might be more intrusive. These observations led investigators (Ainsworth
et al., 1978) to contrast secure attachment with *insecure attachment*, which
was later further subdivided between *avoidant, anxious-ambivalent* and
disorganised (Hesse & Main, 2000). The four attachment classifications
describe different responses to seeking care and imply differences in the
structures that regulate internal experience and guide the development
and maintenance of object relationships.

The attachment behavioural system is underpinned by a set of cognitive mechanisms that are described by Bowlby as *internal working models*.
These are essentially representational systems or, if you like, schemas
of self and other in interaction. In secure attachments, we find a representational system within which the attachment figure is experienced as
accessible and responsive. In insecure attachments, we find a representational system where the responsiveness of the caregiver is not taken for
granted and the child has to develop strategies for managing the perceived
unresponsiveness.

Consistent with Bowlby's theory, these different attachment styles have
been found to be closely associated with differences in caretaker warmth
and responsiveness. Secure attachment to the mother in infancy reflects
the mother's reliable and responsive provision of security and love as well
as the meeting of more basic needs such as food and warmth. Insecure
attachment is more typically associated with unresponsive or inconsistent
responses from the caregiver.

Investigators have also applied the concept of attachment theory to the
study of adult behaviour and personality. This has led to the development
of the adult attachment interview (Main, 1995), which allows for the
investigation of adults' internal working models, that is, the security of
the adult's overall model of attachment and of the self in attachment
experiences. In several research studies, adult attachment styles have
significantly predicted relationship outcomes, patterns of coping with
stress and couple communication (Brennan & Shaver, 1994; Kirkpatrick &
Davis, 1994).

Attachment theory and the fascinating developmental research that it
has spawned lends support to the continued relevance of developmental

history to the psychoanalytic process, for the psychoanalytic construct of internalised object relationships and the likely origins of these models in actual relational transactions, even if these are most probably partly distorted, through the processes of projection and introjection, as suggested by the Kleinians (Fonagy, 2001).

Conclusions: One Psychoanalysis or Many?[19]

Freudian and object-relational approaches are often contrasted. Freud's theories underwent multiple revisions, yet throughout he remained loyal to the centrality of the drives viewing them as the fundamental motivational force in development. As far as Freud was concerned, it was the baby's helplessness that resulted in the attachment to caregiving figures. The attachment was thus understood as developing secondarily in response to the baby's oral needs (e.g. feeding) that the caregivers could satisfy. Nevertheless, it is apparent while reading Freud that he never ignored the importance of relationships in shaping the development of the individual. His views on transference, identification and the development of the superego, to name but a few, highlight his awareness of the influence of the "other" on the developing mind.[20]

Nevertheless, it is fair to say that in spite of his appreciation of the importance of others, Freud's theory was sensation dominated rather than relationship dominated. Klein took Freud's ideas further and refined them in a very innovative manner, both emphasising the importance of very early developmental experiences and highlighting the role of unconscious phantasy in psychic life. Whereas Freud's focus on early development placed sexuality at its epicentre, Klein was more concerned with the role of innate destructiveness and on how anxiety was managed from the very beginning of life.

---

[19]Please refer to the paper by R. Wallerstein (1988), 'One Psychoanalysis or Many?' *International Journal of Psychoanalysis*, **69**: 5–21.

[20]Although some Contemporary Freudians still subscribe to the above-mentioned classical Freudian views, there is now more interest in the role of unconscious phantasy and in object relations. This reflects the more systematic integration of object-relations theory within the Freudian approach as exemplified in the work of Kernberg (1985). He argues that libido and aggression are constructed from good and bad experiences with others. He suggests that affect and cognition are integrated by intrapsychic experiences which in turn link libidinal and aggressive drive systems. Internalised object relationships, which are internalised in selfobject dyadic units, are characterised by a particular affective tone. He has proposed that the development of mental life involves the laying down in memory of "units of experience" involving the self and other around an affect (e.g. the infant crying in hunger and the mother's response of feeding). Object relation units, according to Kernberg, are therefore major building blocks of intrapsychic structure.

Just as Freud can be criticised for not sufficiently emphasising the importance of relationships in the development of the psyche, Klein can be criticised for overemphasising the importance of internalised relationships, the quality of which she attributed as much to innate phantasies as to external factors. The work of the post-Kleinians has mostly concerned itself with redressing this imbalance and paying due attention to the experiences of real trauma and deprivation and their interaction with internal phantasies.

Kleinian thinking evolved into an alternative metapsychology to the one put forward by Freud. Along with that an alternative theory of technique ensued. Klein's contribution was unquestionably vital to the richness of analytic ideas that have developed since Freud's time. In particular, it inspired the development that came to be known as the British Object-Relations School and the British Independents who have produced some of the most interesting writing within psychoanalysis.

The diversity in theoretical thinking that dominates the British psychoanalytic scene stands in contrast to the stronghold of ego psychology in North America for many years. Steadily, however, other perspectives have risen to prominence. Kleinian thinking took root more slowly and hesitantly in North America as compared to the popularity of her ideas in Britain. Kohut's self psychology – which has remained comparatively neglected in Britain – emerged as an alternative metapsychology and technique, providing a helpful contrast to the technical neutrality and impersonality of the ego-psychological tradition. Significantly, Kohut developed a psychology of deficit that contrasted with the psychology of conflict, central to the ego-psychological tradition.

In North America in particular, hermeneutics, subjectivist and interactional approaches have also gained a strong foothold now. The interpersonal, intersubjective and interactional have gradually replaced the intrapsychic. These approaches have in common an abiding concern not to place the person of the therapist beyond the reality testing of the patient and to acknowledge the impossibility of achieving neutrality, as originally suggested by Freud.

Grouped under the heading of "psychoanalysis", we thus find multiple and divergent theories of mental functioning and of treatment. Exciting though all these developments are, these theoretical frameworks are nothing more than metaphors that we employ to help us in our clinical work. Strenger (1989) describes two visions of human nature that help situate different psychoanalytic approaches on a continuum ranging from those therapists who share what he calls the *classic vision* to those who espouse a *romantic vision* of human nature. The classic vision approaches psychopathology in terms of an internal conflict, whereas the romantic vision views psychopathology in terms of deficit. These stances, in turn, reflect differences at the level of clinical practice. The classic therapist views transference as a recreation of early object relationships and views the therapist's role as technical and interpretative. The romantic therapist views transference as also containing a search for a new object and views the therapist's role as mutative via empathic relatedness. Analytic therapists situate themselves somewhere along this continuum and this determines, in part, what they choose to privilege in their patient's communications and how they approach this in the consulting room.

There is some common ground in the high-level general theories that the different schools of psychoanalysis have put forward. Table 1.1 summarises what are considered in this book to be key assumptions that are broadly shared by the various schools. Nevertheless, schisms continue to abound around such core issues as to whether problems are pre-Oedipal (i.e. their onset is associated with experiences that predate the possibility of verbal articulation) or Oedipal, whether we are dealing with a one-person versus a two-person psychology (i.e. intrapsychic focus versus interpersonal/intersubjective focus) and whether pathology is the result of conflict or deficit.

The question of deficit as contrasted with conflict pathology regularly emerges in clinical debates. Notwithstanding their differences, both Freud

Table 1.1   Key psychoanalytic assumptions

- We have a conscious as well as an unconscious mental life.
- Meaning systems include both conscious (i.e. verbalisable) and unconscious aspects of experience.
- Causality is as much a characteristic of external events as it is of other processes in the psychic world.
- Our early relationships contribute to the development of representations of relationships that are affectively toned.
- We have an internal life that gives texture and colour to each new situation that we encounter: meanings and phantasies shape behaviour and thinking whether or not they are the originators of the behaviour or thought.
- The inner world of process and experience mediates the individual's relationship with the external world.
- The internal world is in a perpetual dynamic interaction with the external world, so that both influence each other.
- We all have a developmental history and a current life: both need to be understood in the context of therapy.
- In therapy, we are always dealing with developmental pathology and conflict pathology, though their respective contributions will vary between patients.

---

and Klein essentially espouse a *theory of conflict*, unlike Kohut's self psychology and many of the intersubjectivists who espouse a *theory of deficit*. A deficit involves an insufficiency of appropriate input from the environment. Kohut argued, for example, that insufficient mirroring of the child by the parent led to low self-worth and difficulty in experiencing oneself as the centre of initiative.

Most contemporary practitioners accept the notion of deficit and believe that many patients' difficulties reflect developmental deficits. In this sense, deficit is understood as an adaptation reactive to difficult early experiences. Acknowledgement of deficit, however, does not mean that we need to reject conflict theory altogether or that we have to subscribe to theories of psychopathology that focus exclusively on traumatic early development. Rather, in most contemporary models, the emphasis is on an appreciation of the interaction between conflict and deficit (Gabbard, 1994). In many patients, we can observe manifestations of deficit at certain times of conflict and in certain specific areas of conflict (Druck, 1998). The patient's level of ego and superego structure, for example, will influence the way the patient manages particular conflicts. For example, the patient, who through the experience of early neglect, has failed to develop a capacity to reflect on his feelings (i.e. a deficit) may struggle to make sense of his wish for intimacy as well as his fear of it (i.e. a conflict). As a result of a specific deficit, the patient may manage the conflict in more concrete, action-oriented ways (e.g. breaking off a relationship without explanation).

While the richness and variety of psychoanalytic theories are the strength of psychoanalysis, they are also its major weaknesses. Whether we should espouse pluralism or monism is essentially a research question; without research evidence it is impossible to rationally decide between the different schools. Since there is no evidence at present that convincingly proves that any one psychoanalytic theory best fits current evidence, uncritical adherence to any one theory must be viewed with a degree of suspicion.

In the midst of this theoretical diversity, we find more convergence at the level of clinical theory, for example, the theory of transference and counter transference. Even in this respect, however, different approaches emphasise different aspects of technique, for example, whether interpretations should focus primarily on transference or not. Clinical experience soon teaches us that our greatest ally is a flexible approach that allows us to be responsive to the sometimes rapid, within-session changes in the patient's state of mind, which reflect changes at the level of psychic organisation (Akhtar, 2000). It is at this clinical level that clinical constructs can be put to some kind of empirical study and test. This will help us develop knowledge that can guide our clinical therapeutic work with more confidence and to answer our critics.

II. PRACTICE

What is Psychoanalytic Psychotherapy?

As human beings, we have an uncanny capacity to translate the question "what is?" into "what is best?" Differences between therapeutic models are not simply "differences" but all too often become the starting point for comparisons between therapeutic approaches so as to identify the so-called winner. Tribal mentality dominates the psychoanalytic world where each group reinforces its own identity by declaring its differences to another school of psychoanalysis. This dynamic is very apparent in the history of psychotherapy generally, as well as in the history of the relationship between psychoanalysis and its offspring, psychoanalytic therapy.

Psychoanalysis, as originally conceived by Freud, was a method of treatment restricted to a highly specified patient population. Freud was clear, and uncompromising, in his position: psychoanalysis could only be of help to those patients with neurotic character structures, who could develop a transference relationship, who were motivated, educated and not in a current crisis. By those standards, psychoanalysis would have little, if anything, to offer to the patients who are now referred for psychological help in public health service settings. As conceived by Freud – and as subscribed to still by some psychoanalysts – psychoanalysis should be restricted to patients ill enough to require extensive work, yet well enough to be able to make use of it. In other words, patients who are in distress but have sufficient ego strength to withstand the challenges and frustrations of the classical analytic setting, that is, the regressive aspects of the treatment such as, for example, the use of the couch and the unstructured nature of a psychoanalytic session.

Freud was no therapeutic optimist. According to him, the best analysis could hope for was to exchange neurotic misery for "common unhappiness".[21] This goal is by no means modest, but, to some, it may appear perhaps unsatisfactory given the significant commitment psychoanalysis requires of the patient. It would be fair to say that Freud was less interested in psychoanalysis as a treatment method than he was in its potential as a science of the mind. Nevertheless, he defended the application of psychoanalysis as superior to the other treatment methods available then, which he viewed as relying on suggestion alone. He warned that the large-scale application of psychoanalysis, ". . . will compel us to alloy the pure gold of analysis freely with the copper of direct suggestion" (1919: 168). Of

---

[21]Freud's therapeutic pessimism was linked to his belief in the power of the death instinct (Freud, 1920), a concept he put forward shortly after the end of the First World War.

course, Freud was well placed to appreciate the power, as well as the limitations, of suggestion, since his own treatment attempts began with the use of hypnosis.

According to Freud and his principal followers at the time, indirect suggestion deflected attention away from the contents of the patient's mind, the analysis of which was believed to be the road to psychological truth (Jones, 1997). Methods reliant on suggestion were duly dismissed as second-class treatments offering quick results, but no lasting cure. To speak of suggestion is, of course, to speak of none other than the influence of the therapeutic relationship. Thus, from the very beginning, interaction, that is, the idea of a relationship between two people was isomorphic with interpersonal influence. However, this fact is often glossed over in discussions about therapeutic action.

Nowadays, no psychoanalytic practitioner, unless totally lacking in diplomacy, would publicly dismiss other therapeutic approaches – psychoanalytic or otherwise – as merely effecting change through suggestion. Yet, behind a conscious acknowledgement of the value of other approaches, lies the fact that psychoanalysis is all too often still viewed from within the ranks as "better than", rather than simply "different to", other pathways to psychic change. Interestingly, this attitude is also present in current discussions about the relative merits of psychoanalytic therapy versus those of psychoanalysis proper.

The alleged differences between psychoanalysis proper and its offspring raise interesting questions. From the beginning, it was clear that even though psychoanalytic therapy shared its theoretical origins with psychoanalysis and employed the same techniques, and was therefore its legitimate offspring, this was not a favoured child. Many regarded it as a dilution of the classical approach arguing that it produced more superficial change, much like suggestion. With the rise of psychoanalytic therapy, the gold of psychoanalysis, as Freud had warned, was felt to be in danger of being diluted. This defensive attitude has not altogether disappeared from current debates:

> While recognising that psychoanalysis is not a universal treatment for all types of psychopathology, and recognising that certain severe psychopathologies require psychoanalytic psychotherapy rather than psychoanalysis proper... a prevalent attitude has been not to investigate these fields within the realm of psychoanalytic institutes and societies. The fear has been that focussed attention on such related and derivative fields might dilute the nature of psychoanalytic practice, threaten the identity of the psychoanalytic practitioner, and tend to confuse the work of psychoanalysts with that of less well, or

idiosyncratically, trained practitioners in the sociocultural environment (Kernberg, 2002: 328).

Conventionally, the difference between psychoanalysis proper and psychoanalytic therapy is conceptualised, partly pragmatically, in terms of
the frequency of sessions where psychoanalysis refers to at least four to
five weekly sessions, whereas psychoanalytic therapy refers to anything
up to three weekly sessions. Psychoanalysis is often also characterised by
an absence of specific goals (i.e. it is open-ended) with the aim of significant character change, whereas psychoanalytic therapy is described as
focusing on more circumscribed goals and aiming only for modifications
of behaviour and character structure. However, these distinctions do not
hold up to close scrutiny: even psychoanalytic therapy can stretch in an
open-ended manner over many years and its goals can be as ambitious
and far reaching as those of a full analysis. Of course, the more frequently
the patient attends sessions, the less skewed the therapy becomes towards
an exploration of the week's events, so that more time can be devoted to
exploring the unconscious and a more intense transference relationship
often develops.

Looked at dispassionately, the aims of the two approaches are not significantly different; nor are there differences in the techniques used or in
the theories that purport to support them. Both approaches focus on the
interpretation of transference, though in briefer and less-intensive psychoanalytic therapies only partial aspects of the transference are interpreted,
consistent with the particular focus of the therapy and the goals of a given
patient. Although some might argue that psychoanalytic therapy makes
use of a broader range of interventions than psychoanalysis proper, for
example, supportive interventions or clarifications, this is unlikely to be
supported by evidence because no analytic treatment relies exclusively on
interpretation alone.

The difficulty in clearly differentiating between the two approaches is
apparent: today what is considered to be, as it were, proper psychoanalysis within one theoretical school or in particular countries is reclassified by
another as being no more than "only psychotherapy". These tensions were
already apparent in Freud's time. Against the background of Freud's strict
and limited criteria of suitability for psychoanalysis, Ferenczi was one of
the most outspoken and controversial thinkers who challenged the ortho-
doxy. He paid a high price for this since, until comparatively recently,
he remained an unfortunately neglected figure within psychoanalysis.
Marginalised as practising "wild analysis", Ferenczi had a keen interest
in the therapeutic effects of a benevolent relationship with the therapist.
In his own approach, he transgressed established parameters for practice,

for example, by experimenting with briefer analyses and advocating a more active stance on the part of the analyst, thus anticipating some of the features of the current intersubjective school of psychoanalysis. His efforts reflected a desire to extend psychoanalysis to a broader patient population than that outlined by Freud. This was a stance later embraced by another analyst, Franz Alexander (Alexander & French, 1946). Alexander advocated the use of more active techniques amenable to working with a more disturbed population. His practice was predicated on a more affectively engaged relationship with the patient in contrast to the more reserved, aloof stance adopted by the majority of analysts at the time. This approach became identified with the notion of cure through a "corrective emotional experience". Although a corrective emotional experience provides perhaps an all too simplistic account of the change process (Jacobs, 2001), it is nevertheless a concept that has recently enjoyed a resurgence alongside the tide of interest in the mutative factors in psychoanalytic therapy besides transference interpretations (see Chapter 2).

For many years, there was considerable resistance to any dilution of psychoanalysis proper from within the psychoanalytic community, but in North America, as psychoanalysis struggled to integrate itself into mainstream psychiatry, it was confronted with a patient population far more diverse and challenging than that originally thought to respond best to psychoanalysis. This fact was instrumental in rekindling interest in the modifications to classical technique that might be necessary to accommodate the needs of more disturbed patients. The debate thus shifted towards a consideration of the differences between so-called supportive and exploratory therapy and their respective suitability for different patients. It is important here to note the distinction between interventions that are experienced as supportive and supportive therapy as an approach.

Supportive therapy draws on key ideas in the psychoanalytic tradition. The main difference lies in the manner in which the ideas are translated into therapeutic intervention. In supportive therapy, the therapist is very aware of the transference and the potential for resistance but these are only rarely interpreted. When the transference is interpreted, this is usually in the context of an intervention that counteracts the patient's projection with the goal of emphasising reality. So, for example, say the patient is experiencing the therapist as critical, a supportive intervention might look something like: *"I can see that you felt very hurt by what you experienced as my criticism but in fact what I was trying to say was not intended as a criticism. . ."* A supportive intervention involves responding to the patient's current reality, including realistic aspects of the transference. The therapist is more interactive and makes more use of psycho-educational information. The therapist may offer praise and encouragement and may, in some rarer situations, even offer a measure of reassurance through normalising interventions, such as: *"Most people in your situation would feel very distressed."* The approach is thus considered to be suitable for patients who are more disturbed or – to use the psychoanalytic terminology – those with less "ego strength" (see Chapter 4).

To clarify the difference between a supportive and an exploratory intervention, let us take as an example a patient who "forgets" to attend one of his sessions. When the patient next sees the therapist, he berates himself for this. Let us also assume that the week prior to the missed session the therapist had cancelled the session due to illness. If this patient was in a supportive therapy, his forgetting the session and his self-criticism might be addressed by saying something like: *"You are not bad for having forgotten."* The supportive therapist might then try to help the patient become more aware of a critical part of himself that puts him under pressure to always behave perfectly. If this patient had been in an exploratory therapy, the therapist might have instead said something like: *"I don't think you are only angry with yourself for having forgotten to come to your session, but you are also angry with me for having cancelled our last session."* The exploratory therapist thus aims to intervene by addressing what lies behind the patient's surface behaviour and takes up the patient's hostility actively by interpreting the unconscious meaning of the patient's behaviour.

Whereas supportive therapy maintains or strengthens existing defences and level of functioning, exploratory therapy fosters an increase in self-understanding through the patient's expression of his conflicts and the defences used and the therapist's interpretation of what is revealed. The therapist's interventions tend to address the problematic reactions of the patient towards the therapist and significant others.[22] Negative feelings towards the therapist are actively explored from the start whereas in supportive therapy they are not actively worked with unless they become a significant source of resistance.

The Aims of Psychoanalytic Psychotherapy: Different Perspectives

Psychoanalysis is an umbrella term that covers a range of theoretical schools. Notwithstanding their differences, all the schools converge on one conclusion with respect to the aims of treatment: if you are seeking to avoid conflict, you are in for a disappointment. Freud (1930) was explicit

---

[22] Brief psychoanalytic therapy may be either supportive or exploratory. It is generally based on the therapist's assessment of a constellation of thematically related dynamic conflicts.

on this matter: he maintained that man's happiness was never included in the plan of Creation and consequently neither does it feature as one of the aims of psychoanalytic treatment. Avoiding conflict is not the aim of therapy. Rather, the analytic approach underlines the importance of keeping conflict alive, even of re-igniting it, if it has been replaced with a defensive acquiescence or resignation to the status quo:

> It could be said that people come for psychoanalysis, people suffer, because they have suppressed a conflict by imposing an authoritarian order... It is illuminating to think of the superego not as the cause of conflict but as a saboteur of conflict (Phillips, 2001: 129).

The aims of psychoanalytic therapy have evolved over time. At first, the aims were formulated in general metapsychological terms, whereby making the unconscious conscious was the core aim of Freud's topographical model. In keeping with his later structural model of the mind, treatment was aimed at strengthening the position of the ego within the overall personality structure, promoting its autonomy and improving control over instinctual impulses:

> Analysis does not set out to make pathological reactions impossible but to give the patient's ego freedom to decide one way or another (Freud, 1923b: 50).

Alongside a more sturdy ego, the other main emphasis of treatment in the 1920s was to bring about a change in the patient's superego, making it more gentle and more indulgent towards the ego.

In the early days of psychoanalysis, the aims were grander – some might even say unrealistic – than they are now. For example, Ferenczi thought that an analysis was "a true re-education" in which the whole process of the patient's character formation had to be followed back to its instinctual foundations. In general terms, the aim was "structural" change based on the resolution of unconscious intrapsychic conflicts as opposed to purely behavioural change. Needless to say the latter was, and often still is, regarded by psychoanalytic practitioners as more superficial and less enduring.

As object-relations theory took hold, the aims shifted. Object-relations theorists believed that the central aim of an analysis was to bring about an improvement in the patient's relationships. This remains to this day the central aim of object-relational approaches. By the 1960s, aims acquired a more idiographic slant whereby the patient's individual psychic structure was taken into account along with their characterological limitations (Sandler & Dreher, 1996). This shift heralded a more realistic interpretation of the limitations of psychoanalysis such that by the 1970s, in the context of greater tolerance of pluralism within psychoanalysis itself, the psycho-analytic approach began to be applied to a more disturbed population. The more disturbed the patient, the more modest the aims of treatment became. The emphasis shifted from the aim of changing personality structure to helping patients "live with" or "manage", as constructively as possible, within the constraints of their personality difficulties or specific conflicts. This also allowed for a more patient-centred conceptualisation of goals such that treatment goals were seen to be related to the life goals of the patient.

The aims of therapy reflect, at their core, the respective models of the mind espoused by the different schools of psychoanalysis. Thus the ego psychologists' aim is the alteration of psychic structure on the basis of conflict resolution, resulting in an increase in the autonomy of the ego that will tolerate conflicts, the pull of different emotions and the irrationality of the unconscious. The emphasis of the treatment is on troubled relationships between unconscious impulses and consciousness. Self psychologists aim to achieve greater coherence of the self. Object relationists focus on a modification of inner representations of significant others and more adaptive external relationships. Kleinians focus on a lessening of persecutory and depressive anxieties and on helping the patient to deal satisfactorily with mourning and integrating split-off aspects of the self. For Klein, the task of psychoanalysis was to facilitate the integration of the psyche through overcoming splits that are maintained by unresolved primitive conflicts. This involves re-owning projections and bearing within oneself aspects of the self that arouse intense anxiety. Therapy aims to help the individual to bear ambivalence, in other words, to bear the burden of guilt arising from destructive impulses as well as helping the patient to have confidence in his reparative impulses.

It becomes apparent that there is no single way of formulating aims. Nowadays, amidst the differences between the schools, many therapists agree that an exploration of the dynamic interplay between the patient's internal world and external reality forms a central part of analytic work to enable the patient to gain a greater appreciation of the distorting impact of projective processes. The ultimate aim is to allow for a more integrated self that does not have to rely on extensive splitting and projection to maintain psychic equilibrium.

Perhaps, the most significant shift in aims, since Freud's time, is that fewer therapists nowadays view the retrieval of repressed memories as the main aim of analytic work. Instead, the creation or enhancement of a capacity for self-reflection is aimed for. The idea of "self-reflection" emerges from the ego-psychological approach (Bram & Gabbard, 2001). It denotes the capacity of the individual mind to take itself as the object of reflection in relation to the behaviour of the self with others and of others towards the self. It refers to the ability to understand one's own and others' behaviour in terms of mental states (i.e. thoughts, feelings, intentions, motivations), along with an appreciation that mental states "are based on but one of a broad range of possible perspectives" (Fonagy & Target, 1996: 221).

The notion of *reflective functioning* has grown out of the attachment theory and research (Fonagy & Target, 1996, 2000). The capacity for reflective functioning in the sense used by Fonagy & Target refers to the ability to mentalise, that is, to put words and images to somatic experience and to integrate them to create psychological meanings. Reflective functioning is believed to underpin our capacity to develop and sustain relationships because being able to attribute others' behaviour to their internal states makes their behaviour more meaningful and predictable and allows for communication and empathy. The capacity for self-reflection exists on a continuum such that it may be more or less operative and mediating depending on the circumstances the individual is in. For example, under severe psychic stress, as a result of a traumatic experience, this capacity may wane thereby leaving the individual to construe the traumatic experience as a personalised attack due to their "badness".

Fonagy *et al.* (2002) argue that all therapies attempt to provide a space where the patient is recognised by the therapist as an intentional being and is helped to relate to himself as intentional and real. The "psychological self" the authors refer to is said to be rooted in the attribution of mental states, and therefore of intentionality, to the self and to others. The focus and aim of the therapeutic work, however it is approached, thus becomes the understanding of mental states. This simple, yet very sophisticated, appraisal of the aims of psychotherapy provides perhaps the most intelligible account of what therapy strives to achieve.

Evidence-based Practice

The aims of psychoanalytic therapy are broader, and perhaps more ambitious, than those of other therapeutic modalities as the focus of the work is on the patient's overall functioning and personality structure. Consequently, they are also harder to evaluate in outcome studies. Indeed, there is a long psychoanalytic tradition of antipathy towards outcome research for precisely this reason. Evaluating outcome by the standards applied to other therapies (e.g. according to the patient's symptomatic profile) is considered meaningless by many psychoanalytic practitioners. For a long time, psychoanalysis eschewed notions of cure. Indeed, Freud would not have fared well in our evidence-based age. He was clear that:

> Therapeutic success is not our primary aim; we endeavour rather than enable to obtain a conscious grasp of unconscious wishes (1900: 120).

The task was to analyse, not cure. If you achieved the latter through the former, this was a perk rather than the goal.

The tidal wave of interest in evidence-based approaches has now shaken the cosy cocoon of psychoanalytic practice, and indeed of psychotherapy more broadly conceived. In a health service culture obsessed with costs and overstretched budgets, proving the effectiveness of treatments has become essential. However, the response to a call for more outcome research from within the psychoanalytic community has been, on the whole, a defensive one reflected in the total disinterest of some and the criticisms of research by others.[23] Green (2000), for example, voices a common position by suggesting that the requirements of research end up being an "oversimplification" of psychoanalytic ideas. Likewise, Wolff (1996) argues that psychoanalysis is "a psychology of idiosyncratic personal meanings and hidden motives", which is not amenable to empirical investigation.

Those who have risen to the challenge have articulated some well-placed criticisms of outcome research pointing, for example, to the complexity of clinical presentations that defy diagnostic categorisations and consequently, undermine a more prescriptive approach to fitting the patient to a particular therapy on the basis of the outcome research. However, some practitioners prefer more prescriptive approaches since they offer certainty. Because research has the ring of respectability, so do our decisions if based on it. This is a slippery slope since how we define science can exclude or include particular fields of enquiry. Those that do not fit the dominant definition of "science" can then be dismissed. But as Brenner writes:

> Science is a matter of attitude... not of subject matter and scientific truth is not something like the Holy Grail, which one eagerly searches out and which, once found, one expects will remain forever bright and unchanged. On the contrary, what is called truth in science is neither

---

[23] There are notable exceptions to this as evidenced, for example, in the work of Peter Fonagy in the UK and the Menninger Foundation in North America.

more nor less than the best conjecture that can be made on the basis of the available evidence (2000: 601).

Although absence of evidence is not evidence of ineffectiveness, the relative lack of outcome research on psychoanalytic treatments has been problematic in an age obsessed with evidence-based practice. For many years, there was a dearth of outcome studies evaluating the effectiveness of psychoanalytic therapy. Those who had braved the research path produced studies that on the whole stand as good examples of how *not* to carry out research. Indeed, criticising research in psychoanalysis is easy. Until recently, the state of outcome research in psychoanalytic approaches read like a litany of research sins: the treatments were seldom operationalised, thereby making it difficult to standardise what was actually being offered to patients and so to replicate it; there were no controls; patients were not randomly allocated to different treatment conditions; follow-ups were brief if non-existent; the samples were small... the list could go on, but it would make for dull reading and, importantly, it is not the aim of this book to review the outcome evidence. For more details on this, please refer to the text by Roth & Fonagy (1996).

Notwithstanding the early resistance to research, we are now witnessing a more sustained interest in outcome studies. The sheer number of studies now available is encouraging (Fonagy *et al.*, 1999). Many are methodologically "state of the art". Although there are no definitive studies that show that psychoanalysis is unequivocally effective relative to an active placebo or an alternative method of treatment, good quality comparative trials of cognitive behaviour therapy (CBT) and brief psychodynamic approaches reveal no difference in outcome (Shapiro *et al.*, 1995). Fonagy *et al.* (1999), in their review of outcome studies for psychoanalysis and psychoanalytic therapy, tentatively conclude the following:

- Psychoanalysis has a beneficial effect for neurotic and psychosomatic disorders.
- More severe disturbance benefits more from psychoanalysis than psychoanalytic therapy.
- Longer treatment has a better outcome.

It is important to remember that outcome research is a method for testing claims for efficacy or effectiveness. But it is not a method for testing the theories underwriting those claims, that is, even if psychoanalytic therapy is effective as a treatment, this does not mean that it is effective for the reasons a Freudian or a Kleinian might suggest (Fonagy, 1999a). Even though we can now assert more confidently that psychoanalytic treatments work, we are unable to assume the same level of confidence about *how* they work. Identifying the key ingredients conducive to a good outcome for the patient is an important avenue for further research.

Key Interventions in Psychoanalytic Therapy[24]

Psychoanalysis, as we have seen, is a broad church. The concern in this section is to highlight common threads, which distil the essence of a psychoanalytic approach as compared to other therapeutic modalities, rather than to espouse a particular psychoanalytic stance. Wallerstein (1992) suggests that despite the theoretical plurality of psychoanalysis, there is common ground within clinical theory. Sandler & Dreher (1996) explain this phenomenon by drawing a distinction between therapists' "implicit theories", which they regard as more pragmatic than their explicit theories. They argue that this may account for the greater convergence amongst psychoanalytic therapists of differing theoretical persuasions at the level of practice.

Interpretation

Traditionally, psychoanalysis has been associated with the notion of *interpretation*. Interpretation was originally defined as bringing the unconscious into consciousness. The main function of the therapist in Freud's time was to interpret, that is, to translate the unconscious meanings of the patient's conscious associations. To a large extent, this remains the mainstay of analytic practice throughout all the different schools. Nowadays, interpretation is also defined as those interventions that address interpersonal themes and make important links between patterns of relating to significant others and to the therapist.

In the early days of psychoanalytic practice, the therapist's interventions were concerned with the patient's past and, more specifically, on integrating current difficulties with past experience. Interpretations thus tended to be based on a reconstruction of past events so as to elucidate current patterns. Whilst transference interpretations (see below) were already an important part of Freud's analytic work, there was a greater tendency to link the transference interpretation to a past or parallel relationship.

Although we might say that a cognitive–behavioural therapist (CBT) also interprets his patient's negative cognitions, an analytic interpretation

---

[24] Adapted from Jones & Pulos (1993) and Blagys & Hilsenroth (2000).

looks quite different. Let us take as an example a patient who is unhappily married, complains about her husband and feels depressed because she feels trapped in the marriage. The CBT therapist who adopts a problem solving approach might approach this by saying to the patient: *"It sounds like you feel there is no way out of this difficult situation. Why don't we make a list of what is making it difficult to make the break"*. The psychoanalytic therapist, on the other hand, might say: *"I know you tell me that you want to leave your husband, but something gets in the way of you doing so. I wonder if what holds you back is that if you didn't have a complaint against your husband you might be forced to look at some uncomfortable feelings in yourself that you would rather avoid"*. The second interpretation focuses not on finding a solution but on understanding the meaning of the impasse the patient finds herself in at that point and the unconscious need she might have to stay in the relationship as the husband acts as a repository for her own split-off feelings. This kind of interpretation is more challenging than the first problem focused intervention.

The analytic attitude

Notwithstanding individual variations due to personality differences, analytic therapists, on the whole, approach their work in quite a specific manner: they strive to be as unobtrusive as possible and retain an anonymous, more neutral and non-gratifying stance towards the patient. This attitude represents in itself an intervention because most patients will relate in highly idiosyncratic ways to the analytic therapist's reluctance to answer personal questions, to offer advice or reassurance or to structure the session. The patient's reactions to the person of the therapist then become the target of exploration and provide a route into the elaboration of the patient's internal world of object relationships.

Here-and-now transference focus

With the development of object-relations theory, the focus of analytic work shifted to interpersonal themes. This emphasis has been systematically reinforced over the last twenty years as psychoanalytic theorising and practice has moved away from a one-person to a two-person psychology. Along with this shift, a greater awareness of the bi-personal field co-created by both therapist and patient has come to the fore. Contemporary models thus focus more on the *here-and-now*. A "here-and-now" emphasis refers to an exploration of the patient's current relationships including, and indeed prioritising, the relationship with the therapist, which is understood as an actualisation of internalised object relationships. Interpretations thus emphasise the process of interaction between the patient and the therapist – that is, a transference interpretation – eventually leading to connections to other relationships in the patient's life.

There remain differences between the schools in the extent to which the transference is interpreted from the first session onwards as is more typical of Kleinian approaches, or whether it is allowed to develop and only interpreted later, as is more typical of classical Freudian approaches, where more attention is initially devoted to the development of a therapeutic alliance (Couch, 1979). Overall, however, contemporary practice has increasingly moved towards the earlier and more systematic interpretation of the transference, with less emphasis on reconstructive interpretations (see Chapters 5 & 7).

Focus on affect

The expression of emotion is central to the psychoanalytic enterprise. Unlike CBT, which focuses primarily on the patient's cognitions, for example, psychoanalytic therapy aims to primarily explore the patient's affective experience. Of course, psychoanalytic therapists also pay attention to the content of the patient's thoughts and phantasies. However, they approach this by listening to the transference implications of what the patient brings and interpreting these so that the latent and manifest affect associated with any particular thoughts/phantasies can be explored in as "live" a way as possible. It is far more helpful to talk about anger or contempt, for example, as the patient experiences it in the here-and-now of the session towards the therapist, than to talk retrospectively about incidents outside of the session, when the patient experienced such feelings. Reporting on an experience produces a comparatively toned-down report and lacks the immediacy of the transference. It is the affective immediacy in the "here-and-now" that allows for a helpful reworking of the felt experience "there-and-then".

Free association

Psychoanalytic therapy is an unstructured approach. Unlike many other therapeutic modalities that invite the patient to explore a given problem and where the therapist's task is to help the patient address the problem through the use of questions or other interventions such as psychoeducation or challenging of core schemas, the psychoanalytic therapist approaches the session without structure and invites the patient likewise to relinquish the need to plan what he will say. The rule of free association urges the patient to say whatever comes to mind irrespective of whether it is connected with what was discussed the previous week or a few minutes earlier in a session. The idea behind this is that it is only when the patient can let go of his need to produce logically coherent and purposeful communications, will he be able to allow unconscious anxieties or meanings to emerge through his spontaneous associations.

Exploration of patient's wishes, dreams and phantasies

The rule of free association highlights the analytic therapist's focus of interest, namely, on the patient's irrational feelings, thoughts and phantasies. Interventions are geared towards facilitating the elaboration and articulation of the more unconscious aspects of the patient's experience, which can be productively explored through dreams, for example. While the external reality of the patient's life is acknowledged and worked with, the psychoanalytic therapist is primarily interested in the patient's internal reality and how this influences the particular meaning ascribed to what is perceived in the external world.

Analysis of defence and resistance

All psychoanalytic approaches focus on an exploration of the patient's attempts to cope with psychic pain. Interpretations will often aim at pointing out to the patient his idiosyncratic ways of avoiding pain or managing it. Likewise, the interpretation of resistance will address those topics that the patient tries to avoid exploring within the context of the therapy and any other behaviours (e.g. lateness, silences) that hinder therapy (see Chapter 6).

Use of countertransference

All therapeutic approaches nowadays consider the quality of the therapeutic relationship to be important to the outcome of therapy. However, it is only within the psychoanalytic approaches that we find detailed attention devoted to the use the therapist makes of her own emotional reactions towards the patient, namely, her counter transference. The use of counter transference dominates the clinical picture across the board. The therapist's experience of the patient and the feelings aroused whilst with the patient are taken very seriously and considered to provide an important source of information about the patient's own mental states through an understanding of such processes as projection and projective identification (see Chapters 6 & 7).

In trying to distil some of the more distinctive features of a psychoanalytic approach, it is important to keep in mind that some of the features outlined above are not the exclusive provinces of psychoanalytic practitioners. Interpersonal patterns are of as much interest, for example, to cognitive schema-focused practitioners as they are to psychoanalytic ones. Humanistic therapists also focus on affect and schema-based cognitive therapists would argue likewise. What is distinctive about an analytic approach in these respects is its *consistent* focus on affect and interpersonal themes within the context of a detailed understanding of the transference relationship that develops with the patient. In other words, the approach does not distinguish itself with respect to any one single feature; rather, it is the way in which these features are woven together in a systematic manner and are addressed through the vicissitudes of the therapeutic relationship that marks the difference. Moreover, as mentioned above, the psychoanalytic therapist adopts a very particular attitude (see Chapter 3). A psychoanalytic session often *feels* distinctively different, say, to a cognitive-behavioural one. This is because the more neutral and questioning manner in which the therapist conducts herself in an analytic session sets a very different therapeutic ambience to the one created by a more active, structured therapist who is prepared to answer a range of questions rather than exploring with the patient why he may be asking the question in the first place.

What Makes the Difference?

The simple and honest answer to this question is that we know relatively little about the key ingredients of a successful therapy. Although cognitive behaviour therapy CBT and Interpersonal Psychotherapy (IPT) for example, have been shown to be effective, we do not know which components of these therapies are the agents of change. What we do know, however, is that several therapeutic approaches have been shown to be effective notwithstanding their differences. Moreover, although there are distinctive emphases and techniques that are typically associated with psychoanalytic work, none is exclusively the province of psychoanalysis. Indeed, the suggestion emerging from research is that there is more commonality at the level of techniques across different therapeutic modalities than the theories they emanate from might at first suggest.

Although the process of therapy is often qualitatively different between say CBT and psychoanalytic therapy, there is evidence of a degree of rapprochement between developmental approaches in CBT and psychoanalytic approaches. More generally, as Bateman points out:

> ... the brand name of the therapy no longer indicates what happens in practice and even theoretical differences appear narrower than hitherto (2000: 147).

Overall, research indicates that the more experienced the practitioner, the less differences there appear to be at the level of practice. For example, Goldfried & Weinberger (1998) found few between-orientations differences in sessions that master therapists of differing theoretical persuasions (i.e. analytic and non-analytic) identified as significant.

In a book on psychoanalytic therapy written by a psychoanalytic therapist, it would be reasonable to suspect a degree of bias towards the approach. However, the therapeutic value of psychoanalytic interventions is not just a matter of personal bias. On the contrary, process research, which addresses not just the interventions used but those associated with change, has exposed some interesting results as it points to the helpfulness of what have been traditionally regarded as "psychoanalytic interventions". Jones and Pulos (1993), for example, looked at the process in thirty brief psychodynamic sessions and thirty-two sessions of CBT. They found that better outcome in CBT was not predicted by cognitive techniques but was associated with psychodynamic exploratory interventions (e.g. "evocation of affect", "bringing troublesome feelings into awareness" and "integrating difficulties with past experience"). Wiser & Goldfried (1996) found that in sessions identified as important for change, CBT therapists commonly used interpretations defined as "statements that provide the therapist's perspective on the patient's experience", but the study did not control the content of interpretations. Ablon & Jones (1999), in a re-analysis of the NIMH[25] tapes found that the more features the process of brief therapy shares with that of a psychodynamic approach, the more likely it is to be effective.

Style and Technique in Psychotherapy

What psychoanalytic therapists do with their patients relies on the use of particular techniques, such as the interpretation of transference, *and* the personal manner in which these techniques are deployed. Therapists vary widely in their therapeutic styles ranging from being more aloof and silent to being more interactive and self-disclosing. Some use humour to engage the patient; others view it as an enactment that should be understood and interpreted. Some are willing to answer personal questions; others approach them as a manifestation of the patient's anxiety or as an enactment if the therapist chooses to answer. Some smile as they greet their patients; others look sombre.

---

[25]National Institute for Mental Health study of treatments for depression.

The variations are as infinite as human nature. No matter how neutral we strive to be, each therapeutic session will feel different and will draw out different aspects of our own personalities along with our blind spots.

Technique is therefore interpreted differently depending on who we are and our own analytic experiences. The relationship between these stylistic differences and the outcome is poorly understood. It is very likely, however, that the therapeutic value of an interpretation is not solely dependent on its content. *How* the interpretation is given, for example, whether it is given in a manner that invites the patient to think for himself about whether it makes sense, or whether it is dispensed as the "the truth" by the therapist, is likely to be important. This is so because what matters is the intent behind the words. Patients are interested in their therapist's state of mind in relation to them, not solely whether their therapist generates accurate interpretations. For example, a therapist may be intellectually very adept at picking up her patient's hostile phantasies but may interpret this in a triumphant manner, displaying her intellectual prowess. Another therapist may interpret accurately but do so in such an aloof manner that the patient feels objectified. The quality of the engagement between therapist and patient is a critical variable. Some styles of communicating are probably more conducive to the establishment of a good therapeutic alliance than others.

The impact that therapeutic style has on technique is seldom formulated. It is well recognised that the way Freud practised deviated significantly from the technical prescriptions he recommended (see Chapter 3): he was much warmer and interactive than many of the therapists who have since assiduously tried to approximate the neutral, blank-screen persona advocated by Freud in his writings. We have much to learn about the influence of such non-specific factors on outcome. It would be surprising, however, given the emphasis that psychoanalysis places on the relationship between therapist and patient, if the person of the therapist did not emerge as a salient factor influencing outcome.

FURTHER READING

Bronstein, C. (Ed.) (2001) *Kleinian Theory: A Contemporary Perspective*. London: Whurr Publishers.

Fonagy, P. & Target, M. (2003) *Psychoanalytic Theories: Perspectives from Developmental Psychopathology*. London: Whurr Publications.

Frosh, S. (1997) *For and Against Psychoanalysis*. London: Routledge.

Gomez, L. (1997) *An Introduction to Object Relations*. London: Free Association Books.

Mollon, P. (2001) *The Legacy of Heinz Kohut*. London: Whurr Publishers.
Sandler, J., Holder, A., Dare, C. & Dreher, A. (Eds) (1997) *Freud's Models of the Mind*
    London: Karnac Books.
Smith, D. (1999) *Approaching Psychoanalysis*. London: Karnac Books.

2

THE PROCESS
OF PSYCHIC CHANGE

Our models of the mind inform how we practice psychotherapy. As our understanding of unconscious processes has become more sophisticated, it has shed new light on how psychic change might occur and how psychoanalytic therapy can assist this process. In this chapter, we will examine the nature of unconscious perception and the workings of memory as a springboard for addressing the question of therapeutic action in psychoanalytic therapy.

THE EVIDENCE FOR UNCONSCIOUS PROCESSING

Consciousness is considered as a distinctive feature of human beings. However, the influence of unknown factors on the human mind has long been recognised. It was certainly not Freud's original discovery that human conscious behaviour was driven by forces that were not immediately accessible to us. Before the notion of a dynamic unconscious was formulated by Freud, Gods or destiny were convenient repositories for unknown – and often destructive – forces that exerted an impact on behaviour and were experienced as alien to the individual.

Freud's early theories described a rational, conscious mind separated by a barrier from a non-rational part of the mind pictured as hedonistic, self-seeking and destructive. The Freudian unconscious consisted of unsatisfied instinctual wishes understood to be representations of instinctual drives. He posited an intermediary zone called the preconscious, involving not conscious processes but ones capable of becoming so. This model was subsequently further refined into the structural model with the three agencies of the mind, the id, the ego and the superego (see Chapter 1). It soon became apparent that not only was the id unconscious but that many of the functions ascribed to the ego and the superego were also unconscious.

Since Freud, the evidence for unconscious mentation has steadily accumulated. Studying unconscious processes has never been as exciting or promising as it is today because of a gradual rapprochement between psychoanalysis and neuroscience. Factors operating outside of conscious awareness are now recognised in many cognitive psychological theories. Unconscious activities are understood to constitute far more of mentation than consciousness could ever hope to explain. Findings from cognitive psychology and neuroscience have repeatedly demonstrated that a significant proportion of our behaviour and emotional reactions is controlled by autonomous, unconscious structures, bypassing consciousness altogether (Damasio, 1999; Pally, 2000). Psychoanalysis and cognitive psychology nowadays also converge on the recognition that meaning systems include both conscious and unconscious aspects of experience.

The most compelling evidence for the unconscious has emerged from studies of perception. What we perceive is the end result of a very complex neurophysiological process. To perceive an object, the brain processes all of the object's individual environmental features and compares it with patterns stored in memory. When a match for the current pattern is found, perception occurs.[1] Our perceptual system has evolved in response to the need to perceive not only accurately but also speedily. The brain has thus developed a split perceptual system (LeDoux, 1995). The slower perceptual system involves the cortex and can thus include conscious awareness. This system allows for more detailed information to be gathered, which in turn, helps us to inhibit responses and initiate alternative behaviours. The other system "fast tracks" perception bypassing the cortex. This system does not involve any conscious awareness. The problem with the "fast-track" system is that it does not allow for a more fine-grained appraisal of what we are perceiving. However, many situations in our day-to-day lives rely on just such a system. This means that when we fast track perceptions, past experiences always influence the current perceptions and hence may contribute to patterns of behaviour or feelings that closely resemble past experiences.

Some of the most interesting examples of unconscious processing are to be found in the neurological literature. Damasio (1999), for example, describes face-agnosic patients who can no longer consciously recognise people's faces but yet can detect familiar faces non-consciously. In experimental situations where these patients are shown pictures of faces, they are all unrecognisable to them whether they are familiar ones (e.g. friends or

---

[1]Pattern matching is of interest because as Pally (2000) highlights, it provides some explanation for the clinical observation that patients often repeat certain experiences. It suggests that rather than repeating a particular experience, it may be more accurate to say that we fall into repetitive behavioural patterns because we tend to interpret situations with a bias towards what has occurred in the past (Pally, 2000).

family) or unfamiliar ones. Yet, on presentation of every familiar face, a distinct skin conductance response is generated, while on presentation of unknown faces no such reaction is observed. This suggests that even though the patient is consciously unaware of any level of recognition, the physiological reaction tells a different story: the magnitude of the skin conductance response is greater for the closest relatives. It would thus appear that our brain is capable of producing a specific response that betrays past knowledge of a particular stimulus and that it can do this bypassing consciousness totally.

Learning too often occurs without consciousness. So, much of our so-called "knowledge" is not acquired in a conscious, purposeful way. For example, knowledge acquired through conditioning remains outside our consciousness and is expressed only indirectly. The retrieval of sensory motor skills (e.g. how to drive or ride a bike) without consciousness of the knowledge expressed in the movement is perhaps the most common everyday example of how our behaviour does not require the mediation of consciousness. This is referred to, within cognitive science, as *implicit processing*. This type of processing is applied to mental activity that is repetitive and automatic and provides speedy categorisation and decision making, operating outside the realm of focal attention and verbalised experience (Kihlstrom, 1987). Indeed, it is precisely because we can rely on such implicit processing, and we are therefore not dependent all the time on a conscious survey of our behaviour, that we are freed up in terms of attention and time. The device of consciousness can thus be deployed to manage the environmental challenges not predicted in the "basic design of our organism" (Damasio, 1999).

Such is now the evidential basis for unconscious perception and processing that no therapeutic approach can dispute the existence of an unconscious, at least in the descriptive sense. However, even though there is evidence for unconscious processing, that is, for learning and perception that occurs without conscious awareness, the notion of a *dynamic* unconscious is more problematic. In Freud's original formulations, the dynamic unconscious was depicted as a constant source of motivation that makes things happen. In this sense, what is stored in the unconscious was said not only to be inaccessible but Freud also suggested that its contents were the result of *repression*. Repression was a means of protecting consciousness from ideas and feelings that were threatening and hence the source of anxiety. At first, Freud, along with Breuer, suggested that repression operated on memories of traumatic events excluding them from consciousness. Later, he suggested that repression operated primarily on infantile drives and wishes, rather than on memories of actual events.

The concept of repression raises an interesting question because it is only when an experience can be known and represented that it can it be hidden. To be able to maintain a specific idea at an unconscious level, we must first have a stable ability to specify an experience. Developmental psychology has shown that the ability to represent our experiences in a stable and meaningful fashion only develops over time. This suggests that from a cognitive point of view, repression is not a defence that can operate from the very beginning of life. Freud too understood repression as a mode of defence against unwanted impulses that develops over time:

> Psychoanalytic observation of the transference neuroses... leads us to conclude that repression is not a defensive mechanism which is present from the very beginning, and that it cannot arise until a sharp cleavage has occurred between conscious and unconscious mental activity (Freud, 1915a).

On the basis of the current evidence, the notion of repression as a fully unconscious process, or as one directed primarily at infantile wishes, finds little empirical support. Although we can still speak of a dynamic unconscious and of repression as a defensive process, this requires a redefinition of the concepts in keeping with what we now know about the workings of memory. We shall now turn our attention to this.

PSYCHOANALYTIC PERSPECTIVES ON MEMORY

The question of memory, of what we can, cannot or do not want to remember is of central concern to psychoanalytic practitioners and researchers. In his early formulations on the nature of hysteria, Freud understood the hysteric's problem as one of "suffering from reminiscences" (Breuer & Freud, 1895: 7). Freud and Breuer (1895) suggested that the source of the hysterical patient's psychic pain was the inability to forget traumatic events that had occurred in childhood but which could not be consciously remembered. The goal of therapy was therefore to bring back to the surface the repressed traumatic events. Although Freud changed his ideas about hysteria later, this early link between disturbances of memory and psychopathology can still be traced in the implicit thinking of some psychoanalytic practitioners who view the excavation of the past as a necessary goal of psychotherapy. As our knowledge of memory has become increasingly more sophisticated, the classical psychoanalytic view of memory and hence of the nature of therapeutic action has been challenged.

A feature of memory that is of special relevance to clinical practice is that memory is by definition always reconstructed and, importantly, influenced by motivation. Memory is influenced as much by present context, mood, beliefs and attitudes, as it is by past events (Brenneis, 1999). Memories are not direct replicas of the facts per se. On the contrary, memory undergoes a complex process of reconstruction during retrieval. This means that memory of some autobiographical events may be reconstructed in ways that differ from the original event or may never be recalled at all. The view that memory is continually being constructed rather than retrieved from storage in original pristine form is consistent with current thinking in cognitive psychology and neurobiology. However, it would be mistaken to infer from this that early memories are mostly inaccurate: research suggests that there is in fact substantial accuracy in early memories (Brewin *et al.*, 1993) even though the more fine-grained details of an experience, even if vividly recalled and reported by the patient, are unlikely to be entirely accurate.

We are now all too aware of the heated debates about so-called false memories. The interest, and indeed controversy, about the reliability and accessibility of early memories gained momentum over ten years ago when the media drew attention to a groundswell of reconstruction of incestuous sexual abuse within the context of psychotherapy. Dreams, puzzling body sensations, specific transference and countertransference patterns and dissociative episodes were taken by many therapists as evidence that their patients had repressed a traumatic experience. This conclusion was predicated on the assumption that analytic data can reconstruct and validate consciously inaccessible historical events. In other words, it reflected a belief that analytic data was "good enough". Any of the symptoms listed above, which have been taken as evidence of repressed trauma, may occur in conjunction with trauma, and often do, but they do not occur *exclusively* with trauma. The danger lies in inferring the nature of unremembered events solely from the contents of any of these repetitive phenomena.

Suggesting that memory is reconstructed does not mean that psychoanalytic reconstructions are necessarily false or that recovered memories are invariably, or mostly, false. It does mean, however, that we must approach notions of "truth" based on reconstructions within the context of psychotherapy with some caution. All that we can assert with any certainty is that what our patients believe to be true has important consequences for how they feel and act in the world. Our role as therapists is neither that of an advocate or a jury: we are facilitators of the patient's attempts to understand his internal world and how this impacts on his external relationships and day-to-day functioning. I am not advocating disbelieving what patients say. Patients who have experienced a trauma need to have their traumatic experiences validated. However, all we can validate is their emotional experience of an event and their individual narrative about it. Importantly, we often have to bear the anxiety of not knowing what *may* have happened so that we can help our patients to bear it too. When our patients have no conscious recollection of any trauma but we, as therapists, infer trauma from their symptomatic presentation, we need to caution against an overeagerness to fill in the unbearable gaps in understanding with the knowing certainty of formulations that may, or may not, be correct. There exists in us and in our patients, as Brenneis suggests, ". . . a balder desire to locate an original event that unlocks the mysteries of present experience" (1999: 188). This desire can mislead us at times because, as Kris wisely reminds us:

> . . . we are [not], except in rare instances, able to find the events of the afternoon on the staircase where the seduction happened. (1956: 73).

Research on human memory helps us to understand the need for caution in these matters. It suggests that there are different kinds of memory systems and hence different types of memories. Certain sets of memories are consistently reactivated moment by moment. These memories concern the facts of our physical, mental and demographic identity. They orient us in the world. Conventionally, this is variously referred to as *declarative* or *explicit*[2] or *autobiographical memory*. Declarative memory – the term I will use from now on – is the underlying organisation that allows us to consciously recall facts and events. It refers to the conscious memory for people, objects and places. It involves symbolic or imaginistic knowledge that allows facts and experiences to be called into conscious awareness in the absence of the things they stand for. This kind of memory includes *semantic memory* for general and personal facts and knowledge and *episodic memory* for specific events.

There are also contents of memory that remain submerged for long periods of time, some never to be retrieved. Many aspects of our behaviour rely on us remembering "how to do things", and we can do this without consciously remembering the details of how to carry out a particular behaviour. This kind of memory is conventionally variously referred to as *procedural* or *implicit* or *non-declarative* memory. It includes *primed memory* (e.g. for words, sounds or shapes), which facilitates the subsequent identification or recognition of them from reduced cues or fragments, *emotional memory* and *procedural memory*, that is, memory for skills, habits and routines.

---

[2]"Explicit" and "implicit" refer, respectively, to whether conscious recollection is involved or not in the expression of memory. Long-term memory may be both explicit and implicit. Both involve the permanent storage of information: one type is retrievable (i.e. explicit memories), the other most probably is not (i.e. implicit memories).

Emotional memory is the conditioned learning of emotional responses to a situation and is mediated by the amygdala. There is a difference between emotional memory, that is, a conditioned emotional reaction formed in response to a particular event, and declarative memory of an emotional situation, that is, the recall of events felt to be of emotional significance. Classically conditioned emotional responses (e.g. classically conditioned expectations, preferences, desires) constitute the affective colouring of our lives. They orient us unconsciously to aspects of our environment and to particular types of relationships. Often, there is no conscious memory connected with this learning. LeDoux (1994) suggests that a focal point for cognition – the hippocampus – can be involved in the activation of emotions before cognitive processes take place. His research indicates that emotions can bypass the cortex via alternative pathways leading from the thalamus to the amygdala. This makes it possible for emotionally charged schemas to be repeated without the mediation of consciousness.

Like emotional memory, *procedural memory* is unconscious and is evident in performance rather than in conscious recall. This type of memory refers to the acquisition of skills, maps and rule-governed adaptive responses that are manifest in behaviour but remain otherwise unconscious. It includes routinised patterns or ways of being with others. For example, we may have a coordinated procedural system for "how to ask for help". In turn, these procedures shape, organise and influence a person's unconscious selection of particular interpersonal environments. Moreover, emotionally charged events are particularly prone to repetition when events of a similar nature are anticipated.

Neuropsychology has demonstrated complete independence of the declarative and procedural memory systems. Declarative memory is located in the hippocampus and the temporal lobes. Procedural memory is located in sub-cortical structures such as the basal ganglia and the cerebellum. The declarative and procedural memory systems are relatively independent of each other. Studies of amnesic patients provide evidence for the potential dissociability of the two forms of knowledge contained within these memory systems: amnesic patients, for example, demonstrate evidence of prior learning of words, as shown in a word-recognition task, but display no conscious recollection of whether they had ever seen the word before. This suggests that procedural knowledge was acquired in the absence of any conscious recall of the learning experience. This finding suggests that a change in procedural forms of learning may thus come about through different mechanisms than a change in conscious, declarative forms of knowledge. As we shall see later in this chapter, this has important implications for psychotherapy.

In normal adult development, both declarative and procedural memory systems overlap and are used together. Constant repetition, for example, can transform a declarative memory into a procedural one. Likewise, repeated avoidance of particular thoughts or feelings may result in the associated behaviour becoming automated, thus resulting in a so-called "repression". Procedural memory influences experience and behaviour without representing the past in symbolic form; it is rarely translated into language. Whilst we can say that procedural memories operate completely outside of conscious awareness (i.e. they are unconscious), they are not repressed memories or otherwise dynamically unconscious. This means that they cannot be directly translated into conscious memory and then into words: they can only be known indirectly by inference.

In the very early years of childhood, declarative memory is impaired because of the immaturity of the prefrontal cortex and hippocampus, whereas the basal ganglia and amygdala are well developed at birth. During the first two to three years, the child relies primarily on her procedural memory system. Both in humans and in animals, declarative memory develops later. In other words, a child learns how to do things before she is able to recall an actual event in her past. Research suggests that it is highly unlikely that we can remember events predating our third or fourth year of life. This means that there may be procedural memories for infantile experiences in the absence of declarative memories. Indeed, amongst many analytic therapists there is a shared assumption that pre-verbal experiences are expressed indirectly and can only be grasped through the skilled use of the countertransference.

Declarative memories emerge around three years in line with the increasing maturity of the relevant brain systems. This finding suggests that the infantile amnesia Freud spoke of may have less to do with the repression of memory during the resolution of the Oedipus complex, as he suggested; rather, it may reflect the slow development of the declarative memory system. Lack of verbal access to early experiences may therefore have little to do with repression as an unconscious defence process. On the contrary, it probably results from the fact that these early experiences are encoded in a pre-verbal form and are expressed indirectly, for example, through somatic symptoms. In this sense, it is both true to say that we do not forget *and* that we cannot remember very early events, thereby explaining their continued hold over us in the absence of conscious recollection of the formative experiences in our early childhood.

The very early events that may exert a profound influence on the development of the psyche are most probably encoded in procedural memory. Procedural memory stores a lot of knowledge, but the experiences out of which such knowledge is born are seldom retrievable. In procedural memory, we thus find a biological example of one component of unconscious mental life: the *procedural unconscious*. This is an unconscious system that is not the result of repression in the dynamic sense (i.e. it is not concerned with drives and conflicts), but it is nevertheless inaccessible to consciousness. By contrast, the world of the psychoanalytic unconscious, in its dynamic sense, has its roots most probably in the neural systems that support declarative memory. Repression can occur here, but it is a process that can only act on events that are experienced at a developmental stage when encoding into declarative memory is possible.

Taken as a whole, our current understanding of perception and memory points to a fundamental fact, namely, as Gedo put it, *"What is most meaningful in life is not necessarily encoded in words"* (1986: 206). This, as we shall see in the next section, has important implications for how we might understand the process of change in psychoanalytic therapy.

THERAPEUTIC ACTION IN PSYCHOANALYTIC THERAPY

Given that so many therapeutic approaches successfully promote psychological change, it is clear that psychoanalytic treatment is not unique in this respect. Yet, the attention psychoanalysis has assiduously devoted to the therapeutic *process* sheds helpful light on those factors that might contribute to psychic change.

All schools of psychoanalysis subscribe to the view that clarifying and resolving the patient's idiosyncratic ways of perceiving the world and other people in light of internal reality will help him to perceive the external world more clearly. Broadly speaking, the origins of psychic pain are understood to be not simply the result of an external event(s) that was traumatic but also of the way the event itself is subjectively interpreted and organised around a set of unconscious meanings. Notwithstanding a broad agreement over these questions, there is lesser consensus over how psychic change occurs through psychotherapy and the techniques that drive change. The lack of agreement partly reflects a dearth of empirical research on these matters. This opens the way for hyperbolic claims to be made about a variety of techniques that purportedly lead to change.

There are several versions of the process of psychic change. Each version emphasises different, though sometimes overlapping aspects of the therapeutic process and of the techniques believed to facilitate change. Let us briefly review the most dominant accounts. I shall, however, focus in particular on the account that I find the most persuasive and consistent with the available research.

The Excavation of the Past

The archaeological metaphor originates from Freud's topographical model. Compelling in its simplicity, and revolutionary in its time, this version suggests that change results from remembering past events that have been repressed and from exploring their meaning and impact on the patient. Change is said to occur through the lifting of repression, the recovery of memory and the ensuing insight. This is the model most lay people identify as characteristically psychoanalytic.

Not inconsistent with this version is the emphasis placed by Freud's later structural model on the importance of helping the patient to build a stronger ego that is better able to withstand the pressures of the id and the superego. Therapy is said to assist the latter by engaging the patient's ego in an alliance with the therapist to combat, as it were, the other sources of pressure. In particular, the relationship with the therapist is thought to allow for the internalisation of a more benign superego. Remembering the past and making connections with the present behaviour nevertheless remains a key aspect of the therapeutic work.

The central function accorded in this account to the recovery of memory leads to a view of the therapist's role as that of reconstructing the past through the patient's associations. Reconstructive interpretations that make genetic links back to the patient's early experience and lead to insight are considered to be important agents of change.

Working Through in the Transference

The Kleinian version of change focuses on the working through of paranoid anxieties and the associated defences to allow the patient to reach the depressive position. Change is linked to the development of the capacity to mourn the separateness from the object and to bear the guilt and concern for the state of the object as a result of the phantasised, and real, attacks on it. As the depressive position is established, feelings of guilt and concern contribute to a wish to repair the perceived damage to the objects. The capacity to constructively manage depressive anxieties without resorting to paranoid modes of functioning leads, in turn, to a strengthening of the ego.

One of the main goals of treatment is to achieve greater integration of split-off aspects of the self rather than on insight. This task is said to be largely assisted in therapy by the detailed exploration of transference phenomena so as to help the patient to understand how he manages intolerable psychic states. The interpretation of transference is believed to facilitate a change in the patient's relationships to his internal objects, paving the way for a more realistic appraisal of the significant others in his life. This allows for a greater discrimination between the internal and the external world. Kleinians therefore suggest that change results not from a conscious exploration of the past but from a modification of underlying anxieties and defences as they arise in the therapeutic relationship and are worked through in the transference.

In this view of change, understanding (i.e. insight) and the relationship with a therapist who lends meaning to the patient's communications through an analysis of the jointly evolving interaction are inseparable. The transference relationship is held to be a key to the change process because of its focus on affect – itself regarded as an agent of psychic change – and because the Kleinians subscribe to the view that the here-and-now relationship is an enactment of the past, that is, it is thought to be isomorphic with the infantile past. By interpreting the transference, the therapist is said to be interpreting concurrently the past and the present (Malcolm, 1988). Given this, reconstruction of the past is not regarded as the most significant aspect of the technique; rather, it is the enactment in the present and its interpretation that is the effective agent of psychic change. Linking present patterns to the past is nevertheless acknowledged to offer the patient "a sense of continuity in his life"(Malcolm, 1986: 73).

The Healing Power of the Narrative

Language allows us to begin to form an autobiographical history that over time develops into the narrative of our life. This is the story that the patient presents to the therapist, a story that is likely to evolve during the therapeutic process. Currently, there is a trend towards understanding therapeutic action in terms of the integration of accounts from the patient's past, leading to the achievement of narrative coherence. In this version, it is the stories we tell that make the difference. Narrative truth is considered to be just as "real" as historical truth. Spence (1982), for example, has suggested that people seek help when they feel confused by their life stories or when they are felt to be somehow incomplete, painful or chaotic. Psychotherapy helps patients by providing them with an opportunity to create or rewrite a narrative about their lives, through the relationship with the therapist, which brings greater cohesion. Therefore, within this model, reconstruction of the past retains an important therapeutic function.

The Corrective Emotional Experience

All therapies aim to establish a relationship between the therapist and the patient, which allows for a safe exploration of the patient's mind. The majority of psychoanalytic therapists converge on the assumption that change occurs through the relationship with the therapist. How this relationship exerts its therapeutic effects and thus facilitates change remains nevertheless a hotly debated question. For example, is it because the therapist becomes a transference object thereby allowing the patient to examine patterns of relating in the here and now (as many contemporary therapists suggest), or do people get better through involvement with an emotionally responsive therapist who provides a new interpersonal experience that disconfirms negative expectations of others?

Those who subscribe to the idea of therapy as a corrective experience suggest that the therapeutic encounter offers an opportunity for a new object relationship that becomes internalised and disconfirms more pathogenic assumptions about the self and the other. Put simply, the therapist becomes the "good" object that the patient never had. This position suggests that benefits accrue from a relationship with a new object along with the internalisation of new perspectives and ways of responding. In this respect, it is important to make a distinction between the patient's use of his experience with the therapist as a new object that leads to a revision of internalised object relationships, and in this sense "corrects" the old models, and the more common usage of the term *corrective emotional experience* to denote the therapist's deliberate attempts to act in specific ways to provide the patient with a new experience instead of interpreting the patient's internalised object relationships as they manifest themselves in the transference. Under the influence of infant developmental research, therapeutic changes are sometimes understood as a kind of new development analogous to the emotional development of infancy, but other clinicians argue that change takes place alongside rather than replacing faulty development whereby we become more tolerant of the aspects of the self and of early phantasies.

Until comparatively recently, the notion of a corrective emotional experience was perhaps all too readily dismissed. As we shall see below, some contemporary thinking on the change process converges on the notion that the patient's experience with a new object who responds qualitatively differently towards the patient may indeed be contributing to change at the procedural level, bypassing language.

Present Change: Making Implicit Models of Relationships Explicit

Led by research, and originating primarily within the Contemporary Freudian tradition (Sandler & Sandler, 1984, 1997), lies an account of the process of change that brings together coherently several of the strands mentioned above. As we have seen, contemporary models of the mind have developed out of an appreciation that much of our relational experience is represented in an implicit, procedural or enactive form that is unconscious in the descriptive sense though not necessarily dynamically unconscious.

This version of psychic change suggests that we all have formative early interpersonal experiences that contribute to the development of *dynamic templates* or, if you like, schemata of self–other relationships. These templates are encoded in the implicit procedural memory system. This system stores a non-conscious knowledge of how to do things and how to relate to others. Sandler and Sandler (1997) see mother–infant interactions as the contexts for the earliest formulations of self and object representations and as providing the basic unit of self-representation. The Sandlers refer to this as the *past unconscious*. Its contents are not directly accessible. Nevertheless, it stores procedures for relationships that may well be stamped into the developing frontal limbic circuitry in the brain and provides strategies for affect regulation, thus influencing the processing of socio-affective information throughout the lifespan (Schore, 1994).

The so-called *present unconscious,* on the other hand, refers to our here-and-now unconscious strivings and responses. If there is any kind of repression or censorship, it is said to occur here. Although the contents of the present unconscious may become conscious, they are still frequently subject to censorship before being allowed entry into consciousness. The lifting of repression in the present unconscious gives us access to autobiographical memories; it does not give us access to the past unconscious with its procedural memories. The distinction between a past and present unconscious highlights that our behaviour in the present functions according to templates that were set down very early on in our lives while simultaneously acknowledging that the actual experiences that contributed to these templates are, for the most part, irretrievable.

Procedural models for being with others are organised, to begin with, according to the developmental level of understanding available at the time when they are taking shape. Children internalise their expe-riences with significant others. Internalisation, in this sense, occurs at a pre-symbolic level, predating the capacity to evoke images or verbal representations of the object. The primary form of representation is not of words or images but of enactive relational procedures governing "how to be with others" (Stern *et al.*, 1998). Depending on the environment, and the experiences the individual is presented with, the procedures may or may not become reorganised over time with the aid of more sophisticated levels of understanding. They may be, for example, less integrated with other procedures or more likely to involve fearful or hostile interpretations of others' behaviour that are not open to revision. Moreover, models of self–other relationships reflect networks of unconscious expectations or unconscious phantasies:

> The models are not replicas of actual experience but they are undoubt-
> edly defensively distorted by wishes and fantasies current at the time
> of the experience (Fonagy, 1999b: 217).

The internal models of relationships that are stored as procedures and that organise our behaviour are retained in parts of the brain that are separate from the storage of autobiographical memories. This suggests that the models of how-to-be-with-others that are re-enacted in the transference become autonomous and that the events that may have originally contributed to their elaboration need not be recalled in order for therapeutic change to occur.

In any therapeutic encounter, several models of self–other relationships will be activated and the patient may produce stories about experiences relevant to the model that is activated (Fonagy, 1999b). In this version of therapeutic action, therapy thus aims to bring to awareness possible meanings of the patterns of current relationships. In turn, therapeutic change is said to result from the elaboration and re-evaluation of current models that are implicitly encoded as procedures, leading to a change in the procedures that the patient uses in his relationships. In this respect, the excavation of the past as memories is not considered to be the route to change.

MUTATIVE EXCHANGES

It will no doubt be clear by now that I lean towards the type of model put forward by the Sandlers. The idea that change occurs at the procedural level has been further refined by those theoreticians and clinicians influenced by both psychodynamic and developmental ideas who underscore the importance of the co-construction of new contexts by the meeting of two subjectivities (Beebe & Lachmann, 1988, 1994; Sameroff, 1983; Stern *et al.*, 1998). Like the Sandlers and Fonagy, these practitioners also propose that psychic change occurs partly at a procedural level. Their contribution builds on these ideas and specifies more explicitly the implications for technique, namely, that verbal interpretations by the therapist may have become overvalued tools overshadowing the importance of the quality and the nature of the interactions between therapist and patient that bypass language itself. The underlying assumption in these accounts is that both patient and therapist contribute to the regulation of their exchanges, even if their respective contributions cannot be regarded as equal. From this perspective, regulation is an emergent property of the dyadic system as well as a property of the individual. Within this context, there is room for a variety of interventions, other than transference interpretations, which may have mutative potential.

The research that has inspired these perspectives originates from the field of developmental psychology. A notable contribution from this field has been the description of interaction as a continuous, mutually determined process, constructed moment to moment by both partners in the mother–infant dyad. Approaching the question of the patient–therapist relationship from the standpoint of infant research, Lachmann & Beebe (1996) propose three organising principles of interactive regulation, namely, ongoing regulation (i.e. a pattern of repeated interactions), disruption and repair (i.e. a sequence broken out of an overall pattern) and heightened affective moments (i.e. a salient dramatic moment). They suggest that the three principles serve as metaphors for what transpires between patient and therapist. Moreover they believe that:

> At every moment in a therapeutic dyad there is the potential to organise expectations of mutuality, intimacy, trust, repair of disruptions, and hope, as well as to disconfirm rigid, archaic expectations (Lachmann & Beebe, 1996: 21).

In the therapeutic situation, ongoing regulations range from postural and facial exchanges to greetings and parting rituals. The way in which these are regulated promotes, according to Lachmann & Beebe (1996), new expectations and constitutes a mode of therapeutic action. In other words, they are suggesting that the qualitative nature of the interactions between patient and therapist, even if not verbally articulated, are nevertheless potentially mutative. Their work underscores a view of psychoanalytic interaction consisting of non-verbal communication signals that closely resemble the exchanges between mother and baby.

I would like to draw attention, in particular, to Lachmann & Beebe's (1996) notion of "heightened affective moments". Pine (1981) originally described particular interactions between mother and baby, which were characterised by a heightened affective exchange, either of a positive or of a negative nature. This might denote, respectively, for example, the experience of united cooing by both mother and baby or moments of intense arousal in the absence of gratification. Pine suggests that such events are psychically organising, that is, they allow the infant to categorise and expect similar experiences and so facilitate cognitive and emotional organisation. Beebe & Lachmann (1994) propose that heightened affective moments are psychically organising because they trigger a potentially powerful state[3] transformation that contributes to the inner regulation. If the regulation is experienced positively as, for example, when the mother and baby are engaged in facial mirroring interactions in which each face crescendos higher and higher, subsequent experiences of resonance, or of "being on the same wavelength" with another person, are organised around such a heightened moment. The notion of heightened affective moments is by no means new, and most therapists would agree that such exchanges are essential in developing an emotionally meaningful relationship with their patients.

Stern *et al.* (1998) elaborate some of the above ideas. In their paper, they grapple with the notions of the "real" relationship and "authenticity". They observe that what we often remember as patients of our therapeutic experiences are "moments of authentic person-to-person connection" with the therapist:

> When we speak of an 'authentic' meeting, we mean communications that reveal a personal aspect of the self that has been evoked in an affective response to another. In turn, it reveals to the other a personal signature, so as to create a new dyadic state specific to the two participants (1998: 917).

They refer to these particular exchanges as "moments of meeting". These "moments", in a general sense, are interpersonal events that provide opportunities for new interpersonal experiences (Lachmann & Beebe, 1996). Stern *et al.* (1998) propose that they rearrange "implicit relational knowing" for both patient and therapist. This rests on an important distinction drawn by the authors between "declarative knowledge", which they hypothesise is acquired through verbal interpretations and "implicit relational knowing", which is acquired through the experience of actual interactions between patient and therapist. They suggest that moments of meeting contribute to the creation of a new intersubjective environment that directly impinges on the domain of "implicit relational knowing", thereby altering it. Such interventions are therefore believed to be mutative. They bring about change through "alterations in ways of being with", which facilitate a recontextualisation of past experience in the present,

---

[3]"State" is used here to denote the arousal and activity level, facial and vocal affect and cognition (Lachmann & Beebe, 1996).

... such that the person operates from within a different mental landscape, resulting in new behaviours and experiences in the present and future (Stern *et al.*, 1998: 918).

In contrast to the suggestion that it is primarily the interpretation of transference that allows for an elaboration of the object relationships dominating the patient's internal world, Stern and colleagues underscore the importance of moments of interaction between patient and therapist that represent the achievement of a new set of implicit memories that facilitate progression to a new level of interaction in the therapeutic relationship. The therapist's task is to facilitate the deconstruction of established but unsatisfying ways of "being with" while simultaneously moving towards new experiences. Moments of reorganisation involve new kinds of intersubjective meeting that occur in a new opening in the interpersonal space, allowing both participants to become agents towards one another in a new way. In the course of their exchanges, patient and therapist find themselves being with each other in a different way that reflects an emergent property of their unique and complex system of intersubjective relatedness.

The clinically relevant implication of the position outlined by Stern *et al.* (1998) is that psychic change may not rely on the patient becoming aware of what has happened. In other words, this account of therapeutic action suggests that insight may not be necessary to facilitate psychic change. Rather, the opportunity that therapy provides for qualitatively different types of interactions promotes an increase in procedural strategies for action, which are reflected in the ways in which one person interacts with another. The therapeutic relationship is conceptualised here as a source of information that is implicitly communicated (Lyons-Ruth, 1999), that is, it bypasses language. Elsewhere, I have described the use of humorous exchanges between patient and therapist as providing an opportunity for relating differently (Lemma, 2000). If we approach the therapeutic interaction in this manner, prosodic elements of language such as rhythm and tonality emerge as influential features of the interaction, at least as much as, if not more than, the actual words exchanged between the therapist and the patient. It thus encourages us to pay attention to the affective components of language.

As we develop, the increasing integration and articulation of new enactive procedures for "being-with-others" destabilise existing enactive organisations and act as the engine for change. The relationship with the therapist provides opportunities for new experiences, which challenge existing enactive procedures. Attachment research has shown that enactive procedures become more articulated and integrated through participation in coherent and collaborative forms of subjective interaction. The development of coherent internal working models of relationships is tied to the experience of participation in coherent forms of parent–child dialogue. Such dialogue is characterised by the quality of the caregiver's openness to the state of mind of the child. In such interactions, the child's affective or motive states are recognised and elaborated so that the child is helped in regulating her affective experience. The parent provides "scaffolding" (Lyons-Ruth, 1999) to the child's emotional experience.

To illustrate the idea of emotional scaffolding, let us take the example of a child who has just tipped over a pot of paint over the drawing she has been working on for some time. When this happens, the child bursts into tears. In one version, the mother rushes over and comforts the child telling her: "Sometimes these things happen and it's really upsetting. Do you think we should try again?" The mother here acknowledges the child's emotional experience, invites the child to re-engage in her drawing thereby also implicitly suggesting that nothing too catastrophic has happened, but also leaves it open for her to decide not to pursue it. In other words, she respects the child's experience, but also conveys that the child's internal state of frustration and disappointment can be overcome. In another version, the mother rushes over and says: "Look what you've done. I'm going to have to clean this up now. You're a 'bad' girl. Go to your room." In this scenario, the mother, who for all sorts of reasons may be very stressed, reveals that her mind is so full of her own preoccupations that she reacts to the event in an accusatory way, depriving the child of an opportunity to process the experience emotionally. Importantly, she makes a crucial attribution: she conveys to the child that this has happened because she is "bad". This latter exchange is neither collaborative nor coherent.

In the account of change that I favour, we can trace echoes of the notion of a corrective emotional experience. Here the patient is seen to benefit from the experience of a new object/therapist[4] who has the capacity to mentalise and whose way of relating implicitly attributes significance to the patient's emotional experience and acknowledges the patient's separateness from the therapist's own mind. This version of psychic change provides a more fine-tuned account of *how* the new experience with the therapist can lead to change by altering implicit procedures. It proposes that non-declarative processes (i.e. procedurally unconscious) underlie much of the non-interpretable changes in psychoanalysis. In other words, as Lyons-Ruth put it:

---

[4]I am not advocating that the therapist should actively behave in ways that, for example, aim to "correct" early parental failures. The therapist's role is to understand the impact such deficits may have had on the patient and, in so doing implicitly provides the patient with a "new" experience.

... the medium is the message; that is, the organisation of meaning is implicit in the organisation of the enactive relational dialogue and does not require reflective thoughts or verbalisation to be, in some sense, known (1999: 578).[5]

This perspective challenges psychotherapy's traditional emphasis on the spoken word as the mediator of psychic change. Rather, it proposes that translating, or if you like "interpreting", enactive knowledge into words may be an overvalued therapeutic tool:

> If representation of how to do things with others integrates semantic and affective meaning with behavioural and interactive procedures, then a particular implicit relational procedure may be accessed through multiple routes and representational change may be set in motion by changes in affective experience, cognitive understanding or interactive encounters, without necessarily assigning privileged status to a particular dimension such as interpretations (Lyons-Ruth, 1999: 601).

In a post-modern zeitgeist that has so emphasised the relativity of the stories we tell about our lives, psychotherapies of different persuasions have increasingly viewed the therapeutic process as one that provides the conditions of safety that allow the patient to narrate and rewrite his life. This may well be one of the functions of therapy and it may contribute to its eventual outcome. However, as Frosh so aptly captures:

> Many stories can be told about something not because they are all equivalent, but because of the intrinsic insufficiency of language. The real is too slippery, it stands outside of the symbolic system (1997a: 98).

What is so unique and privileged about the therapeutic encounter is that it provides an interpersonal context for the narrative process. It may therefore be that change takes place in the interpersonal space between therapist and patient and that what is experienced may not be verbalisable, but may yet be mutative.

CONCLUSIONS

Ask any psychoanalytic therapist whether understanding the past is important if we are to help the patient and most would agree that it is. Our childhood years are considered to be the most formative period of our lives. However, the question of how the past influences the present had, until comparatively recently, remained unclear, adding confusion to the question of therapeutic action.

---

[5]This is very reminiscent of Bollas' (1997) evocative notion of the "unthought known".

When Freud first started to practice psychoanalysis, he believed in the therapeutic importance of discharging affect and bringing latent instinctual wishes to consciousness so as to overcome resistances to their acceptance. Retrieving early memories that had been repressed was seen to be the legitimate goal of psychotherapy. To this end, reconstructive interpretations linking the present to the past were the mainstay of analytic practice. A minority of Freudians continue to model themselves on a more classical approach conceiving of change as an essentially intrapsychic process that relies on the retrieval of memories and on the reconstruction of early events.

However, if, as some of the contemporary models reviewed here suggest, change rests on the elaboration and refinement of implicit procedures for being with others in a range of emotionally charged situations, then making the unconscious conscious does not do justice to the process of change in psychotherapy. Indeed, nowadays many therapists – irrespective of theoretical group – devote their analytic efforts to an exploration of the here-and-now transference relationship and the understanding of the patient's internal reality. The frequency of references to the past varies, but reconstructive interpretations no longer hold the centre stage afforded to such interventions by the early Freudians.

Contemporary Freudians influenced by developmental perspectives also view change as occurring in the here and now. Accordingly, their interventions are often indistinguishable from those of the Kleinians, the object relationists and the intersubjectivists. If there is a difference, it is probably that the Freudians are more inclined to refer to the past than the others. Although Freudians and Kleinians approach the patient's communications differently in terms of the extent to which they focus on the interpretation of transference versus reconstructive interpretations, they nevertheless share in common the belief that the present is isomorphic with the past. This sets them apart from the British Independents who adopt a developmental view, thereby understanding the here-and-now situation as a highly modified derivative that is transformed through experience at different developmental stages.

All contemporary accounts of change broadly converge on the importance of the relationship between patient and therapist although, as we have seen, this is conceptualised in different ways. We do not yet know which version is the most valid. We need research to help us understand what function(s) the therapist performs that facilitates psychic change. If we model our understanding of therapeutic interaction on the function performed early on by the good enough parent who helps the child to develop a capacity to mentalise, that is, to think about her own and other people's behaviour in terms of mental states, then we can hypothesise that psychic change occurs through finding a new object in the therapist who deciphers the patient's communications and lends meaning to them, ascribing intentions and desires to him. This introduces the patient to a new experience of being with another who can think about his mental states without distorting them. Being able to pull together into a narrative sometimes inchoate experiences can feel very relieving most probably because creating a narrative is a part of creating meaning *and* because it is jointly created with another person who shows an interest in the contents of the patient's mind, lending meaning to his experiences. This may be one of the functions of psychoanalytic work. As Fonagy suggests:

> Psychoanalysis is more than the creation of a narrative, it is the active construction of a new way of experiencing self with other (Fonagy, 1999b: 218).

Whilst this new experience will depend in part on the therapist's verbal interpretations of the patient's experience in the transference, it is also likely that the way in which therapist and patient interact will convey a great deal of information implicitly. Change is thus likely to also rest on the quality of such implicit communications, leading to change at the procedural level.

The current interest in the "something more than interpretation" (Stern *et al.*, 1998) may pave the way for research into other features of the therapeutic process that contribute to change. Much will be gained in our understanding of how psychotherapy works if we become more aware of the functions of the relationship between patient and therapist in its broadest sense:

> Change can only take place if an interpersonal process between patient and therapist is created, establishing a climate of seeing things differently, of recognising what we can do and what we cannot do, of understanding what is ours and what is not (Bateman, 2000: 153).

The interpretations that we make are more than words leading to insight. At its best, an interpretation is a reciprocal mode of interaction that in itself provides an opportunity for the patient to experience a different way of relating. As we approach the delicate task of helping our patients to change, we do well to remind ourselves to focus less on the content of the verbal exchanges we have with them and more on the qualitative process underpinning these exchanges.

FURTHER READING

Sandler, J. & Dreher, A. (1996) *What do Psychoanalysts Want? The Problem of Aims in Psychoanalytic Psychotherapy*. London: Karnac Books.
Sinason, V. (Ed.) *Memory in Dispute*. London: Karnac Books.

3

THE ANALYTIC FRAME AND THE ANALYTIC ATTITUDE

All human activities are framed: they unfold in a given physical and psychic space. Therapy is no different. The pragmatic features of the analytic frame such as the consistency of the setting, the set length of time of sessions and the use of the couch demarcate the therapeutic space as different from other spaces within which relationships take place. This demarcation is further supported by the analytic attitudinal stance therapists are encouraged to adopt: a relatively unobtrusive, neutral, anonymous, professional stance that requires the therapist to inhibit, to an extent, her so-called "normal" personality so as to receive the patient's projections, thereby providing fertile ground for the development of the transference (see Chapter 7). Whilst the patient may discuss feelings and thoughts with a therapist that he might also share with a friend, the therapist adopts a very specific attitude in response to the patient's communications that is qualitatively different to that adopted by other people in the patient's life: she does not give advice, offer practical help or reassure. Rather, she listens and interprets the unconscious meaning of the patient's communications (see Chapter 5).

The analytic setting along with the analytic attitude creates a space that is as unique as it is at odds with many other social and professional encounters. Most human relationships unfold in contexts that are not timed to the very last minute, and where shaking each other's hand or talking about the weather, smooth social interaction rather than potentially become the focus for a discussion of unconscious wishes. Even professional and boundaried relationships such as those with medical or legal practitioners do not approximate nearly as much the "oddness" of the analytic situation. It is therefore unsurprising to find that for the uninitiated the analytic setting can give rise to anxieties and paranoid phantasies[1] – conscious and/or unconscious.

The core features of the analytic frame read like the top five best selling ideas in psychoanalytic practice: consistency, reliability, neutrality, anonymity and abstinence. Deviate from this frame and you could easily find yourself having to contend with the analytic superego many practitioners internalise during training. There are of course exceptions to the rules, embodied in Strachey's (1934) original notion of "parameters", developed to accommodate the deviations from the so-called standard technique with those patients who could not undertake clinical psychoanalysis. With few exceptions, the rules laid down by Freud have become the mainstay of contemporary views on the frame. It is of note, and not merely of historical interest, that Freud's own practice was more lax with respect to the frame: tea, sandwiches and kippers, for example, were not untypical occurrences in his work with the "Rat Man".

Rules exist for good reasons. It is one of the aims of this chapter to outline why the therapeutic frame *ideally* strives towards certain practical arrangements and encourages the adoption of a particular attitude by the therapist. However, rules also need to be challenged, not out of a perverse desire to be defiant, but because they are otherwise in danger of becoming reified and inflexible in the face of clinical situations, even with less disturbed patients, that call forth a different response to the one set out by the rules. Moreover, rules get adopted as standard practice on the basis of the hearsay tradition that unfortunately underpins so much of psychoanalytic practice, rather than because certain practices have been empirically tested and shown to be effective. Until such research is carried out, we can at best only assume that we do what we do because this is how it has always been done and it "works" in practice, rather than because this is what works better than another way of doing it. If this is the case, then rules are guiding posts that need to be flexible and open to revision. Indeed, the frame may be an unhelpful term as it conjures something fixed rather than responsive to the unique needs of each patient–therapist dyad.

THE FUNCTIONS OF THE ANALYTIC FRAME
The Frame as Contract

At its most basic, the establishment of the parameters of the frame marks the beginning of the therapeutic work. It indicates to the patient that the

---

[1]The patients who seem the least perturbed by the therapist's more distant stance tend to be more avoidant personalities who are threatened by intimacy. They thus find the distance reassuring.

therapeutic relationship is distinctly different to other relationships and that it operates along certain rules that both patient and therapist agree to subscribe to. When we outline the basic parameters of the frame, we are essentially outlining the working contract. This sets out unambiguously the boundaries of the relationship in such a way that any deviations from these established boundaries, for example, attempts to lengthen sessions or arriving late become open to interpretation. If we have not made it clear to our patient that the sessions will last fifty minutes, it is then difficult to interpret the fact that he takes ten minutes to leave our room. We can only interpret a deviation from the frame as meaningful if the terms of the frame were fixed at the outset of the therapy.

The more pragmatic aspects of the frame are very explicit and easy to specify, for example, the fee and the timing of sessions. Others, such as the analytic attitude, are never explicit, but always implicit in the manner we carry out the initial consultation and in all our subsequent interactions with the patient. Unlike an assessment for cognitive behaviour therapy (CBT), for example, an assessment for psychoanalytic therapy will not be very structured or therapist-directed. This is because one of the aims of an assessment is to give the patient a flavour of what it might be like to work psychoanalytically and to give us an opportunity to gauge the patient's capacity to make use of a less structured therapeutic space (see Chapter 4).[2]

The Frame as Reality

One of the key functions of the frame is to anchor the therapy in reality. The fact that we are only available for a set amount of time on a particular day provides a sharp, reality-oriented contrast to the host of phantasies that the patient may be developing about us and the primitive longing for care and nurture that are activated by the intimacy of the situation. Our limited availability may also bring to the fore feelings of neglect or rejection as the patient's longing for care is frustrated by the reality of the therapeutic situation. The frame thus serves to remind the patient that however intense his wish for unlimited care might *feel*, therapy on demand is not possible. Although it is hoped that our empathy and care will be experienced as containing – and for some patients as providing a new emotional experience – the therapeutic relationship also invariably frustrates and disappoints the patient. How the patient manages this becomes a focus for the analytic work. The frame, as agreed at the outset

---

[2]It is important to retain some consistency of approach and stance between an initial consultation and subsequent sessions. Marked changes in approach between consultation and therapy might confuse or disturb the patient.

with the patient, becomes part of how the patient relates to us, that is, we become for the patient, for example, the therapist who is always on time, always sits behind the couch and always takes a break at Christmas and Easter. These features are experienced as integral to the object we become in the patient's mind. It is part of what the patient feels he knows about his object/therapist. Consequently, any change to this frame challenges the patient's subjective experience of knowing his object. For example, if I have always been on time and I am late once, my patient has to factor this into his experience of me as the kind of therapist who is not always on time. This can be experienced as very disturbing for those patients who have difficulty with feeling separate or different.

The secure frame creates a space free from impingements so that the patient can "use" the therapist (Winnicott, 1971). The space needs to be safe because within it the patient may need to give expression to a range of feelings that arouse significant anxiety, often of a persecutory nature. Winnicott outlined the developmental importance of the infant's experience of destroying an object that survives the attack and does not retaliate. This allows the object to become "objective" – that is, the infant realises that it exists outside the self. This marks the beginning, according to Winnicott, of "object usage". If we apply some of these ideas to the therapeutic situation, we might say that one of the functions of the analytic frame is to create a setting in which patients can experience both omnipotence and deprivation in the knowledge that the therapist will survive the patient's attacks.

It is not only the patient who benefits from being anchored in reality by the frame. We benefit too. The work of psychotherapy plunges both patient and therapist into what is a very intimate, intense and sometimes highly arousing relationship. Just as the patient can come to experience us as an all-powerful figure, so can we experience the patient, for example, as the needy child part of ourselves. Such projections by us can contribute to a wish to repair past hurts through the patient, thereby actualising feelings that need to be understood, not acted upon. The boundaries set in place by the frame help remind us that the relationship with the patient should never become a substitute for resolving personal conflicts or thwarted desires. It helps us self-monitor: for example, if we extend a session beyond the agreed time, our deviation from the frame acts as a warning signal that something in the relationship and/or in ourselves needs to be attended to.

The Holding Environment

The frame that supports the analytic relationship is also referred to as the *holding environment,* an expression that highlights its containing function.

Bion (1967) drew a parallel between the mother's capacity to receive the raw intensity of her baby's projections, to empathise and to bear them, thereby rendering them eventually manageable for the baby, and the therapist's function of receiving, containing and transforming the patient's communications. This helps the patient eventually to internalise the capacity to manage feelings in himself and to think about them.

Just as mothers provide the baby with a dependable, secure environment that maximises the opportunities of physical and psychic growth, the therapist's function to an extent mirrors the early parental function with its emphasis on responding to the patient's needs without impinging on them. Winnicott, who suggested that the function of the analytic frame was to provide the necessary conditions for the development of ego strength so that the therapy could proceed, also proposed this view. The frame was, according to Winnicott, a potent symbol of the maternal holding that he so emphasised in his writings; he believed that it was this holding function that allowed the baby to manage difficulties in early life. When we transpose these ideas to the therapeutic setting, it becomes clear that the holding function of the frame depends primarily on the therapist's *mental* holding that is supported and protected by the pragmatic aspects of the frame.

The frame thus acts as a container. It allows for the unfolding of the patient's story and an understanding of his internal world within safe confines. The safety or otherwise of the so-called container is communicated in practical terms through the respect of the boundaries of the analytic relationship. The safeguarding of a secure frame is a core part of analytic technique. It involves managing the physical boundaries of the relationship, namely, the provision of a space where therapist and patient can meet without interruptions, where confidentiality can be assured, where the therapist can be relied upon to turn up on time, at the same time, week after week, as well as to finish the sessions on time. The thoughtful administration of these boundaries conveys a great deal of information to the patient about what kind of person he is entrusting his pain with.

A therapist who starts her sessions late or cancels sessions repeatedly is conveying a very different message to the one who strives to adhere to the agreed boundaries. We are human and fallible, however, whatever projections the patients may make on us. This means that the ideal frame we try to provide is just that: an ideal. In reality there will come a time when we will be late for our patient or we may overrun the session, or someone will walk into our room whilst in a session. This may well encourage self-recriminations (e.g. "I am not a good therapist") or anger at the colleague who interrupts the session. There will always be a reason for every deviation from the frame, but whatever feelings we might have about it, what matters in the therapeutic work is the meaning the deviation acquires for the patient.

Tony was a forty-year-old man who had been orphaned at age three after both his parents were killed in a car accident. He had been brought up at first by his maternal grandmother, but after her death, when he was aged ten, he was placed in the care of various relatives and eventually spent one year in residential care. On our first meeting, he described how, after his grandmother's death, he had never lived anywhere for longer than two years.

As an adult Tony was very precise and a stickler for routines – a propensity that verged on the obsessional. He arrived to his sessions punctually and would monitor the time often announcing, before I could, that the session had come to an end. I felt that this was one of his many ways of retaining control in our relationship.

On one occasion, I am delayed on a train and arrive five minutes late for the session. As I collect Tony from the waiting area I sense his tension: he does not establish eye contact with me and utters a barely audible "Hello". When he sits down, he starts by saying there is not much to say today. He adds that he had not wanted to come because he was busy at work and it bothers him when he cannot finish a task he has started. He speaks a bit about pressures of work and deadlines not being met by colleagues, which he finds "infuriating". He barely looks at me as he speaks. As I listen, I feel that he is very angry with me but I also know it is one of Tony's characteristic patterns never to express directly what he feels.

Approaching my intervention, I take into consideration that Tony began the session non-verbally displaying signs of anger (e.g. he did not look at me) and verbally telling me that he did not have much to say and that he had not wanted to come to the session. This kind of start to a session invites me to think about what might have triggered Tony's stated resistance to talking and coming to the session. Here, I note that his not wanting to come to the session may have only come to his mind once he arrived and did not find me waiting for him, as was usually the case. Given Tony's early history of loss and discontinuity in his carers, I hypothesise that my lateness was most probably a trigger for his silent rage towards me.

Through his complaints about work and people not meeting deadlines, I hypothesise that Tony is giving expression indirectly to his infuriation with me for having missed our "deadline". His choice of the word "deadline" makes me think about his parents' death and I speculate that, given his traumatic history, my lateness has also aroused terrifying anxieties about whether I would ever arrive and whether he would be left, once again, orphaned.

This hypothesis was supported by a question Tony had put to me in a previous session about what would happen to a patient if his therapist had to move to another country. My attempts to explore the meaning of the question had been met with resistance. At the time of asking this question, Tony had insisted that he was simply curious about this and rejected my interpretation that he was worried about what would happen to him if for some reason I could no longer see him. It now seems important to return to the anxiety that I thought had fuelled this earlier question, namely, the anxiety arising from his growing dependency on me and his fear that I might also leave him, just as his parents had done. Although Tony had rejected my earlier interpretation, the theme of being abandoned is recurring and therefore needs to be pursued. I therefore hypothesise that Tony's rejection of my first interpretation may have been a sign of resistance to thinking about the possibility of my leaving him and the painful affects this gave rise to.

In my interpretation, I decide to reflect back to Tony, not only his rage about my lateness but also to acknowledge what the rage defends against. However, rather than giving the interpretation all at once, I start with the most conscious feeling, namely, the rage. This way Tony may be more receptive to what I have to say than if I offer him an interpretation that confronts him too quickly with feelings that he would rather not think about. Bearing this in mind I begin by interpreting: "You start off telling me that you don't have much to say today and in fact you did not really want to come to the session. You also express infuriation with work colleagues who do not meet deadlines. I think that you are saying to me that my lateness has made you feel infuriated with me. It's like you experience my lateness as me not doing a very good job and keeping to our deadline. But we both know you find it hard to express such angry feelings directly."

Tony is able to think about this and acknowledges that he had been angry as he had made a real effort to get to the session on time and was angry when I did not arrive. He then falls silent. He resumes speaking and reports an upsetting dream he had a few days earlier in which his cat ran out into the street and Tony waited for a long time but he did not come back. He could not remember anything else about the dream. This dream is thematically consistent with feelings of loss and abandonment; it reinforces my hunch about the underlying anxiety of being abandoned and I therefore decide to share with Tony the second part of my interpretation: "I think that your anger with me when I did not come to get you on time today covers up the anxiety you felt as if inside you feared that I would never arrive."

Adhering assiduously to the boundaries of the frame is not a question of being pedantic or inflexible – accusations often levelled at therapists who are very strict about their boundaries. On the contrary, such an attitude of respect for boundaries reveals an appreciation of the importance of stability and reliability for the patient's psychic development. For patients such as Tony who have experienced early losses, unsettled childhoods or grew up in an unpredictable family environment, the safeguarding of the boundaries of the analytic relationship may represent for the patient the very first experience of a person who can be trusted and depended upon. It creates a safe psychological space in which the patient may explore his deepest longings and fears. The importance of this frame cannot be overstated. It is a concrete expression of the containment we can offer the patient – an indication of what the patient can expect from us and can therefore rely on.

The boundaries of the therapeutic relationship ensure that anxiety provoking phantasies and feelings about the self and others can be explored and expressed in the context of a non-retaliatory relationship that will carry on being irrespective of the feelings the patient may need to voice. This does not mean, however, that "anything goes". Being truly containing requires knowing when understanding is not enough, that is, when words simply cannot contain the patient. There are clearly behaviours that undermine the therapeutic process and have to be managed, for example, arriving to sessions under the influence of alcohol or attempts to self-harm during a session. Such behaviours need to be addressed promptly and understood as unconscious communications. In many cases, this will defuse the need to act out.

An important part of our role is to allow ourselves to become the receptacles for the patient's projections and his need to act out feelings that cannot be verbalised. However, it is also our responsibility to keep the boundaries and to remind the patient of this if his behaviour threatens to undermine the therapy. Lending oneself to the patient's projections involves knowing when the enactment of a projection is too concrete for it to be of any use. Not retaliating does not mean passively accepting that the patient is abusive towards us because of what has happened to him. The therapeutic relationship may well be subjected to familiar patterns prominent in the patient's interpersonal repertoire, but it also has to be one with a difference, namely, one where these patterns, and their consequences for relating, are made explicit and can be thought about. The survival of the object that Winnicott spoke of results from our ability to use our own mind when under interpersonal pressure to abandon thinking and to act. Where understanding is not enough to defuse the need to act out, the therapy may, in rare situations, need to end.

Regressive Aspects of the Frame

The analogies frequently drawn in the literature between the therapist's function and the maternal function highlight the regressive quality of the analytic relationship. This has raised concerns about the potential for exploitation of the patient. To an extent, the analytic "set-up" does invite a degree of regression. The analytic setting frames a level of reality that is separate from that of ordinary life – an area of illusion. The rules and rituals of the frame demarcate this reality. This is most concretely evident in the use of the couch on which the patient lies and the rule of free association, itself a regressive phenomenon, urging the patient to suspend ordinary censorship, to abandon strict logic and coherence in his communications. Even though there are regressive features of the analytic setting, we should most certainly not exploit the consequent vulnerability of the patient. When used therapeutically, the regression enables the patient to explore infantile longings and anxieties that shape present relationships and attitudes to life.

As with any relationship, the therapeutic relationship is open to abuse, but this is by no means specific to analytic treatment. Nevertheless, it has been argued that the analytic process, through its use of interpretations and the fostering of a transference relationship, places the therapist in a more powerful position in relation to the patient than in other forms of therapy. That there is a power imbalance is true, but this is an intrinsic feature of *any* therapeutic relationship. The patient is, by definition, vulnerable. The intensity of the relationship will almost certainly arouse intense emotions and longings that the patient may put us under pressure to gratify. This places us in a powerful position vis-à-vis the patient. The actual abuse of this power merely reflects an aspect of human behaviour that is all the more shocking when it occurs in the context of a relationship that sets itself up as offering a measure of healing.

The Frame as Intervention

How we set up the frame and manage it, or deviate from it, are all interventions, just like an interpretation. An intervention carries communicative intent – conscious and unconscious. Hence, if we strive to maintain a secure frame, we are conveying something important to the patient. If we deviate from it, for example, by being late or by introducing a new picture into the consulting room, we are also communicating and hence intervening. This is why it becomes important when deviations from the frame occur – and they invariably do – that we work with the patient to understand the meaning of the deviation for him and that we work out within ourselves why we have deviated. Of course, the odd situations when we arrive late because of transport problems, as in Tony's example above, are probably not best understood as an enactment, but merely as an unavoidable reality that nevertheless has meaning for the patient.

One Frame for All?

Psychotherapy does not take place in a vacuum. It unfolds in given cultural and social systems that give it shape and meaning. This immediately raises the question of the cross-cultural validity of the frame as conceived of in the West. I became very aware of the ethnocentric assumptions embedded in the very structure of the analytic frame when I worked in Bangladesh some years ago (Lemma, 1999). Compared with the privacy that we strive to provide to our patients in the West, the sessions in Bangladesh took place in a wide variety of settings that cut through the cultural landscape: in open, public and overcrowded clinics, where the whole family expected to accompany the identified "patient". The concept of time was also quite different to our Western tendency to clock every activity and hence to notice and lend meaning to the transgressions from such established boundaries. The majority of the patients were very socio-economically deprived, travelled long distances and had no access to more reliable means of transport. It would not have made any sense to interpret their lateness as a sign of resistance.

Therapy works through, or at least acquires, the flavour of wider cultural activities. The setting in Bangladesh could hardly have been more different than its British sanitised counterpart. Nevertheless, in their own idiosyncratic ways, both settings develop their own particular rituals imbued with the meaning and emotional colours of the local cultural spaces in which they are rooted. Over time, these become reified as "practice". If this is so, then the interesting question is not which setting is best, but which setting makes most sense in a given culture. It is only once the culturally meaningful boundaries are established that it becomes possible to interpret deviations from them.

THE PHYSICAL FRAME

Time

Why this obsession with time? Is running a session a few minutes over the set fifty minutes significant? Is it not worse for the patient who has finally managed to get in touch with his feelings to have to stop abruptly rather than extending the session by five minutes? These are reasonable questions to ask ourselves.

When we contemplate the time boundary in psychoanalytic practice, it becomes evident that the agreed upon length of sessions is an arbitrary custom. A forty-five minute session is probably little different to a sixty-minute session or an eighty-minute session except in so far as the longer the session the more material one can cover. However, whether this correlates with greater or quicker improvement is another matter for which we lack evidence. The fifty-minute hour is customary practice most probably developed and adhered to because it helps therapists manage their time efficiently so that patients can be seen on the hour, allowing for a ten-minute break in between sessions.

Even if the actual length of the session is arbitrary, it is nevertheless essential that the agreed length is respected and not changed in response to pressure from the patient or from internal pressures arising within us. For example, if a patient becomes very distressed just as we are about to call time, it may feel insensitive or cruel to have to end the session. Experiencing oneself as cruel may well conflict with the preferred image of ourselves as caring. This internal pressure may lead us to extend the session. In such a situation, this would represent acting out on our part. In turn, the patient may, for example, experience the extended time as confirmation that we do not trust he can manage without us.

Time boundaries can be a source of frustration, anxiety, relief or indifference. For one patient, the words *"It's time"* may symbolise a mother's refusal to feed on demand, while for another it may relieve him from the burden of intimacy. Molnos helpfully reminds us that, "Real time is a mental and cultural construct" (1995: 6). The time boundaries will thus assume different meanings depending on the patient's internal reality. They will also be coloured by the prevailing cultural attributions linked to time.

Whatever idiosyncratic meanings time boundaries acquire for the patient, they introduce reality within the therapeutic relationship and challenge the oceanic feelings of eternal union that the intimacy of the therapeutic relationship can re-evoke (Molnos, 1995). They present the patient with a mini-separation, which is likely to elicit quite specific feelings. For the patient in the throes of discussing something very important to him, the time boundary may lead him to feel misunderstood, uncared for, deprived, neglected, rejected, abandoned or punished. For the patient who finds intimacy difficult or even unbearable, our words "It's time" may bring about immense relief whereas our extension of the time might, for this same patient, elicit claustrophobic phantasies of being trapped or being seduced by an overbearing, intrusive other.

The agreed time boundary and our adherence or deviation from it stim-ulates in the patient an unconscious phantasy about the therapist's own state of mind in relation to him. Extending the time boundary, for example, is loaded with meaning for a patient who may interpret the extension in a variety of ways, for example, *"The therapist can't bear to let me go. She's lonely."* or *"I'm so interesting she wants to extend the session."* or *"She thinks I'm so ill she doesn't trust I can manage without her"*.

If a deviation has taken place, it will be important to intervene once we have formulated the meaning it holds for the patient. This involves naming the unconscious phantasy it gives rise to. This phantasy relates to the internalised object relationship that is activated by the trigger. As an example, let us assume that we have arrived late for a session and that this is the relevant trigger. The patient we have kept waiting is one who experiences a lot of conflicts related to rivalry. He is the eldest of three; the siblings were all born in close proximity to each other. The patient has spoken in the therapy about his frustration when he fails to get attention. He recognises that this was an issue in his family as he felt that his mother was always too busy. One of the themes in the therapy is his insistent curiosity about the other patients we see and his conscious fantasy that we see more interesting patients than him. On the day we are late the patient informs us that he has been having thoughts about taking a break from therapy to go travelling for six months. He has not voiced this before. To formulate our intervention we could go through the following steps in our mind:

- Name what the deviation is (e.g. *"I was late getting you from the waiting area today."*).
- Identify the unconscious phantasy that is elicited (e.g. *"I think that when I fail to get you on time you feel as though I have someone else on my mind other than you."*).
- Name the feeling that accompanies the unconscious phantasy (e.g. *"When you believe that I am not keeping you in mind, I think this leaves you feeling as if I'm abandoning you and that I prefer a more interesting patient over you."*).

- Name the consequence of the phantasy (e.g. *"When you feel abandoned, that's when you get angry and decide that you are going to leave me and go travelling."*).

The Physical Setting

The physical environment of therapy requires careful planning. Its most important feature is the extent to which it enables us to ensure confidentiality and minimise interruptions by others. The room we see patients in needs to be well soundproofed and clear signs need to indicate whether a session is in progress. These particular features of the setting may be hard to provide if working within public services in which walls are often paper-thin and colleagues regularly walk into ongoing sessions despite notices on the doors!

The physical setting is also ideally one that is relatively neutral. By this I am not suggesting that the room needs to approximate a monastery in its austerity and lack of any visual distractions. Clearly, the environment we work in is going to reflect who we are to a greater or lesser extent. We need to create environments we feel comfortable working in as we will be spending many hours in them. Nevertheless, because of our chosen profession there are some constraints on how personal we can make this space. We are seeking to minimise intrusions into the patient's space so that he can more freely project onto us any conscious and unconscious phantasies that he might have. For example, if we display photographs of our children in the consulting room, we may be depriving a patient from exploring his fantasies about whether we have children or not and what this means to him. The reality of our having children as indicated by displaying family photographs represents an intrusion into the patient's exploration of his fantasies. Sometimes such intrusions are unavoidable, for example, if we work from home and the patient can hear children playing in the room above the consulting room. This needs to be worked with but given that some intrusions cannot be avoided, it is best if we minimise them wherever we can.

The choice of the art we display in the consulting room will require some thought. For example, if we have a penchant for nudes this is not appropriate. In setting up a private practice, attention will also need to be given to the provision of a waiting area, even if this consists of no more than a chair outside the consulting room and of toilet facilities. My practice is to point out to the patient at the end of the first consultation these practical arrangements. I have heard from some patients, and a few colleagues, that some therapists appear not to give any indication about such matters seemingly either thinking that it will be obvious – which in some instances it is – or where it is not obvious, the therapist has sometimes taken up as potentially meaningful, for example, the patient's query about where he should wait. In such instances, it strikes me that what is interesting is not so much the patient's most probably reasonable question but the therapist's assumption that it is therapeutically beneficial to take up absolutely everything the patient says or does as having unconscious meaning. Importantly, meeting a patient's quite normal question about where to wait with silence may represent a shaming experience as the patient may feel that he should not have asked and that he has done something "wrong".

Confidentiality

Confidentiality is of the utmost importance. It is also all too easy to breach confidentiality without even realising it. After a difficult session, it may be tempting to discuss the patient with another colleague or even with a partner. Whilst the intention is to gain support, and not gossip, we are nevertheless breaching the patient's right to confidentiality.

Confidentiality may be seriously compromised when working in teams where information about patients is regularly shared. If working in such a setting, it behoves us to carefully think through the limits of confidentiality and to spell these out to the patient. Besides the usual proviso that confidentiality will be breached if the patient's life or that of another is at risk – a condition that should prevail, in my opinion, whether working privately or in health or social services – there may be other added limitations that need to be explained to the patient when working in multidisciplinary teams.

Patients, on the whole, have a very different understanding of confidentiality to ours when we work in public services. Most patients have no idea that we discuss them at team meetings, with other colleagues or with a supervisor. If working in a team, it may be helpful to explain the implications of this for confidentiality to the patient, as follows, *"What we discuss together remains confidential but as I also work in a team who is responsible for your overall care there may well be occasions when I will be asked to provide reports or updates on how our work is progressing. I will not disclose the details of what we discuss but just give a general overview of how you are doing. Do you have any thoughts about this?"*

My practice is to give limited information to other professionals unless there are clear clinical reasons for being more specific. For example, if a patient was harbouring homicidal fantasies about his psychiatrist and I considered the potential for acting out to be even remotely probable, I would disclose this detail, for obvious reasons. In the majority of cases, however, I do not see any reason for letting others know, say, whether the patient was abused and how, or the specifics of their sexual difficulties. Generally speaking, all that the other professionals need to know is:

- who referred the patient,
- the date of the first assessment,
- brief summary of the presenting problem and formulation in general terms,
- whether there are any risks to self and others,
- how long the patient will be seen for.

As a rule, one sheet of A4 is enough. People are busy and do not have time to read long reports. The only exception to this would be cases in which there are concerns about risk to self or others. In these situations it is best to err on the side of more information than too little.

In public services, the GP is contacted as a matter of course even if he is not the referrer, providing the patient consents to this. In private practice, the question of whether or not to contact the patient's GP needs to be considered. Although it is always important to ask for the GP's details, it may not always be imperative to write to him. The only conditions under which it is essential to liaise with a GP at the outset are as follows:

- The patient is at risk of harm to self or others.
- The patient appears to have needs beyond psychotherapy.
- The patient is receiving medication for psychological problems.

Sometimes patients deteriorate during therapy or their needs become clearer and therefore other professionals need to become involved at a later stage. It is because of this possibility that it helps to make a note of the GP details at the outset so that it is easy to contact him in an emergency. However, it is important to let the patient know our intention before contacting the GP. The only exception to this would be if the patient was so disturbed that he could not take in what we were saying or may become violent towards us at the suggestion of calling another professional.

Fees

There is no such thing as "free" therapy. Even when we work within publicly funded services and the patient is not directly responsible for paying us, the therapeutic relationship unfolds in the knowledge that if we were not remunerated by the patient himself or by an organisation, there would be no such relationship.[3] Of course, most patients receiving publicly funded treatment are not consciously thinking about this arrangement, but its meaning and implications are never too far away, if only we listen out for this. Nevertheless, because there is no physical exchange of money between patient and therapist, the unconscious meaning of money within the therapeutic relationship can be more easily sidestepped in public health service settings.

Therapists who work privately are, however, often faced with patients' feelings about having to pay for treatment and the different meanings of money. Psychoanalytic treatment that is open-ended requires as Phillips put it "The kind of investment no rational person could make" (1997: x). Indeed, as he points out, the patient is asked to pay in exchange for fifty minutes of our time, for an indeterminate length of time for an uncertain outcome. The only certainty in analytic treatment is that the process will be painful. For some patients, having to pay for this may only add insult to injury.

Clinically, we often note that the fact of the fee can be used in different ways by the patient. The exchange of money for services received can, for example, create the illusion that the subjective inequities within the analytic relationship (e.g. the needy patient versus the all-knowing therapist) are cancelled out by the fee. The fee can seduce both patient and therapist into the belief that "obligation, reciprocation and service are perfectly aligned" (Forrester, 1997), thereby diluting the intensity of the transference. For some patients, the fee may be used to confirm deeply held beliefs that they are being exploited. For others still, the fee may act as a painful reminder that the therapist can never be a surrogate parent, that is, at the end of the day no matter how caring the therapist might be, the patient knows that she would not be doing this unless she was paid. All these possible meanings and others need to be borne in mind and interpreted if they become a form of resistance, for example, as with the patient who repeatedly forgets to pay.

Perhaps the most complex aspect of the fee arises from the fact that money creates the illusion that it cancels out indebtedness (Forrester, 1997). Yet, in therapy, we are usually dealing with symbolic debt. The existence of a fee glosses over the fact that symbolic debt can never be absolved by money. How we calibrate emotionally what we feel we owe to another, what we feel the other might expect of us and what we feel we want

---

[3] Even in many voluntary/charitable settings the patient is often asked to make a financial contribution, however minimal.

to give him or take from him are important questions that hover in the background of the reality of the fee. Conflicts over dependency can also attach themselves to the patient's relationship to the fee. Where these are salient relational themes for a given patient, we will need to work hard at exploring what phantasies lie behind the exchange of money.

Robin was a thirty-year-old, highly successful, intelligent man. He had made a lot of money very quickly working in the financial world. He was seeking therapy because he wanted to settle down and felt dissatisfied with the series of brief affairs he had been drawn to since his early twenties. His partners had accused him of never getting emotionally involved. Robin acknowledged that he was good at going through the motions of relationships, such as buying presents or taking his partner out to the theatre, but he felt uneasy with the expression of affection. Alongside his acknowledgement of his discomfort with this, Robin defensively emphasised that he was generous and caring. He told me that if he had arguments with a friend or partner he would send flowers the next day or book the best seats at the opera, as a way of "making up".

Robin described a very close relationship with his mother. He was the second born. His sister had died at 4 months of a rare heart condition. He told me that after her death his mother had quickly got pregnant with him. Robin felt that his mother had been overprotective of him and he explained this with reference to his sister's tragic death. His father figured as largely absent emotionally, but very generous financially. Robin said that he had never wanted for anything as he was growing up. When I asked him how his parents had responded to him as a child when he was upset, Robin explained that he would be promised a new toy or a special outing. In his family, it appeared as though money represented an attempt to smooth the cracks, as it were, but feelings were never openly discussed.

After a period of three weeks over which I assessed Robin, we finally agreed to start a once-weekly therapy. At this point I discussed my fee with him. Robin replied that my fee was "More than reasonable", adding that it was in fact much lower than another therapist he had consulted before me. I invited him to think about how my "lower fee" made him feel. At first Robin replied that it made him feel like he was seeing someone who did not value herself enough and that he preferred to mix with people who, as he put it, "went for gold". He punctuated the end of this sentence with raucous laughter. I responded by saying that he was perceiving a difference between us that was making him quite anxious though he was doing his best to cover this up. Robin stopped laughing, paused and added, "Actually there is something I feel uncomfortable about: money does not matter to you, so you may not understand what it means to me." This struck me as very important even if I suspected that Robin did not grasp the full import of what he was saying. As I found Robin to be interested in what went on in his mind and receptive to being helped, I ventured into offering a more elaborate interpretation than I might do at such an early stage with someone who was less psychologically minded. I interpreted: "I think you are right when you say that you fear that I may not understand what money means to you. It's as if you feel that we speak a different language when it comes to the meaning of money. I also hear this as you saying to me that you are worried that if we run into some difficulty in our relationship that demands of you that you connect with me in a more emotional way, then you won't know how to manage this because you are more comfortable with money currency than emotional currency. You won't be able to pay me more to reassure yourself in your mind that you are attending to what may be going wrong in this relationship and somehow putting it right".

It is not only patients who struggle with the meaning of the fee. Being paid for this kind of work can arouse conflicts in the therapist too. Our unease around money is well worth considering. It is not uncommon, especially early on in our professional development, to struggle over such questions as how much to charge or whether to charge for missed sessions. One of the reasons these decisions can feel very complicated is because we may be projecting our own needy, injured self into the patient with whom we identify. If this happens, we may then feel it is unfair to charge for a missed session. We may perhaps even idealise the patient's neediness and our own meeting of this need, setting up the patient as the unfortunate victim and ourselves as the saviour. "Saviours", of course, don't charge for missed sessions; they meet the need sacrificing their own self. If this internal scenario is a familiar one for us, we do well to remind ourselves that omnipotence sometimes lurks beneath apparent acts of generosity. An identification with the "underdog" deserves analysis since it frequently masks omnipotence.

For some therapists, the reluctance to charge for missed sessions arises from ambivalence about their professional competence and worth. The image of the profession and its origins are partly responsible for this. As a profession that originated out of the tradition of pastoral care provided by clergy, payment to heal one's soul may seem unfair. However, psychoanalytic therapy is a specialised intervention that requires years of training and significant emotional and financial investment. Being remunerated for it in financial terms is legitimate. Unless we examine honestly within ourselves our own ambivalence about money, the management of the fee will attract the potential for acting out on our part. In public health service settings in which there is no exchange of actual money, we have to work even harder to make sense of its meaning and how it is being unconsciously used by the patient.

Holidays and Cancellations

1. Cancellations

At the outset of therapy, it is important to specify the cancellation policy. In the analytic situation, the therapist avails herself to the patient at a given time during a given period. Breaks are an integral part of the relationship from the outset – another reminder that we have our own life separate from the patient – something that is likely to give rise to phantasies in the patient about what we do when we are not seeing him. Patients may choose to take breaks additional to those set by us. In private practice, this usually incurs payment of the fee for the cancelled session(s). Although some patients readily accept this aspect of the contract, some take objection to it, feeling that it is "unfair".[4]

Some therapists too find it uncomfortable to charge patients when they go on holiday at a different time from them. It is helpful to think through why we might not charge. The conflicts that arise for both patient and therapist around these issues are themselves important to examine. For some therapists there is a wish to be the ever-adapting parent who meets the demands of the patient/child. This often masks an anxiety about being perceived as inflexible or uncaring and thus eliciting the patient's hostility. But, as I have emphasised repeatedly in this chapter, therapy does not aim to create a relationship in which every wish is met, but one in which frustration or disappointment can be understood and managed more constructively.

If we are not clear within ourselves about why we charge or do not charge for missed sessions, it becomes more difficult to stay with the patient's feelings about the stance we adopt. It is unhelpful, however, to be prescriptive in these matters; what is essential is that the arrangements are made clear to the patient at the outset. It is surprisingly easy to omit to specify the cancellation policy after the first meeting, often because the therapist fears the patient's response. It is easier to meet the patient's

---

[4]In public health service settings, what the patient may regard as unfair is the therapist's refusal to offer an alternative session to replace a missed one, especially if working within a brief contract.

ambivalence at the outset than to have to face the patient, who, having just booked his holiday is told that he will be charged for the two weeks he will be away: this is bad practice. If the patient has entered the relationship assuming he only pays for the sessions he attends, we have no right to demand payment and the patient is justified in feeling angry at the demand for payment. This is why it is important to spell out our policies.

My own position on these matters has become clearer over the years. I do not believe that there is anything immoral or unfair about charging patients if they choose to have a break at a time different to my own breaks. This is because when I enter into an agreement to work with a patient I commit myself to offer them a specific time during specific periods. This is their time, nobody else's. This means that unless there are exceptional circumstances, I will not change that time and use it for another purpose. In other words, I am "booked" for that time.

Patients may, of course, at times have to take unplanned breaks to tend to what life unexpectedly throws their way, for example, bereavements, illness or childcare arrangements that have fallen through. A related question that thus needs to be thought through is whether we are willing to reschedule missed or cancelled sessions in these kinds of situations. I find this is a reasonable request and I endeavour to offer replacement sessions wherever possible. However, I explain to the patient at the outset that since my time is quite committed it may not always be possible for me to offer him an alternative time and if I cannot do so then he will be responsible for paying for the missed session.

If the patient made a habit of requesting to reschedule, I would be more guarded in my approach to offering alternative sessions. I would always consider the possibility that the request may be a form of acting out that needs to be understood (of course, sometimes, there may be a legitimate reason that is nevertheless also used for unconscious ends). Under these circumstances, I would take it up with the patient as a pattern that might help us both to understand a resistance or impasse in the work. For example, it may reflect the patient's wish to test the extent of my care or it may express his difficulty in making a commitment.

Offering alternative sessions may be a reasonable response in most cases but may pose particular problems if working within health service settings or within brief contracts. Repeatedly rescheduling appointments may be a way of prolonging a brief contract. In these cases, the request for a different session time becomes the focus of exploration.

There are also those patients who want to have therapy but whose work makes it impossible to commit to a regular time, for example, actors and journalists. It is true that people choose particular professions that give them conscious justification for always avoiding commitments. When this is the case, it needs to be explored rather than colluded with by offering to see people infrequently or constantly re-arranging times. Yet, it is important to also be realistic: some professions make it very hard indeed to make a regular commitment. Does this mean that therapy is impossible or should we be flexible under these circumstances? After all, we might argue, people have to work to afford therapy. My own view on this is that it depends on each individual case. There are people in impossible professions – from the point of view of the practical demands of analytic therapy – to whom I suggest waiting until such a time as their job allows them more stability. There are others, however, with whom I feel it is possible to work making allowances for the fact that they may be away at times for extended periods. This does interfere with the therapy as we, the therapists, have been taught to do it. Yet, I can think of cases in which the patient in such less than ideal circumstances managed to derive significant benefit from therapy. An attitude of openness is most probably the best policy in these situations so that each case can be considered in relation to the patient's individual needs and their personality organisation.

2. Therapists' planned breaks

The patient needs to know that we will be taking regular breaks. For most therapists, these will usually occur around established holiday times such as Christmas and Easter and the summer. However, there will be exceptions to this and this needs to be made explicit. Wherever possible we should give ample warning of breaks. How we manage our absences – planned or unplanned – conveys a great deal to the patient about how serious we are about our commitment to them. It also sets the within-therapy culture for how the patient's own absences will be approached, that is, as an event that is potentially meaningful.

Even though it will be part of our contract that we are away at certain regular times, the reality of this may nevertheless take the patient by surprise. At the time of the break, the patient may behave as if we had never alerted him to the fact that we would be away and will feel let down and angry. This is because the conscious aspects of the frame – such as holiday arrangements – often have an unconscious meaning that may not come to light when the contract is first discussed with the patient.

3. Therapists' unplanned breaks

Unplanned breaks, for example, in response to illness or other life events cannot be anticipated but it is helpful to have contingency plans in place.

It helps to have on hand contact numbers of patients at which they can be reached at different times. Nowadays, mobiles make it possible to forewarn the patient before he sets off for his session and so spare a wasted journey. Illness that is very serious and may make it impossible for us to directly contact the patient requires sensitive handling. Forethought on this matter spares us added anxiety at a time when we are already feeling unwell.

We generally prefer to avoid contemplating the worst, yet in choosing this profession we have chosen one in which our absence will have repercussions on our patients who may be in particularly vulnerable states. It is therefore incumbent on us to make provision for those situations in which we may be unable to contact the patient. The best way to approach this is to entrust a colleague with a list of all patients that are being currently seen along with their contact numbers. In case of an emergency, this colleague can phone patients on our behalf and we can be assured that they will handle it with sensitivity and tact. This is far preferable to asking a partner or a friend to do it, as they may be unprepared for the patient's anxiety, concern or occasional anger. The patient list needs to be updated regularly.

In cases in which there is likely to be a prolonged absence, contingency plans will need to be made for managing the practice. These plans are hard to pre-empt, as each patient is likely to have very individual needs. However, it is at times like these where having good referral networks that we are familiar with and can trust alleviates significantly the anxiety associated with having to ask another colleague to cover us in our absence.

The Couch, Evenly Suspended Attention and Free Association

Lying on the couch has been likened to a form of "sensory deprivation" (Ross, 1999). Deprived of face-to-face contact with the therapist, the patient relies more on fantasy than on actual visual information to make sense of what the therapist may be feeling towards him. By breaking the flow of communication, the couch deprives the patient of interpersonal data, allowing the patient more scope for "completing the gestalt with his or her subjectivity" (Louw & Pitman, 2001: 760). It facilitates a liberation from the social cues that constrain normal communication that allows unconscious phantasies to emerge more freely. Importantly, as it avoids visual contact, the expression of feelings or thoughts that elicit shame, is facilitated.

Like many aspects of the frame, the use of the couch is most probably as much for the benefit of the therapist as it is for the patient's benefit. Indeed, Freud was quite explicit about this: he is reputed to have remarked that sitting behind the patient, out of sight, was a safe haven that freed him from the burden of being stared at all day (Ross, 1999). When not engaged in face-to-face contact with the patient, it is easier for us to look inwards and not to feel under pressure to respond. It is commonplace for many therapists to feel uncomfortable with silences. The temptation to say something can be very strong when we are under the stare of the patient whose own anxiety about the silence may exert considerable pressure to speak – not because this is helpful but because it relieves both parties of an anxiety that could be more productively understood rather than being temporarily soothed by having spoken.

Out of the glare of the patient, we may find it easier to adopt the stance advocated by Freud:

> The attitude which the analytic physician could most advantageously adopt was to surrender himself to his own unconscious mental activity, in a state of evenly suspended attention, to avoid as far as possible reflection and the construction of conscious expectation, not to try to fix anything that he heard particularly in his memory, and by these means to catch the drift of the patient's unconscious with his own unconscious (1923: 239).

With an attitude of "evenly suspended attention", Freud encouraged the therapist to give equal weight to all of the patient's free associations. The distinctive features of this attitude were later articulated, somewhat paradoxically, by Bion:

> ... there is a psychoanalytic domain with its own reality... these realities are intuitable. In order to exercise his intuition, the psychotherapist has to let go of memory, desire and understanding (1970: 315).

Here Bion is advocating relinquishing our own preconceptions that may otherwise interfere with our capacity to listen unencumbered by our desires.

The use of the couch is linked with another "rule", namely, the invitation to the patient to *free associate*. This was Freud's fundamental rule, and the cornerstone of his technique, whereby his patients were asked to share all their thoughts as they came to mind without any regard for logic or order. Once on the couch, out of the therapist's direct line of vision, the patient turns inwards, he begins to focus less on his perceptions of material objects in the room and more on the images that flash through his mind, the fleeting thoughts that emanate from the stream of consciousness and are so difficult to catch. This presents the patient with a further paradox since he is effectively "moved to be pre-verbal yet enjoyed to speak" (Ross, 1999: 93), as we invite the patient to articulate his free associative linkages.

Free association has been defined as the "breathtakingly imperialistic requirement to reveal all" (Forrester, 1997: 4). It asks the patient to suspend censorship over what he says. This is a true paradox because as Phillips so aptly put it, "Telling the truth in analysis means relinquishing one's wish to tell the truth" (1997: IX). Indeed, Freud was well aware of the demand he placed on his patients:

> In confession, the sinner tells us what he knows; in analysis the neurotic has to tell more (1926: 289).

Freud insisted on the rule of free association because he realised that whatever the seemingly plausible reasons for the appearance in his patients' conscious minds of certain thoughts or images, these were used, as it were, by deeper forces pressing for expression. In encouraging patients to share everything that came to mind, Freud hoped to be led to their inner conflicts through their associations. In free associating, patients certainly reveal a lot about themselves – often far more than would be the case if we asked questions or structured the therapeutic session.

Free association is an ideal towards which the patient strives but in practice it is very difficult indeed to share all the contents of our thoughts. While Freud encouraged his patients to freely associate, he was soon confronted by their reluctance to do so: the hesitations, the silences, the self and other deception, the "nothing comes to mind" in response to the encouragement to the patient to speak his mind. Over time, Freud became aware of a force within the patient that opposed the treatment. He understood this as a *resistance* to treatment – the same force that prevented unconscious ideas from becoming conscious. The purpose of this resistance was, according to Freud, one of defence. His patients' claims that they did not know something were understood by Freud as their "not wanting to know". The primary task of the therapy was therefore to overcome the resistance thereby allowing the patient's gaps in memory to be filled in (see Chapter 6).

THE ANALYTIC ATTITUDE

Abstinence

Freud (1919) emphasised the need to abstain from responding to the patient's sexual wishes and renouncing any over-gratifying attitude towards the patient. Abstinence ensured that the patient did not derive any substitute satisfaction from the therapeutic encounter that would otherwise inhibit progress. This is deemed unhelpful because in the absence of a degree of pain or conflict there is usually no desire to heal.

Freud proposed that once the therapist becomes an important object to the patient, that is, once she becomes invested as the target of transference wishes, the therapist should leave these wishes ungratified and instead analyse the defences that develop. Clinical experience repeatedly demonstrates that affect soon emerges in response to the experience of frustration along with the accompanying phantasies that are elicited and the defences to manage this. This allows the therapist to help the patient examine his conflicts. Abstinence is thus believed to give rise to a state of deprivation crucial to treatment. Freud (1919) did acknowledge that some "concessions" should at times be made, but he warned:

> ...it is no good to let them become too great. Any therapist who out of the fullness of his heart perhaps, and his readiness to help, extends to the patient all that one human being may hope to receive from another, commits the same economic error as that of which our non-analytic institutions for nervous patients are guilty: their aim is to make everything as pleasant as possible for the patient, so that they may feel well there and be glad to take refuge there again from the trials of life, (1919: 164).

Given the rather inhospitable state of so many of our in-patient psychiatric settings, Freud's remarks may at first appear ridiculous. However, even if the physical environment many patients have to contend with in institutional settings leaves a lot to be desired, it is nevertheless the case that the relationships they are likely to establish with ward staff may gratify some of their wishes for companionship or for attention on demand. By contrast, the fixed boundaries of the therapeutic encounter can become a source of frustration and deprivation for the patient who wishes for exclusive attention on demand. The fifty-minute hour, as we saw earlier, provides one such frustration.

Nowadays most therapists would agree that the therapeutic situation should not gratify, or if you like, become too "comfortable". Gratification, in the analytic sense, may arise in myriad ways and needs to be considered along a continuum. For example, we gratify patients by a smile, common courtesy, offering hope of help, understanding and empathy. This kind of gratification is mostly considered appropriate and, I would argue, essential so as to create a therapeutic atmosphere of collaboration and respect. What we try to avoid is inappropriate gratification of regressed wishes that would undermine the analytic work and the patient's autonomy. For example, agreeing to see the patient out of hours (unless it was a very serious emergency) or accepting his invitation to attend his wedding would all constitute inappropriate degrees of gratification.

Being mindful of the dangers of overgratification is important. Nevertheless, the indiscriminate application of the principle of abstinence represents a manipulation of the transference. The iatrogenic effects of an overly austere approach can contribute to unnecessary suffering or discomfort and give rise to an unproductive exaggeration of psychopathology. For example, greeting the patient with silence and no smile will almost certainly heighten anxiety, especially if the patient is prone to paranoid anxieties. Whether this is helpful remains an open question. We do well to remind ourselves in this respect, as Inderbitzin & Levy (2000) suggest, that any treatment modality that has the power to cure also has the power to harm.

Anonymity and Self-disclosure

Freud advocated anonymity on the part of the therapist; hence, he regarded any previous acquaintance with the patient or his relations as a serious disadvantage. Freud (1912) described how the therapist should function as a "mirror" to the patient's projections so that the reactions to the therapist could then be analysed to throw light on the patient's relationships more generally. The notion of the therapist as a blank screen, receptive to the patient's projections was, however, gradually challenged (Balint and Balint, 1939). Gitelson (1952) and Heimann (1950, 1960) were amongst those theorists who drew attention to the notion of a "fit"[5] between patient and therapist whereby some patient–therapist couples might fit together better than others.

It soon becomes apparent when we practice that complete anonymity is impossible to sustain: those who make referrals to us may give something away about us to the patient and, in any event, the patient will almost certainly pick up a lot of clues about us by the way we are with them, our accent or our dress or through publications, where applicable. Even where we strive to maintain as anonymous a stance as possible, for example, by decorating neutrally our consulting rooms, or by not seeing our patients within our own homes, patients will often be curious about

---

[5]The "fit" can only be said to be a function of technique or skill in so far as these are "conditioned" by the therapist's personality.

us and draw conclusions about our person – sometimes from the most improbable sources.

Some patients are explicitly curious about their therapists. Behind such curiosity we often find unconscious motivations or wishes worth exploring. It is also of equal interest when the patient displays no curiosity whatsoever, as lack of curiosity may be, for example, a defence against erotic feelings in the transference or rivalrous feelings about the therapist's phantasised other patients or children.

Freud (1913) suggested that the therapist should not reveal to the patient her own emotional reactions or discuss her own experiences. Especially at the beginning of our training many of us will have struggled with whether or not to answer personal questions about what we think or feel or other personal facts. By and large, the rule of thumb in psychoanalytic work is that no question is ever "innocent" and therefore our task is to interpret its unconscious meaning.

Sarah was a thirty-year-old woman who had been in three-times-weekly psychotherapy with me for four years. Some months after the traumatic events of September 11, 2001, she arrived for her session clearly irritable. Everything I said was rebuffed. She remarked that we were going round in circles and she could not see the point of what I said to her. She complained that she had come into therapy to be able to have a relationship and she was still not succeeding in this. The night before a man she had started to date made it clear that he had no wish to pursue the relationship further. Sarah was very hurt by this rejection and felt despondent about any future relationships.

In the session Sarah went on to talk about the difficulties at work since the events of September 11 and the number of redundancies in her profession. She was worried that sooner or later her name would be called out and she would be left without a job. She sardonically said to me "Without job *and* a man! You've done a good job. You must be pleased with yourself. I just don't know why I bother with therapy". I was feeling anything but pleased with myself under the sway of her hostile attack. Sarah then fell into silence. After a few minutes she said, in a softer, more childlike tone that she felt sorry for the Jewish people, that the attacks on the Twin Towers were fundamentally attacks on the Jews. She thought the Jewish people would have to retaliate. She then paused and added: "I've been meaning to ask you for some time, are you Jewish?" I did not say anything and Sarah added, "I guessed you would not answer. I don't get it. Why will you never answer my questions?" Sarah went on to criticise me for not answering. She then paused and added, "But I suppose that if you are Jewish you must have been feeling quite bad".

Sarah's personal question cannot be considered to be simple curiosity about the therapist she has been seeing for four years whose religious affiliation had never concerned her before this point. Answering her question directly is unlikely to be of any benefit to her: she does not need to know whether I am Jewish or not in order for her to get the most out of the therapy. However, understanding why after four years in therapy with me she thinks to ask me about my religious affiliations could help her at this particular juncture. I therefore decide to intervene but not to answer the question directly.

My intervention is informed by tracking the sequence of the material Sarah had produced. Sarah arrives for the session hurt and angry. She begins by complaining about the therapy and its uselessness and then lets me know that she has been rejected by her partner. She then expresses her concerns about being made redundant at work. This represents a consciously realistic preoccupation and is thematically related to her first story of being rejected/made redundant by her partner. She follows this up with an attack on me: I have not helped her and she does not know why she bothers with therapy.

Tracking the sequence of the session and the various themes allows me to formulate my first hypothesis, namely, that Sarah manages her painful feelings of rejection by projecting them into me: I become the useless therapist who is not worth bothering with and is going to get dumped.

My thoughts then turn to the fact that Sarah is overtly hostile towards me and I wonder what the anticipated consequence of being hostile might be for her. Again, following the sequence of her associations, and in particular her question to me about whether I am Jewish, is helpful in this respect. After her attack on therapy, Sarah switches tack: she talks about the Jewish people probably wanting to retaliate against the attacks. She is thus introducing a preoccupation with how people manage an attack that is very personal (i.e. it is not a random attack but it is linked in her mind with the personal attribute of being Jewish). Sarah lets me know that in her own mind such an attack could only provoke a counter-attack. She then asks her direct question: "Are you Jewish?" In light of the preceding sequence of associations I hear this question as expressing Sarah's anxiety about her own hostile attack towards me. This was a very personal attack and it is as if she is saying to me: "I have attacked you and you are now going to retaliate."

This is what I eventually interpret: " I think you are feeling very hurt by X's rejection and you are angry with me for not having helped you to make this relationship work. But your anger towards me also leaves you feeling very anxious that the Jewish me who feels attacked is going to strike back and you will be punished by being left alone, redundant with no job or man."

This intervention allowed Sarah to then talk about her anger towards her mother whom she felt had set a very bad example as she had "given up" on relationships. Sarah feared she would end up alone like her mother, depressed. However, she felt guilty for criticising her mother in this manner as she recognised that her mother had sacrificed a great deal for her, having relinquished her own career after Sarah's father left her. By not answering Sarah's question directly, Sarah was able to begin to explore a painful dynamic with her mother, highlighting her identification with a mother who had "given up", her anger about this and her feeling about having somehow been the cause of her mother's depression. Her attacks on her mother, in turn, gave rise to considerable guilt.

If we answer a question directly without thinking about its unconscious source, we are depriving the patient of an opportunity to understand himself. Etchegoyen (1991) argues that "direct satisfaction takes away from the patient the capacity to symbolise." Leaving the patient to struggle with why he may need to know, for example, whether we have children encourages the patient to verbalise something that might otherwise be enacted. If we answered such a question, for example, saying that we do not have children, the patient does not have to think about, and therefore represent, his experience of, say, feeling excluded in relation to his possible phantasy about not being our only and special child/patient. Likewise, had I answered Sarah's question directly I would have deprived her of an opportunity to make sense of aspects of her relationship with her mother, of how she managed her angry feelings and the paranoid anxieties this gave rise to. Not complying with the patient's curiosity[6] also emphasises the frustrations entailed in the position of being a third who is excluded from a phantasised couple. Answering questions directly in these situations therefore bypasses an opportunity to understand the patient's experience of triadic relationships.

---

[6]Not only is it unhelpful to satisfy the patient's curiosity about our personal lives, it is also unhelpful to satisfy our own curiosity by pursuing particular topics mentioned by the patient that interest us but may not be relevant to the work.

Although our own personal lives and preoccupations should not impinge on the therapeutic space, it is clearly impossible to sustain anonymity if by this we mean the withholding of all personal information – whether verbalised or enacted – or the inhibition of the therapist's "real" personality, beliefs and values. In outlining these views I am not advocating self-disclosure by the therapist – in the vast majority of cases I can see no good rationale for doing so from the vantage point of the best interests of the patient. Rather, I have in mind here the *inevitable* disclosures of the real person of the therapist through the way we dress, talk, decorate our rooms, how much or how little we intervene, what we choose to focus on and what we may or may not laugh about with the patient. Moreover, our *considered* disclosure, for example, of our uncertainty through the use of self-deprecating humour, can promote a climate where an acceptance of limitations can be faced without fear of being admonished, as well as helping to demystify the therapeutic process itself (Bloch *et al.*, 1983).

The therapeutic benefits, or otherwise, of self-disclosure are an ongoing preoccupation within psychoanalysis. Besides the controversy over whether we should answer personal questions, for example, about our sexual orientation or religious affiliation, there is also division over when, and if, the therapist should openly acknowledge mistakes. Some think that to acknowledge a mistake to a patient rather than just exploring the patient's perception of what occurred is an error. This school of thought maintains that such self-disclosures are frequently motivated by the therapist's feelings of guilt and a need to "confess" in the hope of obtaining forgiveness or to undo an error. In so doing, it is argued, the therapist burdens the patient and forecloses exploration.

There is another school of thought, however, which views the therapist's retreat into exploratory mode when faced with a mistake as:

> ... itself a mistake and creates a serious – and sometimes insuperable – problem in the treatment; one that, in fact, places a heavy burden on the patient (Jacobs, 2001: 666).

This is a very important observation. If we have erred in any way, there are three options open to us:

- We can acknowledge the mistake and then explore the meaning it holds for the patient.
- We can remain silent, allow the patient to elaborate the meaning the error holds for them and we can then acknowledge our mistake.

- We can use silence as a way of encouraging further elaboration of the patient's phantasies about our error without acknowledging our part in it.

When we employ the third tactic, the patient can feel rebuffed and distanced rather than producing helpful material. Acknowledging our error – which may or may not be understood as an enactment reactive to the patient's projections – does not mean that we necessarily burden the patient with our guilt. It is possible to acknowledge an error, take responsibility for it as well as invite the patient to explore how it has made him feel and how it may have changed his view of us. When I have made mistakes that I deem to be the result of my own "blind spots", I have typically allowed the patient first to talk about how it has affected him. In my intervention I have then acknowledged what I have done, or failed to do, and conveyed understanding of how this has made the patient feel in relation to the version of me that became dominant in his internal world, for example, a me/therapist who is negligent or insensitive. Especially when working with patients whose own grasp on reality is tenuous, not acknowledging something that has happened in the relationship and our part in it may only serve to confuse the patient further.

Neutrality

The question of the therapist's neutrality has always been central to psychotherapists' attempts to lend credibility to their work. This is largely because psychoanalysis has needed to disown any association with the possibility that it is no more than mere suggestion. Freud grappled with the demon of suggestion from the outset. Suggestion and neutrality stand as polar opposites, the former aligned with hypnosis, the latter with a more respectable scientific pursuit.

Levy & Inderbitzin (2000) have proposed that Freud's technical recommendations were an attempt to manage the problem of suggestive influence.[7] In his papers on technique, Freud (1912) advocated that the therapist should not give the patient direction concerning life choices nor assume the role of teacher or mentor. He emphasised that he should remain neutral in the sense that what the patient says, feels or phantasies about is responded to impartially by the therapist. Laudable though these prescriptions are, in practice we all make suggestions, if only to

---

[7]They further suggest that Freud tried to co-opt suggestive influence by capturing it and subsuming it as part of what he called "the unobjectionable transference" – in other words, as part of what we would nowadays call the therapeutic alliance.

indicate the use of the couch, the rule of free association and, most importantly, what we choose to draw attention to via our interpretations or silences. Our interventions therefore always influence to varying degrees the patient's material. Although Bion's (1967) recommendation that we should approach each session "without memory or desire [to cure]" helps to remind us of the unconscious forces always operating on the therapist, there is little doubt that we all enter the therapeutic situation with implicit therapeutic intent. We persuade, steer and reward our patients in different ways, often without even realising that we are doing so. If we practice psychoanalytic therapy, we are implicitly making a clear statement about our beliefs, about what is important in therapy and what helps people to get better and this will inevitably affect how we listen to the patient and what we choose to focus on. Phillips has an original take on the position of neutrality that captures the problems inherent in this notion:

> . . . The therapist, like the democrat, would be vigilant about attempts to suppress both the possibility and the sustaining of conflicts within the individual and culture. The therapist would position herself as a democrat wherever the patient places her through the transference. In my version of analytic neutrality, neutrality would never be the right word because to think of oneself as neutral in a democracy does not make sense. It would only make sense that the therapist would be finding ways of sustaining that conflict which is a form of collaboration. The therapist and the analytic setting would be like a rendezvous for the conflicts involved in the suppression of conflict (2001: 131).

Phillips is describing how the analytic role can never be neutral as we are actively invested in helping the patient keep conflict alive when it has been repressed. Indeed, there are no neutral interventions as such. Any intervention is, by definition, aim-directed: we ask a question or take up a theme in the patient's narrative because we want to expand a field of exploration in keeping with what we believe to be the aims of psychoanalytic therapy. Klauber (1986) was one of several psychoanalysts to challenge the notion of neutrality arguing that the therapist's efforts to sustain this illusion were in vain and merely reflected a failure to "give credit to human intelligence and the human unconscious" (1986: 130). He adds:

> Alongside the distorted image of the therapist due to the patient's transference, which is modified by treatment, goes a considerable perception of his realistic attributes, with the result that the patient identifies with the therapist's real personality and value system (1986: 136).

Whilst advocating that therapists should monitor their contribution to the analytic relationship, Greenberg notes that

> The suggestion that we can be blank screens or reflecting mirrors seems a kind of conceit; the idea that we can judge and titrate abstinence appears arrogant and evenly hovering attention seems both epistemologically and psychologically naïve (1996: 212).

The classical analytic position presumes the therapist's capacity for objectivity, and so neutrality, thus bestowing on the therapist a privileged status about knowing or discovering a hidden "truth". The therapist is seen to be an objective presence interpreting to a subjectively distorting, unrealistic, self-deceiving patient. The therapist's objectivity is justified on the grounds that she will have undergone a necessary personal analysis, which is thought to confer insights yet unknown by the patient. However, for the most part, unconscious processes that are largely opaque to introspection govern patient–therapist interaction, even if we have had twenty years of personal analysis. The latter is no guarantee against personal bias. If anything, it may be a liability as it may lull us into a false sense of security and arrogance on account of the assumed self-knowledge acquired through personal analysis. The intersubjectivists, of course, find the whole notion of neutrality problematic, arguing that, along with abstinence and anonymity, it is "antithetical to the proposition of inherent mutual interaction" (Gill, 1994: 683).

Anonymity, Abstinence and Neutrality: Help or Hindrance?

Freud is usually credited with the rules that structure the analytic relationship and that so many therapists internalise during training. Nevertheless, since he never allowed anyone to observe his work, all that we really know about how Freud carried out his own practice is inferred from his published case studies and the written accounts by his ex-patients. These make for interesting reading and suggest that his own technical recommendations were not rooted in his practice. As Gay (1988) noted, in several of his cases Freud's actual methods differed markedly from his recommendations: he had a pre-existing relationship with some of his patients, namely, Max Etington and Sandor Ferenczi and he was certainly warm and quite active in his treatment of the Rat Man and the Wolf Man. Lipton (1979) concludes that it was Freud's actual practice to establish a personal relationship with the patient. However, because he took this for granted, it was never included in his technical recommendations.

David & Vaillant (1998) reviewed Freud's case studies between 1907 and 1939 and obtained data on forty-three cases. In all forty-three cases they found that Freud deviated from strict anonymity and expressed his own feelings, attitudes and experiences. These experiences included his feelings towards his analysands, his worries about issues in his own life, his attitudes, tastes and prejudices. In thirty-one cases, Freud participated in an extra-analytic relationship (not of a sexual nature) with his analysands obviating the anonymity and opacity prescribed in his recommendations. Interestingly, as Gay observes:

> It was the rules that Freud laid down for his craft far more than his licence in interpreting them for himself, that would make the difference for psychoanalysis (1988: 292).

Lipton elaborates the dangers of adhering too rigidly to the analytic rules imparted to many contemporary therapists in training:

> Paradoxically, modern technique can produce just what it may have been designed to avoid, a corrective emotional experience, by exposing the patient to a hypothetically ideally correct, ideally unobtrusive, ideally silent, encompassing technical instrumentality rather than the presence of the therapist as a person with whom the patient can establish a personal relationship (1977: 272).

The central theme that pervades Lipton's position is straightforward: the therapist as a person is a variable that cannot and should not be ignored. Moreover, it is a variable that – even if it was possible – we need not try to eliminate as it contributes to the analytic ambience of collaborative work that provides the essential backdrop to analytic work. Without this we might as well recount our sorrows to a computer. Lipton is not just referring to such qualities as warmth and respect for the patient, which are of course important. Rather, he is suggesting that patients live in a real world as well as in their phantasy world and that the exchanges with the therapist's humanity involve confrontations with their limitations as much as with their strengths. In other words, an important aspect of the therapeutic relationship is that it involves a confrontation with the reality of the therapist as a real person, capable of spontaneous responses and, hence, inevitably fallible.

The negotiation of disappointments and frustrations with a therapist who is real, in the sense just outlined, provides a potentially mutative interpersonal experience as long as this can be worked through. Just as a therapist compromises her potential effectiveness if she remains too fully a real person with no sensitivity to the distortions of projection, she will be equally ineffective if she remains solely a "symbolic object" (Szasz, 1963). The therapeutic situation requires of the therapist that she functions as both and of the patient that he perceives the therapist as both. Relative neutrality and anonymity – "relative" insofar as they can never be absolute – are important components of the therapeutic stance towards which we should strive, without which the analytic work is compromised. This does not, however, preclude an empathic, warm and sometimes even humorous attitude (Lemma, 2000).

If we anchor psychoanalytic practice in rules that encourage the kind of therapist who approaches her work with objectivity and a degree of so-called neutral dispassion, this lends to psychoanalytic therapy a more "scientific", respectable feel, but we need to guard against superficial allegiances to a version of so-called science at the expense of what is helpful to patients and what is, in fact, possible. What may feel neutral to one patient may feel persecutory to another. With the more disturbed and damaged patients we need to be mindful of this if we are to create the conditions that will allow them to let us into their world.

It might be tempting to see Freud's recommendations as superior to his actual technique. But the discrepancy between his written rules and his practice begs the question of what is effective, that is, which aspects of the analytic frame and attitude are essential to a good outcome. It is interesting to speculate as to who benefits from the adherence to the classical analytic frame and attitude. The frame and its prescriptions of neutrality, abstinence and anonymity exist not only for the patient's benefit but also for the therapist's – a fact frequently overlooked. The prevailing analytic persona may provide a safe screen for our own apprehensions about more spontaneous exchanges as it legitimises a more withdrawn, grave stance. Working analytically generates anxiety for both participants since any such exploration is an invitation to enter the uncharted territory of our own unconscious as well as that of our patients'. By keeping a careful reign on our spontaneity, we protect ourselves from the anxiety inherent in the analytic enterprise viewing ourselves more as receptacles for the patient's projections rather than as active participants in the process. Through the highly prescriptive rituals that surround the therapeutic relationship, we have found a way of sustaining the illusion that we are observers, onlookers into another's unconscious, whilst our own is kept neatly in check.

Research on the quality of the therapeutic alliance brings to the fore the reciprocal nature of the therapeutic relationship. The person of the therapist emerges as a critical, if neglected, variable that should be researched. There is indeed a dearth of research offering a detailed phenomenology of the patient–therapist system or of its boundaries and frame. Research that devotes attention to the patient and therapist as an interactive, mutually determining system may eventually lead to the possibility of specifying which styles of interaction contribute to effective (i.e. curative) emotional exchanges.

The Frame and the Analytic Superego

The technical provisions of all analytic schools model restraint for the therapist. In an enterprise as delicate and uncertain as the discovery of another's unconscious, we need to closely monitor our own interventions. While claims to a pure objectivity and neutrality fly in the face of what we know transpires between patient and therapist, and some therapists' aloofness is counter-therapeutic, so too are there problems with those positions upholding the therapist's "irreducible subjectivity" (Renik, 1993). Such a stance leaves the patient potentially open to unsubstantiated, intrusive interpretations based on the therapist's countertransference, with the accompanying danger of a denial or misrepresentation of the patient's experiences. Bringing our own subjectivity into the therapeutic equation represents an important acknowledgement of the influence of the therapist's own personal psychology, but it is not a license for self-analysis on the back of the patient's analysis.

The more we rely either on ideas of inevitable subjectivity or on a self-deluding belief in neutrality and objectivity, we get further away from the reality of the therapeutic situation. The onus is on us to remain grounded enough in our own subjectivity to realise when that may be clouding our perception of the patient *and* to take responsibility for our own mind so that we are able to give the patient a perspective on his mind.

The physical frame, along with all the technical recommendations, provides an ideal baseline we can strive towards but from which we will at times fall short. This is cause for concern but not for obsessional manoeuvres to control the therapeutic environment. The aim of therapy is to help patients manage reality, not to manage the very controlled environment that psychotherapy can become. Whilst we should strive to minimise intrusions wherever possible, we must also be realistic about the fact that we have lives outside of the consulting room and that the patient will have phantasies about this. Our task is to engage with his phantasies and acknowledge to ourselves when we collude or act seductively through our own impingements. We need to be always alert to the idiosyncratic meanings that such deviations from the ideal frame might hold for a given patient, and to be receptive to the disappointment or hostility they can give rise to.

Although anonymity and neutrality are advocated on account that they facilitate the transference, I do not believe that the transference is impeded if a therapist is warm, uses humour, or displays paintings in her consulting room. We are deluding ourselves if we think that the transference can be manipulated through the environment. If the transference is the ubiquitous phenomenon we believe it to be, it will unfold wherever we see patients and whether we are warm or aloof towards them. Clearly, some behaviours will most probably call forth particular responses or they may exaggerate particular responses.

The analytic frame is unique in offering the possibility to express ourselves freely in a confidential setting. In the consulting room, no subject is beyond the pale of analytic interest and understanding. Our most shameful thoughts and our greatest fears can be expressed and received by the therapist who does not impose restraint, judgement or punishment. It helps us to safeguard this space if we are mindful of our own subjectivity and if we administer sensitively the more pragmatic aspects of the frame.

FURTHER READING

Gray, A. (1994) *An Introduction to the Therapeutic Frame*. London: Routledge.

4

ASSESSMENT AND FORMULATION

Most psychoanalytic therapists regard formal psychiatric diagnosis with justified suspicion. They view it as insufficient for determining suitability for psychotherapy. This is because clinical experience repeatedly demonstrates that it is meaningless to make a diagnosis on the basis of the manifest problems alone. The disease and behaviour model underpinning psychiatry and behavioural psychology assumes an underlying disturbance that results in a symptom or behavioural problem. It suggests that this is primary and creates secondary problems in living that can be addressed by treating the symptom or behaviour itself. By contrast, psychoanalytic practitioners assume that the symptom or disorder is a secondary effect rather than the cause; it is seen to be a consequence of presumed psychological processes in conflict at the time, even if consciously inaccessible to the patient. In many cases, the manifest problem leading to referral masks other more complex difficulties.

One of the strengths of a psychoanalytic approach to formulation lies in its appreciation of personality structure. If we are to arrive at a meaningful formulation of the patient's difficulties in addition to symptoms, we need to consider *in whom* these symptoms are occurring. In other words, we need to take into account the person's character. For example, panic attacks in a person with a narcissistic personality are lived out very differently than in a characterologically anxious person. The aim of a psychoanalytically informed assessment is therefore not to diagnose in the psychiatric sense, but to formulate the problem in dynamic terms. Formal psychiatric diagnosis may form part of the assessment, but it is not usually the primary aim of the assessment.

In this chapter, we will review the core areas of the patient's functioning that provide necessary information about a person's *dynamic* functioning and that we can profitably explore in an assessment.[1] The way assessments are carried out most probably reflects individual differences between therapists at the level of their explicit and implicit theories about the mind and the process of psychotherapy, as well as personality differences. There is no right or wrong way to carry out assessments. This fact will either relieve you or panic you further as you grapple with the complex task of assessment.

ASSESSMENT IN THE AGE OF EVIDENCE-BASED PRACTICE

In an age of plenty, assessment for psychotherapy has become a hotly debated topic. With so many therapeutic approaches to choose from, the question of what approach works best for a particular problem can no longer be ignored. Unfortunately, the growth of psychotherapy as an industry has far outstripped the pace of research; although we now have some knowledge about aspects of the psychotherapeutic process that make a difference – not least the research highlighting the link between a good therapeutic alliance and outcome – we still know relatively little. Our ignorance is strikingly apparent when one surveys the literature on assessment. The word *assessment* might well evoke a scientific frisson, but it is in fact an imprecise process reliant more on intuition than science, limited by the therapist's theoretical allegiances and constrained, especially within public health service settings, by the reality of limited resources.[2]

Prior to the surge of research interest in the outcome of psychotherapy and attempts to empirically study the fit between presenting prob-lem/diagnosis and treatment modality (see Roth & Fonagy, 1996), patients were all too frequently offered what the therapist/department had to offer rather than what would ideally have been helpful to them. The drive towards evidence-based practice has encouraged many practition-ers to use research as a guideline for which treatment works best for a given diagnostic group. Although this type of guidance is helpful and should be considered when formulating patients' problems and deciding on treatment interventions, there is also recognition, especially among psychoanalytic practitioners, of the limitations of such an approach. This

---

[1] The framework offered here should not be seen as prescriptive. It merely reflects my own personal approach to assessment.
[2] In publicly funded services, many therapists are forced to make decisions about what will be most beneficial to the patient in the shadow of a limited choice of therapeutic models and long waiting lists.

is because when we see a patient who presents with so-called depression or anxiety, the individual formulation of the patient's difficulties is probably going to be a far more reliable guide as to what help he needs and can use than the formal diagnosis.

The current emphasis on evidence-based practice has challenged the work of many therapists, especially those employed within health service settings. Funding is now closely dependent on the evidence base that has accrued and important treatment decisions are informed by research studies that at times poorly reflect the reality of everyday clinical practice. The highly selected patient populations that comprise randomised controlled effectiveness trials (RCTs) – the "gold standard" of outcome research – often bear little resemblance to the complex presentations most clinicians encounter in their everyday practice where Axis 1 disorders (DSM, IV) often coexist alongside Axis 2 disorders, that is, characterological disorders, which often undermine even the most skilled therapeutic efforts.

The limitations of research should not be ignored, just as ignoring the research evidence should not be encouraged. If we know that cognitive behaviour therapy has been shown to be effective in the treatment of panic disorder, then we do need to ask ourselves why we are recommending psychoanalytic therapy to a patient with panic attacks. In other words, the benefit of an evidence-based approach is that it reminds us of the need to justify our decisions. It compels us to make explicit what is all too often implicit. This is important since what is implicit is susceptible to the vagaries of our own unconscious – not the most reliable guide in a decision-making process. Nevertheless, when we are dealing with a process as complex as that of understanding another person's mind, research evidence should not be taken as the most important criterion or as the sole criterion. Rather, it needs to be considered alongside our experience of the patient in the room, the patient's response to our interventions and the accumulated clinical evidence of those psychological and social factors that have been most frequently found to be associated with a good outcome in psychoanalytic therapy.

THE AIMS OF ASSESSMENT

Evidence-based practice has highlighted an important issue, namely, the thorny question of generic assessment versus single model assessment. If we are assessing a patient for therapy, then we should be, strictly speaking, approaching the patient with the possibility in mind that our own approach may not be best suited to the patient's needs. Whilst it is impossible to be trained in all models of therapy, carrying out assessments for psychotherapy is a highly skilled task. It requires considerable knowledge of different therapeutic modalities, how they work, what demands they make on the patient and whether they are effective for treating particular problems. Even when one's own style of assessment is influenced by psychoanalytic thinking, unless the patient has been specifically referred for this type of therapy the assessment that is carried out needs to reflect the therapist's openness to the possibility that an approach other than psychoanalytic therapy might be required. This poses a challenge since a traditional psychoanalytic assessment is unlikely to elicit the range of information that might be required to thoughtfully decide about the relative appropriateness of different therapeutic modalities. For example, a family therapist might be more interested in family composition, a cognitive therapist might want information about the patient's cognitions during a panic attack and a psychoanalytic therapist might focus her assessment on her countertransference reactions and gather relatively little information about the patient's external life. Depending on our primary theoretical orientation, we will each approach the assessment situation with a different emphasis and we will also report the contents of the assessment differently. Since this chapter is intended to cover a specifically *psychodynamic* assessment, I am merely highlighting this important issue but we will not review the components of a generic assessment here.

The challenge of psychodynamic assessment reflects its dual task:

- To enable us to make an informed decision about whether the patient can be helped by a psychoanalytic approach.
- To enable the patient to get a feeling for the approach and to decide whether this is an approach they want to use.

In private practice, most therapists will see the patients referred to them if their approach is indicated. Those working in the National Health Service (NHS), on the other hand, may be assessing patients who will be treated by another colleague. The task of assessment is even more delicate in these situations as the transference has to be managed and contained, bearing in mind the fact that the patient will need to transfer the intensity of this initial transference to the treating therapist.

The information we obtain from the patient needs to be digested and structured in such a way that it allows us to arrive at some conclusions about the appropriateness, or otherwise, of psychoanalytic therapy. The facts of the patient's narrative that we select as important are brought together in a hypothesis. Inevitably, as we endeavour to structure and categorise the information we collect, we are unavoidably doing so in light of our own theories. The theories we subscribe to thus bias us towards certain facts and prompt us to follow particular lines of enquiry to the exclusion of others. We all approach the assessment situation with implicit categories that structure the way we filter the information the patient gives us through what he says, does not say or merely hints at. This is why two therapists, even when both are psychoanalytically trained, will most probably elicit and report on different aspects of the patient's functioning depending on the school of psychoanalysis they respectively subscribe to.

Assessments are conventionally distinguished from therapy per se. Yet, they are often of profound significance to the patient. More often than not, the assessment will lead to a recommendation for some form of therapy, but occasionally they may be an end in itself, an encounter that will have given the patient a unique space to take stock of his predicament and to move on from an impasse without requiring ongoing psychotherapy.

For those patients who have little or no experience of therapy, the assessment is a critical encounter. It is not only an opportunity for the assessor to accurately identify the problem in a way that brings some relief or hope to the patient that things might be different in the future but it is also the patient's first experience of what it might feel like to be in psychoanalytic therapy. The assessment therefore sets the scene for what is to follow and thus represents a crucial crossroad that will influence whether the patient takes up the offer of help. In this sense, as assessors, we are in a position of great responsibility vis-à-vis the patient's current and future psychological well-being. Although our so-called science may be imprecise – or indeed may not be a science at all – our role is nonetheless one that can make a significant difference to the patient's life. I am not wishing to encourage placing ourselves in an omnipotent position, nor am I suggesting that psychotherapy cures all ills. I simply want to emphasise that our responsibility for the patient who consults us is no different from that of the medical doctor who may pick up, or fail to diagnose, the presence of a physical illness.

INTRODUCTIONS: SETTING THE BOUNDARIES FOR THE ASSESSMENT

In our assessment role, we aim to create the best possible conditions for the patient to show himself as he is so that we can assess his problems and steer him towards appropriate help. Accordingly, our assessment style is worthy of consideration. Assessments are not approached in a uniform way by psychoanalytic therapists. Some clinicians advocate a more aloof stance in the context of an unstructured approach that gives the patient few cues about what is expected of him. This style of assessment would most probably orient the patient minimally to the purpose of the assessment, if at all. Milton describes such an approach as approximating:

> ... at first technically to an ordinary analytic session. The patient is greeted courteously but gravely, and subjected from the outset to an intense scrutiny, with the minimum of instruction, or measures that might be described as 'putting one at ease'... no automatic social responses are given, for example, smiles (1997: 48).

The rationale usually given for such an approach is that it very quickly brings to the fore the patient's more primitive anxieties. This is indeed often the case. Possibly armed with little understanding of what is likely to transpire in an assessment, the patient coming to meet a therapist for the first time, who welcomes him "gravely" and actively avoids the usual social responses he might reasonably expect from a professional person, will quickly feel anxious and possibly a little paranoid. This is a risky approach since it might well alienate some patients who would feel too persecuted by the experience and may therefore decide not to follow-up the offer of psychotherapy.

Even though the unstructured approach to assessment is a high-risk option, it does present some distinct advantages. The less structure is imposed on the session, the more readily the unconscious wishes and anxieties of the patient make themselves known through the stories the patient recounts without prompting from the therapist. The patient entering this kind of assessment would also get a good feel for the analytic space. The patient's response to this may alert the therapist to the appropriateness or otherwise of a psychoanalytic approach. The patient who responds well to structure and prompts may become paralysed and highly anxious in an unstructured therapy. Without any exposure to such an approach at the assessment stage, it may prove hard for both patient and therapist to realistically consider the appropriateness of an analytic approach.

Notwithstanding the advantages of an unstructured approach, in my own work I favour an assessment style that is as least directive as possible without becoming overly ambiguous at the initial stage. This is because I find that anxiety needs to be manageable for the patient or he may leave or be too inhibited to speak freely about what troubles him. Anxiety, usually of a paranoid nature, proportionally increases in direct response to the unavailability of cues that would otherwise orient the patient to the task in hand. The fact that the patient feels more paranoid in the presence of an aloof therapist tells us little about him as most people become disoriented and therefore more anxious when they have few cues as to how to behave. It is possible that by making it more comfortable for the patient, as it were, we may not be able to get a comprehensive feeling for the patient's functioning. However, in my experience, as long as the assessment remains unstructured enough to see how the patient operates without too many prompts, it is possible to arrive at meaningful recommendations for treatment, with the added advantage of avoiding the risk of losing the patient altogether. Indeed, Sullivan (1953) advocated that therapists should be sensitive to their patients' needs for "interpersonal security"; an overly distant and uncommunicative therapist is unlikely to foster such security.

In my work, I open assessments with a brief statement like, *"I would like to explain to you the purpose of this meeting. This is an initial consultation. It will last about an hour and half. Hopefully this will give us both an opportunity to understand what brings you here and to arrive at some decisions as to what may be of help to you. At this stage I cannot know whether I can help you but if I cannot I will endeavour to help you find someone who can."* After I have said this, I pause to see if the patient is able to start talking without further prompting from me. Many patients at this stage might say, *"I don't know where to begin"* or *"I don't like the silence"*, or *"I would prefer if you asked me questions"*. At this early stage, I try to avoid the temptation of launching into questions as a way of easing the tension that silence can give rise to. I prefer to wait in silence for a minute or so to gauge how the patient manages the lack of further structure.

As a rule of thumb, I find it helpful to be more interactive and facilitative with the less integrated patients. With highly anxious or paranoid patients who cannot think about their anxiety, I will help to ease them further into the assessment with some questions. Before doing so, however, I may simply say: *"It can be difficult to know where to start. Why don't you start by telling me what's on your mind/how you are feeling right now"*. If they are unable to comment on their own internal processes, I might then follow this up with something like: *"What would make it possible for you to feel able to speak to me today about what brings you here."* If this fails to ease the patient, I would start to question in my own mind whether an analytic approach was indicated and I would be inclined to ask questions more liberally and so to structure the assessment more than usual.

With the majority of patients, an hour and a half is sufficient to arrive at some *preliminary* understanding of the patient's predicament and to gain a good enough sense of how the patient functions within the parameters of a therapeutic frame. It is important not to get too carried away with one's own ambitions of capturing the patient's problem in a clear and definitive formulation. It is highly unlikely that we can arrive at such a clear understanding on the basis of one session. Formulations are of necessity speculative and need to be re-visited regularly.

One of the advantages of lengthier assessments (e.g. over two or more sessions) is that they will lead to a more in-depth understanding of the patient; they may be necessary for those patients with very complex presentations or for those patients who have so much difficulty disclosing themselves that a one-off assessment may lead to an inaccurate formulation. Assessments that are spread out also allow both patient and therapist to realistically assess the patient's capacity to manage the breaks and to see what use the patient is capable of making of the sessions. A patient who acts self-destructively between two assessment sessions would alert the assessor to the possible unsuitability of a psychoanalytic approach within the private sector, but this same patient might be capable of using such an approach in the context of a psychiatric setting in which medical back-up would be readily available. This raises an important consideration for all assessments. In assessing the suitability of psychoanalytic therapy, we need to think about the advantages and limitations of the setting in which the therapy will take place. The setting can make all the difference; nowadays very disturbed patients can access psychoanalytic psychotherapy because it is provided within NHS settings to which the patient may be admitted in case of an emergency or in which other resources (e.g. community psychiatric nurses or outpatient meetings with a psychiatrist) provide the necessary infrastructure for the psychotherapy to be viable.

HISTORY TAKING VERSUS HISTORY MAKING

Psychiatric assessments are structured around the elicitation of a personal history. Psychiatrists typically question the patient systematically about his childhood history, his sexual and relationship history, his occupational history and his previous treatments. A great deal of information is thus collected. Asking about a patient's occupational history or knowing about his sexual history may yield valuable information that will inform an understanding of the problem. Nevertheless, reading through standard psychiatric reports and then meeting the patient in question, soon makes it apparent that this type of detailed, factual information about a patient tells us comparatively little about his capacity to use therapy or, indeed, about his problems and their dynamic meaning.

In order to gain a more in-depth perspective of the patient, we need to pay attention to the *process* of the assessment. In other words, as Hirshberg (1993) suggests, we are not taking a history but "making a history", that is, we are attuned to how the patient constructs his narrative and what use he makes of us in doing so. We listen for omissions, for emphases, for topics that are flirted with but not engaged in, for idealisation or denigration, for the tone of voice, for the word the patient cannot find or for the word he knows in one language but not in another. Whenever a narrative appears unified, clear, complete, something always has to be suppressed in order to sustain the illusion of unity (Chessick, 2000). It is often in the gaps, in the moments when words fail to capture something of the patient's experience, that we begin to come close to the patient's psychic pain.

Listening in this way is very different to "taking a history". The skill lies in managing to combine this very specialised type of listening that is the hallmark of analytic listening (see Chapter 5), along with a capacity to weave in and out of the patient's narrative and cover certain areas of the patient's life and functioning that we need to know about in order to meaningfully assess his capacity to make use of psychoanalytic therapy. For example, the patient may well respond to an interpretation about his internal world and this may lead us to conclude that he could use psychoanalytic therapy. However, if we know nothing or little about who is actually in his current life and who could support him through the demands of therapy, we may be arriving at a wrong conclusion. Some patients are unable to manage the space in between the sessions if they have few or no support systems. It is therefore imperative that by the end of an assessment we know something not only about the primitive figures that populate the patient's internal world but also about who exists in the patient's external world and the quality of those relationships (see below).

SUITABILITY CRITERIA AND CONTRAINDICATIONS FOR PSYCHOANALYTIC THERAPY

In Freud's time, the selection criteria for psychoanalysis were seductively straightforward: psychoanalysis was only indicated for those patients who suffered from neuroses, whose psychopathology was rooted in the Oedipal phase and who could reveal their infantile neurosis in the transference through the so-called *transference neurosis*. Although there still exists a minority of therapists aligning themselves with Freud's original views on the matter, since the 1970s cases of patients diagnosed as psychotic or personality disordered have been treated by psychoanalytic therapists of all persuasions.

In the NHS, psychoanalytic therapy is a very scarce resource, weighed down by long waiting lists. It is usually offered primarily to those patients who present moderate to severe difficulties that have taken a chronic course. Generally speaking, such an approach seems most indicated when the patient presents problems of a characterological nature or where there are interpersonal difficulties. Nowadays, the patient's formal diagnosis, for example, whether he is psychotic or suffers from borderline personality disorder, is considered less relevant than whether the patient shows some capacity for engaging with the therapeutic process.

Our understanding of psychotherapy is becoming more sophisticated, but we are a long way from being able to confidently assert which pre-therapy criteria can reliably predict the best outcome for psychoanalytic therapy. Research on suitability criteria reveals correlations with outcome that are small such that multiple factors must be combined to meaningfully predict outcome.[3] Although there is little research evidence as to their validity and reliability, this section will briefly review some the most commonly recommended criteria.

- *Psychiatric diagnosis* is often cited as an important criterion. Svanborg *et al.* (1999) found that recommendation for psychoanalytic therapy was predicted by absence of a personality disorder and high GAF[4] scores, but not by the presence of a psychiatric disorder. Most studies suggest that it is those patients with a predominantly neurotic personality organisation and with inhibitions as the most prominent defence who do best, most probably in any type of psychotherapy. Nevertheless, in practice, the majority of the referrals for psychoanalytic therapy in public health service settings are of patients with personality disorders who present with quite diffuse problems that do not lend themselves to structured and briefer interventions.
- The need for a *focus* is imperative in brief therapy (Malan, 1980). Brief therapy is most indicated where the conflict is at a neurotic, Oedipal level and is less appropriate where the patient's problems are indicative of borderline or pre-Oedipal problems. Hoglend *et al.* (1993) suggest that a circumscribed focus addressing problems that are Oedipal, such as assertiveness with the same sex, ambivalence about triangular situations as opposed to more oral problems such as dependency, trust and separation predicts a more positive outcome in brief focal psychoanalytic therapy. Involvement in complex and pervasive dynamic issues usually excludes a patient for brief psychoanalytic therapy but he may still be suitable for a long-term approach.

---

[3] Broadly speaking, the criteria for brief psychoanalytic therapy, overlap with those for long-term psychotherapy.

[4] GAF is a composite measure, which in addition to current symptomatic suffering, assesses more stable characteristics such as aspects of ego strength, quality of interpersonal relationships, level of psychosexual development and anxiety tolerance.

- The *analytic frame* itself places particular demands on the patient that need to be considered when choosing psychoanalytic therapy. Moore & Fine (1990), in their classic text, suggest that some of the requirements for suitability stem from the very nature of the analytic process and thus include the ability to free associate, to make the sacrifices of time and money, to tolerate frustration and anxiety and other strong affects without recourse to flight or acting out.
- The patient's capacity to sustain the therapeutic relationship in the absence of immediate gratification is essential. For some patients, the more aloof therapeutic stance may prove too persecuting in the face of a relatively weak ego. Indeed, the patient's *ego strength* (see below for a fuller discussion) is another important factor; patients with weak egos whose capacity to discriminate between the object and the self is impaired, or those with poor impulse control or with limited capacity to accept the limitations of reality, pose special challenges in psychoanalytic therapy. This is especially so when the therapeutic contract is brief and this is often contraindicated.
- A *good history of interpersonal relationships,* or at least evidence of one positive object relationship, is often thought to be a good prognostic sign. Intuitively this makes sense: if the patient has some demonstrable capacity – however rudimentary – to engage with and trust another person, then it will enable the patient to engage more readily with the analytic process and to tolerate the intimacy of the relationship. The patient's *ability to get actively involved with the therapeutic processs* is thus a related criterion. Frayn (1992) found that those patients with previous positive relationships with parents, bosses, teachers and other therapists, where applicable, were less likely to terminate psychoanalytic treatment prematurely. Those who recreated disinterested, chaotic, narcissistic or exploitative relationship dynamics were the most likely to drop out. Hoglend *et al.* (1993) and Hoglend (1993) found that interpersonal relationships, characterised by mutuality, gratification and stability and where the patient related to the other person as autonomous rather than as need-gratifying, were positively correlated with outcome after four years, but not after one year of brief focal psychoanalytic therapy. Similarly, Piper *et al.* (1991) found that those patients with a high level of object relations (i.e. with a history of good relationships) had the best outcome in brief psychoanalytic therapy.

Absence of any so-called "good" objects in the patient's life is not in itself an absolute contraindication. Some patients who do well in psychoanalytic therapy may start off with a very deprived internal world, yet give the therapist the impression they could hold on to a good object. Our experience of the patient in the room is therefore an important additional source of information that complements the relationship history.

• The patient's degree of *psychological mindedness* is frequently mentioned as an important criterion. There is little research on psychological mindedness as a pre-treatment variable related to eventual outcome. It is one of those concepts we often invoke as if we all know what it means, yet it is perhaps the most overused and least well defined of all. It purports to refer to the patient's capacity to reflect on himself in psychological terms. So, for example, a patient who has suffered a bereavement and insists concretely that his headaches are the problem and cannot entertain the possibility of a link between the experience of loss and his physical symptoms would not be deemed to be psychologically minded.

Psychological mindedness, like the psychiatric notion of "insight", is potentially problematic since at times it can synonymous with the patient's capacity to work, and to agree, with the psychological concepts and formulations of a particular therapist. This criterion is also something of a paradox: the patient's so-called psychological mindedness is used to determine suitability but, it could be argued, it is also a legitimate goal of treatment. One of the aims of psychoanalytic therapy is, after all, to build or strengthen self-reflective capacities when they are weak, thereby helping the patient to become psychologically minded.

Just as any of the above criteria for suitability would be an unreliable guide when used in isolation, so are the contraindications for psychoanalytic therapy. All of the above are contraindications when couched negatively (e.g. the patient is *not* psychologically minded). The presence of psychosis and substance abuse are also often cited as contraindications. However, although psychoanalytic therapy is rarely recommended, for example, in the treatment of psychosis, it may be very helpful for some patients who have had brief psychotic episodes or those who suffer from manic depression. Nevertheless, working psychoanalytically with psychotic patients is a highly specialised application of psychoanalysis that should never be undertaken without adequate consultation and supervision (see Jackson & Williams, 1994).

Suitability criteria (see Table 4.1) are best thought of as pointers we refer to during the assessment process, but in order for them to be helpful they need to be carefully considered in the context of our own experience with the patient in the room.

Table 4.1   Suitability criteria for psychoanalytic psychotherapy

When assessing a patient with a view to psychoanalytic treatment, consider the
  following:
- whether the patient is interested in and has a capacity for self-reflection,
  however rudimentary;
- whether the patient has sufficient ego strength to withstand the inherent
  frustrations of the therapeutic relationship and to undertake self-exploration;
- whether the patient can tolerate psychic pain without acting out (e.g. threats
  to the self or others);
- whether the risk of acting out, if present, can be managed within the setting
  the therapy will take place in;
- whether the patient will be adequately supported personally and/or
  professionally to sustain him during the difficult times in therapy.

If considering a brief psychoanalytic approach, also think about the following:
- whether the patient's difficulties lend themselves to focusing on one theme or
  core conflict;
- whether during the assessment the patient responds to interpretations
  concerned with the identified focus;
- whether the patient is motivated to work with the chosen focus.

WHAT SHOULD AN ASSESSMENT COVER?

The Symptom/Problem from the Patient's Point of View

As with any assessment, the starting point has to be the patient's own
understanding of the problem. Some patients are able to tell their story with
little prompting from us, whilst others need more encouragement to speak.
In my experience, inviting patients to speculate about how they have ended
up in their predicament is very revealing of how they make sense of their
symptoms and hence gives some clues as to what kind of therapeutic
approach may be more congenial. For example, some depressed patients
approach their problem as one purely due to a chemical imbalance and
however hard we might try to engage them in an exploration of other
possible triggers, they steadfastly hold on to a biochemical explanation.
Others may discuss their depression in terms of negative thoughts and
how they wish they could change the way they think. Others still explicitly
link the onset of their depression to either childhood problems or more
recent interpersonal events and express a wish to understand "why" they
have ended up becoming who they are.

Every patient comes to the assessment with his own language and frame
of reference for emotional distress. Each patient has his own theories
consonant with cultural idioms for the expression of emotional distress.
Often the assessment provides an opportunity for the sharing of different

narratives about the problem and the patient may find that our formulation is meaningful and helpful and he may thus shift, say, from his biochemical explanation to a more psychological one. This is not always the case, however. It is therefore important to listen out for whether the patient's own narrative maps onto a psychoanalytic one. We are looking for some compatibility between treatment rationale and the patient's own theories. There is little point offering psychoanalytic therapy to a patient who is convinced his problems are related to a genetic predisposition or who believes that it is all down to his faulty thinking. The aim of assessment is not to work towards getting the patient to take on our point of view but to find a good enough fit between our knowledge of the patient's difficulties and the therapeutic approach most congenial to the patient's own way of thinking or philosophy of life that could best address those difficulties.

Motivation

Any psychological treatment relies on the patient's motivation. Psychoanalytic therapy, perhaps more than most, makes a lot of demands on the patient. Frayn (1992) found that patients with poor motivation, a lack of commitment to self-understanding and symptoms that were egosyntonic (i.e. they do not generate conflict) were more likely to terminate treatment prematurely. Ensuring that the patient will persevere with the therapy even when the "going gets tough" is therefore important. How one assesses motivation is complicated. Motivation is a complex, multidimensional concept. There is, in fact, little agreement over the term. It is sometimes defined so broadly that it becomes synonymous with suitability for psychoanalytic therapy (Truant, 1999). It can include some, or all, of the following:

- the motivation to change
- a capacity for insight
- self-understanding
- active participation in the therapeutic work
- a desire to relieve psychic pain
- taking responsibility for oneself
- positive expectations of therapy.

Clinical work makes one thing very clear, however: motivation does not refer to a static state of mind. Patients will traverse periods in therapy when their motivation is high and at other times the secondary gains from illness gain the upper hand and motivation wanes. The relative predominance of a motivation to change over unconscious gratification from the symptoms, which acts as a resistance to change, is an important factor to assess especially if brief therapy is being considered.

The assessment of motivation is of necessity inferential. It can be gleaned from a thorough exploration of the patient's previous experience of therapy where applicable and of his expectations of the new treatment. To assess motivation, it may be helpful to explore the following areas with the patient:

- *What is the patient's relationship to help?* What did the patient find difficult or helpful in his former therapy, if anything? How realistic are his expectations of therapy? What difficulties does he envisage in relation to the treatment you are proposing to them? Does he display an active or passive stance? Is he hoping to be "cured" or does he give some indication that he appreciates that therapy will make demands on him and is not just down to the therapist?
- *Is the patient's relationship to you an overly idealised one?* Some positive investment in the person of the therapist and her capacity to relieve suffering is necessary for a working alliance to be established, but this is quite different from the patient who takes a back seat and is expecting a magical transformation at the hands of an all-powerful therapist. Tempting though it may be for our own narcissistic reasons to collude with such an omnipotent projection, it is just as well to remind ourselves that denigration reliably follows idealisation. This is because idealisation serves the function of protecting the object from what we know we could do to the object in our mind, that is, it protects it from our hatred. Idealisation or denigration of a previous therapist should sound alarm bells and can be a poor prognostic sign.
- *Is the patient motivated internally or by external sources?* This question is typically related to the "why now" question. It is important to explore this because those who enter therapy at the behest of partners or other mental health professionals may establish a weaker alliance or misalliances that can undermine the treatment process. Generally speaking, the patient is motivated to work in therapy if he experiences his problems/symptoms as ego-dystonic (i.e. they generate uncomfortable conflict because they are experienced as unacceptable to the ego). It is important here to distinguish between motivation for self-understanding (e.g. "I want to know why I always end up in abusive relationships") and a search for concrete relief from symptoms or particular life situations (e.g. "I want to get out of the council estate I am in, that's getting me down"). Although in both cases the patient will be motivated to get some form of help, it is unlikely that the second patient will find psychoanalytic therapy congenial.

Assessing the Patient's Internal World and the Quality of Object Relationships

"Memory relating to external events and to the corporeal reality of loved figures as beings distinct from ourselves, is one facet of our relation to them, the other facet is the life they lead within us indivisible from ourselves" (Riviere, 1936: 320).

To understand our patients in dynamic terms, we not only explore their actual lives and what is happening in their external world. We also, and perhaps even primarily, devote attention to their *internal world* and their *internal reality*.[5] We owe this distinctive emphasis to Freud. Freud argued that whether material events make a direct impact on the mind is irrelevant to understanding neurosis; what matters in the unconscious is not the memory of external events but how the patient experiences them, that is, the subjective meaning of events. Freud arrived at this understanding through a dramatic, and controversial, turnaround in his theorising.[6] At first, Freud hypothesised that his hysterical patients were suffering as a result of real trauma. He believed that they had been abused and that the repression of this sexual trauma accounted for their hysterical presentation. In 1897, however, Freud retracted his so-called *seduction theory* and replaced it with the *wish theory*. This latter theory suggested that instead of actual trauma, the patients' hysterical symptoms were the result of disguised memories of infantile wishes, not memories of real infantile experiences. The retraction of the seduction theory firmly placed internal psychic events as having the same potential impact on the patient's functioning as events in external reality. This viewpoint was later reinforced by Klein through her emphasis on the impact of projection on the process of perception (see Chapter 1).

Essentially, both Freud and Klein suggested that internal and external forces shape the mind. From a developmental point of view, it is important that we acquire a capacity to keep what is internal and what is external separate yet, paradoxically, in some way related. The ability to decouple the immediate experience of psychical reality from what is externally real is an essential precondition for recognising that others perceive, and feel, the world differently from us. It is only when we recognise that how we perceive something, or how we feel about it, is not the same as how the

---

[5] These terms are used interchangeably here.
[6] It is beyond the scope of the aims of this chapter to discuss this interesting shift in theorising but for those interested in reading more about it there is a very good chapter in Smith (1991).

thing is, that we have the basis for imagining that another person may not share our point of view.[7]

The way the patient presents his history will give us important clues about his capacity to think about himself in relation to others and of others in relation to himself, that is, it tells us something about his capacity for self-reflection. Obtaining a relationship history including past and current relationships with significant others, and noting carefully how the patient talks about these relationships, is central to the task of assessing the patient's internal world and his capacity to reflect on it and so have perspective on it. One helpful way of thinking about the quality of the patient's narrative and what this reveals about the quality of his attachments can be found in the work of Mary Main and her colleagues who developed the Adult Attachment Interview[8] (Main, 1995). The latter is a research tool for assessing the subjective meaning of attachment experiences revealing an adult's attachment status. Depending on how the person responds to questions about his early attachments, he is classified as being securely or insecurely attached.

When we listen to the way the patient constructs his narrative, we are paying attention to how he presents his relationship to the significant

---

[7]Fonagy & Target (1996, 2000) have written extensively on the nature and development of psychic reality. They put forward the idea that in the earliest stages of development psychic reality takes the form of a dual mode of experience. In the *psychic equivalence* mode, an inner experience is isomorphic with external reality in terms of power, causality and implications. The child at this developmental stage assumes that everyone shares the same experience of an event. In the *pretend mode*, feelings and ideas are experienced as totally representational. This means that they are not felt to have any implication for the world outside. In the pretend mode, the child is able to think about mental states in the context of play, but perceives them as unrelated to external reality. In this mode there still exists a strict separation from external reality. The child does not appreciate yet the dialectical nature of the relationship between internal and external reality. Fonagy and Target argue that normal development rests on an integration of the modes of psychic equivalence and the pretend mode. This process is hypothesised to start around the second year of age right up to the fifth or sixth year. This leads to a psychic reality in which ideas are known as internal and yet related to what is outside.

[8]The AAI classifies responses as either

- *autonomous* (i.e. the patient speaks of the past, including painful past experiences, in a coherent manner that reveals an appreciation of his own and other people's mental states);
- dismissing (i.e. the patient dismisses or devalues the significance of relationships or minimises the impact of traumatic experiences);
- *preoccupied* (i.e. the patient reveals confused feelings about childhood experiences and relationships and their impact on current functioning, displaying anger, fear and confusion);
- unresolved (i.e. the patient has experienced past trauma and still feels emotionally entangled with it as it has not been processed).

figures in his life. For example, if there are difficulties in a relationship we note whether the patient shows evidence of an awareness that how he feels about the difficult situation may be different to how the other person feels about it. Coherent narratives tend to include an acknowledgement of conflict and pain; in speaking about his difficulties the patient demonstrates an appreciation of the complexity of his own and other people's motivations. By contrast, those narratives typically associated with an insecure attachment status reveal more contradiction, denial, confusion or strong negative affects such as anger or fear. The patient may, for example, recount abusive experiences and yet talk about them in a very cut-off manner, dismissing their significance, or he may relate a very confusing story, leaving us feeling that he is still in the thick of his emotional experience and cannot have perspective on it.

As the patient tells us his story, we begin to listen out for *patterns* in his relationships that will assist us in building a schematic picture of his internal world. It is helpful to note what repetitive conflicts emerge as we explore these relationships, for example, whether the patient repeatedly engages in relationships where he is submissive or where he feels secretly triumphant over other people. Likewise, we note which dynamics are absent, for example, whether relationships are reported to always be conflict-free. Recurring interpersonal configurations alert us to internalised object relationships that have taken root in the patient's internal world and are likely to have shaped the personality. The patient's pattern of relating can become entrenched such that he can only function by adopting a very specific role in relation to the other or he filters what he perceives in highly predictable ways, for example, the patient who always hears criticism even when praised.

The internal world consists of prototypic schemas involving invariant dimensions of early affectively charged relationships organised, for example, around experiences of frustration and gratification. In early life, heightened affective exchanges (see Chapter 2) are psychically organising: they allow the baby to categorise and expect similar experiences. For example, a negative experience is internalised as a working model of "self-misattuned-with-a-dysregulating-other" that is linked with painful affect (e.g. terror). Once learnt, a schema sets a template for interpreting later events in a similar way, that is, it generalises. External relationships at any stage of the lifecycle may trigger the affects associated with particular relationship constellations and the associated relational phantasy (e.g. of being deprived or intruded upon). These mental representations of "self-affectively-interacting-with-other" therefore contain both conscious and non-conscious cognitive and affective components derived from significant interpersonal experiences. Although, as we have seen in Chapter 2, the experiences that contributed to these schemas remain for the most part inaccessible to us, they nevertheless structure how we think and feel about ourselves and others. This is why even though we may not be able to recall early events, we nevertheless continue to organise the present according to developmental models.

As we listen, we are looking for evidence of the patient's ability to confide, to trust and to see others as potentially helpful as opposed to feeling paranoid and mistrustful of others' intentions towards the self. One of the key questions that we need to be able to tentatively answer by the end of an assessment is *"What kind of relationship(s) does the patient typically create?"* We are therefore interested in formulating the relationship models that organise the patient's experience, modulate affect and direct behaviour. This involves identifying some of the key internal object relationships that dominate the patient's internal world and so influence his external relationships. A useful way of formulating these dominant internal relationships is to think in terms of prototypes of positive and negative relationships that consist, according to Kernberg, (1976) of:

- a self-representation (e.g. a demanding, frustrating infant),
- an object representation (e.g. an inattentive mother/father),
- an affect linking the two (e.g. anger or terror).

To assist us in our formulation of these self and object representations, three sources of information are available to us:

- the patient's narrative account of his childhood history with significant others;
- the patient's current relationships;
- the relationship the patient develops with us.

Tanya was a 26-year-old woman who sought therapy for help with her eating problems. Since the age of eighteen, she had alternated between restricting her food intake and bingeing. At the time she entered therapy she was regularly bingeing and vomiting. She binged, as she put it, as a way "of shutting down my feelings". When I asked her what she thought she might feel if she did not binge, Tanya replied "A terrible loneliness".

Tanya found it difficult to establish relationships; she felt that people were often trying to get away from her and she had been told that she could be "suffocating" – a description of herself with which she broadly agreed. She told me that if she was in a relationship, she phoned her partners several times a day to check on them, asking them for reassurance that they loved her. With her girlfriends she was more relaxed but she noticed a heightened sensitivity to feeling easily rejected, for instance, if she was not always invited out by them.

Tanya described a close, yet anxious, attachment to her mother whom she praised for her courage and emotional resilience. Her parents separated when she was six and she described her mother as coping very well with the upheaval. After the divorce her mother had gone back to university and eventually developed a very successful career. Tanya maintained a relationship with her father but as he moved to a different country after the divorce, regular contact was not possible.

Prior to our initial meeting Tanya had phoned twice to confirm that she was coming. I was struck by this behaviour since we had agreed on our meeting over the phone the first time we spoke. I felt as though Tanya could not take for granted that I had registered her and would keep the space open for her, hence her need to check by phoning me just as she told me she had to phone her partners to reassure herself she was on their mind.

In the assessment, I invited her to think about therapy and what she wanted from it. She had had a spell of twice-weekly therapy whilst at university and was thus familiar with psychoanalytic therapy. Tanya said that she was eager to attend three times per week. She even wondered whether she should come more often because she recognised that her problems were severely restricting her life. Although all this was in fact true, I was struck by what I experienced as her over eagerness to come into therapy, to have sessions all the time as if she could not bear to be left alone with any gaps when she might have thoughts that could be too disturbing. I began to think about her wish for intensive therapy as like a binge. Rather than agreeing to this request without thinking it through further with her, I suggested that we needed another meeting before we could make final decisions about the intensity of the therapy.

In the first assessment session Tanya had described her mother as a very self-sufficient woman whom she admired greatly. She had berated herself by comparison because she could not "get her act together" like her mother had done after her father had left her. In the second assessment session Tanya spoke to me some more about her mother. She told me that she had missed her mother a great deal as she was growing up. The woman that the week before had been presented as the perfect role model, took on a qualitatively different colouring: her mother was now described as unavailable, at times even selfishly pursuing her own career leaving Tanya in the care of nannies. When her mother used to come back from her business trips, Tanya recalled being very clingy towards her mother and begging her to stay at home with her. When her mother left for another business trip, Tanya would cry and she remembered her mother saying "Big girls don't cry". Tanya recalled that she would try very hard to stop crying as she did not want her mother to think she was weak. She told me that she had become so good at putting on a mask that she sometimes did not even know what she felt anymore. Tanya also added that once her mother had left on one of her trips she did not think of her anymore and just got on with her life at school. It was only when her mother returned that Tanya experienced her longing for her. She recalled asking her mother how many hours she could spend with her before she left again.

On the basis of this additional information about Tanya's experience of her relationship with her mother, using Kernberg's framework, I began to formulate that one significant internalised object relationship might be as follows: a needy, deprived self relating to a dismissive, unavailable other. The conscious affect associated with this was, in fact, a lack of affect: Tanya describes dissociating herself from her feelings, retreating into an "I have no feelings state" which, as a young adult, she recreated in her binges. However, she had also told me that what she feared most was "a terrible loneliness". Hence, I hypothesised that the defended against feeling was that of loneliness and even panic. This formulation could then be applied to the emerging transference and Tanya's wish for a very intensive therapy. It suggested that in coming into therapy the internal model that was activated was one where Tanya felt like a very needy child/patient who is so deprived that she has to clock up as many sessions as possible with me to keep a check on my state of mind in relation to her as she anticipates an unavailable mother/me who will take off on my 'trips' leaving her behind.

In asking the patient questions about his relationships (see Table 4.2), one of our aims is to gain some sense of who the patient identifies with, both consciously and unconsciously, focusing on building a preliminary sketch of those qualities that have been assimilated or repudiated. A helpful question in this respect is to ask the patient what his father and mother were/are like respectively. If the patient gives a very global reply, for example, "They were good parents", we can prompt him to be more specific, perhaps even to think of a few adjectives that best describe the parents. This exploration not only begins to put some flesh on the bones of the various significant figures in the patient's life but the quality of the patient's descriptions is also informative as it gives some clues as to whether we are dealing with a predominantly borderline/psychotic or neurotic personality organisation (see below). Borderline and psychotic patients tend to portray others in global, dichotomous terms reflecting a split between their overall goodness or badness. Alternatively, they portray significant others

Table 4.2   Some prompts for assessing the quality of object relationships

Be curious about the quality of early relationships by asking the patient:
- What is your earliest memory?
- What kind of a person is your mother/ father/sister etc?
- Can you recall a time in your childhood when you needed help? Who did you turn to?

When assessing object relationships think about...
- ...the flexibility, adaptiveness and maturity of representations of self and other,
- ...the degree of differentiation/relatedness of self and object representations.[9] For example, whether there is evidence of...
- self/other boundary compromise (i.e. basic sense of physical integrity is lacking/breached as in psychosis)
  - self/other boundary confusion (i.e. self and other are represented as physically intact/separate but feelings are confused/undifferentiated)
  - cohesive/individuated self and other representations
- ...the maturity of representations of self and other:
  - people are described primarily in terms of the gratification or frustration they provide
  - people are described in concrete, literal terms (usually on the basis of physical attributes)
  - people are described primarily in terms of their manifest activities/functions
  - descriptions integrate external appearances and behaviour with internal dimensions, i.e. contradictions can be managed
- ...the thematic content of the descriptions of others, for example, are others experienced as...
  - affectionate
  - withholding
  - successful
  - strong/weak
  - ambitious
  - malevolent/benevolent
  - cold/warm
  - intellectual
  - judgmental
  - nurturing
  - punitive

in terms of the function they serve in the patient's life, that is, more as part objects, devoid of their own autonomy and omnipotently controlled by the patient. Neurotic patients, on the other hand, tend to provide more balanced, multidimensional accounts of other people, revealing some appreciation of their distinct qualities, separate from the self.

---

[9]Adapted from Blatt *et al.* (1997).

In an assessment, we are therefore simultaneously thinking about the quality of the object relationships and making inferences about the level of maturity of these relationships, that is, whether the patient relates to whole or part objects and the patient's capacity to be separate from others. In this respect, it is important to make a distinction between a narcissistic involvement where the other is an appendage or extension of the self and an object relationship where the other is seen as separate from the self (Mason, 2000). It is helpful to consider too whether the self is experienced as cohesive or vulnerable to fragmentation if others are not available.[10]

The Transference Relationship

A major focus of assessment is the kind of relationship that the patient initiates with us from the outset, including his initial telephone or written contact. The dominant internal object relationships that emerge through the assessment of past and current relationships will give some initial clues about the quality of the transference that is likely to be established. Many patients typically arrive to the consultation in a state of need, looking for an authoritative person to relieve the distress. The underlying initial transference may therefore be to a powerful, omniscient parental figure. In turn, this may set up a conflict between the wish for, and fear of, a dependent relationship as it immediately establishes the therapeutic relationship as unequal in the patient's mind.

The quality of the phantasies the patient has about us is vitally important to the future of any psychotherapy:

> It is not the diagnosis that makes or breaks the psychoanalysis, but the nature of the patient's phantasies (Waska, 2000: 31).

At the outset, many prospective patients are likely to turn to us with a mixture of fear and hope that activates latent phantasies regarding authority figures and caregivers, phantasies into which we will be unconsciously fitted. The patients most difficult to treat are those with persecutory phantasies that shape virtually all aspects of their mind as they relate to the world with phantasies organised around controlling, tormenting or rejecting the object as a defence against the risk of becoming the victim of phantasised retaliatory attacks.

---

[10]Identity diffusion where the patient is not the same over time regardless of external circumstances suggests that different self-representations, split off from one another, are vying for dominance.

In order for the patient to use and benefit from a psychoanalytic approach, it is important that he can report on the therapeutic relationship and so work with, and experience, the transference whilst maintaining reality testing. The relationship that we hope patients will be able to develop with us will be emotionally "live". It will arouse a host of feelings – positive and negative – some of which may feel terrifying. The patient's grip on reality and hence his appreciation of the "as if" quality of the transference is vital. When this is absent the patient no longer experiences us, for example, as if we were an abusive parent; rather, in his experience we are the abusive parent. A symbol is experienced as representing an object. The capacity to symbolise allows the symbol to stand for the object whilst remaining distinct from it with its own qualities. It is its distinctiveness that allows the symbol to be used creatively by the mind to represent things.[11] When the symbol and the thing it symbolises cannot be distinguished, it reflects a breakdown in symbolic functioning, which is psychically devastating. We can observe this in varying degrees of severity and disruption in children. For example, both very young and also disturbed children cannot distinguish speaking about an experience from being in it or acting upon it: for them language is still an enactment and not a form of reference.

Social Networks

People enter *individual* psychotherapy, but they remain in reality and in their phantasy related to others. In addition to eliciting a relationship history (as above), which will have enabled us to build a picture of the patient's internal world, it will be important to also assess the patient's wider social networks and the quality and patterning of the interactions between the patient and their friends/acquaintances (e.g. issues of relationship to authority, dominance and submission, dependency and autonomy, intimacy, trust). This allows us to identify recurring interpersonal configurations and to identify a possible focus for the work if brief therapy is considered.

The patient's external relationships and their support or otherwise of the patient's wish to engage in therapy also deserves consideration. Patients with inadequate supports tend to do poorly and terminate prematurely (Frayn, 1992). Lack of support from work or family may undermine further a fragile therapeutic alliance and tenuous motivation for change.

---

[11]Segal (1957) draws a distinction between a *symbolic equation* and *symbols*. In the symbolic equation, that which becomes the symbol is experienced as the original object (i.e. "as if" quality of the symbol is not recognised such that the signifier is not distinguished from the signified).

With more psychically fragile patients, the question of who will support them during therapy breaks needs to be carefully considered. For the most disturbed patients with a proneness to acting out, special provision may need to be made to ensure they have additional professional supports for the duration of their psychotherapy.

Even those patients who are relatively high functioning (e.g. capable of sustaining a job or studies or who are not suffering from chronic interpersonal deficits) will find undertaking psychoanalytic therapy demanding because it is not only a significant emotional investment but it is also one of time and money. This is likely to impact on those close to the patient and therefore it is important to assess whether the external environment will support the therapeutic enterprise. Jealous partners, for example, might find the intimacy of the therapeutic dyad threatening and may seek to undermine it. In these situations it is important to realistically appraise the extent of support available as well as how the lack of support may collude with the patient's own ambivalence about embarking on the therapy. In some cases, provision may need to be made for the partners/families who may also require intervention.

Ego Strength

The assessment of the patient's ego strength is essential. It involves identifying whether the patient's difficulties restrict his self-observational capacity and other executive ego functions that would contribute to diffuse boundaries and encourage acting out. A patient's ego strength is inferred from presentation at assessment. It reflects those personality assets that will enable the patient to overcome anxieties and acquire more adaptive defences. At its most basic, ego strength refers to the patient's capacity to be in touch with reality whereby perception, thinking and judgement are unimpaired. A psychotic patient, for example, when in the grips of psychosis would be deemed to have very limited, if non-existent, ego strength. Ego strength reflects the patient's capacity to hold on to his identity in the face of psychic pain, without resorting to excessive distortion or denial.

Ego weakness manifests itself in poor frustration tolerance and impulse control, a lack of tolerance of anxiety and an absence of sublimatory activity. For example, a patient who is angry and has weak ego strength is more likely to be unable to reflect on the source and meaning of his anger and may instead act on it and hit another person. The patient with more ego strength will either be able to think about his anger or might manage to sublimate it and channel it into some other more constructive activity, for example, exercise.

The capacity to symbolise is an important indicator of ego strength. A key developmental task from infancy onwards is the acquisition of the capacity to interpose thought between impulse and action. If this capacity breaks down or fails to develop the consequences are serious; when mental experiences cannot be conceived of in a symbolic way, thoughts and feelings have a direct and sometimes devastating impact (e.g. thinking is felt as words that have been spoken and cannot be retracted). Hobson summarises the advantages of symbolisation eloquently:

> ... symbolising enables us to think of absent realities but also to conjure up imagined worlds; symbolising allows us to fix objects and events as experienced, and then to think about them; symbolising gives us mental space in which we can move to take up one and then another attitude to things (2002: 99).

To assess ego strength, we look for evidence that the patient is oriented in time and place, that thinking is rational and the capacity for judgement is unimpaired either by organic or by psychological problems. The patient's capacity to persist with relationships and occupational or vocational endeavours in the face of challenges provides us with another opportunity to indirectly assess ego strength. This is why it is important to take an educational and occupational history: patients who present with histories of dropping out of education, being fired from jobs or flitting from job to job, would raise the question of whether they have a sufficiently well-developed capacity to persevere with stressful situations. Difficulties in this area would not bode well for a course of psychoanalytic therapy, especially of a brief nature.

Superego Integration

The superego is that agency of the personality that can either function as a relatively benign, guiding presence in the patient's internal world or as a more persecutory, ruthless presence. Superego integration refers to the patient's ability to abstain from exploitation and manipulation of others, to maintain honesty and a capacity to think about, rather than act out, aggressive and/or perverse fantasies in the absence of external controls. This is especially important to assess when working with impulsive individuals and those who have forensic histories.

As with ego strength, the patient's superego integration is inferred indirectly. A forensic history or the expression of violent fantasies would act as cues for a consideration of potential problems in this respect. In a more general sense, however, to assess the quality of the superego we are interested in how the patient relates to his own goals and aspirations, for example, whether the goals appear to be realistic ideals or whether the patient is relating to an overly demanding, even ruthless, internal object.

Defences

Defences act as the gateway to change; flexible defences that are open to challenge allow for a destabilisation of the psychic status quo that maintains the problems. Rigid defences, instituted to protect the individual from intolerable psychic pain, may prove harder to shift. Assessment of defences is therefore critical for determining the patient's ability to respond to psychoanalytic treatment. Although rigidity of the defensive structure is usually a contraindication for brief therapy, it may also indicate the unviability of a psychoanalytic approach altogether. It is thus important to assess the balance between defence and motivation alongside the strength of the therapeutic alliance. The key questions we ask ourselves as we approach the patient's defences are as follows:

- What is the patient's core pain/anxiety?
- When he is afraid or in pain, how does he manage this?

We will be looking at defences in more detail in Chapter 6. For now, suffice to say that to assess defences it is important to pay attention to the non-verbal behaviour that might indicate the operation of defences such as the avoidance of topics, incompleteness in the patient's accounts, vagueness, preoccupation with excessive detail, tangentiality and externalisation of problems. Once we identify the operation of defences, we gently challenge these in an assessment. We do so to assess their flexibility by gauging the patient's willingness to examine or elaborate further on our interpretation. If interpretation elicits more defensive behaviour, this is suggestive of an entrenched defensive system that would prove hard to shift in a relatively brief intervention. If the interpretation of defence leads to regressive behaviour on the part of the patient, this would suggest the possibility of defences protecting the patient from a breakdown. For example, I once saw a patient who, after the first assessment session in which I had made a trial interpretation, reported having been incontinent on the way home from the hospital where I saw her. In such cases it is advisable to proceed cautiously and to recommend a more supportive therapy, at least until there is more evidence of ego strength.

Developmental Level of Character Organisation

As the assessment unfolds, we are building in our minds a picture of the patient's character. This allows us to tentatively distinguish between character and responsivity. Certain situations elicit aspects of our personality that may be latent under other circumstances, that is, they do not reflect enduring ways of being that have become integral to the fabric of our character. When stressed, for example, we may at times respond to the situation by somatising but this manner of responding would not be considered to be an enduring trait. It is the more enduring interpersonal, defensive and behavioural patterns that reflect character.

To understand character, we need to appreciate the patient's developmental level of personality organisation along with his defensive style. From a psychoanalytic perspective, one of the tasks of assessment is to determine whether the patient operates *predominantly* at a neurotic, borderline or psychotic level. I say 'predominantly', because even within a so-called normal personality there may be fluctuations in levels of functioning that are activated under different circumstances. For example, if placed under undue stress we can all revert to more primitive, paranoid thinking and perception that would place us, at that point in time, as functioning at a more borderline level of personality organisation. Conversely, a paranoid person may be organised neurotically *or* psychotically.

In assessment, we are looking for the dominant level of personality organisation that colours how the person feels and acts in the world. Each level of organisation is characterised by:

- the use of specific defences,
- the overall quality of the internalised object relationships,
- the experience of self-identity,
- the patient's relationship to reality.

Let us now look at the three levels of organisation.

1. Neurotic level

Neurotic patients tend to seek help when they encounter a conflict between what is wished for and the obstacles, often self-generated or maintained by an intrapsychic momentum, that stand in the way of a resolution. The conflicts are typically of a more Oedipal nature reflecting concerns around sexuality and aggression in the context of an ego sturdy enough to remain rooted in reality even when in the grip of powerful affects or wishes.

A neurotic personality organisation reflects the operation both of more mature defences and, more broadly, of the flexible uses of defences. This does not mean that primitive defences are never used – they are sometimes. It is the absence of any mature defences that would point to a more borderline or psychotic organisation.

Whilst this level of organisation does not immunise the patient against the ebbs and flows of narcissistic equilibrium, he is nevertheless more likely to present an integrated sense of identity capable of incorporating a more complex self-representation (e.g. he may see himself both as hardworking and reliable but also at times as manipulative). When invited to describe himself, the patient is capable of doing so. His experience of self through time and across situations is more stable than for the borderline patient whose predictable instability reflects greater discontinuity in his self-representation. Just as with his own self-representation, his representation of others reveal more colour and depth than the more black and white description readily elicited from borderline patients.

This level of organisation confers significant advantages that are also a great asset to the therapeutic enterprise: these are the patients whose observing ego can be more readily engaged. They are able to stand back from their problem(s) and think about what may be happening.

2. Borderline level

A degree of confusion accompanies the label borderline as it refers both to a psychiatric diagnostic category – borderline personality disorder – and to the description of a particular type of personality organisation found in the analytic literature. The most striking feature of a borderline organisation – in the analytic sense – is the distressing inconsistency and discontinuity in the individual's self-experience. Threats to self-image often act as precursors to self and/or other destructive behaviour, reflecting a desperate attempt to maintain some self-integrity. Identity confusion is prominent. The borderline patient has some notion of being separate from others but this is fragile and hence the patient's identity is invariably diffuse. Unlike psychotic patients, the borderline patient only experiences transient, reversible psychotic episodes.

Lacking the resources to manage affect, the borderline patient attempts to simplify emotional experience through splitting. Descriptions of others are typically two-dimensional, that is, they are "black and white", revealing only sporadic appreciation of people's mixed motives or conflicting feelings. Similar difficulties are apparent in his relationship to himself.

Shame-based experiences dominate the subjective world of the borderline patient. Although he may be concerned with a malevolent power residing inside him that can be destructive, more often he is preoccupied with an internal experience of powerlessness and vulnerability. Badness is projected outwards into the world and other people, leaving the patient feeling paranoid, at the mercy of persecuting forces.

The inflexible use of primitive defences, such as splitting and projection, is the hallmark of a borderline organisation. In this respect, it is closely akin to a psychotic organisation. This is especially so when a borderline patient is regressed. However, the borderline patient has a greater capacity to be in contact with reality than the psychotic patient even if his behaviour may at times be very disturbed.

3. Psychotic level

The patient who operates predominately at a psychotic level reveals the most fragile psychic structure. He struggles to define a sense of person-hood. His core anxieties are commonly centred on issues of trust and dependency. He experiences a terror that is often pre-verbal and is only inferred indirectly through careful use of the therapist's countertransfer-ence. He displays a core disturbance at the level of his own identity, at times doubting his own existence and/or that of others. Essentially, he is not anchored in reality and is thus often feeling confused and estranged from a sense of shared community with others.

Pattern of Affect Regulation

Psychoanalytic therapists influenced by a developmental framework argue that the cognitive-affective structures of self and other representa-tions regulate children's behaviour with a caregiver and all behaviour in subsequent significant relationships.

Observations of mother–baby dyads attest to the rhythmic, coherent con-figuration of verbal and non-verbal reciprocations. Stop-frame analyses reveal that the interactions between mother and baby follow a cyclical pattern of looking–not looking, of engagement–withdrawal. This rhythm is critical to the baby's need to regulate his comparatively immature psy-chophysiological system and in so doing he learns a great deal about basic self-regulation (Brazelton & Cramer, 1991). Parents play a very significant part in regulating the baby's emotional experiences. Despite neurological maturation, the baby's innate potential requires an inter-active and intersubjective environment to be optimally actualised. In this unique environment, co-created by both participants, most of the baby's and parents' time is devoted to active mutual regulation of their own or the other's state.[12] Regulation of states within the mother–baby

---

[12]State is used here to refer to the "semi-stable organisation of the organism as a whole at a given moment" (Stern *et al.*, 1998).

dyad is jointly choreographed through the flowing exchanges of information from perceptual systems and affective displays. Some of the states that are regulated in the early months are hunger, sleep, activity and arousal, to name but a few. From a psychoanalytic standpoint we consider it important that so much of what the baby will feel is only possible in the presence of, and through interaction with, another person who acts as mediator and consequently whose own emotional states will colour the baby's experience. Brazelton & Cramer (1991) underline this point:

> As infants achieve an inner balance and then go on to experience expectation and excitement within a safe, predictable relationship, they begin to discover the capacity for emotion and cognition with which they are endowed (Brazelton & Cramer 1991: 128).

The emotional state of others is thus fundamentally important to the baby's own emotional state. This is not on account of passive processes such as mirroring. Rather, it results from the baby's active use of the mother's emotional expression in forming her appreciation of an event and using it to guide behaviour. The function performed by the mother is that of transforming the baby's experience into something emotionally digestible.[13]

The earliest forms of communication take place without any mediation by verbal symbols. The baby often conveys his feelings to the mother in a very raw manner. This leads the receptive mother to experience as her own feelings that the baby is not yet able to articulate or indeed emotionally process within himself. The mother who is not overly preoccupied with her own difficulties is able to respond to the infant's behaviour. As she responds, the mother provides the baby with an experience of being understood that enables him to gradually build up a sense that his own behaviour is meaningful and communicative (Fonagy et al., 1991). The quality of these exchanges lays the foundations of the child's internal world and of his capacity to regulate affects.

As we saw in Chapter 1, the internal world is a primitive, fantastical psychic landscape that develops in response to what is mirrored back to the child by his parental figures. The child's experience of affect, and so the emotional colouring of the child's internal world, is organised via

---

[13]Within psychoanalysis, the mother's function has indeed been likened to that of a container for the painful states of being which the baby experiences but has not yet developed the capacity to process (Bion, 1962a, b).

the parents into secondary representations of the child's states of mind and body:

> In individual development, communication commences with actions carried out without communicative intent but interpreted by observing others as indicators of the infant's state of mind (Fonagy & Fonagy, 1995: 369).

Fonagy and Target (2000) suggest that it is the creation of an internal experience resembling "reflection" that is established through interpersonal interaction of this qualitative nature. As the child develops he can deploy this capacity to make sense of his own behaviour and affective experiences in relation to the self and to other people. Fonagy & Target refer to this capacity as *reflective functioning*.[14]

The capacity to reflect on what we are feeling underscores our capacity to regulate affect. Each patient's pattern of affective arousal is different and we can only understand it over time as we work with a patient. In listening to the patient's narrative at the assessment stage, we are therefore looking out for how the patient manages strong feelings and whether some feelings cannot be allowed. We are interested too in whether the patient can engage in an exploration of how he feels and whether he relates to himself as a feeling being.

At the assessment stage, our understanding of the patient's pattern of affect regulation can only be rudimentary. It will consist of hypotheses about:

- the affects that need to be kept in check by defences;
- the affects that function as defences, that is, those affects that protect the individual from feeling other emotional states;
- how particular affects are managed or discharged (e.g. through self-harm or substance abuse).

An important aspect of the assessment of affect regulation is to establish whether:

- the patient is able to distinguish between affect and action (something psychotic and borderline patients have difficulty with, for example);
- the patient can represent affective experience in words. This is linked to the capacity for symbolisation, which may be severely challenged in both psychotic and borderline patients.

---

[14] Reflective functioning is "an ingrained way of thinking about the mental states of self and others that is activated based on the interpersonal context" (Bram & Gabbard, 2001: 692). The development of reflective functioning involves shifting from a teleological stance in which behaviour is explained on the basis of the physical constraints of what is observable, to a stance of intentionality in which behaviour is explained in terms of beliefs and desires.

The Body

Our patients bring their minds *and* their bodies to psychotherapy. Freud (1923b) suggested that our earliest experience of an ego is a *body ego*, that is, the physical sensations of the corporeality of the self and an understanding of its possibilities and limitations. Yet, it is surprising how often we neglect the body both in ongoing therapy and at the assessment stage. In order to bring the body into the therapeutic discourse, it is helpful to take a brief developmental history to check for any complications at birth or any physical illnesses and/or disabilities, especially in childhood.

A rich source of information about the patient's experience of himself can be found in how he relates to his physicality. The limits of the body influence how we relate to ourselves and others. Visual or auditory impairment, for example, not only affects the individual on a pragmatic level but also profoundly influences the confidence with which he approaches the world and, importantly, the way others relate to him.

We can begin to reflect on the patient's subjective experience of his body by observing his use of the physical space in the consulting room and the way he holds himself in his body. For example, a very tall patient may walk into our room stooped, while another may walk into the room and bump into the furniture. It is seldom appropriate at the assessment stage to comment on any striking features of someone's physicality since at this early stage any thoughts we will have about the matter are likely to be highly speculative. Referring to them may feel very intrusive to the patient. Unless the physical appearance suggests a serious medical condition, for example, if the patient is severely emaciated, I would not draw attention to this fact. However, I would feel free to note in my own mind my own reactions to the patient's physical presence.

Sociocultural Factors

Historically, psychoanalysis has placed the greatest emphasis on the patient's internal world to the relative neglect of the patient's external reality. As our practice is nowadays truly multicultural, our work needs to embrace very varied experiences and ways of thinking about emotional distress.

We do not develop in isolation. From the moment of birth, we are a part of a family system but also of wider systems, such as the culture we are born into. This wider system needs to be acknowledged in our assessments. The same life event or "given" may acquire very different meanings or implications for a person depending on the culture they are born into. For example, being an only child and being a girl may influence the development of the child differently if the girl is born into a culture where male children are more highly valued.

The internal world is always in a dynamic interaction with the external world. Although there is never a direct correspondence between external and internal as what is internal reflects the operation of defensive processes that distort what is taken in from the outside, our assessments need to reflect the reality of our patients' lives as much as what they idiosyncratically make of this reality. The reality of racism and sexism, of socio-economic deprivation, of illness or disability and of religion, will all have a bearing on our patients' lives. In order to have the best possible understanding of our patients and of their needs, we need to be curious about the world they live in externally. If we do not ask about it, we may never know and we can jump to erroneous conclusions. For example, an often neglected question in an assessment is how people manage financially. This is an important question not only if the patient is paying for therapy. It is also important when the patient is seen in publicly funded services as it can tell us a lot about how the patient lives and alerts us to the real pressures he may be under and which might undermine the therapy (e.g. homelessness).

Culture is important too because the very notions of self, of separation and of individuation that are so commonplace within western models of therapy may not be as relevant for other cultures. In the West the individuated self is the goal of therapy. It is a self that values differentiation. In the East, the relational self is more permeable and we encounter more fluid self–other boundaries; the unit of identity is not an internal representation of the other but of the family or community.

The relationship with the assessor will also be influenced by cultural factors. By virtue of our own cultural identifications or our race, we may find it easier to relate to some patients than others and the same will apply to our patients. Being open and receptive to these transferences and countertransferences is essential to a good assessment. Patients do not always seek likeliness in their therapists with respect to cultural background. Instead, some actively seek difference and in so doing may be communicating something very important about their own cultural identifications. For example, one mixed race young woman I once saw specifically requested a white therapist. In our work, it soon became clear that the "white" self was good and the "black" self was bad, hence she defensively wanted to identify herself with the white me/therapist.

THE TRIAL INTERPRETATION

Traditionally, an assessment for psychoanalytic therapy will include what is referred to as a *trial interpretation*, sometimes of the transference, to assess the patient's capacity to make use of such interventions. It helps us to explore whether:

- the patient can decentre and observe his own thought processes;
- the patient can receive and make use of what we can offer;
- the patient can work to a focus, especially if brief therapy is being considered.

Transference interpretations in an assessment are best used sparingly and only if they are required in order to overcome an impasse. For example, if the patient cannot speak, an interpretation that acknowledges the possibility that the patient might be worried about our assessment of him, might be very helpful. Reconstructive interpretations that point out patterns or themes to the patient are more indicated as a part of an assessment. I encourage limited use of transference interpretations because at this stage we do not yet know whether we will be taking the patient on for therapy and we must ensure that we do not foster too intense a transference only to then tell the patient that we cannot see him. Moreover, the purpose of an assessment is not to begin the treatment, even though good assessments are often experienced as very therapeutic by patients. The assessment relationship should stimulate the patient to examine himself but it should strive to not be too arousing so that the patient can manage the possible gap between assessment and therapy itself.

CONCLUDING ASSESSMENTS

It is not unreasonable for patients at the end of an assessment to want to find out what we think. They may be preoccupied with whether they are "mad" or "bad", or whether we think they will get better or not. It is important to avoid colluding with the patient's wish for a definitive answer to his problem by offering a formulation based on insufficient evidence. Nevertheless, it is part of the responsibility of an assessment to convey to the patient our understanding of his predicament. Merely interpreting his questions about what we think as reflecting anxiety about the process or his fear that he might be going mad or is "bad" is unhelpful, though such speculations will be true for some patients. In our response, we can offer some opinion about what kind of help he needs as well as attend to the anxiety that may lurk behind the question.

Our task is a delicate one: we need to find the words to convey that our understanding is tentative and that our work does not always lead to precise outcomes, yet we also need to convey that if we are recommending treatment either with ourselves or with a colleague, that we believe this will help. Fortunately, we now have more evidence that does indeed suggest that psychotherapy is better than no treatment at all.

At the end of an assessment, assuming we have agreed to offer therapy, some patients will ask about our training and qualifications or about how we work. As with any question that a patient asks us, it is important to first reflect on why this question is being asked. We may pick up clues about this through how the question makes us feel: whether we feel intruded, challenged, provoked or eager to answer. Depending on the impact the question has on us, it will influence whether we approach the question with a focus on its latent meaning and function or whether we answer it straightforwardly or both. When it comes to a question about qualifications, I think it is important to answer it briefly and matter-of-factly. This should not be taken as an invitation to reel off an impressive CV. It is sufficient to say what our professional background is and to mention the body we are registered with. A question about qualifications may, of course, also mask anxiety about engaging in the process and this needs to be explored, but we have a duty to inform our patients of the service they are receiving, just like any other service. It is churlish to reduce such questions purely to manifestations of the patient's anxiety. Patients both have a right to know *and* are also possibly anxious for their own individual reasons.

Some patients may ask about how psychoanalytic therapy works. In one respect this is a reasonable question. I am, however, less inclined to give long explanations in response to such a question. Any explanation we might give is likely of necessity to be cursory and thus probably rather meaningless. Nevertheless, I think that it is helpful to orient the patient to the nature of future psychoanalytic sessions, especially if the assessment has demanded a more discursive approach. In this situation, all I say might be something along the lines of, *"You will find that in our future sessions I will ask you few questions. I will be interested in what is on your mind when you come here and in your dreams. Together we will try to make sense of patterns in your relationships or in your life and of some of the thoughts and feelings that trouble you. But you will set the agenda, as it were."*

SETTING THE CONTRACT

If the conclusion of the assessment is that we will be taking the patient on for treatment then a few practicalities need to be discussed. This will involve clearly outlining the following to the patient:

- *The use of the couch*: where indicated (*Note*: usually not indicated if once weekly therapy as we do not want to encourage too much regression but there are exceptions to this, for example, the patient who has used the couch before and has sufficient ego strength to tolerate the regressive aspects of lying on the couch).
- *The time and frequency*[15] *of sessions*: (*Note*: when mental representations have permanence once weekly work is possible because the patient can make use and hold on to the experience of the therapeutic relationship in his mind in between sessions. With more fragile patients, the gap between sessions may be difficult to manage so that frequent sessions will be more containing).
- *The fee*: where applicable (*Note*: specify clearly if and when this is reviewed).
- *The cancellation policy*: including holiday arrangements (*Note*: be specific about whether you are willing to offer alternative sessions).
- *Who else might need to be involved*: (*Note*: ask for GP details and explain under what circumstances you will contact them).
- *Confidentiality*: (*Note*: outline the limits of confidentiality).

Any of the above issues could potentially be meaningful and elicit very emotive responses from the patient. Some patients may balk at the idea of having to pay for missed sessions, whilst others may feel threatened by the suggestion of several sessions rather than just once weekly therapy. In light of this, it is advisable to allow a bit of time at the end of an assessment to discuss these issues or to discuss alternative arrangements should you both decide that the patient needs to be referred on to another colleague or agency.

PSYCHODYNAMIC FORMULATION

A psychodynamic formulation is the final stage of the assessment. It is a provisional hypothesis that will most likely be refined as the work progresses. It is incumbent on us to monitor whether we become so wedded to our hypothesis that we no longer remain alert to what the patient may be trying to communicate that does not fit, as it were, with our hypothesis.

The formulation will inform the direction and goals of treatment. A formulation will aim to bring together an understanding of the problem that will reflect the relative contribution of developmental deficits and conflicts to the presenting problem. (see Chapter 1). Because maturation can be

---

[15]The question of frequency is a complex one that deserves more careful consideration than I am able to give in this introductory text.

very uneven, a formulation is likely to include the patient's well-adapted capacities that coexist with deficits and/or conflicts in particular areas.

A formulation strives to identify both the external and the internal factors that have contributed to, or are maintaining, the problem. The emphasis on internal factors is linked to the special importance assigned to internal reality within psychoanalysis. As we have seen, psychological development is in large part a process of taking in external objects. Psychoanalysis continues to be preoccupied with whether the real relationship – as opposed to the child's inherent drive development and other biological factors – shapes the development of the mind. Fonagy (2001) has argued that psychoanalytic theories poorly integrate the impact of the external world in their formulations. Nevertheless, many contemporary practitioners now acknowledge that the influence between the child and her environment are reciprocal. Difficulties may be expected to develop where constitutional vulnerability or predisposition meets with an external environment incapable of responding to the child's needs. Trauma is understood as a process rather than as an event to be considered in isolation from the context in which the trauma occurred and the supports available to the individual at the time of the trauma.

Even where we know of a real trauma in the patient's life that we predict will have significant consequences for development, it is difficult to be very specific about the longer-term consequences of childhood events. This is particularly so since we all vary tremendously and people exposed to the same adverse experiences respond quite differently and show different degrees of resilience in the face of adversity. The social and personal context within which an event occurs may determine its meaning for us and influence its impact. For children, for example, the impact of a traumatic life event is in part mediated by the parent's response. In a time of crisis, a supportive and cohesive family environment may help a child to process its experience without adding further undue stress. Moreover, our resilience is not solely the result of positive experiences we may have had, which could be seen to act as protective factors in the face of adversity. Not all protection stems from desirable events in our lives – it may well be that for some people the experience of actually overcoming adverse circumstances is used constructively as evidence that they can manage in the face of adversity and therefore lead them to feel stronger within themselves.

Temperament is also likely to play a part. Stressful life events result in different effects on children as a consequence of individual differences in temperament (Goodyer, 1990). This, in turn, is likely to contribute to their developing personality as well as to the quality of their interactions with adults and peers. For instance, children with "adverse" temperamental characteristics such as impulsivity and aggression have been found to be twice as likely to be the target of parental criticism (Quinton & Rutter, 1985b). Temperament thus appears to exert its main effects through influencing the parent–child interaction thereby setting up a particular pattern of interaction which may become self-perpetuating.

On the basis of the evidence currently available, it would appear that the past does play a part in who we become and how we are able to function in the present and may influence the choices we make in the present. However, its relationship to the present is by no means a simple, linear one. Temperamental dispositions, early experiences, family environment, social and cultural factors all interact. As adults, we might find the resilience to manage better the painful consequences of early trauma. We may have formed significant relationships that help us find the courage to face the past and diminish its hold on the present. Moreover, a strict deterministic position is no longer tenable as modern physics has highlighted the problems with such a position: events are now no longer regarded as inexorably and absolutely determined but their occurrence is more a matter of high or low probability. This perspective is vital to a balanced formulation that reflects not only the patient's difficulties but also his resilience and the interaction between the two.

Constructing a Formulation

A psychological formulation has several components:

- It describes the problem as seen by the patient.
- It contextualises the problem in a developmental framework taking into account temperamental dispositions, physical givens, traumatic experiences/life events, past and present relationships and sociocultural factors.
- It makes some recommendations for treatment based on the above.

A *dynamic* formulation includes all of the above but its distinctive feature is that it identifies recurring themes or conflicts in the patient's relationships to self, to others, to his body and to work. Hinshelwood (1991) proposes three sources of information that can mould a formulation:

- The patient's infantile experiences.
- The present situation which acts as a trigger for help.
- The transference relationship with the assessor.

Using the psychodynamic formulation aide-memoire in Box 4.1 let us return to my patient, Tanya (see pages 99–101), and formulate her problems in psychodynamic terms.

Step 1: Describe the problem

Tanya presents with bulimic symptomatology. She uses this, according to her, as a way of not feeling anything. She also describes relationship problems: she fears that she is not kept in mind and seeks constant reassurance from others.

Step 2: Describe the psychic cost of the problem

Tanya acknowledges that she has problems in establishing relationships and that she can be suffocating. This alienates others and makes her feel lonely.

Step 3: Contextualise the problem

Tanya reports a difficult early life. Her parents separated when she was six and she subsequently lived with her mother. Her mother was a busy professional woman who travelled extensively and left Tanya in the care of nannies. Because her father did not live in the same country as her, she could not turn to him for support and she did not have any siblings. Tanya therefore often felt lonely, longing for her mother's return.

She describes her mother telling her not to cry when she felt upset saying goodbye to her. Tanya thus learnt early on that the best way to manage her affects was to switch herself off from them, so that she did not have to feel her mother's absence and her loneliness.

In her adult life, Tanya encounters more loneliness because she appears incapable of establishing an intimacy without taking the other person over in an attempt to control an object whose attention she internally fears she cannot sustain.

Step 4: Describe the patient's most dominant and recurring object relationships

Tanya experiences herself as easily rejected. She needs constant reassurance in her relationships as if she finds it hard to believe that she is kept in mind. She experiences the other as unavailable to her such that she has to chase the other, as with her partners whom she phones several times a day, to concretely reinforce her presence in their mind. In the assessment relationship, these patterns manifest themselves in her need to confirm twice the time of our appointment and in her wish to be my patient every day of the week as if anything less might mean that I will not keep her in mind and that another patient will replace her in my mind.

Step 5: Identify defences

Tanya's anxiety and fear of being alone are managed by controlling behaviour towards others and an embargo on her own feelings, which she manages by bingeing, thereby creating temporarily the illusion that she can feed herself without recourse to the unavailable, uncontrollable other. Tanya can at least have control over what she ingests and to have as much as she wants. If she were to relinquish this defence she might be faced more often with the terrible loneliness she has been escaping since early childhood.

Step 6: Identify the aims of treatment

Tanya is clear that she wants help with her eating. Although eating is clearly a significant symptomatic presentation, Tanya is also aware that the eating is somehow linked with her problems with intimacy and her fear of confronting what she feels inside. Part of the work will therefore be to help her acquire a capacity to manage her affects without recourse to bingeing and to help her address her pattern of controlling and suffocating relationships based on her expectation of the other as unavailable to her.

BOX 4.1 PSYCHODYNAMIC FORMULATION AIDE-MEMOIRE

Step 1: Describe the problem

- The problem as seen by the patient: what or who is the patient reacting to?
- What is the patient's "core pain": what is he most afraid of/trying to avoid?

Step 2: Describe the psychic cost of the problem

- What limitations in the patient's functioning or distortions in his perception of others and self have resulted from the problem?

Step 3: Contextualise the problem: Identify relevant predisposing factors

Ask yourself: How do the environmental and biological givens relate to the presenting problem? (e.g. how do they modulate or exacerbate it)

- **Environmental factors:**
  - History of trauma
  - Developmental factors influencing processing of trauma

- • Family constellation
  - • Other relevant life events
- • **Biological givens:**
  - • Body
  - • Temperament
  - • Disability

Step 4: Describe the patient's most dominant and recurring object relationship(s)

Ask yourself: How does the patient experience himself in relationship to others?

- • What object relationships dominate the patient's internal world?
- • Identify who does what to whom and the associated affect.
- • How are these internalised object relationships manifest in the patient's current life?
- • How might the representations of self/others influence and be influenced by current relationships?
- • Highlight how these internalised object relationships manifest themselves in the relationship with you.

Step 5: Identify defences: how does the patient protect himself from psychic pain?

Ask yourself: What are the possible consequences of change?

- • Describe the patient's habitual ways of managing psychic pain.
- • Specify if using neurotic or primitive defences.

Step 6: Identify the aims of treatment

Ask yourself: What does the patient want and what does the patient need?

- • Specify what kind of help the patient wants and your reasons for recommending, or not, a psychoanalytic approach.

FURTHER READING

Cooper, J. & Alfille, H. (Eds) (1998) *Assessment in Psychotherapy*. London: Karnac Books.
Gabbard, G. (1994) *Psychodynamic Psychiatry in Clinical Practice*. Washington, DC: American Psychiatric Press.
Waddell, M. (2000) *Inside Lives: Psychoanalysis and the Growth of the Personality*. London: Duckworth.

5

UNCONSCIOUS COMMUNICATION

Starting with Freud's (1900) work on dreams and their hidden meaning, psychoanalysis has always focused on what lies behind the surface content of what the patient recounts. The psychoanalytic therapist is not sidetracked by the detailed or colourful content of the patient's narrative; rather, we painstakingly listen out for what the patient may be trying to convey indirectly through the stories he chooses to recount and, more importantly, through the way he recounts them. In this chapter, we will explore the key features of analytic listening as a basis for how to approach unconscious communication in the consulting room.

LEVELS OF LISTENING: TEXT AND SUBTEXT IN COMMUNICATION

We owe to Freud the notion of "levels" of communication. In his study of dreams, Freud (1900) suggested that the trick to understanding dreams was, quite simply, not to take them literally. He urged us to go beyond their *manifest content* so as to gain access to the meaningful subtext, namely, the *latent content*. He likened the dream thoughts (i.e. the latent content) and the manifest content to two versions of the same topic in different languages. Freud's exploration of dreams led him to one of his finest contributions, as he articulated the inferred psychological operations by which the underlying latent content is translated into the manifest content. It is this class of mental operations that he referred to as the *dreamwork*. The latter is a kind of psychodynamic translation system – psychodynamic, because the translation from one level to another tends to be based in the service of motives, especially of defence. The transformation of the latent content into the manifest content involves not just translation but actually *mis*translation as the underlying text is in effect tampered with, so as to diminish or eliminate altogether its threat value to consciousness.

Freud described several processes that allow disguise. He noted that when we look at a dream we are often struck by how brief it is in comparison to the dream thoughts that instigate it. He explained this phenomenon as the result of the process of *condensation*. This involves the compression of several ideas or people into one. The manifest dream is a highly condensed version of the thoughts, sensations and wishes that make up the latent dream content. *Displacement* was the term Freud used to describe the process by which the real focus of the dream is shifted and displaced elsewhere, for example, the manifest dream may be about a problem with the plumbing in a house but may reflect deeper anxieties about the person's physical health. *Symbolisation* represents one of the more fascinating operations of the dreamwork whereby elements of the latent content are expressed not directly but symbolically in the manifest content. For example, using "plumbing" to represent the workings of the physical body.

The processes of condensation, displacement and symbolisation reflect the operation of primary-process thinking. They are operative in any narrative structure the patient presents. This means that when a patient recounts a story, the characters in the manifest story may well represent a number of significant other people and conflicts other than those appearing in the manifest story. Condensation, in particular, offers us an opportunity to combine features of different significant people into one figure, which is unconsciously associated with a number of latent thoughts or feelings or preoccupations.

When we approach communication in the consulting room, we are essentially concerned about how to translate the patient's manifest level of communication into its latent content, bearing in mind, just as we would if we were approaching a dream, how the surface communication disguises a latent meaning.

Modes of Listening

Listening is not a passive process. It involves actively being with the patient, moment by moment, and tracking the often subtle changes in his state of mind, which indicate shifting identifications and projections. These changes are imperceptible to the untrained ear.

Analytic listening has been variously described. Freud spoke of the therapist's need to maintain "evenly suspended attention", giving equal weight to all of the patient's communications whilst remaining sensitive to peripheral perceptions. Freud evocatively suggested that the therapist should turn his own unconscious, like a receptive organ, towards the transmitting unconscious:

> Everyone possesses in his own unconscious an instrument with which
> he can interpret the utterances of the unconscious of other people
> (Freud, 1913: 320).

No matter how open we strive to be in our listening, we invariably filter what our patients say to us through our theories of the mind, thus altering and expanding what we give back to the patient through our interpretations. The intent of Freud's "evenly suspended attention" is not to produce blank minds – an impossibility – but, to strive for, as Pine (1998) put it, "uncommitted and receptive ones".

Common to many of the descriptions of analytic listening is the suggestion that the therapist needs to avail herself of the patient's projections, to be "used" by the patient, as it were. Sandler (1976) thus speaks of a "free-floating responsiveness" whereas Reik (1948) advocated the development of "a third ear" that allows the therapist to attune herself to the patient's subjective experience. Bion (1970) writes about the therapist's "negative capability" – a kind of listening with "no memory or desire", which resists the sway of certainty or preconception. Bion's call to listen "without memory or desire" is both helpful and misleading. It misleads because "listening is not naïve" (Meissner, 2000: 325). It neglects the inevitable backdrop of ideas, theories and orientations that inhabit the listening mind; theory creates basic assumptions and expectations about possible meanings. Nevertheless, Bion's dictum serves as a helpful reminder of our responsibility to divest ourselves of the shackles of preconception and overvalued ideas, which may interfere with listening; it urges us to relinquish as much as possible any "commitment" to our own needs.

All these descriptions of modes of listening reflect the central importance of the therapist's receptivity to the patient's conscious and unconscious communications. They all point to a key aspect of analytic listening, namely, that it is impossible to listen with an analytic ear without involving ourselves. This confronts us with a paradox:

> It is necessary for the analyst to feel close enough to the patient to
> feel able to empathise with the most intimate details of his emotional
> life: yet he must be able to become distant enough for dispassionate
> understanding. This is one of the most difficult requirements of
> psychoanalytic work – the alternation between the temporary and
> partial identification of empathy and the return to the distance position
> of the observer (Greenson, 1967: 279).

Bollas (1996) approaches this dual demand on the therapist by distinguishing two types of listening that he refers to respectively as the "maternal mode" and the "paternal mode". The maternal mode denotes a more receptive, "holding" therapeutic stance whereas the paternal mode reflects a more active and interpretative therapeutic stance. Bollas argues that both modes play complementary roles in the analytic process. Analytic work calls for different stances at different stages of the therapy, often within the same session. For example, if a patient is very distressed he may require us to operate in a more maternal mode than during times when he can withstand a more challenging interaction. Neither stance is better than the other; rather, they complement each other.

Analytic listening, unlike ordinary listening, takes place simultaneously on multiple levels and in reference to multiple contexts. This kind of layered listening acknowledges the complexity of the patient's communications and the hidden agendas. The patient's physical presence in the consulting room suggests that at least a part of him wants to be there, but there are always resistances working against the therapeutic process and change (see Chapter 6). As Meissner aptly points out:

> Given the patient's wish to conceal and the analyst's possible motivation for not hearing or not wanting to hear, the opportunities for miscommunication and faulty listening are ample (2000: 327).

Alert to the possibility of miscommunication, listening with an analytic ear involves taking nothing for granted. This is not about being a sceptic who questions everything the patient says and never takes what the patient says at face value; rather, it is about a kind of listening that is attuned to the human tendency towards self-deceit and the resistances that are operating to shield the patient from painful affect. For example, some patients present well-rehearsed, seemingly coherent narratives. Yet, as we listen, we find ourselves struggling to hear what the patient really feels. Or the patient explicitly tells us what he feels and we find ourselves unable to connect with this. Or we hear the opposite of what the patient consciously says he is feeling. Sometimes the most important communication lies in the way something is relayed to us rather than in what is actually said. At other times, it is the silence that speaks volumes, whereas the words are like shallow vessels.

We listen to what is not quite there, not yet spoken, perhaps never to be spoken. We guard against being seduced by the spoken word or by the assumption of shared meaning. Words carry with them a personal and uniquely individual meaning. In order to understand what our patients are trying to communicate, we need to check what they are intending. We can only do so by gently questioning something that appears to make sense but may instead conceal a great deal that doesn't yet make sense. It becomes important to encourage patients to fill the gaps, to explore what they mean and to get their associations to dreams or images or unformed thoughts. Ambiguous and uncertain implications can only be approached over time by uncovering associative linkages. As Meissner put it:

> The meaning of words can never be fully grasped but only pursued (2000: 330).

Analytic listening is thus a highly sophisticated skill that encourages us to be attuned to, and to monitor multiple levels of discourse simultaneously (Adler & Bachant, 1996). The manifest content is but the tip of an iceberg of reference and implication. Communication, however, would fail if we did not take the first level of implication of what the patient says to us at face value. Sometimes, psychoanalysis' abiding concern with process and latent content has been interpreted by some therapists in such a way that the actual content of what the patient says is not responded to. An overemphasis on what the patient is *not explicitly* saying to the exclusion of what they are saying does not contribute to the development of a good therapeutic alliance. For example, the patient who after a break tells his therapist that someone close to him has died during the break may well be using the story about his bereavement to convey something of his experience of losing his therapist during the break, but to take this up before acknowledging the actual loss of someone close to the patient would be insensitive and unhelpful. Our interventions ideally convey both an acknowledgement of the manifest content of what the patient communicates as well as the possible latent content. Patients are less likely to feel misunderstood, bemused or angered by our interpretation of an unconscious meaning if we acknowledge first what they have actually said before making a link to the unconscious content.

James was a successful businessman. He had been in once-weekly therapy only a few weeks when he began a session talking about his business partner. He was concerned that his business partner might be dishonest. He had heard rumours about him but had chosen to ignore them at the time he set up his business with him because he had found him to be impressive. However, he was now aware of some irregularities that made him wonder whether there had not, in fact, been some basis to the rumours he had heard.

Together, we identified a wish to align himself with "impressive" people and James worried about his capacity to discriminate the good from the bad as a result of his wish to be seen mixing with high-profile people. As I listened to James, I was reminded that when we first spoke on the phone to arrange to meet for an initial consultation I had arranged to see him on a Saturday as I work on Saturdays. His reply to my suggestion had struck me at the time: "On a Saturday? I didn't think that therapists did that", James had said sounding bemused.

This exchange now came back to my mind and I wondered whether unconsciously James had perceived this as an "irregularity" in our work, which led him to be suspicious of me too. Although I felt quite confident that this might well be the case, I was nevertheless also aware that James was very worried about the work situation and it sounded as though he had good reason to be so. In my eventual interpretation, I therefore acknowledged the anxiety about his work problem adding: "I am also thinking that having only recently started working with me you are perhaps letting me know that you are not sure whether I can be trusted to run the business of our therapy with integrity."

Vehicles for Unconscious Communication

There are numerous vehicles for unconscious communication that are non-verbal, for example, posture, gesture, movement, facial expression, tone, syntax and rhythm of speech, pauses and silences. These non-verbal modes of communication are of interest to us. In psychoanalytic therapy, we are working with what lies beyond language. Meaning and unconscious phantasies may be expressed through the way the patient speaks rather than in what he says: a harsh tone, a soft, barely audible voice or a fast-paced delivery can convey far more about the patient's psychic position at the time the words are spoken than the words themselves.

Gestures, including bodily postures and movements, always accompany the speech process. Fonagy & Fonagy (1995) suggest that the power of *gestural messages* rests in the concealment that they afford, thus offering an opportunity for splitting and denial and so become ideal vehicles for the communication of preconscious and sometimes unconscious mental contents. Fonagy & Fonagy (1995) further suggest that pauses, silences or incomplete sentences and syntactic irregularities should draw our attention to the presence of possible hostile transference and counter-transference reactions. Indeed, patients' preconscious attitudes are often expressed at the paralinguistic level preceding their emergence in the patients' verbal utterances.

Sandra stood at the door of my consulting room for the first time and extended her hand to shake mine. Her gesture was strong and confident. She was wearing a scarf that she took off and threw across the back of the chair she sat on. She looked around the room and said, confidently: "I like it".

Sandra did not need any prompting from me to speak. She launched into her acrimonious divorce and the unfair financial settlement. She spoke about her work with the same businesslike tone. I felt swamped and controlled by her as if she had appropriated my room through her confident "I like it". From the moment Sandra arrived, non-verbally as well as verbally, I felt that she was letting me know she would find it very difficult to be vulnerable and dependent on me.

Indeed, as the session progressed, a clear pattern emerged: whatever I interpreted, Sandra would somehow find a way of letting me know that she had known this already. For example, she would say "Good point, yes, I read that in a book", or "I agree. I've always known that", or "That's exactly what I told my friend." It seemed as though the first few seconds of our non-verbal exchange had already conveyed a great deal about what we were eventually able to identify as a conflict about her own dependency.

Listening to *silence* is also important. At times silence indicates a quiet reflective mood, which is beneficial. At other times it can be a sign of resistance or an attack. The pregnant pauses can feel like a pressure to relieve the patient from his own introspection or the responsibility of thinking for himself. Or the silence may feel difficult to bear because it is being used as a weapon. No matter how difficult silences may feel, we must caution against premature impingement and pressurising the patient to overcome them. We too, may use silence as a way of discharging our own hostility towards a patient. Therefore, it is important to monitor our own silence and ensure it does not veer into withholding or neglecting the patient and perpetuating a misalliance.

Traditional psychoanalytic listening has focused on the process of listening to content, themes, symbolic and denied meaning and metaphors. Nowadays, the *structure* of the patient's narrative is also considered to be pregnant with latent meaning. The attachment research by Main and colleagues urges us to focus on the meaning that is inherent in the organisation of language itself. Main (1995) makes an explicit distinction between coherent and incoherent narratives. She distinguishes between language that is collaborative and coherent and language that is incoherent, distorted or vague. Incoherent narratives make it necessary for the listener to infer linkages of which the speaker may be unconscious so as to create organisation and to deduce real or underlying meaning in the story that is being told. The distinction drawn by Main encourages us to listen closely to moment-to-moment changes in linguistic fluency and to shifts in voice, to lapses in meaning and coherence and to the fragmentation of the narrative, all of which have been found in research to be indicators of attachment insecurity in adult speech (Main, 1995) (see also Chapter 4).

Slade (2000) suggests that the application of Main's work translates in a focus on the structure of language, syntax and discourse, which may be understood to unconsciously represent the dynamics of an individual's early object relationships. Indeed, Fonagy's (2001) work suggests that secure or reflective patterns of language and thought indicate the presence of an internalised other who can contemplate or contain the breadth and complexity of the child's needs and feelings. In this sense, the breaks, incoherencies and contradictions observed in the narratives of insecurely attached adults are said to imply a break in the caregiver's capacity to respond to the child's need for care and comfort. Listening to the structure of the patient's narrative sensitises us to the quality of his early experiences of attachment and how this might be translated into the patient's current relationships. An important task in therapy then becomes that of reflecting on, and mentalising, those aspects of the patient's story so as to provide a patient with, as Slade puts it:

> a secure base for the patient's mind that leads to healing and internal consolidation (2000: 1158).

WORKING WITH UNCONSCIOUS COMMUNICATION

Listening to Latent Content

As we saw earlier, Freud's work on dreams led him to approach the remembered dream as the end result of a complex psychic work of disguise through processes such as displacement and condensation. Any story or dream that the patient brings to a session is understood to carry meaning at different levels of consciousness. Not only can an aspect of the environment, or its image, be used metaphorically, but the people the patient refers to may represent – stand-in, as it were – for other people. They may represent the patient himself as a whole or as a part. In the evolving dialogue between the patient and the therapist, the patient gives voice to complex schemata of self and others that indicate different states of mind (e.g. the self as a child raging at a dominating parent may give way to the self as a child yearning for an absent parent). Within a session, the patient may oscillate between being the subject of angry impulses and, at other times, may feel like the object of someone else's rage. These shifts are seldom conveyed directly through language, but we can infer them from the stories patients recount and how they recount them.

Symbolic transformation means that a threatening mental event – for example, a murderous wish – is not simply abolished from consciousness but often remains in symbolic disguise. The detection of unconscious

Table 5.1   Levels of listening

- *The level of content:*   what the patient is consciously saying (e.g. who is doing what to whom and who is feeling what?)
- *The level of structure of the narrative:*   is the narrative coherent or incoherent?
- *The level of function:*   what effect is the narrative having on you and how is it making the patient feel in relation to you? (e.g. is it being used to impress, to implore, to ignore or to distance).

---

aspects of communication – the bulk of our analytic work – thus becomes a matter of symbolic decoding, that is, of interpretation. Unlike other therapeutic approaches, the emphasis in analytic approaches is on decoding the patient's unconscious communication. Listening to unconscious communication is demanding (see Table 5.1). It requires patience because unconscious meaning is seldom immediately obvious. Freud's principle of *overdetermination* cautions us against facile formulations that invoke simplistic links. On the contrary, Freud argued that any behaviour or dream or phantasy is the end result of multiple, interacting factors. Our interpretations thus need to reflect this complexity. Sometimes, several sessions will pass before we can make sense of what the patient may be desperately trying to convey. We may feel stupid or incompetent in the process, especially if we are under pressure from the patient to provide an interpretation that will be a cure-all. To work analytically, we have to divest ourselves of the need to know and let go of our wish to solve the problem. This does not mean that we ignore the problem; rather, it means that we try not to get caught up in providing an answer before the problem has been identified.

The primary vehicles for unconscious communication are narratives, dreams and free-associative linkages. We play a significant part in creating a space ripe for unconscious communication. This requires, first and foremost, a capacity to bear silence so that free associations can emerge. The more we structure a session through questions or other interventions, the more we inhibit the spontaneous production of unconscious communication. Having created a space that is safe and conducive to free associations we begin to listen. When listening, we always need to ask ourselves if there is a *subtext* to the story recounted (see Table 5.2). This is the starting point for our eventual interpretation. In the following example, I have bracketed my own thought processes as I listen for the subtext in Tom's narrative.

Tom was a forty-year-old man with mild learning disabilities. He was a large man whose personal hygiene had been a problem. He had been

Table 5.2   How to listen to the subtext

- Don't be tied to the apparent content of the patient's narrative. Listen to the story in terms of relationship patterns, for example, who is doing what to whom. Note how roles can switch. For example, the patient may be describing shifting from being passive to active in different situations.
- Observe prosodic elements of language (e.g. rhythm and tonality) – they can be a manifest form through which crucial material excluded from consciousness can be glimpsed.
- Whatever the patient tells you, resist the temptation to jump in and interpret. Asking for associations (e.g. "What comes to mind?") can be helpful whether it is associations to elements of a dream or to an incident the patient recounts (e.g. "What do you make of what happened with X?").
- Explore with the patient the affective experience that dominates the narrative. For example, in telling you about a colleague's achievements is the patient feeling anxious, shamed, hostile, envious?
- Make a note of how you feel (i.e. your own countertransference) as you listen to the patient. For example, as the patient tells you about a blind date he has been on, do you feel curious, anxious or excited?
- Consider the possible transference implications in what the patient is recounting. Sometimes patients will recount a dream a week after they dreamt it or they will tell you about an argument that took place at work months after the event. The first question in your mind needs to be, "why is this story being brought *now*?"

referred because of inappropriate sexual behaviour towards staff in the hostel where he lived. In the session reported here, he had arrived for his penultimate session of a year-long once-weekly psychotherapy.

In the session, Tom starts off talking about difficulties with his parents whom he feels do not care about him. [*Mindful that this is our penultimate session and that Tom has feelings about this, I consider the possibility that he is letting me know about a difficulty in our relationship but displaces it onto the relationship with his parents*]. He goes on to express anger at his parents for not visiting him often at the hostel. He thinks they prefer to visit his brother who is a chef. [*The theme is of being neglected by parental figures who have a preference for another son who is experienced by Tom as being the favoured son. I hypothesise that Tom is letting me know that he has a phantasy that I am stopping therapy with him because I want to devote my time to someone else whom I prefer to him*]. He then stops talking and looks to his feet. His face looks sad. When he resumes talking,

Tom says: "I smell bad. No one wants to have sex with me. I haven't had sex in fifteen years. If I had sex I would squash the woman. I'm too heavy." [*Tom has now given very rich free associations. He begins by identifying two personal attributes – his smell and his weight – which, in his mind, are associated with other people's rejection of him. But it is more complex than this, since Tom also says that if he had sex he would squash a woman. Through this powerful image Tom is communicating his own rage and murderous feelings and the phantasy that intimacy is impossible because if he gets close to a woman he would squash/kill her*].

To understand the meaning of Tom's communications we need to contextualise what he is saying, that is, we listen to the content of his story bearing in mind that this is the penultimate therapy session. The dominant themes in his narrative are about being neglected/not visited by his parents and a perception of himself as repellent to others thereby preventing any intimacy. I note here that he switches from being angry with his parents to focusing on what it might be about him that makes it impossible for others to get close to him. If we consider these themes in relation to the fact that this is the penultimate session we begin to hear a different story. Tom is angry with me for not seeing him anymore. In his phantasy I have another non-smelly, non-heavy patient who I would rather see than him and this is why I am stopping the therapy. Behind the initial anger about the therapy ending lies Tom's anxiety that he destroys relationships and that is why people/I need to get away from him.

THE NATURE OF PSYCHOANALYTIC INTERPRETATION

Interpretation is not an exclusively psychoanalytic technique. Cognitive-behavioural therapists also "interpret" when they make explicit to their patients, the links between their thoughts and behaviour. To interpret, in the more strict analytic sense, refers to verbal interventions that make something unconscious[1] (i.e. an aspect of their psychological functioning) conscious.

Jane was a deprived, young single mother who came into therapy because she had become post-natally depressed after the birth of her first child. She told me that her own family had rejected her and the father of her daughter had not shown any interest. She described her daughter as difficult as she

---

[1] I am using the term here in its descriptive sense.

cried most of the time. She felt exhausted by her demands and struggled to breastfeed her. She said that her daughter was always hungry, but that her breasts had little milk and it hurt her and that she was going to give her daughter the bottle. She was so exasperated at times that she was contemplating giving the baby up for adoption. She said that her social worker visited her once a week but that this did not help.

Presented with this material, I ask myself what internal experience Jane might be trying to convey through her description of her struggle with her baby. Jane consciously knows that she is depressed, and as the material indicates she links her current state with the demands of what she perceives to be a difficult baby. What is missing in her manifest narrative is a sense of why her baby becomes, in her mind, such a voracious, demanding baby that she reaches the stage of contemplating giving her up for adoption. What I know from her history is that Jane has a difficult relationship with her family who have rejected her and with her partner who has also rejected her. She also has a social worker but she does not feel the weekly visit is a good feed. I hypothesise that she is most probably feeling internally deprived and additionally has to contend with the very real demands of a small baby. A dominant theme of the narrative is conveyed by the powerful image of her depleted, aching breasts: she feels she has nothing left to give and that her baby has taken everything from her. In an interpretation we might therefore approach this material as an unconscious communication about a very needy part of Jane that cannot be soothed, just like her daughter who cries and is always hungry. In her own needy state, she experiences her daughter as a rival for limited resources. The fantasy of giving her up for adoption represents a way out in her mind when she feels that her daughter is taking too much away from her.

An interpretation is a hypothesis. It invites the patient to comment on it if he wishes or to ignore it. This is why an interpretation is ideally couched as a tentative statement, question or formulation that conveys to the patient "This might be one way of understanding what you are saying". An interpretation is not a statement of truth where we tell the patient what he is *really* thinking even if he does not yet know it; rather, it is an invitation to consider another perspective that may, or may not, fit.

Interpretation involves an inescapably subjective dimension. Interpretations are neither true nor false, only more or less helpful. It is of course the case that when we know our patients well and have worked with them over a period of months or years, our interpretations will become less hesitant and we can "cut to the chase" when recurring patterns manifest themselves. This may lend to the interpretation, a quality of "certainty", but usually this is not how the patient experiences it. This is why some published case histories are problematic: taken out of the context of the history of the therapeutic relationship, some interpretations may misleadingly come across as unfounded, wild guesses.

THE CONTENT, FUNCTION AND TIMING OF INTERPRETATIONS

Three key aspects of interpretations need to be considered, namely, their function, content and timing.

Content

One of the differences between the schools of psychoanalysis can be found at the level of the *content* of the interpretations that dominate the clinical picture. "Content" refers to whether the interpretation relates, for example, to defences, to intrapsychic factors or to the transference. Content is not just determined by what the patient says, but by the level at which the therapist interprets is. For example, a patient may discuss a difficult work situation with a boss whom they are experiencing as hostile towards them. He describes the boss as insensitive, a bully, who always does things his own way. In dealing with the boss, the patient reveals his character-istically passive stance: he will endure the situation while secretly giving expression to his hostile feelings about the boss through his contempt for him. The patient thus presents himself as self-righteous and passively aggressive in the face of a bullying boss. Such a narrative could be taken up in different ways. In a classical Freudian model, the emphasis might be more on interpreting the impulse (e.g. to wish to attack and humil-iate the boss) and the defence (e.g. the passivity). More contemporary, object-relational models might place less emphasis on the interpretation of defence and impulse and more on relational and interactional perspec-tives. For example, they might take up the relationship with the boss as an instance of transference and examine the patient's experience of the therapist as a bully along with his secret contempt for the therapist.

There are no definitive "rules" about how to determine the focus of an interpretation. Nevertheless, if the patient is primarily struggling with the experience of fragmentation and boundary diffusion, this exposes a lack of a sturdy-enough ego structure (i.e. weak ego strength) due to an absence of a constant, defined self-representation; this experience is generally prioritised in the content of an interpretation over issues of subtle meaning, affect and wish (Greenspan, 1977). For example, focusing an interpretation on the patient's conflictual wishes when the patient's main concern is with a sense of inner fragmentation misses the patient's core experience and is thus unlikely to be helpful. With neurotic patients, whose personalities are more integrated, interpretations can afford to focus on the meaning of what the patient says. With more disturbed patients, who have very disorganised object relationships and who cannot regulate their emotional states, interpretations can more helpfully address the patient's affective experience, that is, the focus is on helping them to identify what they feel before meanings are explored.

Psychoanalytic interpretations can focus on a wide range of thoughts, feelings or behaviour:

- They can draw attention to contradictory pictures of people, including the therapist, and the anxieties that lie behind the construction of such contradictory representations.
- They can address specific defensive manoeuvres that compromise the patient's self-awareness and connection to the therapist in the session, that is, transference interpretations (see Chapter 7).
- They can be directed at the patient's self-representations, helping him to explore positive and negative attributes and how these might be linked with particular representations of other people. Such interpretations can be made at different levels, that is, they may invoke unconscious meaning or they may, at first, simply make explicit covert attitudes and feelings the patient has. When working with patients who are more concrete in their thinking, interpretations of this latter kind can provide a gradual entry into a more exploratory mode.
- They can centre on the identification of patterns in the patient's actions, thoughts and feelings, especially in the context of relationships to self and others, including the therapist, highlighting the underlying object relationships and the associated unconscious phantasies that are enacted or implied. We infer the presence of unconscious phantasies[2] from the patient's behaviour or beliefs. For example, the phantasy *"I am filled with badness"* may manifest itself in the transference as a constant vigilance by the patient for critical comments. The phantasy *"I am omnipotent"* may manifest itself as the patient talking about risk-taking behaviour without any sense that he might get hurt.

Function

At its simplest, one of the functions of an interpretation is to convey to the patient that his communications, however incoherent or confused, are

---

[2]Britton (1991) helpfully distinguishes between unconscious phantasy and belief. In his view, phantasy exists in the non-experiential realm of implicit memory whereas a belief reflects the mental contents generated by the procedure activated in an object relationship.

meaningful. An interpretation puts into words the patient's experience, focusing in particular on the unconscious aspects of the experience. Many interpretations serve the function of validating the patient's experience; they are essentially sophisticated reflections of empathy that convey to the patient that we have understood his predicament by going one step beyond an acknowledgement of what the patient feels. For example, if the patient is describing a dispute with a friend who disagrees with him over some issue and he tells us that he is upset by the argument, our interpretation would go beyond recognition of the patient's stated distress. We would be, additionally, trying to formulate why a disagreement feels disturbing to the patient, for example, we might hypothesise that the patient experiences any kind of difference as threatening to his internal psychic equilibrium.

When we interpret to our patient his state of mind, we are implicitly communicating our own stance in regard to the patient, that is, we are relating to him as a thinking and feeling being who has a complex mental life that can be understood. This, in turn, includes an element of reflection that will eventually become transmuted into the patient's self-reflective function by a process of internalisation (see Fonagy *et al.*, 2002). An interpretation is thus potentially mutative not only by virtue of its content, but also because it provides the patient with an experience of an external and different object who can think about his experience in addition to validating it (Kernberg, 1997).[3]

Many interpretations serve the function of linking what the patient experiences internally with external reality. This helps the patient – particularly the more disturbed patient who has blurred ego boundaries – to establish connections between powerful affects or states of mind and perception. Such interpretations provide a gentle introduction to the idea of an unconscious mind that exerts an impact on behaviour.

Interpretations are often said to "contain" the patient's distress. By bringing together disparate aspects of the patient's experience, an interpretation metaphorically "holds" the patient. The mere act of interpreting may be experienced by the patient as a concrete expression of our interest in him and this too may be felt to be very containing. At times, containment may be all that the patient can manage: some patients come to us to be understood but not for understanding (Steiner, 1993). Understanding presumes the patient's active involvement in the process such that he is emotionally sturdy enough to take on responsibility for his own mind and

---

[3] Fonagy and Fonagy (1995) suggest that when the mother responds to the baby's distress by giving it a dual-tone message that acknowledges both the child's experience alongside the expression of another emotional state that is incompatible with the baby's, this conveys to the baby that her emotional experience has been contained.

its impact on others. Although the containing function of interpretations is important, and with more disturbed patients it is essential, containment is not an end in itself (Steiner, 1993). As Frosh aptly puts it:

> If containment is all that therapy provides, then the real thing, the existence of contradiction and loss, is never faced (1997b: 108).

As we approach any of our patients' communications we always need to be mindful of the ever-present pressure from the patient to relieve him of his suffering. Of course, this is one of the aims of any therapeutic enterprise. But there are different ways of easing psychic pain. One is to engage in some activity, such as giving advice or providing reassurance. Such interventions, while providing short-term relief to the patient, may also communicate to the patient that we cannot bear to stay with his pain and to think about it. Keeping to an interpretative mode conveys to the patient, even if painfully, that unbearable states of mind can be reflected upon with another person who validates the patient's experience. After all, as Frosh suggests, perhaps all that therapy can offer is a "... metaphor of interpersonal recognition, a sign of not being alone" (1997a: 98). Interpretation may be one of the means of conveying this kind of recognition. It signals to the patient that he is "not alone", that another mind is grappling with his mind. We should not underestimate this simple, yet powerful, function.

In our work we need to balance an open, receptive, supportive attitude with one of searching and "facing up to". An interpretation may both validate and contain a patient, but it also needs to bring together disparate elements in a way that is ultimately challenging. Ideally an interpretation is more than revelatory: it is also destabilising. The act of interpreting is more than a reflective statement that captures the patient's experience. It also introduces a new perspective on the patient's experience. It is important, therefore, to create the conditions of safety within which the patient can withstand the challenge that is a necessary part of the therapeutic enterprise.

Timing

An interpretation can be resisted if it is felt to threaten an existing internal state or established views of the self or others. Timing is therefore of the essence. Just like a badly timed joke, an interpretation, even if correct, will fall flat, may shame or may alienate the patient if it is offered when the patient is not psychologically ready to hear it. If a particular behaviour is interpreted before the patient can fully grasp its psychological significance, the patient may feel forced into a passive position where our perspective is privileged. Premature interpretations can unhelpfully lend the therapist an omniscient quality that serves to protect both participants in the therapeutic process from core anxieties elicited by "not knowing". The patient's inner sense of the analytic relationship must be stable or be stabilised in order for him to utilise the destabilising impact of interpretations, which, by definition, bring something new to the patient's attention.

The best interpretations are no more than well-timed prompts that enable the patient to arrive at his own interpretation. These prompts are skilled interventions informed by our dynamic understanding of the patient and of the particular transference matrix dominating the relationship at the time. The aim of analytic work is to foster the patient's self-analytic capacity, not to make him reliant on a therapist who delivers clever interpretations. Although we may be tempted to make an interpretation we need to guard against approaching the therapeutic situation as a forum for exposing our analytic prowess. If we always pre-empt the patient's efforts to understand himself, we are like the mother who upon seeing her child reaching out for an object always leaps in and hands it to him, depriving him of an opportunity to experiment with his own abilities. This is why, when it comes to interpreting, less is often more. Tarachow observes:

> An interpretation should rarely go as far as possible. It should by preference fall short even of its intended goal. This gives the patient an opportunity to extend your interpretation, gives him greater share in the proceedings and will mitigate to some extent the trauma of being the victim of your help (1963: 49).

A good interpretation is simple, to the point and transparent. By "transparent" I mean that the interpretation shows the patient how we have arrived at our particular understanding. This is especially important in the early stages of therapy when the patient might be unaccustomed to working with the unconscious and may therefore experience an interpretation as "plucked out of the blue" unless it is grounded in the content of what he may have been talking to us about in the session or in the dominant feelings expressed. Importantly, this minimises the patient's experience of us as omniscient and provides a model that the patient can adopt to make sense of his own unconscious.

During her penultimate session before a two-week break, Sara asked me during the session whether I had seen a programme on television, which dealt with people's attitudes towards death. As she spoke I was aware that her speech was quicker, her voice brittle. Sara told me that she had found the programme helpful as it validated her own experience of how difficult it is to talk about death. She had lost her own mother to cancer two years previously and since that time she had painfully struggled to reconcile

THE PRACTICE OF PSYCHOANALYTIC PSYCHOTHERAPY

herself to her death. She did not like the word 'death' and actively avoided it in the sessions.

In approaching this material I had two things in mind: Sara had indeed come into therapy to explore her grief about the loss of her mother on whom she had been very dependent. The session reported here took place a few months before the second anniversary of her mother's death. It felt important, therefore, to respond to her comments both as related to her mother's actual loss as well as to consider the possible latent communication. In this respect, I was mindful of the forthcoming break in the therapy and of Sara's dependency on me. We had explored, on a few previous occasions, her fear that I would not be there for her at the time of her session and how she struggled to allow herself to rely on my being there for her. She was characteristically quick to dismiss her dependency on me while at the same time reassuring me that she valued my input a great deal.

In light of this background history in our relationship and the material in this particular session I made the following intervention, taking into account her conscious preoccupation and linking it to my own understanding of what else it might also mean: "I am aware that we are approaching the anniversary of your mother's death and we both know that this makes you feel very anxious. I wonder too whether our forthcoming break is making you feel anxious but to speak about it feels too dangerous. Just like the people in the TV programme you were telling me about who confirmed your experience that death talk is avoided, I think that you are telling me that 'break talk' is also difficult today."

Our interpretations will serve different functions depending on the developmental level of the patient. This is a crucial consideration in relation to the timing of an interpretation. Whether an interpretation is experienced by the patient as liberating or horrifying has everything to do with the degree to which language is freed from some of its ties to the body and to primitive impulses. Only when language has truly become a system of signifiers will interpretation help. With very disturbed patients, especially psychotic patients whose symbolic capacity may be severely compromised, an interpretation will not necessarily contribute to an experience of validation, containment or understanding.

Knowing when and what to interpret therefore relies on our ongoing assessment of the patient's overall degree of disturbance and his shifting states of mind within a session. There is a distinction between an interpretation that makes the patient conscious of patterns he is unaware of and an interpretation that makes the patient conscious "in the sense of helping the patient acquire a previously non-existent representation" (Edgecumbe 2000: 19). With more damaged patients who may have had little, if any, experience of another person helping them to make sense of their emotional experiences, our work is often not about uncovering meaning; rather, it is about helping the patient to find or to make meaning. That is, we help the patient discover what he feels before we can begin to explore why he feels in a particular way.

The Interpersonal Context of Interpretation

Before we can consider the type of interpretation we might make, we need to think about the quality of the interpersonal context in which the interpretation is made. If one of the functions of interpreting is to challenge the patient's perspective on a given issue, this is a risky strategy. The pull of the internal psychic status quo can be powerful and an interpretation may therefore be experienced as an unwanted intrusion that threatens to disrupt a fragile equilibrium. This is why it is preferable to interpret in the context of a good therapeutic alliance that can withstand the patient potentially experiencing us as unhelpful, attacking or persecuting. Nevertheless, there will be occasions when the patient will experience us as unsupportive precisely because of the distortions of transference. In these circumstances, it will be important to interpret this as a way of re-establishing a context of support. As with any relationship, the therapeutic relationship will suffer the strains of misunderstandings and misattunements. What matters is that such experiences can be thought about and survived constructively. The therapeutic relationship is strengthened by the experience of ruptures that can be repaired.

Types of Interpretation

There are two main types of analytic interpretations: *reconstructive or genetic interpretations*[4] and *transference or here-and-now interpretations*. A reconstructive interpretation draws attention to the patient's feelings or thoughts, for example, by linking them to their developmental origins (e.g. *"I think that you feel angry when your husband does not share his work with you just as you felt when your parents excluded you from their discussions"*). Until Kleinian thinking established itself in mainstream analytic practice, reconstructive interpretations had been the quiet staple of analytic work (Brenneis, 1999). As we saw earlier in Chapter 2, some contemporary

---

[4]These are also sometimes referred to as extra-transference interpretations. The latter effectively covers any intervention that is not transference interpretation.

approaches now stress the importance of understanding childhood events as being shaped into procedures based on early experiences that may never be retrieved. This position has challenged the function and prominence of reconstructive interpretations.

In our work we need to pay attention to the very psychic structures that organise our behaviour. It is through addressing these structures – not the experiences that have contributed to these structures in the first place – that therapeutic change will take place.[5] The interpretative focus is on the patient's patterns or procedures as they manifest themselves in the transference relationship. These interpretations are often referred to as "here-and-now" or transference. Although they can include links to figures from the patient's past, they retain their primary focus in the present relationship with the therapist as it unfolds in the consulting room (see Chapter 7).

We infer the transference from the patient's associations, affect and behaviour that recreate or re-enact the past. Nowadays this is mostly regarded as a new experience influenced by the past rather than an exact replica of it. A transference interpretation makes explicit reference to the patient-therapist relationship and is intended to expose, elucidate and encourage an exploration of the patient's conflict(s) as it makes itself known in the relationship. Although the emphasis of the interpretation is not on the patient's past, work in the transference leads to an understanding of the past, as Roys points out:

> It is the experiencing of the live interaction with the therapist, rather than an intellectual explanation from the therapist that leads to the reconstruction of infantile anxieties and defences (1999: 37).

The aim, in many contemporary approaches, is not to arrive at the truth in terms of what really happened to a patient but to reach an understanding of the patient's affective experience (Flax, 1981). Consequently, many contemporary therapists concentrate their therapeutic efforts on the formulation and interpretation of the patient's *current* representations of himself in relationship with other people. This focus reflects a move away from the illusion that there is an objective truth to be found in reconstructing the patient's past.

In practice, few therapists restrict themselves exclusively to either transference or reconstructive interpretations though there are differences in emphasis typically associated with different schools. The respective use of these two types of interpretation produces quite different experiences

---

[5] I am describing here what I consider to be important, rather than a definitive, psychoanalytic stance.

within the consulting room. A reconstructive interpretation locates the origins of the patient's behaviour firmly in the past. As such the patient's current feeling of anger, say, can be redirected by the therapist back to a past significant figure, thereby protecting the therapist and patient from a potentially too immediate emotional experience in the room. By contrast, a transference interpretation is bolder: it invites the patient to examine his emotional reaction, however uncomfortable or distressing, in the immediacy of the therapeutic relationship. In this sense, a transference interpretation involves more direct exposure to the affect that the patient might want to avoid. By implication, it involves the therapist directly as a protagonist in the patient's unfolding narrative. It renders the therapist the target of emotions that may also feel uncomfortable to the therapist. Indeed Waska observes that:

> Many patients and analysts use genetic reconstruction, free association and dream recall to defend against the exploration of transference fantasies. The ability of both the patient and analyst to keep returning to the centrality of the patient's fantasy life and the intricacies of that internal motion as it plays out in the treatment relationship is what defines the treatment as psychoanalytic. (2000: 28).

Another common distinction is drawn between surface interpretations and depth interpretations. A *surface interpretation* restricts itself to material that is very close to the patient's consciousness, that is, a more manifest level of communication. Generally speaking, in response to such an interpretation the patient is unlikely to feel bemused; rather the patient is likely to more readily recognise that which the therapist points out even if he had not himself consciously made the connection. When in doubt as to what the patient can tolerate, it is best to avoid starting with interpretations that are potentially too threatening or farthest removed from what the patient is consciously aware of, such as interpretations relating to the patient's destructive feelings or phantasies.

A *depth interpretation* typically involves bringing to the surface those elements that are most historic and so farthest from awareness. Busch (2000) helpfully suggests that by the time we make a depth interpretation, this should ideally not seem very deep at all to the patient. Ross argues further that:

> ... interpretation of conflicts that are still unconscious and that there-fore can only be inferred [are] violations of the analysand's mental autonomy – as premature schematisations to which the analyst resorts when a patient requires some kind of frame or guidepost to assuage terror of the unknown. (1999: 98).

Busch and Ross both advocate an approach that follows the patient's pace warning us against the perils of over-interpreting and ascribing meaning prematurely as a defence against uncertainty.

The most helpful interpretations are those that help the patient understand himself in a way that is emotionally meaningful, not intellectually seductive. An approach that relies on frequent so-called depth interpretations privileges our agenda whilst remaining distant from what the patient may be capable of at any given point.

Another clinically helpful distinction is drawn by Steiner (1993) between "patient-centred" and "therapist-centred" interpretations. This distinction reflects Steiner's view that some patients, whilst wanting to be understood, cannot bear understanding. The patient who wants understanding is actively engaged in a process of self-exploration. This kind of patient can make use of *patient-centred interpretations*. These interpretations focus on what the patient is doing or thinking, revealing to the patient his projections into the therapist. These kinds of interpretations invite the patient to assume responsibility for having an effect on the therapist:

> Responsibility is a key trigger for depressive anxiety and some degree of working through of that position may have to be achieved before the patient's role in phantasy can be interpreted. That is to say, the patient's responsibility for the analyst's mind brings on feelings of guilt and blame which may involve a sense of deserving punishment (Hinshelwood, 1999: 804).

By contrast, the patient who simply wants to be understood, according to Steiner, uses the therapist to evacuate unwanted thoughts and feelings but is not able to take back these projections in the form of interpretations. If the patient cannot tolerate self-understanding, Steiner advocates using *therapist-centred interpretations* that focus on the patient's view/phantasy of what might be going on in the mind of the therapist (e.g. *"You experience me as..."; "You are afraid that I will feel..."*). Such interpretations have a more containing function.

Table 5.3 summarises the main considerations for how to approach making an interpretation. At the risk of repeating myself, our primary concern, when we interpret, is to make an assessment of the patient's state of mind at the time of the interpretation and the implications of this for his receptivity to what we have to say. A patient in the grip of paranoid anxieties will struggle with a so-called patient-centred interpretation, but this same patient, when in touch with more depressive anxieties may be able to make use of such an interpretation.

Table 5.3   Guidelines on how to approach the task of interpretation

- The first stage of an interpretation is the clarification of the patient's subjective experience.
- The second stage involves interpreting what the patient may not yet be aware of and/or may be avoiding becoming aware of.
- The patient's state of mind is an important consideration when making an interpretation: ask yourself what he can bear to know.
- The interpretation needs to reach the patient: it must take into account his level of personality organisation.
- The interpretative focus should be on material infused with the most affect, whether it is a transference or extra-transference interpretation.
- Consider the interpersonal context: it is less risky to interpret in the context of a good therapeutic alliance.
- Interpretations early on in therapy need to be delivered cautiously and in the context of some evidence, not pure guesswork.
- As a rule, refrain from making elaborate genetic reconstructions about matters outside a patient's awareness and usually outside of your own knowledge. It is far more reliable and productive to stay focused on the here-and-now conflicts and patterns as they arise in the therapeutic relationship.
- Monitor how you are using both transference and reconstructive interpretations. Historical reconstruction may be used defensively to avoid the present situation.

Interpretation: The Patient's Experience

Asking for help is a complex psychological process: it requires an acknowledgement that we need help, that we are therefore vulnerable and hence that we are in some important respects dependent on those who help us and who are not within our omnipotent sphere of control. Being understood by another person before we can understand ourselves is not universally experienced as supportive. For some patients, it is evidence that they are a failure or that they are weak or dependent, and hence it is at its core a potentially humiliating experience (Mollon, 2002). Being in therapy can therefore be experienced as shameful by the patient who may view it as an admission of weakness or inadequacy that threatens a fragile psychic equilibrium. The patient's experience of an interpretation will most likely reflect his state of mind and dominant self-representation at the time of the interpretation.

"Analysing" means breaking things into their component parts. The interpretation tries to make sense of what emerges through this process. It is therefore an exposing experience for the patient who is being presented with a version of himself that he may not like and may indeed feel very ashamed of. Shame experiences result from sudden awareness that we are being viewed differently than we anticipated. In a shame experience, there is a split in awareness (Spiegel *et al.*, 2000): the self is experienced as deficient, helpless, confused and exposed and the shaming other is experienced as if inside the self, judging and overpowering.

When we make an interpretation, our intention is to help the patient to understand something about himself that will be of help to him. Nevertheless, when we speak we can never know what the patient hears and whether it is what we intended. Just as we listen to the patient's non-verbal behaviour, so does the patient listen to ours. Sometimes the patient may "mishear" intentions, or at other times he may "hear" accurately intentions we are not even aware of but that may in fact hold a degree of truth. Our patients often turn out to be our best supervisors. Even if we are sitting out of sight, what the patient hears happening behind the couch, such as our possible restlessness or our tone of voice can be interpreted rightly or wrongly as signs of boredom, lack of concern or critical judgement.

An interpretation is a hypothesis, but it can be experienced by the patient as an action (i.e. the therapist doing something to the patient). Interpretations can thus be experienced as attacks or invasions that must be warded off. When working with patients who have been in some way abused it will be crucially important to bear this in mind. Because interpretation involves externalising, and thereby exposing, the contents of the patient's mind at a given point in time, this can be experienced as the therapist entering the patient's mind. In more disturbed patients this can provoke a violent reaction, not necessarily directly towards the therapist but possibly displaced onto someone else.

In part at least, the patient's experience of an interpretation will be determined by what he is seeking from us. As Steiner (1993) points out, for those patients who are not looking for self-understanding, the therapist's role is to carry the burden of knowing. Interpretations that put back to the patient his disturbing state of mind – that is, patient-centred interpretations – may be experienced as a burden rather than feel containing. Disturbed patients, such as those with more borderline personality organisations, alert us to the importance of the interpersonal dimension of the act of interpreting. This kind of patient lacks trust in his objects. He has little or no confidence that his objects will understand him and may therefore feel defensively hostile to a therapist who tries to understand him. Where shame-based experiences dominate the patient's internal world, an interpretation may be destabilising – a potential threat to a fragile self. The safety and consistency of the setting are key aspects of the intervention that such a patient needs. For a long time turning up for the session at the same time each week may be all these patients are able to manage.

The act of interpreting itself communicates to the patient that we have a separate mind, capable of entertaining different thoughts from those held by the patient. This reminder of difference may be intolerable for some patients. Britton (1998) suggests that as the therapist produces interpretations this may be experienced by the patient as a painful, even unbearable, separateness that challenges the illusion of being one and the same with the therapist. Britton is referring here to the difficulties some patients experience with triadic relationships where the interpretation is experienced as the therapist being engaged with her own thoughts – in a couple as it were – that excludes the patient. When we introduce our thoughts, we may be experienced as:

> . . . a father who is either intruding into the patient's innermost self or pulling the patient out of his or her subjective psychic context into one of the analyst's own (Britton, 1998: 49).

A transference interpretation, in particular, introduces us as an external object, separate from the patient and therefore is a reminder to the patient that we are not within the patient's omnipotent sphere of control. Along very similar lines, Kernberg (2000) understands the therapist's interpretative function as representing "the excluded third party". In giving an interpretation, Kernberg suggests that the therapist replicates the role of the Oedipal father in disrupting the pre-Oedipal, symbiotic relationship between infant and mother. The therapist's interpretation is a reflection of the third position, introducing triangulation into the symbiotic nature of transference and countertransference entanglements between patient and therapist:

> When the analysand reflects on his communications and the analyst provides an interpretation, he always bears the name of the father: the outside who breaks the unhindered movement of desire and defence. (Bollas, 1996: 3)

Interpretation does not always assist the therapeutic process. It can also be used defensively by both patient and therapist. The therapist's interpretation and the patient's response to it may be no more than "a means of joint disposal" (Britton, 1998: 94), an intellectual way of reassuring both parties that they are doing the work of therapy when they are, in fact, avoiding something unsettling in the transference. The illusion of understanding may be pursued to defend against the pain of not understanding. Ideas or the construction of a narrative may be used to reassure:

> An interpretation can become a means of seeking security rather than enquiry and its constancy may be more highly valued than its truth (Britton, 1998: 106).

Britton is making a very important observation because it is all too easy to forget the potentially defensive function of the search for understanding.

In our eagerness to restore coherence in our patient's confused and distressing life story, we may use interpretations to fill the gaps in understanding and to foreclose the open-ended, at times tormenting, nature of exploration.

CONCLUSION: THE LIMITS OF INTERPRETATION

As I have repeatedly stressed throughout this chapter, an interpretation is a hypothesis. As such it is our best guess, in light of the knowledge we have, about a patient at any given point in time. I am using the term "knowledge" to provoke since we filter what we hear of the patient's narrative and therefore the knowledge we arrive at through our own personalities, with our own blind spots and no-go areas and through our theoretical allegiances. Meissner suggests that:

> Listening is limited by the conditions of hearing – namely, that our access to the mental life of another is constrained by audible expressions of that subjective experience conveyed by external behaviour. We have no direct or immediate access to the subjectivity of another: we can only read that subjectivity by way of inferring from its external expressions (2000: 326).

Interpretation is a subjective act. It is easy to forget this. We can all get "married to a hypothesis" trying to fit the patient into our ideational mould.

> A good Skinnerian will remind us that the interpreter of psychoanalytic material is on an intermittent reinforcement schedule and that therefore his verbal behaviour and his belief system will be maintained, despite numerous trials, that constitute potential refuters (Meehl, 1994: 31, quoted in Pine, 1998).

In analytic work, the scope for misunderstanding or faulty inferences and hence conclusions is impressive. The more we engage in psychoanalytic work, the more we learn to appreciate that when it comes to matters of the mind nothing can be stated with absolute certainty and that exploration only reveals further questions.

If interpretations are inevitably subjective acts, then how do we know whether our interpretations are correct? Do we assess correctness in relation to whether the interpretation reflects the truth or, as Frosh (1997b) suggests, does its value lie in its effects and not necessarily in its truthfulness? Such questions inevitably lead us to consider whether interpretations lead to a revelation of facts or the creation of a new narrative.

Traditionally the validation of an interpretation has been thought to require the generation of new memories or affects in the patient's free associations thereby amplifying his exploration: the patient runs with the interpretation, as it were. A deepening of affect after an interpretation is often taken as a good indicator that the interpretation is "on the right track" and strikes an emotional chord. If the interpretation falls flat and the patient does not elaborate on it we would note this and remain open to the possibility that we are either on the wrong track or that the patient may not be ready to hear the interpretation.

In analytic work what we take as evidence of confirmation of an interpretation leaves room for considerable debate. The fact that the patient can make use of what we have said is not necessarily evidence of the accuracy of an interpretation. In some cases it may reflect no more than the patient's compliance and wish to please us:

> When there is a desire for agreement from the primary object with a dread of misunderstanding there is an insistent, desperate need for agreement in the analysis and the annihilation of disagreement (Britton, 1998: 57).

It is beyond the scope of this chapter to enter into the kind of debate these questions deserve. They are eloquently discussed by Frosh (1997b). In raising the question, my aim is simply to reiterate that because interpretation is by definition a subjective act, we must proceed cautiously and remain open to the possibility that the patient's agreement or disagreement with it may tell us very little about its correctness and/or helpfulness. It is worth noting that this is a problem shared by all therapeutic approaches, not just psychoanalytic ones.

Not only do we need to be concerned with how we evaluate our interpretations, but we will also do well to ask ourselves whether interpretations are the main vehicle for change. If psychic change is not solely related to the verbal articulation of procedures that have become implicit – as suggested in Chapter 2 – interpretations, whether of a reconstructive or a transference kind, are unlikely to be either the sole, or indeed primary tool, at our disposal to help our patients. Our ways of being with our patients, which are so often implicit and perhaps can never be adequately captured by language, may present the patient with a new experience of being with another that contributes to a reworking of internal expectations of self and other and may lead to subtle, yet ultimately significant, changes at the level of implicit relational procedures. These unquantifiable, hard-to-teach qualitative aspects of the therapeutic process, owing as much to therapeutic style and personality as to technique, may prove to be important variables determining outcome.

FURTHER READING

Casement, P. (1985) *On Learning from the Patient*. London: Routledge.

6

DEFENCES AND RESISTANCE

At the core of all psychoanalytic theories we find the notion that development cannot occur without a measure of psychic pain or anxiety.[1] A common thread cutting across the different schools of psychoanalysis is the abiding concern to understand the nature of the patient's anxiety and how the patient copes with it. In this chapter, we will explore the psychoanalytic perspectives on anxiety and the defence mechanisms deployed to manage it. We will also address the manifestation of defences in the psychotherapeutic situation, that is, resistance.

PSYCHOANALYTIC PERSPECTIVES ON ANXIETY

Freud placed the experience of anxiety at the core of our psychic functioning – the defining psychic burden of a human being. Because of the existence of the life and death instincts and their unavoidable conflict, Freud emphasised the inevitability of anxiety.

Freud put forward two theories of anxiety. In his first theory he understood anxiety as a reaction to the build up of instinctual tensions. Anxiety was not connected to specific ideas or thoughts that were felt to be dangerous, but was said to result from an accumulation of sexual energy as a consequence of sexual abstinence. This situation, in turn, was said to give rise to unpleasure. This view was consonant with the drive model (see Chapter 1) that hypothesised an inherent motivation towards the discharge of instinctual tensions.

In 1926, Freud put forward his second theory of anxiety. Here he described anxiety acting as a danger signal to the ego, alerting it to the occurrence of

---

[1] These two terms are often used interchangeably in psychoanalysis and I shall also use them interchangeably throughout this chapter.

a trauma or an otherwise "danger" situation (e.g. separation from, or loss of, a loved object). The role of trauma becomes important in Freud's second theory such that anxiety is the outcome of a traumatic state in which the ego feels helpless. In this model, anxiety has a signalling function for real or imagined danger, protecting the ego from being overwhelmed. *Signal anxiety* – as it is referred to because its function is to signal a danger situation within the ego – defends against *automatic anxiety*, that is, a primitive anxiety resulting from fear of total disintegration. It is in the context of this second theory that we encounter Freud's object-relational perspective as he discusses infantile danger situations, including fear of loss of the object or loss of love, castration and superego condemnation, as well as loss or fragmentation of the self.

Freudians formulate anxiety within the structural model of the mind identifying particular types of anxiety originating from either the id or superego. *Superego anxiety* involves fear of punishment for unacceptable sexual, aggressive or dependent strivings. *Id anxiety* involves the fear of loss of control of aggressive or sexual impulses. Nowadays conflicts, and hence anxiety, are also understood to result from frustrated needs or deficits. Anxiety is said to be triggered not only by the instinctual drives per se when they threaten psychic equilibrium, but also by the anticipated outcome of the expression of a given feeling or impulse (e.g. fear of punishment).

Klein took Freud's thinking further by arguing not only as he had done that anxiety is inevitable but also that it is present from the very beginning of life. By postulating the death instinct (i.e. the hypothesised presence of innate destructiveness) as active from birth, Klein provides for the original presence of an intrapsychic conflict that already activates defensive mechanisms during the first half of the first year so as to protect the infant from intolerable states of anxiety.

Although both Freud and Klein devoted attention to defences as mechanisms set in place to manage the experience of anxiety, it was Klein who elaborated most richly on the content of anxiety. She viewed anxiety, in moderation, as the driving force of development. Unlike Freud, Klein posited the existence of a rudimentary organising mental agency, that is, an ego, in the newborn. This hypothesis allowed her to develop her ideas on the nature of anxiety; it was the existence of an ego from birth that made it possible for her to suggest that the ego could identify danger situations giving rise to anxiety and therefore could institute primitive defences to protect itself.

Consistent with her notion of psychic positions (see Chapter 1), Klein differentiated between persecutory and depressive anxieties. She believed that the baby is born with a fear of annihilation, a terror of non-existence.[2] Annihilation anxiety refers to a terror that the self will be overwhelmed or engulfed by another or cease to exist altogether. This kind of primitive anxiety was said to be typical of the paranoid-schizoid position. This position, or mental state, is characterised by a predominance of anxiety based on anticipated fear of retaliation, that is, *persecutory anxieties*. In the grip of such anxieties, we are dominated by feelings of extreme fear and insecurity associated with a belief in a "bad" agency outside the self whose intention is to cause us harm, hence the paranoid quality of this type of anxiety. These primitive and terrifying anxieties result from the effects of the death instinct – a concept that has been largely retained within Kleinian theory.

The depressive position heralds the transformation of persecutory anxieties into a qualitatively different kind, namely, *depressive anxieties*. As the baby realises that the "good" and the "bad" object are one and the same, she is faced with the new experience of ambivalent feelings that give rise to a disturbing internal world now dominated by feelings of guilt. Depressive anxieties reflect concern for the good object and fear of its loss resulting from one's real and/or phantasised attacks when in the grip of persecutory anxieties. Depressive anxieties are not about a self-centred concern as a result of the loss of the object. Rather, they reflect a concern for the state of the object thus giving way to reparative impulses.

The capacity to bear depressive anxieties, according to Kleinians, represents a major developmental achievement and is linked with the capacity to be creative as it spurs us towards reparation. Depressive anxieties that cannot be borne leave us overwhelmed by feelings of guilt and despair as the phantasised and/or real damage done to the object is felt to be beyond repair. We are then left in a state of being "unforgiven", as it were, and experience persecutory guilt, which can then plunge us back into persecutory anxieties.

THE ORIGINS OF DEFENCES

Anxiety is an inevitable part of life but too much anxiety is disabling. One of the most crucial capacities that we need to acquire early on is how to manage anxiety and other strong affects. Our early experiences with caregivers are crucial to the development of a capacity to regulate our affective experiences. Nowadays the regulation of affects is understood to be first mediated by the parental figures the child interacts with in

---

[2]This anxiety was vividly captured by Bion's notion of "nameless dread".

early life (Fonagy *et al.*, 2002). Anxiety, we could thus say, is managed, to begin with, through the earliest relationships with significant others. The presence of an emotionally responsive figure who can process or digest the baby's most primitive anxieties provides the building blocks for a functioning affective regulatory system. The absence of such a figure contributes to the development of potentially enduring systems of defence set up to manage intolerable affective states.

Much of the early analytic literature, with the notable exception of the work of Anna Freud, portrayed a rather static view of defences. Within Freudian theory defences are viewed from a predominately intrapsychic perspective such that they exist so as to deal with an internal conflict. Developmentalists and attachment theorists have since introduced a much-needed developmental dimension. They have contributed to a shift in focus away from an understanding of defences as responses to internal conflict, emphasising instead the origins of defences in the earliest interactions with others. This has allowed defences to be viewed as responses or adaptations to recurring interpersonal conflicts.

Two-person processes are central to an understanding of some defences. Relational models view defences as protective shields that represent attempts – however misguided or pathological – to manage intrapsychic *and* interpersonal conflicts, often in the face of real environmental failures. Lyons-Ruth (1999) suggests, for example, that a particular character stance or defensive strategy may constitute an aspect of a broader interpersonal arrangement that has operated over a significant period of the patient's life. Such an understanding has important clinical implications since it encourages us to approach defences as adaptations to particular interpersonal configurations, which may have become internalised as procedures for being-with-others. These "adaptations" can be explored in therapy as the patient deploys various defensive configurations to manage his relationship with us, that is, in the transference.

Defences are processes that distort or exclude information or affective experiences with a particular emphasis on the formation and maintenance of multiple inconsistent models of relational experience. For example, if in early life the child's anger invites a hostile attack from the parent, angry feelings may be excluded from the child's emotional repertoire. Exclusion of such negative affects from interaction, in turn, most likely precludes an opportunity for the affects to be elaborated and for the subsequent understanding of, say, anger-related behaviour, affects and experience.

Paul was twenty-four when he was referred for therapy. He had two previous hospital admissions following suicide attempts. Both his attempts had been preceded by the end of a relationship.

Paul described a very unsettled early life: his mother died when he was aged four, and he was left in the care of his father and his stepmother. His father was described as a hard, unemotional man who was prone to violent outbursts, typically when under the influence of alcohol. Paul remembered little about his childhood except for his father's outbursts and the various prohibitions and restrictions imposed by his father. He had felt humiliated by his father who had repeatedly told him that he should stand up for himself and "be more of a man". He had been a late developer physically, and his small build had been the source of teasing at school by peers. His school years had therefore also been a lonely and painful experience as he was bullied and he found it difficult to ask for help from his teachers.

At the age of nineteen Paul started to inject heroin and found a place for himself in a community of drug addicts. He referred to this group as his "only family". He had become involved in a lot of petty crimes as a way of supporting his habit and that of his various girlfriends. He had been in a rehabilitation programme by the time he started therapy and had been off drugs for the preceding year. Without drugs Paul had sunk into depression.

Paul was subservient in his relationships. He would go to any lengths to please another person even if the requests were, objectively speaking, unreasonable or placed him at risk. In the therapy he was equally compliant. Whatever I said he agreed with, but his responses were so vague that it was clear that he had not made any emotional connection with what I had said. If I attempted to speak to him about this, Paul would become more anxious, and was keen to reassure me that he valued the opportunity to talk. It felt impossible to get through to him. His fear of being punished or abandoned was so great that there was a complete embargo on the expression of any ambivalence, disappointment or frustration of any kind. He appeared to be relating to me as an object that would punish him for disagreeing with me. Paul had no idea about his own mind, as he was mostly preoccupied with the mind of his father/object whom he had experienced as unpredictable and violent towards him. To manage such an internal object Paul had developed a compliant self that acquiesced and denied any of his own emotions or he managed them through drug taking. This was his main interpersonal defence denuding him of any opportunity to feel his feelings and so making him vulnerable to exploitation, depression and suicide attempts.

Some defences are developmentally necessary if the individual is to survive difficult early experiences. Alvarez (1992) has eloquently, and poignantly, elaborated this position through her work with very disturbed children. She argues for a concept of "overcoming" to complement the classical notion of defences, denoting the importance of considering where the patient is coming from (i.e. the notion of deficit) and where he may yet have to reach in terms of his psychic organisation. In discussing various defences, Alvarez evocatively asks, "Do we need lifelines only to escape death, or also to preserve life?" (1992: 112). This stance encourages us to consider when we work with patients who may have been deprived or traumatised not only what their defences seek to avoid, but also what psychic life they allow. The defence may, in some instances, be best conceived as a developmental achievement, a step towards greater integration rather than a structure that stands in the way of development. Taking the example of obsessional defences, Alvarez argues that we need to distinguish an obsessional defence used to control an object perceived to be separate from its use to achieve some order in a highly unpredictable world. Using the metaphor of a house to refer to psychic organisation, Alvarez suggests:

> In cases where the house isn't yet built, what may look like an attempt to throw somebody out of the house – to project their suffering infantile part into someone else – may really be a desperate attempt to find a house anywhere (1992: 114).

Although projection is a defence, the patient's projection alerts us to a seed of hope in the patient that we might be willing to receive the projection, that is, that we are receptive to him. Alvarez's views resonate with the thinking of Anna Freud and that of some Contemporary Freudians. For example, Sandler distinguishes between defences *against* painful realities and defences *towards*, which exist in order to gain or maintain a good feeling of security or safety.

In approaching defences, we are respectful of the patient's need for them and the psychic implications of being denuded of his defences. Interpreting defences requires that we point out to the patient that we understand how the defences may have helped him to survive and develop even if they now stand in the way of further growth. Indeed, nowadays defences are no longer thought of simply as a sign of resistance that has to be worked through in psychotherapy to access the so-called real content. Rather, they are viewed as a reflection of the patient's mode of coping in relation to his internal world. Defences are approached in terms of their so-called "costs and benefits", sometimes even as creative solutions to internal psychic dramas, reactive to the experience of trauma (see for example Sinason, 2002).

THE FUNCTIONS OF DEFENCE

Freud showed us how we pretend, deceive and conceal in order to keep from ourselves and from others the urges, wishes and needs that constantly pressure us. It was his daughter, Anna Freud (1936), who spelt out in detail how we try to live with all the conflicting impulses Freud had identified: namely, how the vigilant ego and superego work both to allow and to disallow the expression of the id's demands. The mechanisms of defence were seen to be like lifelong habitual ways of responding to perceived danger.

Whether we approach defences as attempts to manage intrapsychic or interpersonal conflicts, they always exist to protect us from perceived danger and the ensuing psychic pain. Defences are mobilised against forbidden impulses and painful affective states – not just anxiety, even though this is often the underlying subjective experience. Defences falsify, negate or distort reality in order to avoid situations experienced as dangerous. They act primarily to obliterate awareness to ensure that anxiety does not break through into consciousness.

Defences are a function of the ego. As we have seen in Chapter 1, large parts of the ego are in fact unconscious. Defences are part of the process rather than the context of mental activity, that is, they are also unconscious. Occasionally we decide that we want to avoid particular thoughts and so implement avoidance strategies quite consciously. For the most part, however, defences are brought into play without any conscious will.

All defences represent ways in which meaning can be distorted, for example, through denial, avoidance or transforming ideas and their associated affect. Vaillant (1971) suggests that defences can alter our perception of ourselves, of others, of ideas or feelings. We have many devices at our disposal that allow us to avoid disturbing ideas, feelings or thoughts. Knapp helpfully divides these into four categories:

- We may exclude the feeling or thought from consciousness altogether (e.g. as in repression).
- We may admit the disturbing feeling or thought but only after it has undergone transformation by being disguised (e.g. as in sublimation).
- We may consciously admit the feeling or thought but it is detached from its emotional meaning (e.g. as in intellectualisation).
- We may substitute one feeling or thought for another (e.g. as in reaction formation).
- We may distort or confuse our perception of ourselves or others thus fundamentally altering our perception of external and internal reality (e.g. as in splitting).

Defences have often been likened to a kind of psychic skin that allows us to manage the psychic blows that are an inevitable part of life. One of their functions is indeed to maintain psychic equilibrium. Defences can also be restitutive of self-esteem. Take, for example, the delusional beliefs of the patient who thinks he is Jesus Christ. The delusion could be said to defensively allow the patient to believe that he is special, whereas, as himself, he would feel worthless.

Just as we cannot exist without physical skin, we cannot exist without psychic skin. Although we all need defences, we can use defences too rigidly or too exclusively too much of the time. Habitual defences can harden into what Reich (1928) called the "character armour". When defences are used rigidly or excessively they prevent us from becoming aware of what troubles us and so prevent us from developing a relationship with both our internal and external reality. From a clinical point of view it is therefore never a question of *whether* someone uses defences since we all do, but of whether the defences are used inflexibly and rigidly within the overall structure of the personality.

TYPES OF DEFENCES

In *Inhibition, Symptoms and Anxiety*, Freud (1926) established the central role of anxiety and conflict in psychopathology. He also broadened the concept of defence. Prior to 1926, Freud had conceived of defence as synonymous with repression – a kind of pushing away from consciousness of disturbing thoughts or feelings. In 1926, he came to understand repression to be one of many defence mechanisms.

Any behaviour or feeling[3] can be used defensively, that is, whatever allows for an alleviation of psychic pain belongs under the heading of defence. Brenner (1982) suggests that "modes of defence are as diverse as psychic life itself". It is the psychic function of a behaviour or feeling that determines whether it is being used defensively, for example, whether it protects self-esteem.

Defences are often used to manage interpersonal anxiety generated, for instance, by a fear of being taken over or controlled by the other or of becoming too intimate. Such *object-related defences*, are once again, varied. For example, some people may use distancing to protect themselves from intimacy; others may become obstinate as a way of controlling others and others still may become passive as a way of discharging hostility towards other people.

---

[3]For example, someone may feel sad when they are in fact angry.

As we have seen, the core function of defences is to ward off threatening psychic impulses or anxiety. The ego can use defensively any perception or alteration of awareness, which minimises distress. There are defences that destroy or attack a mental process and leave the patient bereft of his own mental capacities (e.g. attacks on thinking as a defence against understanding something painful) and defences that destroy a mental representation (e.g. splitting the representation of a significant other reducing them to a part object). Let us look at an example of each.

When I first assessed *Dave* he rather blandly described everything in his life as "Going OK". He had sought therapy because his doctor had referred him as he was suffering from irritable bowel syndrome. He came across as being disconnected from his feelings. His affect was predominantly flat.

As a child Dave had suffered a traumatic experience: aged six he had been left at home alone by his parents when the house was broken into by burglars. He had got up thinking his parents were back. When the burglars saw him they tied him up and blindfolded him. A year after this trauma, Dave's parents separated. Dave experienced problems with bed wetting and stammering but he told me that these had resolved by the age of fourteen though he still occasionally stammered as an adult.

The most striking aspect of Dave's narrative was the matter-of-fact manner in which he related his traumatic experience when aged six. Listening to his story about the break-in, I was puzzled about why his parents had left him at home alone at such a young age. When I asked about this, Dave looked stunned. His response struck me as very significant as it felt as though he had never allowed himself to even entertain any thoughts about his parents' possible neglect of him, which had placed him at risk.

At first Dave denied that his parents were in any way to blame. He told me that they worked hard as they came from a socio-economically deprived background and that they were often out working late. He came across as angry with me for insinuating, as he perceived it, that his parents had not behaved appropriately. It was only a few sessions into the therapy that Dave mentioned, in a different context, that his mother had never been happy in the marriage and that she had affairs whilst his father was out at work. It later emerged that his mother had been out visiting her lover the night Dave was attacked by the burglars, leaving Dave alone at home, whilst his father had been out working. This affair had led to his parents' eventual separation.

Over time, we came to understand how Dave had blocked out of his mind any connection between the terrible experience he had been subjected to and his mother's neglect of him. These thoughts were forbidden as they gave rise to feelings of rejection and anger that Dave could not manage. This defence had profoundly altered Dave's relationship to his own feelings and thoughts. He approached conflictual situations by passively retreating into himself and instead somatised psychic pain. This somatisation located his distress in the body and precluded a mental representation of his psychic distress. One consequence of this was that Dave was unable to think for himself about himself: he presented as 'switched off', such that his overall engagement with life lacked vitality.

Aleda was a borderline patient who had been in therapy with me for several months. She related a painful history of abuse and neglect both by her parents and during various periods of time spent in institutional care. She had experienced many changes in carers and had been abused by the very people meant to care for her. Her mistrust of others was profound. This was very apparent in her relationship to me. She struggled to allow herself to become in any way dependent on me and was suspicious of my intentions; she thought that I was only concerned with my career progression and if I made a transference interpretation she thought this was further evidence of my self-obsession. She rubbished any attempt to help her, reducing me to a useless therapist she simply did not need. Aleda was determined, for defensive reasons, to relate to me as a "bad", useless object. This way she could dispense with me in her mind as someone she did not need, thereby protecting herself from feelings of dependency, which could put her at the risk of being abused again by someone she trusted. In other words, Aleda used splitting as a defence and in doing so destroyed a mental representation of me as a therapist with both "good" and "bad" aspects reducing me instead, in her mind, to a wholly bad object.

Defences can be divided according to whether they are characterological or situational. *Characterological defences* denote relatively constant defensive procedures that occur in most situations. These tend to be defences that are so over-used that they become an integral part of the fabric of the personality. Aleda's defences, we might say, are characterological. Characterological defences can be further subdivided according to their level of psychic organisation, namely, neurotic, borderline or psychotic (see Chapter 4). Where the defence is characterological more resistance to change is typically encountered. These more entrenched defences are commonly observed in patients with personality disorders. By contrast, a *situational defence* may arise only in response to a particular context; its use does not dominate the personality. For example, at times of stress we may resort to a particular defensive strategy that would not otherwise be characteristic of our usual way of being.

Although there is no research evidence to support that defences follow a definitive path paralleling development, there is widespread consensus that different defences reflect either primitive or more progressively mature processes, or if you like, more integrated personality organisations. Indeed, it is often through assessing a patient's defences that we gain insight into the patient's overall level of personality organisation, which has important implications for the kind of psychotherapy the patient is most likely to manage. For example, extensive use of projection and splitting would indicate a more disorganised, probably borderline or psychotic personality organisation. Such a patient may be able to use a psychoanalytic approach but may require other services to also be involved (e.g. psychiatry).

Within the Freudian model defences are only thought possible when there is some rudimentary ego, that is, not from birth. Freud therefore focused primarily on what we refer to as *neurotic defences*. The latter deal with internal boundaries such as conflict between the ego and id (see Table 6.1). The Kleinians, however, believe that the child is born with some ego and therefore they argue that it is possible to speak of primitive defences present from birth (see Chapter 1). *Primitive defences* typically concern the boundary between the self and the external world or others. They reflect a lack of appreciation or tolerance of the separateness and constancy of the world outside of the self. Typically, they operate in a more global way. Primitive defences are characteristic of the paranoid-schizoid position. According to Klein, the baby's mind is prone to fragment as a result of the defences operative at this early stage, which protect him from his own aggression projected outwards into the world. Denial, omnipotent control, idealisation, projection and splitting (see Table 6.1) protect the ego from conflicts by means of dissociation or actively keeping apart contradictory experiences of the self and significant others – often of the self in relationship with significant others.

I am deliberately not devoting much space to a detailed discussion of the various defensive mechanisms. This is because labelling a defence with psychoanalytic terminology often stands in the way of formulating individually the very unique defensive creations our patients present with. It is far more useful clinically to describe in plain language what

Table **6.1**   Common defence mechanisms

Primitive defences

- **Denial** refers to the obliteration of perception rather than memories.
- **Splitting** aims to keep apart two, usually opposing feelings/thoughts.
- **Dissociation** allows an essentially undisguised idea to be placed in a split-off context so that it can be disavowed by the self.
- **Projection** involves attributing some aspect of oneself or a feeling to another person.
- **Introjection** is the process of attributing an aspect of another person to oneself.
- **Projective identification** involves attributing states of mind to another person and relating to them as if they embodied the projection. The interactional force of this dynamic can result in the recipient acting in a manner congruent with the projection. It involves splitting of the object or ego. The split can be coherent (e.g. good vs bad) or fragmenting.
- **Omnipotence** involves the illusion of unlimited power, with no awareness that others have a separate locus of control.
- **Idealisation** involves the conviction that another person to whom one can become attached is omnipotent and benevolent.
- **Manic defences** are a group of primitive defences distinguished by their aim of denying depressive anxiety and guilt. The manic defence relies on denial, contempt, triumph, omnipotent restitution and obsessive-compulsive attempts to undo phantasised attacks.

Neurotic defences

- **Repression** refers to an unconsciously purposeful forgetting. It is the defensive use of memory.
- **Displacement** is the process of substituting one object/person for another.
- **Reaction formation** transforms a disturbing idea into its opposite.
- **Undoing** uses designated actions or thoughts to neutralise something that was said or done.
- **Reversal** involves switching one's position from subject to object or vice versa.
- **Isolation** involves severing the connection between feeling and knowing.
- **Intellectualisation** involves talking about feelings in an emotionally disconnected manner (it is a higher-order version of isolation).
- **Conversion** transforms psychic conflict into somatic symptoms.
- **Acting out** involves discharging into action a disturbing feeling so as to avoid thinking about it.
- **Rationalisation** involves turning something unacceptable into something acceptable.
- **Sublimation** involves directing a forbidden impulse towards a typically socially acceptable end (the original impulse vanishes because its energy is withdrawn in favour of cathexis of its substitute).

the patient is trying to do and why they need to do it than to use the shorthand of labels. For the sake of information, I have nevertheless briefly summarised the most commonly referred to mechanisms of defence in Table 6.1. However, I would like to devote some time to discussing *projection and projective identification* in more detail since they refer to key aspects of psychic functioning that are very helpful clinically and over which there often exists some confusion.

Klein (1946) contributed to our understanding of interpersonal defences by studying in detail the function of projective mechanisms. *Projection* is a prominent feature of all relationships. In the earliest phases of development it is suggested that the baby communicates primarily through projection and that the good enough mother acts as a container for the baby's projections, emotionally digesting them for the baby and lending them meaning. Projection refers therefore to a primitive but not in and of itself an abnormal mode of communication. It underlies our capacity for empathy: it is because of the capacity to project that we can imagine ourselves in another's predicament. Projection may also be understood as a means of communicating our internal state to another or to forcefully evacuate unbearable feelings into another by literally depositing them in the other who then acts as a "container", for example, the patient who describes a traumatic experience with no affect but leaves us feeling very saddened. Many contemporary practitioners understand that the patient may need to split off and project into them unbearable feelings that rather than be immediately interpreted need, instead, to be contained by the therapist on the patient's behalf.

During projection what is inside is misunderstood as originating from outside of the self and is attributed to another person/source. It was Klein's insight that we not only project feelings but also parts of the self thus leading to serious distortions of the recipient of the projection. Projective mechanisms allow us to forcefully allocate, in phantasy, aspects of the self to the object. It creates the phantasy that we can control the object thus also achieving control over externalised aspects of the self. Projection is the underlying mechanism that makes transference possible, as we shall see in the next chapter.

As a child, Martha had been brought up in a very academic family. Both her parents had been academics who expected a lot of Martha: her adolescence was spent working hard for exams and scholarships which she successfully achieved. On those rare occasions when she failed to get the top marks, she recalled feeling humiliated by her father's harsh disapproval.

As an adult, Martha was emotionally brittle and thin skinned. She was deeply insecure even though she was an attractive, intelligent woman who had achieved much in her professional career. She covered up her insecurity by retreating into a contemptuous state of mind from which she viewed those around her as in some way lacking or incompetent. For example, at work she criticised colleagues for not being up to scratch. In her close relationships she seesawed between idealising her friends and bemoaning their disrespect for her needs. She could be very intolerant of others and of any weakness in herself.

Martha was in relationship with a man several years her senior who was her intellectual match but in many respects he was disorganised and incapable of constructively harnessing his potential. He had been unemployed for the duration of their relationship and Martha carried the financial burden. Whilst she complained bitterly about him and blamed him for various problems in their relationship, it was also clear that Martha could not contemplate leaving him. He had become in her mind a repository for the disorganised, incompetent, messy parts of her that she had projected into him. As long as he personified these unacceptable qualities she could shine in her competence against the background of his messy, disorganised self and so reassure her critical internal objects.

Klein and her followers have elaborated the notion of projection and speak of *projective identification*. Klein (1957) understood projective identification as an unconscious infantile phantasy that allowed the baby to project her persecutory experiences by splitting them from her self-representation and making them part of her perception of a part object. Projection and projective identification are often used interchangeably and effectively describe the same underlying process. However, the notion of projective identification clarifies more explicitly the interactional process underpinning projection. In describing splitting mechanisms, Klein showed how splitting is invariably accompanied by another defensive manoeuvre, namely, projection. The latter allows for the split-off feeling to be located outside of the self and omnipotently forced *into* the recipient. The idea that we project *into* another person shows how Klein believed that the person who is projecting comes to believe that the recipient, in turn, may actually contain the disowned aspects of himself, that is, the recipient becomes identified, in the projector's mind, with the projection. The recipient unwittingly becomes an active participant in the process by identifying with the projection and enacting what has been projected. Spillius (1994) refers to *evocatory projective identification* to explain instances in which the recipient of the projective identification is under pressure to have feelings in line with the projector's phantasies (see Table 6.2).

Table 6.2   The sequence of projective identification

- The patient experiences painful feelings that cannot be managed.
- To protect himself from these painful feelings the patient, in phantasy (i.e. unconsciously) projects these feelings into another person and the recipient is identified in the patient's mind with these split-off feelings or attributes.
- There is an interactional pressure arising from the patient with the unconscious aim of making the other person experience these feelings instead of the self.
- If the patient is successful in his projection, and the recipient is not alert to this process, an affective resonance is created in the recipient whose feelings may take on a "sameness" based on identification.

Nowadays, we not only speak of defence mechanisms but also of *defensive or pathological organisations*. This denotes a more sophisticated conceptualisation of complex *systems* of defence. Pathological organisations are "characterised by extremely unyielding defences that function to help the patient avoid anxiety by avoiding contact with other people" (Steiner, 1992: 2). Their aim is to maintain an emotional homeostasis. They are referred to as "organisations"[4] to denote the way in which the patient's personality becomes organised around quite specific – and usually destructive – object relationships. Patients who deploy pathological organisations need to subdue emotional life; therapy with such patients often reaches an impasse as the therapist comes up against the rigid defensive structure and may even become in some way co-opted into the defensive system. It is beyond the scope of this chapter to examine in detail the implications of pathological organisations for clinical practice. This involves work with a very challenging group of patients and deserves the thorough exploration that can be found in Steiner's (1993) book *Psychic Retreats*.

WORKING WITH DEFENCE

Faced with the experience of anxiety three psychic options are open to us. Each one is associated with a different subjective experience of anxiety and reflects different levels of psychic organisation (see Chapter 4).

- We can cope with the anxiety by consciously addressing its source and try to resolve it.
- We can defend against the anxiety.
- We can break down if the anxiety is overwhelming and defences fail.

---

[4]What is being described here is what other therapists might describe as "character".

One of our primary goals is to identify the nature of the patient's psychic pain at any given point in a session and how he manages this. In the clinical situation, we formulate the patient's use of defences gradually. We start by naming the expression and the nature of his anxiety. The experience of anxiety is highly idiosyncratic from a phenomenological point of view. One patient's palpitations are another's obsessive ruminations. Both states, one subjectively located in the body, the other in the mind, denote a state of anxiety. Some patients describe their anxiety as a state of physical and/or psychic tension. Usually these patients reveal a fairly high level of functioning with some awareness, however vague, of the source of their anxiety – at the very least, an awareness of a likely psychological origin. Others channel anxiety primarily or exclusively into the body, presenting with a variety of physical symptoms that are not linked with what may be happening in their own minds. The anxiety is instead unconsciously located in the body (e.g. frequent unexplained headaches, diarrhoea). Such patients may require considerable preparatory work to enable them to make connections between their psychic anxiety and its somatic manifestations. Finally, there are those patients who present with more severe disruptions in their overall functioning as a result of their anxiety. The anxiety appears to cause a disruption in thinking, such that they may lose track of their thoughts, dissociate or discharge their internal affective states impulsively into action. These patients display significant ego fragility and require very careful consideration by us of what they can bear to know about their anxiety. In approaching the interpretation of defences, a very important consideration is therefore what the patient can bear to know (see Table 6.3).

In order to make an interpretation, Malan (1979) suggests that it is important to identify the three corners of what he calls the "triangle of conflict", namely the feeling or impulse that is defended against, the way it is defended and the anxiety it would otherwise give rise to were it not for the operation of defences. This is a very clear and helpful model

Table 6.3   Guidelines for working with defences

- Identify the patient's core pain/anxiety in relation to its trigger.
- Ask yourself what the patient is capable of managing.
- Remember that defences have both adaptive and maladaptive functions.
- Formulate the consequences for the patient of not using defences.
- Think developmentally: consider the patient's level of personality organisation (neurotic/borderline/psychotic).
- Note the flexibility or rigidity of defences and the implications of this for therapy.
- Interpret to the patient the "why and how" of their defensive operations but avoid using jargon.

for conceptualising conflict and I shall therefore use it as the basis for approaching the interpretation of defences.

Stage 1: Identifying the Hidden Feeling/Impulse

Anxiety emerges in response to a **feeling or impulse** that gives rise to conflict. The patient's ability to tolerate consciously the existence of particular feelings within himself will determine whether the emergence of the feeling will give rise to anxiety that is so intolerable that defences need to be instituted or whether this can be named and addressed. In thinking about anxiety, therefore, we need to first consider the patient's capacity to freely access their affective experience and any limitations in this respect.

Stage 2: Identifying the Hidden Anxiety or Core Pain

Once we have identified the feeling that is problematic and that the patient needs to somehow disavow, we can consider the nature of the **anxiety or psychic pain** it gives rise to and whether there is any evidence that the patient can tolerate the conscious experience of the associated anxiety. In other words, we are concerned with assessing the nature of the anxiety in the context of the patient's ego-adaptive capacities (see Chapter 4). One of our aims is to identify whether the anxiety is realistic, neurotic or psychotic. To a large extent, these are false dichotomies as anxiety can emerge in response to a real event that is traumatic, but the way in which it is idiosyncratically elaborated may reflect one patient's neurotic conflicts and another's psychotic interpretation of the same traumatic event. For example, one of my patients who had been involved in a car accident caused by a drunk driver became anxious when crossing roads (a realistic anxiety given her accident) but also developed paranoid symptoms in response to this actual trauma. She became suspicious of everyone, accusing me of being in a conspiracy with her solicitor.

Stage 3: Identifying the Defence(s)

If there is no tolerance for the conscious experience of anxiety the next stage involves identifying the strategy used by the patient to circumvent the associated psychic pain, that is, we need to identify the type of *defences* used. This will involve assessing whether the defences are ego-syntonic or ego-dystonic. If they are ego-syntonic, they will be harder to relinquish as the therapist will be experienced as the one disturbing or attacking an internal psychic balance, however precarious. If the defence is itself ego-dystonic, it is experienced as aversive or problematic by the patient who is often internally motivated to be relieved not only of his problem but also of the defensive solution. For example, some obsessional defences (e.g. extensive rituals) can be experienced as ego-dystonic as they severely restrict the patient in their day-to-day life and thus motivate the patient to seek help.

As we approach defences we aim to establish in our formulations whether the defences are directed internally against the awareness of threatening thoughts and feelings or externally against intimacy with others. Often they serve both functions. We remain mindful that defences exist for a good reason and hence we approach them sensitively, with due respect for the patient's need to protect himself. For example, when working with patients who dismiss attachments and detach themselves from inner experience, it will be important to understand their disavowal of emotion not just as a resistance, but also as a vital protective device. For such patients, intimacy is felt to be dangerous and the self-organisation often revolves around not expressing emotions.

In psychotherapy we explore defences as they manifest themselves in the patient's free associations, also paying attention to the way we can be woven into the patient's worries. Not uncommonly, we are experienced as the person attacking the defensive structure and we pose a threat to the patient's attempts to institute defences to protect himself.

> Lisa was in her early thirties, a successful professional woman who came into therapy because of an inability to establish an intimate relationship. She related a painful early history of being "passed around" professional carers as her parents travelled extensively. As she was growing up she had experienced her parents as very demanding of her. She had achieved academically and was the perfect hostess, yet she found intimate relationships, especially with men, very difficult. She had only managed to sustain one sexual relationship whilst at university but since then she had remained single.
>
> Lisa approached therapy dutifully and with precision. She was exactly on time and even a few minutes' lateness would give rise to self-reproach. She was keen to "do it right" and in so doing she constrained the therapeutic space. I soon became aware of "no-go" areas, especially in relation to her sexuality. She told me that she was wary of psychoanalysis because it was "obsessed with sex" and that whilst she recognised that she had some difficulties in "that area", she maintained that her concerns were

not sexual ones. She had, however, intimated a strong attraction towards a female colleague but had quickly moved away from that as the idea of homosexuality repulsed her. She also skirted around the issue of her weight, tentatively suggesting she could do with losing a few pounds but assuring me that she was not bothered by her weight even though she was in fact quite overweight.

In one particular session, Lisa spontaneously brought up the question of dieting. Her mother had suggested that she should go to a health farm. Lisa had felt incensed by this suggestion feeling that her mother had bought into the "whole feminine trap". I commented that perhaps Lisa also worried about her weight but that she feared raising it in her own mind and in the session as it might open the proverbial "can of worms" that would lead us to think about her sexuality, something she wanted to avoid doing. Lisa, who was otherwise usually restrained in her manner, responded angrily towards me. She felt that weight and sexuality were my agenda. She said that I had let her down and that I was now imposing what I thought she should be working on. I could feel Lisa's pain behind her anger. I tried to approach this by acknowledging that my words had felt like a puncture and had left her feeling raw and exposed. Lisa' denial of any problem with her sexuality was a way of protecting herself from the anxiety her own sexual impulses elicited. My interpretation set me up in her mind as the enemy invading a very private space that she was afraid to explore and that she did not want to think about.

In some cases we may have a sense of how the patient is defending himself but be less sure as to what he is defending himself against. In these situations it may be prudent to take up the defence before that which is being defended against. For example, if the patient suppresses tears in a session, we begin by noting this before moving on to wondering about why he may need to do this. This is what is referred to as interpreting from surface to depth or from ego to id (Greenson, 1967). Generally speaking, this approach is very helpful as it gradually paves the way for the patient to explore defences and their function in his psychic economy.

Stage 4: Taking up Defences in the Transference

Our formulation of the triangle of conflict would be incomplete without attention to the way in which our patients use us in order to avoid anxiety. The use of primitive (i.e. in terms of ego development) defences makes itself known quite rapidly in the form of a strong countertransference. According to Joseph (1981), the more the patient relies on primitive defence mechanisms, the more we are likely to be unconsciously recruited in the maintenance of defences. She refers in particular to the unconscious manipulation by projection where we may collude with the patient's projection and be drawn into an enactment.

Joseph suggests that the patient who relies primarily on primitive defences will probably be experienced by us as in some way intrusive as he tries to co-opt us, unconsciously, into his defensive structure. We need to remain alert to these kinds of interactional pressures, which are likely to make us feel in some way uncomfortable.

Stage 5: Making an Interpretation

To make an interpretation we identify in our own mind the three corners of the triangle and the use the patient may be making of us. This is not always shared with the patient all at once because patients resist the broadening range of their consciousness and may therefore experience interpretations as a threat to their control and identity. Interpretations need to reflect back an understanding of the benefits and cost of defences. Such an acknowledgement will help shift the patient from resistance to change allowing him to forge an alliance with us in working against the defensive structure.

RESISTANCE

In our work, we will encounter varying degrees of resistance in our patients to experiencing and thinking about certain feelings or thoughts or states of mind. The patient will deploy a range of defensive manoeuvres to this end explaining, for example, missing a session as "just forgetfulness". Yet, forgetting is not a passive process, that is, forgetting is dynamically motivated. The patient who "forgets" to come to his session may have forgotten because he wishes to avoid thinking about his problems even though he may not be consciously aware of this.[5]

To understand resistance we need to think about the different, and all too often conflicting, motivations that lie beneath the patient's resolve to seek help. In other words, we need to consider the patient's relationship to help and its internal meaning. Suffering often acts as a spur to seeking help, but not invariably. For every wish to be helped we often find the

---

[5]Such motivated forgetting is no longer a controversial notion. Even cognitive psychologists now focus on "inhibitory processes", such as cognitive avoidance, which may affect the retrieval of specific memories.

converse wish, within the same patient, to maintain the status quo due, for example, to the threat of the therapy to the patient's self-esteem or the patient's need to keep the pain alive (i.e. secondary gain). Often the patient both wants to get better *and* stay the same. In some rare cases, as Joseph points out, some patients are "against understanding" (1983: 139–140).

The patient's relationship to help is organised around procedures for being helped that have most probably been set in early childhood. Such procedures will be activated when beginning therapy and will become known to us in the transference. Enquiring at the assessment stage into the patient's previous experiences of therapy or relationships with other healthcare professionals, friends and family will enrich our formulation and help us anticipate particular difficulties in engaging with the therapeutic process (see Chapter 4).

In the psychotherapeutic situation, defences manifest themselves as resistances. Defences are internally aimed, whereas resistance is externally aimed.[6] The term resistance means essentially opposition. It refers to any defensive manoeuvre, as deployed in the psychotherapeutic situation, which impedes the therapeutic work. Resistance may be conscious or unconscious. Whatever its source, the presence of resistance always implies that some kind of danger is impending.

The process of therapy used to be thought of as a working through of the patient's resistances. Ferenczi suggested that patients are not cured by free association but *when* they can free associate, that is, when they are no longer resisting the therapeutic process. The handling of resistance has indeed remained one of the two cornerstones of psychoanalytic technique, the other being the interpretation of transference.

Nowadays there continues to be an emphasis on understanding resistance along with a greater interest in understanding the anxiety behind it and interpreting this earlier on in the therapy than would have been originally the practice of the classical Freudians.

WORKING WITH RESISTANCE

Working with resistance shares a lot in common with how we approach defences. Resistances can occur at any stage of psychotherapy. It is assumed that a degree of resistance is always operative, as Phillips describes:

---

[6]Freud used the terms synonymously throughout most of his writings.

> People literally shut themselves up in their speaking out, speech is
> riddled with no go areas, internal and external exchange, as fantasy
> and as practicality, is fraught with resistance (Phillips, 2001: 133).

Resistances can be "obvious" as, for example, when the patient arrives late
or they can be "unobtrusive" (Glover, 1955) as when the patient appears
compliant but the compliance masks hostility to the process. Because
resistance occurs in the context of the therapeutic situation it is incumbent
on us to acknowledge the reality/external factors that may compound
a resistance. For example, when working as part of multidisciplinary
teams the patient may quite understandably have some anxieties about
confidentiality, which may translate into a resistance to sharing, for
example, suicidal ideation with the therapist for fear of being admitted
to a hospital. Such resistance is most probably overdetermined, but it is
as well to acknowledge the part the context of therapy may be playing in
reinforcing it.

It is also very important – yet perhaps all too frequently glossed over – to
differentiate resistances from the patient's disagreement with us because
we may have misunderstood him. This can contribute to a difficult impasse
in the work: the patient's "No" sometimes does mean just that. It may also
be the case that we contribute to the resistance. The patient's reluctance
to free associate may be a response to our perceived seductiveness that
makes the therapeutic space feel unsafe. It is incumbent on us to be honest
within ourselves and examine the ways in which we may compound or
create a resistance.

The first stage of working with resistance requires a formulation of
the patient's relationship to help, that is, we strive to make sense of
what internal object relationship is activated when the patient experiences himself as needy and vulnerable in relation to us as the helper.
Many resistances emerge specifically in relation to this dynamic. For
example, one of my patients whose experience of being vulnerable
had become equated early on with being humiliated found it intolerable to take in anything I could offer him because he experienced his
not-knowing as deeply humiliating. He therefore met my interpretations with contempt making me feel, in my countertransference, like
the "stupid" therapist who always got it wrong. This object relationship got in the way of him being able to derive help from our work.
The focus of our work was this dynamic so as to lift the resistance to
being helped.

Once we have grasped the quality and nature of the patient's relationship
to help we can begin to reflect on whether the patient "won't" accept help

or "can't" accept help. This distinction relates to the important consideration of whether the resistance results from an internal conflict or a deficit.
The greater the degree of personality integration typically associated with
a neurotic personality structure, the more likely it will be that the resistance arises from a conflict between a part of the patient that wants help
and another that finds some substitute satisfaction in maintaining the
symptoms. The less integrated patient may, on the contrary, be resisting
help because to allow another person into his world is simply experienced
as too dangerous. This is the kind of patient who feels that he cannot
afford to take the risk to allow us into his world. In the history of this kind
of patient, we often encounter developmental deficits. Our task here is to
find ways of communicating that we understand what the experience of
being in therapy might feel like for the patient. This patient, for instance,
may have no template for being helped that does not involve an abusive
other masquerading as a helper. We thus aim to convey respect for the
defensive structure that has protected him and name the feared risks of
letting us into his world. And then we wait, sometimes for a long time,
until the patient painstakingly lets us in.

One of the most helpful description of how to approach resistance in
a session can be found in the work of Greenson (1967). He suggests a
gradual approach to the interpretation of resistance that distinguishes
between the following:

- The fact that the patient is resisting and how they do it (e.g. lateness,
  silence).
- What is being kept at bay (i.e. what affect is the patient trying to protect
  himself from).
- Why the patient needs to do so (i.e. what would be the consequences
  of not doing so).

Table 6.4 summarises some key points worth considering when approaching resistance.

RESISTANCES IN THE INITIAL STAGES OF PSYCHOTHERAPY

It is beyond the scope of this chapter to exhaustively cover all possible
forms of resistance. Like defences, resistances are varied. I will therefore
restrict myself to firstly describing those resistances that are most commonly encountered in the initial stages of therapy, but not exclusively
so, and secondly, we will review some of the most common resistances
that often invite us into potentially collusive enactments. In so doing,

Table 6.4 Working with resistance

- Consider whether you are faced with a developmental deficit or resistance (i.e. the patient "won't" or "can't").
- Consider the source of the resistance: internal or interpersonal or both?
- Check whether any aspects of the therapeutic frame might be contributing to the resistance (e.g. the patient's reluctance to disclose may be reinforced by concerns about the limits of confidentiality).
- Point out to the patient that he is resisting. Use clear examples of why you think this may be happening (e.g. "It's the third time you arrive late this month").
- Invite the patient to be curious about the meaning of his behaviour before you make an interpretation (e.g. "It's the third time you arrive late this month. Do you have any thoughts about this?").
- Try to grasp the affects the patient needs to protect himself from before interpreting the content of the resistance (e.g. "You seem to feel quite anxious in the sessions of late. I wonder if that might be why you arrive late, so that you have less time here").
- The final step is to make a fuller interpretation that takes into account the unconscious meaning of the resistance.

I make some suggestions on how to approach these resistances. These inevitably reflect my own therapeutic style and are not intended to be prescriptive.

The initial stages of the therapeutic relationship are ripe for the emergence of resistance since starting therapy always represents a threat to the patient's emotional status quo.

First Contact

Resistances begin to emerge even before we meet the patient face to face. During the initial phone call to arrange a consultation, some patients ask a lot of information and express anxieties about whether the therapy will help or not. Questions may point to possible resistance to engaging with therapy. In these situations it is worthwhile reminding oneself of how anxiety-provoking starting therapy can feel. Some questions may need to be answered during this initial phone call. For example, questions about our fee should not be interpreted solely as an indication of anxiety though they may also be that too. However, such a question needs to be answered practically since patients need to know before they arrive for the consultation how much we charge.

With the majority of questions asked during an initial phone call, I tend to avoid answering directly (with the exception of questions about the fee) and might say something like: *"Starting therapy can be quite unsettling and brings up a lot of questions. I would be happy to think about these with you when we meet so that we have time to talk these things through together"*.

If the patient asks a lot of practical questions at the end of the first consultation and I think this is driven by anxiety, I might say: *"Beginning psychotherapy can make you feel anxious because it is frightening and painful to confront certain aspects of oneself. Asking me a lot of practical questions is perhaps a way of letting me know that you are worried about what you are letting yourself in for"*.

In the vast majority of cases, taking up the anxiety behind the question is enough to ease the patient into therapy.

Involuntary Patients

Patients who are referred to us by a third party often approach psychotherapy with considerable resistance: they are actively wanting to avoid it or they arrive passively, reacting to another's wish or instruction to seek help. In these situations it is helpful to acknowledge at the outset that they do not want to see us and to invite them to talk about what they feel they need. If they are obliged to see us or, at some level, feel obliged, then it is best to empathise with their plight and wonder aloud as to how we can make this a worthwhile experience given that they have to come to see us. In other words, we seek to establish some alliance with the patient's resistant self.

Requests for Personal Information About the Therapist

One of the areas that many of us struggle with are requests by the patient for information about ourselves. The analytic approach to questions generally is to avoid answering them and instead take them up as expressions of unconscious wishes or anxieties. This reluctance to answer directly often troubles those approaching psychoanalytic work for the first time. It is important to note that not answering is not driven by a perverse wish to be contrary or to make the patient feel powerless; rather, it is driven by the careful attention paid in psychoanalytic work to the patient's latent communications, as we saw earlier in Chapter 5.

Requests for personal information, especially at the beginning stages of therapy, often belie the patient's fear of being the vulnerable one in the therapeutic situation and the one who is scrutinised. There is of course natural curiosity about the kind of person we are but our emphasis is on understanding the unconscious determinants of this apparent curiosity. It may therefore help to respond to such requests, for example, as to whether we have children with something like: *"We are here to understand you better, so let's try to make sense of why it might make a difference to you if you knew whether I have children. . .".* If we have a clearer hypothesis about the meaning of the question we could share this with the patient as an interpretation.

On the whole I am disinclined to answer any personal questions. Never-theless, if a patient asks me whether I am Italian, for example, it would be churlish of me to remain silent since it is clear from my name and to a lesser extent from my accent, that I am not English and that I am most probably Italian. If the patient asks me about my nationality, I will confirm that I am Italian and explore the meaning of this fact for the patient. Over the years I have discovered that my being Italian has meant very different things to different patients: it has held negative and positive associations but it is has never been related to as a neutral fact of no personal consequence for those patients who have chosen to comment on it. My own experience with questions about my nationality has taught me that it is helpful even under these circumstances in which I am willing to answer the patient's question to refrain from doing so immediately and instead invite the patient first to consider his relationship to the question – I can always answer the question later if it still seems relevant. In these situations, it may help say something like: *"I would be happy to answer that question but before I do, let's think together about why this question is coming up now".*

Omissions and Emphases

Throughout this book I have repeatedly referred to the importance of listening to how the patient constructs his narrative. One feature of this construction relates to the relative emphasis given to different periods in the patient's life. Some patients display from the outset reluctance to talk about a particular period of their lives. For example, the patient's narrative may be skewed in favour of detailed accounts of his childhood experiences or the patient may only talk about his present life and gloss over past history. Omissions or cursory descriptions should always alert us to the operation of resistance. In these situations, the patient may be helped to explore a period in his life if we can recognise first that he feels some danger if he reveals or thinks about the given period.

Requests for Advice

Requests for advice are common in the early stages of therapy, especially from patients who know little about how psychotherapy works and base their expectations of it on the model they are most familiar with, namely, the medical model in which advice is given liberally. The patient's cultural background may also be relevant in this respect: in cultures in which psychotherapy is not common and in which the expectation is that the "Doctor" gives pills or advice, requests for advice are best addressed first by explaining the nature of psychotherapy and then dealing with how the patient feels about this. For example, we might say: *"I can see that in coming here you expected me to give you advice to help you with your difficulties. I wonder what it feels like to discover that I am a different kind of therapist to the one you had expected"*.

In other cases the request for advice may betray the patient's wish for an idealised therapist who is omnipotent and will cure him of his ills or it may reveal the patient's characteristic passive stance in relation to his problems. In these cases it will therefore be important to take this up with the patient and to articulate the possible meaning.

Challenging the Boundaries of the Therapeutic Relationship

Patients often use the therapeutic frame as the focus of their resistance, for example, by coming late or trying to extend sessions or criticising the therapist for being too aloof. Requests for contact in between sessions may represent another means of challenging the boundaries of the therapeutic frame or it may represent an attempt to intrude on us or to deny the pain of separation. The hostility, and sometimes rebelliousness, that underlies criticisms about our rigidity often masks feelings of vulnerability or humiliation.

Prolonged Silences and Absence of Silence

Prolonged silences can occur throughout therapy or may be actively avoided. Either scenario should alert us to the presence of a degree of resistance. In both instances it is important to ascertain what talking means to the patient. For some patients it may be equated with revealing parts of themselves that are shameful, while for others it may be experienced as a form of submission. Silence may also be used as an attack or as an attempt to control us.

RESISTANCES THAT RECRUIT THE THERAPIST INTO A COLLUSION

Overvaluing Facts

Patients come into therapy in search of answers. Some patients, however, convey an urgent need to make sense of fleeting images or recurring dreams or bizarre symptoms that cause distress. The anxiety generated by not knowing what sense to make of disturbing experiences may translate itself into a search for facts. Where the suggestion is, for example, that the patient may have been abused, it is easy for us to get drawn into a search for historical truth that does not help the patient. Whenever we feel drawn to providing answers or we become preoccupied with trying to establish the factual status of what the patient recounts, we need to make a mental note of this as a warning signal that the patient may be trying to avoid anxiety.

The Very Good Patient

It is not uncommon for patients to project their own critical superegos into us so that we are then experienced as judgmental or punitive. When this occurs, the patient may retreat into compliance and will try to say or do the right thing so as to please us and avoid our disapproval. In so doing, the patient is resisting the process since he is not able to examine this dynamic, something that might, in turn, expose him to his own more critical, hostile feelings towards us. The problem for us in these cases is that we can fall into the comfortable trap of being in therapy with the patient who is always nice, appreciative and interested but who simply does not change because we collude with his defence.

Difficulty in Remaining the Patient

One way of avoiding exploring oneself and of denying feelings of vulnerability or dependency is to fight against being a patient. Rationalising, intellectualising or acting seductively may all be deployed as a means of avoiding vulnerability. Such patients may be very adept at drawing us into intellectual – and often very stimulating – discussions that serve the function of abolishing any differences between us and the patient so that his vulnerability is avoided.

Idealising the Therapist

Given our own narcissistic needs, it may be difficult to resist the pull of the patient who thinks we are wonderful. The patient may need to think we are wonderful because any other thoughts and feelings might be too threatening. If we become too identified with being a "wonderful" therapist, we will not be able to stand back and help the patient think about what idealisation defends against.

Seductive Behaviour

Seductiveness by the patient is often used as a means of resisting feelings of vulnerability or powerlessness. Seduction can be quite explicitly erotised or it may be more subtle and therefore even more difficult to grasp. A subtle form of seduction we need to monitor is the way the patient discloses information. Some patients tell their story enigmatically or very colourfully and we find ourselves gripped by the story, wanting to hear more. Often this reflects the patient's attempt to draw us out of our interpretative function through seducing us. What may be avoided is a fear of being thought uninteresting or not the "special" patient.

As I hope will be clear by now, resistance can take many forms. Table 6.5 lists some other common forms of resistance. Any of these behaviours should alert us to the possibility of resistance. They all point to an avoidance of unsettling feelings or thoughts by the patient, which is subjectively experienced by us as being somehow drawn away from the focus of the analytic work. Working analytically involves deploying a range of interventions not all of which are strictly interpretative. However, if we find ourselves too frequently or for too long becoming supportive or if we feel unable to challenge a patient or we long to see one patient in particular

Table 6.5   Common clinical manifestations of resistance

- Silence "I've got nothing to talk about"
- Absence of affect/incongruent affect
- Physical posture
- Avoidance of topics
- Rigid patterns (e.g. client can only lie down on couch after going through a particular ritual)
- Use of language (e.g. use of jargon)
- Lateness
- Forgetting to come to the session
- Overuse of humour

over the others, we need to ask ourselves why this is happening. Very often, our answers will lead us to discovering the operation of resistance in the therapeutic process and our own collusion with this process.

FURTHER READING

Bateman, A. & Holmes, J. (1995) Chapter 4. *Introduction to Psychoanalysis*. London: Routledge.
Freud, A. (1936) *The Ego and the Mechanisms of Defence*. London: Karnac Books.

7

TRANSFERENCE AND COUNTERTRANSFERENCE

Psychotherapy unfolds in a relational context: patient and therapist bring to the relationship their personal motivations and needs. The therapeutic relationship, like all relationships, is infused with our desire and our conscious and unconscious phantasies. It is always "on the move" (Lyons-Ruth, 1999). The analytic literature in particular offers a rich framework that allows for an understanding of the vicissitudes of this unique encounter. The outcome of therapy is indeed held by many contemporary psychoanalytic practitioners to be related to the successful elaboration and re-evaluation of patterns of relating that become accessible through an analysis of transference phenomena, that is, the enactment in the present of implicit dynamic templates of self–other relationships (Sandler & Sandler, 1997).

This chapter will concentrate on working in the transference and the clinical uses of countertransference. We will begin by reviewing definitions and distinctions between different, yet related concepts. We will then examine more closely what working in the transference involves and how we can use countertransference to inform our interventions.

TRANSFERENCE[1]

"Psychoanalytic observation" wrote Bion, *"is concerned neither with what has happened, nor with what is going to happen, but with what is happening"* (1967: 17). Nowhere is this more apparent than in the analytic focus

---

[1] Freud believed that all human relationships are coloured by infantile transferences. It is beyond the aim of this chapter to review the empirical evidence for transference in everyday life. Suffice to say though that there is evidence that the mental representation of a significant other can be triggered by encountering a new person, leading us to make inferences about the new person that extend beyond what we actually know about that person. This triggering process can occur unconsciously (see Glassman & Andersen, 1999).

on working *in* the transference. Within psychoanalysis, the spotlight has long been on the very particular relationship that develops between therapist and patient. The peculiarities of this relationship are most apparent when we consider the conceptualisation of the transference relationship.

Freud first used the term transference in 1905 when he was reporting on his own work with patients. He became aware of changes in the patient's attachment to him, characterised by the experience of strong positive or negative emotions. These feelings were regarded as "transference" coming about as a consequence of a "false connection". Freud came to see transferences as "new editions" of old impulses and phantasies aroused during the process of psychoanalysis with the therapist replacing some earlier person from the patient's past. Those who followed Freud viewed the analytic task as essentially that of promoting a transference regression,[2] so as to establish a *transference neurosis*[3] on the basis of the patient's infantile neurosis. Once the therapist assumed emotional importance and became the target of transference wishes, the therapist resisted gratifying those wishes. This frustration was said to give rise to intense affects so that the patient's conflicts emerged more clearly and could thus be interpreted by the therapist.

Freud (1912) was clear that the transference was not created by the therapeutic situation; it merely revealed it. Most psychoanalytic therapists would concur with this and suggest that the therapist's activity only shapes the manifest forms of the transference and provides a context by which, for example, the patient's idealising tendencies or his relationship to authority, already formed in the patient's mind, come to light as he engages with the therapist.

In the classical Freudian position, the therapist understood the transference as a repetition of the past, in line with Freud's notion of the *repetition compulsion*. This reflected Freud's belief that repressed early experiences could not be communicated verbally. Instead, Freud suggested, they are acted out, that is, they are transferred into compulsively repeated actions.

> The patient does not say that he remembers that he used to be defiant and critical towards his parents' authority

wrote Freud,

> . . .instead he behaves in that way to the doctor. . . He does not remember having been intensely ashamed of certain sexual activities and

---

[2] Classical Freudians and ego psychologists, on the whole, tend to retain this view.
[3] A transference neurosis is a regression in the transference to the infantile neurosis so as to arrive at the origins of neurotic symptoms.

afraid of their being found out, but he makes it clear that he is ashamed of the treatment on which he is now embarked and tries to keep it secret from everybody... This is his way of remembering (1914: 150).

Transference was therefore understood to be a resistance to memory in so far as it represented a bypassing of memory, leading instead to a re-enactment of wishes and conflicts in relation to the therapist.

Since Freud, the use of the term transference has been extended (Sandler *et al.*, 1973). Some therapists now view all aspects of the patient's relationship to the therapist as transference (Joseph, 1985). Often accompanying such a position is the belief, expressed originally by Strachey (1934), that the most mutative interpretations are transference ones. There appears to be a continuum along which therapists broadly situate themselves on this question. This ranges from those who believe in the "total transference" (Joseph, 1985) and who focus almost exclusively on the here-and-now transference interpretation, and those who draw a clear distinction between real and distorted aspects of the relationship and whose range of interventions include the so-called "extra-transference" interpretations (e.g. reconstructive interpretations) (Hamilton, 1996). For the former group of mostly Kleinian clinicians, the transference "... *is not... merely a repetition of old attitudes, events and traumas from the past; it is an externalisation of unconscious phantasy here-and-now*" (Hinshelwood, 1989: 15). This is an important difference by comparison with the Freudian conceptualisation of transference because it proposes that the transference is more than just a repetition of the patient's patterns of relating to significant figures in the past; rather, it is seen to be primarily about the patient's internal world as it becomes manifest in his total attitude to the therapist and to the analytic setting. What is enacted in the here-and-now is an internalised object relationship, for example, we become, in the patient's experience, a critical other who humiliates him.

Originally Freud conceptualised the therapist as a mirror *onto* which the patient projected. Nowadays, we often speak of the patient projecting *into* the therapist. This marks an important shift in understanding whereby the patient's perception of the therapist is not only said to be distorted so that his behaviour towards the therapist is based on this distortion but the patient also acts, in phantasy, on the therapist's mind, by projecting *into* the therapist, such that the therapist herself may be affected by the projection. This is the idea of projective identification that was introduced in the last chapter.

Unlike Freud, who viewed transference as a misreading of the present in terms of the past, many contemporary practitioners of different theoretical persuasions now understand the transference as a process in which *current* emotions and parts of the self are externalised into the relationship with the therapist. This involves the projection of object relationships infused with benign, positive feelings and phantasies, namely the *positive transference*, and those infused with more hostile feelings and phantasies, namely the *negative transference*.

Contemporary analytic practice is dominated by the interpretation of the here-and-now transference. It would be a mistake, however, to conclude from this that no attention is paid to the historical dimensions of trans-ference. Links to the patient's past are made in varying degrees by all therapists. Nevertheless, for many contemporary therapists spanning all three psychoanalytic groups, working in the transference involves pri-marily an exploration of the patient's unconscious phantasies as they arise in relation to the therapist without too frequent, so-called "genetic" or reconstructive links to the past.

COUNTERTRANSFERENCE

Countertransference, the phenomenon accounting for the therapist's emo-tional reactions to her patient, has been variously defined. In Freud's time, therapists regarded their emotional reactions to the patient as manifesta-tions of their own "blind spots". In 1912, Freud stated that the therapist should behave:

> ...as a surgeon who puts aside all his own feelings, including that of human sympathy and concentrates his mind on one single purpose, that of performing the operation as skilfully as possible.

The metaphor of a surgeon who performs a clean-cut incision without the interference of his feelings profoundly shaped the analytic persona that many therapists internalised, supported by the armoury of the rules of abstinence, anonymity and neutrality (see Chapter 3). To this day, amongst some of the ego psychologists, the therapist's emotional reactions continue to be considered primarily a sign of unresolved issues in the therapist. Provided the therapist can monitor and analyse further her blind spots, she is thought to be free to function as the objective observer and interpreter of the patient's unconscious. It has been argued, however, that by restricting the countertransference to technical errors caused by the therapist's blind spots, Freud and the ego psychologists obscured the "pervasiveness of the therapist's subjectivity" (Dunn, 1995: 725) in the therapeutic situation.

It was Heimann's (1950) work that redressed this skewed attitude towards the therapist's emotional responses. She drew attention to a different ver-sion of countertransference, one that favoured the therapist's emotional response to her patient as a technical tool, not a hindrance. This viewpoint profoundly influenced current contemporary practice. Bion's (1967) plea to resist the temptation of "memory and desire"[4] in the clinical situation in favour of reliance upon our emotional experience as the only "facts" available to us, signposts the contemporary emphasis on countertransference as a privileged source of knowledge about the mind of the patient. This position implies that we have access, through our own emotional reactions, to knowledge about the patient's state of mind without this knowledge needing to be communicated explicitly through the spoken word. Over the years, there has therefore been a marked shift from seeing countertransference as something that interferes with technique to viewing such responses by the therapist as a means of understanding the patient's unconscious communications, thereby acting as a direct guide for analytic interpretations of the current material.

From Kleinian and many object-relational perspectives, countertransference includes all the therapist's reactions to the patient, no matter what their source, allowing for greater tolerance of the therapist's subjectivity. In these approaches, our task is to understand who we come to represent for the patient and the internalised object relationships that are activated at any given point in time whilst simultaneously remaining connected with who we are when divested of these projections. This, as we all know, is easier said than practised because, as Dunn observes:

> ...the analyst's perceptions of the patient's psychic reality are also constructed through, and distorted by, the lens of unconscious fantasy. It is untenable to assume that the analyst is an objective observer, simply mirroring the patient's transference (1995: 725).

It is indeed difficult to see how it would be possible to reliably separate out our emotional reactions as a response to the patient's unconscious communication from our own so-called neurotic reactions. As Kernberg reminds us:

> The analyst's conscious and unconscious reactions to the patient in the treatment situation are reactions to the patient's reality as well as to his transference, and also to the analyst's own reality needs as well as to his neurotic needs. This approach also implies that those emotional reactions are intimately fused (1965: 49).

In the course of any therapeutic relationship, we will experience temporary partial identification with our patients but our commitment is to relate

---

[4]Bion argued that memory was misleading because it was subject to the distortion by unconscious processes and desire (to cure) interfered with the capacity to observe and understand the patient.

to them as an "other" and not be confused with ourselves. This requires vigilant monitoring of our own projections as the interaction that evolves between us and the patient is determined by unconscious forces operating in both. Heimann provides a clear account of why this is so:

> The mind. . .achieves adaptation and progress by employing through-
> out its existence the fundamental and basic processes of introjection
> and projection. . . Such taking in and expelling consists of an active
> interplay between the organism and the outer world; on this funda-
> mental pattern rests all intercourse between subject and object. . . in
> the last analysis we may find it at the bottom of all our complicated
> dealings with one another (1943: 507).

More specifically, the suggestion is that the patient uses projective identification to dispose of unwanted aspects of the self into us. Projective
identification, as we have seen in Chapter 6, assumes "*. . .a kind of
pipeline from the unconscious of the patient to that of the analyst that facilitates direct transmission of mental contents from one to the other*" (Jacobs,
2001: 6). Although the concept is inspired and clinically very helpful,
it is important not to lose sight of the fact that "resonance is not the
same as replication" (Jacobs, 2001). In other words, whatever the patient's
projection onto or into us, this will be altered by our own personal
experiences and phantasies. It can therefore never be the "same as" it
is for the patient, but it may give us an approximate feeling of the
patient's experience that we can employ to further our understanding of
the patient.

The countertransference is now regarded by many, if not most clinicians as
the fulcrum of therapeutic change. This position is, however, potentially
problematic. In moving away from Freud's view of countertransference as
reflecting the therapist's own blind spots that should be worked through,
and therefore act as a cue for more personal analysis, we are now left with
a concept potentially open to abuse. If what we feel, and how we may at
times behave, can always be understood with reference to the patient's
projections, we have here a neat way for explaining away behaviours that
would constitute acting out on our part. Moreover, the importance of our
emotional reactions has at times been so emphasised that the patient's
actual experience and what he reports in a session are overlooked:

> As recently as fifteen years ago, many therapists were reluctant to
> discuss their own feelings about patients, fearful that they might be
> criticised for them and that they were indicative of bad therapeutic
> practice. The situation today is completely different. If anything, it is
> sometimes difficult to get therapists to discuss the patient's material

> because they are talking about themselves and what they feel about
> the patient, rather than the reverse. (Giovacchini, 1985: 447).

Although our countertransference is a useful pathway to the unconscious of the patient, this has been so emphasised that there has been
a neglect of those instances when countertransference responses interfere with our understanding of the patient. For example, there is some
evidence to suggest that therapists who do not feel competent or have
concerns about damaging their patients tend to have patients who break
off treatment (Vaslamatzis *et al.*, 1989). Likewise, therapists who are con-
flicted over their own aggression and have difficulties around loss tend
to experience more problems working within brief therapy (Ursano &
Hales, 1986). In Freud's initial meaning of countertransference, therefore,
it is apparent that our own unresolved issues get in the way of helping
the patient.

Countertransference in its more modern usage could therefore be said to
both facilitate *and* potentially interfere with analytic work. As therapists,
we do well to remind ourselves that we are not beyond the reality testing
of the patient, nor are we beyond making mistakes. Therapeutic work
presents us with opportunities to help our patients as well as opportunities
to gratify our own needs, especially our need to be liked, to be needed or
to be a saviour:

> It is our natural and normal self-esteem needs operating as ever-
> present forces in analysis as they do in life that may, at times, constitute
> a significant source of difficulty for the analyst (Jacobs, 2001: 667).

Jacobs (2001) suggests that for defensive reasons patients often suppress,
deny or rationalise their accurate perceptions of countertransference elements (i.e. the therapist's needs and conflicts) and do not confront their
therapists with it. He helpfully reminds us that even though perception is
filtered through transferential and projective identificatory processes, the
patient may yet accurately perceive aspects of our behaviour.

When misused, the concept of countertransference gives us licence to
discharge onto the patient our own unresolved conflicts. Nevertheless,
when approached thoughtfully and with integrity, our emotional reactions
to the patient are helpful guides to what the patient cannot articulate
verbally. They provide us with important sources of information about the
patient's mental state and his needs moment-by-moment. Taken together
with our formulation of the patient's difficulties, and the history of the
therapeutic relationship that we have developed with the patient, they
provide one source of evidence for our eventual interpretations.

THE THERAPEUTIC ALLIANCE AND THE SO-CALLED "REAL" RELATIONSHIP

The concepts of transference and countertransference represent one of Freud's most important and inspired contributions: he was the first therapist to recognise emotional involvement with the patient. Since then, clinicians have been alerted to the intricate projections that may arise in the course of clinical work. These concepts are useful but in practice it can be difficult at times to differentiate a transference or countertransference reaction from an emotional and/or realistic reaction by the patient to the therapist or by the therapist to the patient's report of his real-life experiences. When considering these concepts, it is therefore important to examine the related concepts of the therapeutic alliance and the "real" relationship.

In recent years, the notion of the "real" relationship has enjoyed a resurgence as a result of the growth of perspectives favouring intersubjectivity (see Chapter 1), where the idea that the therapist should be "real" – in the sense of authentically and personally available – has been taken seriously. Elsewhere, it has remained a more nebulous dimension of the therapeutic relationship. It may be that this has continued to be a comparatively neglected area in analytic thinking as consideration of the therapeutic alliance and its influence may represent, as Levy & Inderbitzin suggest:

> ...an interesting instance of analytical technical theory attempting, with varying degrees of success, depending on the assessment, to come to grips with the role of suggestion (2000: 746).

The notion of a therapeutic or treatment alliance has its origin in Freud's writings on technique. Originally, it was subsumed within the general concept of transference. The therapeutic alliance essentially denotes conflict-free aspects of the ego. Greenson & Wexler (1969) regard the core of the treatment alliance as being anchored in the "real" or "non-transferential" relationship. They argue that in order for patients to develop healthy ego functioning and the capacity for full object relationships, the analytic situation must offer them the opportunity for experiencing in depth both the realistic and unrealistic aspects of dealing with the therapist. That is, both the therapeutic alliance and the transference are considered important for therapy. Nevertheless, in practice, it is difficult to disentangle the therapeutic alliance from transference. For example, while appealing to the patient's rational co-operation, we know that the patient's participation in therapy will inevitably also be governed by unconscious wishes to please, to appease and to defensively identify.

Approaching the question of the therapeutic alliance from a more explicitly clinical as opposed to theoretical perspective, some clinicians have expressed concern that a focus on the therapeutic alliance and extra-transference interpretations can lead to an avoidance of transference phenomena and to resistances masking as collaborative activity and identification with the therapist. This viewpoint suggests that if we restrict ourselves to the surface level of the patient's communications and his conscious motivation to be in therapy, we are effectively avoiding working with the unconscious and we will be handicapped in identifying the resistances that are always operative in therapy.

In the midst of this ongoing controversy, some clinicians have grappled with the complex nature of the therapeutic relationship. Couch (1979), for example, proposes two aspects of the real relationship, which he differentiates: first, the realistic nature of the communication between the therapist and the patient; and second, the realistic nature of the personality of both therapist and patient as real persons. In other words, he is referring to communication between therapist and patient when they are functioning as their "real selves"; that is, "relatively free from transference or countertransference influences" (Couch, 1979). Such a distinction is nevertheless problematic since it assumes that it is possible to separate a so-called "real self" from one whose relationship with others is distorted through the transference projections.

In his original formulation, Greenson (1967) helpfully distinguished three levels of relationship: the transference (and countertransference) relationship, the therapeutic alliance and the real relationship:

> The term 'real' in the phrase 'real relationship' may mean realistic, reality oriented, or undistorted as contrasted to the term 'transference' which connotes unrealistic, distorted, and inappropriate. The word real may also refer to genuine, authentic, true in contrast to artificial, synthetic, or assumed relationship between therapist and patient. (1967: 217).

These different levels of relationship are intimately connected to one another. It is indeed difficult to establish criteria for clearly distinguishing between the real relationship and the therapeutic alliance and the transference and none are forthcoming in the literature. Notwithstanding the divergent views about whether it is possible to distinguish between these levels of relationship, the analytic literature is most certainly not devoid of references to the clinical usefulness of the therapist's "real" emotional responses (Winnicott, 1947; Heimann, 1950; Little, 1951). A paper by King is a good example:

> I do not, however, assume that every communication between patient
> and therapist relates directly to transference, and it becomes important
> to differentiate those feelings and moods which are related to the
> operation of the transference, from those related to my reactions as a
> human being working with another human being. . . (1977: 33).

In a similar vein, Anna Freud alert, as she put it, to the "technically
subversive nature" of her suggestion, remarked that:

> . . .we should leave room somewhere for the realisation that therapists
> and patient are also two real people, of equal adult status, in a real
> personal relationship to each other. I wonder whether our, at times
> complete, neglect of this side of the matter is not responsible for some
> of the hostile reactions which we get from patients and which we are
> apt to ascribe to 'true transference' only. (1954: 618–619).

Those therapists who approach all their emotional reactions in therapy
as responses to the patient's unconscious communication overlook the
distinction drawn by King and Anna Freud. In a critique of "modern"
technique, Couch (1979) offers an alternative perspective. He argues that
the "vast majority" of the therapist's reactions (feelings and thoughts) are
best understood as quite "ordinary responses" to what the patient reports
about his inner and outer life. Some of these responses can assist the
therapist in an empathic understanding of the patient and may therefore
contribute to an interpretation. Their primary function, however, is to
contribute to the maintenance of a therapeutic situation that is not totally
"divorced from real life" (Couch, 1979). While I am in broad agreement
with the spirit of the position outlined by Couch (1979), it is nevertheless
difficult to operationalise the way in which we can reliably distinguish the
"real" responses that he advocates from the so-called countertransference
in its modern usage.

If we can speak of a distinction between a so-called real and a transferential
relationship, this is best articulated by Gill (1979). He emphasises the
non-transferential element in any therapeutic dyad, describing how the
patient may experience the therapist in a particular way because of an
actual event in their relationship. The patient's selective attention to this
particular event is an instance of transference, but it does not necessarily
involve a distortion of reality. For example, let us imagine that in a session
we are preoccupied with something in our own mind relating to a personal
concern. As a result, we are less attentive to the patient's communications
and might say less than what would be our usual practice. The patient may
consciously or unconsciously pick up on this and may become withdrawn
and uncommunicative in response. The session becomes heavy with
silence that feels hostile. Eventually, the patient reports a memory of his

mother listening to music in her study at a time when, as a child, he wanted her attention. The patient expresses anger at not having his needs met by his mother. In turn, we might understand this as a manifestation of transference, that is, we might take it up as an indication that the patient is experiencing us as unavailable and that this makes him angry. In this hypothetical example, the patient's transference reaction is not based on a distortion as it is triggered by a "real" behaviour on our part, that is, we are distracted. Nevertheless, the idiosyncratic way in which the patient relates to this fact is a manifestation of transference as it relies on the activation of an internalised object relationship that is particular to this patient, given his history.

It is not so much therefore a question of whether transference occurs, since it does in all relationships in so far as we all bring past experiences to bear on our present interactions and this colours our interpretation of what we perceive to be "out there". Rather, the question is whether in the specific context of the therapeutic relationship, the transference distorts *all* aspects of the relationship with the therapist. Gill would suggest that it does not and I find myself in agreement with this position. Perhaps, the important question is not whether we can distinguish clearly between these responses as transference or as "real" responses, but whether taking up the transference implications in the patient's communications is always helpful.

These ongoing debates strike at the very heart of the analytic enterprise as they challenge us to examine whether we can sustain a model of the therapist as a relatively blank screen into which the patient projects or whether in our accounts of therapeutic action we need to consider the therapeutic value of the direct expression of the real person of the therapist in a session, not rigidly hidden behind the "orthodox" facade of anonymity, neutrality and abstinence (Viederman, 1991).

WHAT IS A TRANSFERENCE INTERPRETATION?

Working in the transference represents the cornerstone of analytic technique. A transference interpretation makes explicit reference to the patient–therapist relationship and is intended to encourage an exploration of the patient's conflicts and internalised object relationships as they manifest themselves in the therapeutic situation. This exploration is facilitated by the therapist availing herself to become the receptacle for primitive projections. Fairbairn captures this process very well:

> Psychoanalytic treatment resolves itself into a struggle on the part of the patient to pressgang his relationship with the analyst into the closed system of the inner world through the agency of the transference

and a determination on the part of the analyst to effect a breach in this
closed system (Fairbairn, 1958: 385).

If we allow ourselves to be used in this manner by the patient, we can
utilise our understanding of what is projected into us as the basis for the
transference interpretation.

We infer the transference from different sources: the patient's associations,
his affect in the room and the wishes and phantasies that are implicit in the
patient's narratives and dreams. We also infer it from our own counter-
transferential responses. Taken together, these sources of information help
us generate hypotheses about who we become in the patient's mind at different stages and the underlying anxieties that are generated in response
to these different versions of an "other" and the states of mind or feelings
that are projected into us. For example, the therapist may be experienced
as a "judgmental other" or as a "seductive other". Every transference
situates the therapist and patient in an idiosyncratically prescribed relationship to each other, for example, as the critical parent/therapist of a
very frightened child/patient who fears abandonment. The transference
interpretation attempts to elucidate these two interconnected roles and
the affect that links them.

Working in the transference is based on a belief that important aspects
of the past manifest themselves in the present. This is quite different,
however, from the idea that the adult patient can return to an infantile state
as such, that is, a concrete view of regression; rather, the patient's childish
worries and ways of coping are said to be active in the patient's present
reality as implicit procedures and can be helpfully articulated in therapy as
they become manifest in the therapeutic situation as transference reactions.

The patient transfers not just actual figures from the past but internal
phantasy figures that have been construed from the interaction between
real experiences and the patient's own internal reality. This means that
in order to make a transference interpretation, we do not need to know
the actual experiential origins that may have shaped the phantasies our
patient may have developed. In many instances, it will be impossible to
access these facts given what we now understand about the workings of
the mind and of memory in particular. The transference interpretation
merely seeks to capture the emotional, psychic reality of the patient in the
grip of a particular phantasy.

There is not a single type of transference interpretation; rather, there
are what Roth (2001) has helpfully described as "levels of transference
interpretation", namely:

- Interpretations that reflect on links between here-and-now events in the therapy and events from the patient's past history;
- Interpretations that link events in the patient's external life to the patient's unconscious phantasies about the therapist;
- Interpretations that focus on the use of the therapist and the therapeutic situation to enact unconscious phantasy configurations.

As Joseph (1985) has suggested, the transference takes into account what goes on in the room, what went on in the past and what goes on in the external world. All three aspects are important but they are not necessarily all included within one interpretation. Sometimes they are, but generally speaking over the course of a therapy I think of the content of the transference interpretation as undergoing an evolution. It often begins by restricting its focus on the here-and-now interaction, drawing attention to the patient's phantasies and enactments with us. This firmly locates the emotional heat in the therapeutic relationship without diluting it by making links to past or other current figures in the patient's life. This restricted focus is justified since we are unlikely to have a lot of information about the patient in the early stages of therapy, such that links with the past and/or external figures are even more tentative than links to the here-and-now situation, which rely on our first-hand experience of being in a relationship with the patient. Once we become more familiar with the patient's past and current life, our transference interpretations will move on to help the patient identify these patterns in his current external relationships and with past figures in his life.

Although there are varying views on this, in my experience making links between the transference and the current and past external figures in the patient's life is very helpful so as to allow the patient to integrate his emotional experience in the transference with both current and past experience. Riesenberg-Malcom describe the usefulness of such reconstructive interpretations:

> By analysing the past in the present, the ego of the patient becomes more integrated and therefore stronger. By linking interpretations to the historical past we also allow the patient to distance himself both from the immediacy of his experience and from the closeness to the analyst. The distancing from his own immediate experience helps the patient to gain perspective on his problems. . . the distancing from the immediacy of the relationship to the analyst allows the patient at moments to view his analyst as separate and different from his internal object, as someone with whom he is working out his problems (1986: 87).

Reconstructive interpretations offer an opportunity to ally ourselves with the patient's ego. They invite the patient to join us in thinking about him in a way that allows for more distance from the intensity of the patient's feelings. One clinical advantage of these interpretations is that they allow for a de-escalation of the emotional intensity of the transference in situations where the patient may be in the grip of a more psychotic state of mind and can no longer appreciate the as-if quality of the transference, or where the patient is too fragile to reflect on what he may be projecting into us.

In clinical work, both kinds of interpretations are helpful at different stages. It is important, nevertheless, to monitor the use we make of these kinds of interventions. Just as an overemphasis on the here-and-now may detract attention away from the "there-and-then" in a defensive attempt to avoid addressing the pain of a real trauma in the past, tying an interpretation to the patient's past may represent a defensive manoeuvre to avoid current, live feelings in the therapeutic relationship.

When we make a transference interpretation, we are neither interpreting the past nor the present – we are interpreting the past in the present. This is a new experience even if it is organised around relationship patterns that have their roots in the past. When we interpret the transference, we are articulating the actualisation of developmental models that organise the patient's current interactions. In the therapeutic relationship, the so-called "real child of the past is lost". "What survives", writes Green, "is a mixture of the real and the fantasised or, to be more precise, a "reality" re-shaped through fantasy." (2000: 52). This means that in therapy we do not work with a still-life picture of the patient but with an ever changing, interactive system. Our analysis of a patient's historical past is coincident with, and is influenced by the context of remembering. As therapists, we are active contributors to the context in which remembering takes place, and hence to the shaping of the memories that the patient recounts. Our patients' recollections emerge in the context of a highly charged emotional relationship with us. The stories or memories that our patients report have to be considered for their transference relevance – that which may appear in therapy as a recovered memory may be also understood as an indirect, metaphoric, statement about the patient's here-and-now experience with us.

That our patients have memories about the past, which are dependent upon the motivation and context in which they are remembered, was the central message contained in Freud's (1899) notion of *screen memories*. Freud said that vivid early memories were not just historical facts recalled in an archaeological mode but were repeatedly constructed and reconstructed during life. He argued that childhood memories developed like "works of fiction" and were moulded to serve current preoccupa-tions.[5] This means that the patient may locate something in the past in order to avoid analytic turmoil in the present, especially as it concerns something we may have done or not done. This is why, Freud suggested that certain memories "screen defend" against dynamics in the analytic present.[6]

The notion of screen memories has important practical implications. It suggests that if a patient tells us, for example, *"I remember that when I was four my mother told me off and I could not stop crying. I went to hide under the stairs"*, we need to attend to this memory not only as a representation of an experience which is meaningful to the patient, but also as a possible vehicle for unconscious communication about the therapeutic relationship. In this hypothetical scenario, the patient may be feeling "told off" by something we have said in the session. Rather than directly challenging us about this or discussing how it has made the patient feel, he unconsciously uses a memory from the past to communicate to us a current preoccupation in the session.

Johnny was an eighteen-year-old young man referred because of an acute psychotic breakdown. I was seeing him at the time as part of a multidisciplinary team. An implication of this was that I once had to sit in a case conference that he also attended. I felt uncomfortable about this, yet it was felt important by the rest of the team that I attend since I was also Johnny's key-worker.

In our session the week following this meeting, Johnny arrived feeling despondent about therapy. He told me that he felt he had gained all he could from the therapy and that it might be better for him to just keep on attending the day hospital. He spoke some more about this and how fed up he was with everyone meddling in his business. He envied his peers who would soon be off to university. He then paused for a few minutes. He resumed, expressing anger at his mother, whom he felt always meddled in his affairs, not allowing him to develop his own ideas about life and what he should do with it. He then said that he remembered getting very angry with his mother when he was younger. She had this infuriating habit of knocking on his door but opening it even if he had not given her permission to do so. In an exasperated tone, he said to me: "What was the point of

---

[5] A screen memory differs from a phantasy in that it contains some objective perceptual material (Britton, 1998).
[6] This is related to his original concept of "nachtraglichkeit". The latter referred to occurrences in the past which are invested retrospectively with meaning from the present (Good, 1998).

writing in large capital letters 'PRIVATE' if she couldn't even be bothered to read it."

I understood this memory as reflecting not only something important about Johnny's relationship with his mother and his experience of her as intrusive but also as conveying something about our relationship. Clearly, the boundaries of our therapeutic relationship were far looser than is ideal and this is a recurring problem when working in multidisciplinary teams that undermines the confidentiality of the therapeutic relationship. In this sense, we could say that Johnny used a memory from the past to communicate to me something about his experience of me in the present as ignoring his need for privacy and that this intrusion was leading him to want to disengage from the therapy. He could not see the point of continuing with the therapy just as he could not see the point of writing PRIVATE on his bedroom door as his mother did not respect it. He was thus letting me know something of his experience of me as an object he felt he couldn't get through to.

In this clinical vignette, if we were to interpret the transference, we would be essentially aiming to formulate – that is, to make explicit for the patient – the emergence, in the present, of implicit models of relationships that continue to organise the patient's current relationships, simultaneously acknowledging that this model is triggered by a "real" event in the therapeutic relationship, namely, my attendance at the case conference.

THE QUALITY OF THE TRANSFERENCE

A patient can develop a range of transferences – both negative and positive. It is helpful to remember that what is transferred is an object relationship associated with a particular affect(s). This means that in formulating the transference active at any given moment, we keep in mind how the patient experiences himself in relation to an affectively laden representation of the other (e.g. the patient as the abandoned victim of a neglectful therapist).

The Positive Transference

Some transferences smooth the therapeutic process. For example, a positive transference assists the therapeutic work as the patient's positive attachment to us allows for greater ease of communication and fosters engagement with the process. However, an idealising transference can become a resistance to treatment. The patient who wishes to recreate an all-gratifying relationship with us may find it hard to relinquish this kind of relationship and would be inhibited in exploring the range of feelings and phantasies that he probably has towards us. Such an idealising transference may appear early on to be associated with dramatic changes in the patient. This would be understood as a *transference cure* whereby the patient bypasses a working through of loss, frustrations and disappointments. Such a flight into health is not usually accompanied by long-lasting change.

If the transference contains painful or terrifying impulses (either loving or aggressive), it may cause resistance. At times, the patient may persist in a particular transference towards us as a way of avoiding less tolerable feelings; for example, the patient who strives to be agreeable all the time as a defence against more paranoid anxieties about the therapist's intentions (Joseph, 2000). It is important to interpret these feelings so as to free the patient to relate to us as he needs to at any given moment and to show the patient that we can bear to be experienced as the object not only of his love but also of his hate.

The Erotic and Sexualised Transference

More has been written about resistances arising from aggressive impulses than those arising out of loving or sexual feelings towards the therapist. It is not the aim of this general chapter to enter into a detailed discussion of specific types of transference, but a few words on the erotic transference are perhaps indicated since it usually elicits considerable anxiety in the therapist.

Freud helped us to understand that love is not only problematic in life but also in therapy. Freud (1915b) demolished the boundary between transference love and real love, arguing that the difference between the two was a matter of degree rather than kind. Normal love shares many of the unrealistic aspects of transference love. Like transference love, it has infantile prototypes, it is repetitive and idealising. Freud proposed that when erotic feelings emerge in the therapeutic relationship, they represent an attempt to disrupt the therapeutic work by recruiting the therapist into being the patient's lover.

The intimacy of the therapeutic relationship can be very arousing, especially if the patient is otherwise quite isolated or has difficulty in sharing himself with others. When this kind of a patient finds a receptive therapist who listens to him and by whom he feels cared, this can give rise to a wish for the intimacy to go beyond the consulting room. When we consider the intensity and regressive features of the analytic experience, it is not surprising to discover that it has the potential to arouse very powerful, and often erotically charged, feelings in both patient and therapist. Loving and erotic feelings in the transference are ubiquitous. The neurotic versions of the erotic transference need to be understood, but they seldom significantly interfere with the analytic work – they are grist for the analytic mill. Absence of any loving and/or erotic feelings would in fact be unusual and may indicate the operation of resistance as if the patient cannot tolerate within himself the emergence of such feelings. However, the emergence of erotic feelings in the therapeutic relationship can be more problematic, and when it is, then it is usually referred to as the *eroticised transference*. The latter is more tenacious and resists interpretations as the patient becomes insistent on the gratification of his erotic feelings and fantasies. Such problematic transferences can develop, for example, when working with a patient who has been sexually abused or where his relationships in childhood were sexualised even if actual abuse did not occur.

The emergence of erotic feelings in the therapeutic relationship is problematic for both parties:

> As psychotherapy offers an opportunity for the re-working of parent-child dependency issues, it follows that its erotic components will carry the illicit quality characteristic of incestuous feelings (Rosenberg, 1999: 134).

Erotic feelings may thus be experienced as illicit or "bad" and may have to be suppressed. Yet, they typically continue to exert their impact on the relationship:

> In the analytic couple, both members fear the activation of eroticism, and this renders the erotic dimensions of transference and countertransference one of the fundamental problems of analytic treatment (Kernberg, 2000: 877).

Effective exploration of sexual behaviour, phantasies – conscious and unconscious – and dreams is often hindered by resistances that affect both patient and therapist. This precludes an understanding of the meaning of such feelings and leaves the therapeutic situation at risk of impasse or of acting out: between five and seventeen percent of mental health professionals admit to sexual intimacies with their patients (Pope *et al*, 1995).

The confusion for us as therapists arises because the intensity and passion of the feelings that the patient may develop towards us is often compelling. Instead of being pleased for doing a good enough job, we may begin to feel like a long sought-after perfect friend, lover or parent. We may confuse being the object of realistic love and the powerfully seductive experience of being the object of the patient's idealisation, passion and dependence. These reactions, if unanalysed, can seriously compromise our therapeutic effectiveness. The lure of becoming the perfect partner who will cure the patient of his ills can lead us down the slippery slope of enactment. To avoid such enactments, we need to remain alert to the difference between the positive pleasure that we can derive in competent functioning and the "illusory gains of omnipotent fantasy gratification" (Novick and Novick, 2000) that are an occupational hazard.

From a clinical point of view, the critical question is how we intervene when erotic feelings arise. In a general sense, we need to be receptive to any feelings that the patient experiences towards us, including erotic ones. Given that such feelings are also frequently associated with shame or fear, we help the patient if we can approach this exploration without judgement or anxiety on our part. Working with the erotic in therapy elicits anxiety, no matter how experienced we are. A very helpful discussion of these issues can be found in an excellent paper by Rosenberg (1999). For the purposes of this chapter, I am restricting myself to emphasising only a few aspects of working with erotic feelings:

- *Notice the emergence of erotic feelings* in your patient and/or in yourself and take them to supervision.
- *Think about whether the erotic feelings have an infantile quality.* This suggests that they probably reflect the emergence, in the relationship, of attachment needs infused with incestuous longings. For example, one of my patients who had been brought up in care developed a very strong attachment towards me. Six months into the therapy, he hesitantly declared that he loved me and that he often entertained conscious fantasies of the two of us living together. As we explored these feelings, it became clearer to both of us that he was giving expression to a wish for closeness to an attachment figure that he had never experienced in his life because of being placed in care. This wish was infused with more sensual feelings related to a fantasy of being held in my arms and soothed to sleep. This patient's longing for closeness with me had an erotic dimension, but these feelings and wishes originated from a more childlike part of him.
- *Think about whether the patient is sexualising the relationship.* In contrast to the patient I described above, the one who sexualises the therapeutic relationship is using sexual feelings and fantasies to attack the therapy and the therapist. Another of my patients who was very disturbed would often come to the session reporting the previous night's sexual exploits with young prostitutes. He gave me detailed descriptions of what he did to the young girl and I regularly found myself both repelled and intimidated by these revelations. I felt as if he was relating to me as

the powerless young prostitute in relation to whom he felt powerful. This kind of sexualisation is very hostile. In the countertransference, it is often experienced as an assault or intrusion.

- *Think about whether the type of relationship that the patient strives to establish is a defence against the erotic.* For example, the patient's search for a more dependent, childlike relationship with us may be a defence against the activation of the erotic: the patient may defensively retreat into wishing to be seen as a child in relation to the therapist/parent and deny any sexual feelings that threaten to overwhelm him.

- *Think about how erotic feelings are being used in the transference.* The erotic transference can be used in many different dynamic ways, for example, as a cover-up for hostility or in an attempt to seek reassurance from us. Whatever its use, it denotes an attempt to seduce us away from our analytic role and this represents a form of resistance. Working through an erotic transference has important implications:

> If the patient can tolerate sexual feelings while deeply accepting that they will not be gratified in the analytic situation, then mourning, working through... and sublimation may consolidate an intense relationship in the transference while helping both patient and analyst to begin their process of separation (Kernberg, 2000: 878).

The Negative Transference

A positive transference is not uncommon in the early stages of therapy as the patient is mobilised by his wish to get better and usually hopes that we will be of help to him. Nevertheless, as with any relationship, the therapeutic one will also need to stand the test of the patient's hostility or his mistrust. These feelings are not always expressed at the outset. Some patients may find it very threatening to own such feelings in themselves and/or to express them. Consequently, they may be displaced onto other relationships in the patient's life so as to protect the therapeutic relationship. The patient will, for example, report arguments or conflicts with a partner or boss safely keeping their anger "out there" rather than in the relationship with us. Most of the time, negative feelings are more readily voiced when the patient trusts that we can tolerate their expression without retaliating or trying to minimise their significance. The experience of such feelings in the therapeutic relationship is referred to as the *negative transference.*

There are differences between the three schools as to how to work with the emergence, in therapy, of negative feelings and attitudes towards the therapist. Emphasis on the negative transference and its early interpretation are characteristic of Kleinian technique. Anna Freud and those who followed her argued, on the contrary, that interpretation of the negative transference should be avoided early on, prior to the establishment of a solid therapeutic alliance. Nowadays, there is more attention paid to the negative transference across the different schools and its interpretation early on in the therapy.

Interpretation of the negative transference is a risky intervention since it brings into focus the patient's hostile feelings and phantasies. Once exposed, such negative feelings may leave the patient fearing our retaliation. The anxiety that this generates could lead a patient to break off treatment and at the very least, demands of the patient, a capacity to bear his own aggression and paranoid anxieties. In light of these considerations, it is thus often preferable to interpret the negative transference in the context of an established therapeutic relationship in which the patient has felt supported and has had experience of relating to a helpful therapist.

Nevertheless, there are clinical situations in which the interpretation of the negative transference – even if in the context of a relatively new therapeutic relationship – may be necessary so as to help the patient to remain in therapy by giving him the experience of being with a therapist who can understand and think about more aggressive feelings without retaliating. In other words, even though the negative transference will often be apparent in the first session, whether we interpret this will depend on our assessment of how helpful it will be at that stage of therapy. In my experience, the interpretation of the negative transference in the initial sessions is justified where the patient's ambivalence about being in therapy is pronounced and could undermine the viability of the therapy, or where the patient's hostility is so evident that not interpreting it could be experienced by the patient as our inability to manage such feelings. This in itself could lead the patient to break off treatment as he would not have had the experience of us being able to survive, and think about the meaning of, his hostility. Managing the patient's negative feelings towards us with equanimity is important, but under their pressure we may be tempted to seduce the patient away from their distrust or anger. This is another instance when supervision is vital as it supports us to stay with such uncomfortable feelings.

Matthew was the eldest of seven children. He had been married twice when he started therapy. His second marriage was breaking down at the time and acted as a spur to seeking help.

In the assessment session, Matthew described the end of his first marriage in some detail. He had been very much in love with his wife, but he noticed that he became distanced from her when she was pregnant with their first child. Within a year of the birth, Matthew had moved out of the family home. As he was telling me this, we could hear noise outside my office coming from the waiting area. Matthew stopped talking and looked irritated. He said: "It's impossible to think straight with all this noise outside. I guess the NHS can't afford soundproofing". I thought to myself that Matthew was angry with me for not ensuring a space all to himself without any interruptions or intrusions. Although there was a lot of noise outside, and it was intrusive, the degree of irritation and the contemptuous tone in his voice as he referred to the NHS alerted me to the emergence of strong negative feelings in the relationship. However, since we were only fifteen minutes into the assessment, I did not comment on this as I did not have sufficient evidence to make an interpretation.

Matthew resumed talking and continued to describe his first marriage. As he spoke, I was struck by the fact that he referred to his child not by name but as "the child". It felt as though his child was an impersonal object in his mind that had somehow got in the way of his relationship with his first wife. When I later enquired about his second marriage, Matthew described his wife as a very beautiful, intelligent woman who had many interests, "too many" he added as an after thought. When I elicited an elaboration of this throwaway comment, he described finding it increasingly difficult to manage her hectic schedule. He hated coming home from work and not finding her at home waiting for him. As he was finishing off this sentence, there was a loud bang outside my office. Matthew abruptly stopped talking and grabbed his briefcase in one hand. He looked at me sternly and said: "This is just not good enough. I can't hear myself think. It's like a circus out there".

At this stage, I felt that Matthew would leave unless I took up with him why he had felt so perturbed and angry about the noise outside my office. Although taking up his anger felt risky, it seemed the only intervention that might engage him. I was guided at this point by the quality of the interaction between us, his relationship to the setting and the themes in his story as they had unfolded, and as I had tentatively formulated them in my own mind as the session progressed. Firstly, I noted that he was clearly disturbed by the noise. Secondly, his approach to this external reality was angry and indignant, as if he was saying to me: "How dare you expect me to talk under these conditions". Thirdly, his expression "I cannot hear myself think" made me wonder about the nature of his anxiety at that point: I speculated that he was in fact worried about whether I could hear him and whether my mind was uncluttered enough to give him undivided attention, that is, whether I could think about him. Fourthly, I speculated that being one of seven children probably meant that competition and rivalry were themes salient in his experience of relationships and, more specifically, relating to his experience of wanting undivided attention.

These strands formed the basis of my interpretation: "I can see that the noise outside has disturbed you and that you feel very angry about it, so much so that you are ready to leave. You may well decide that's what you would rather do but I think there is something worth understanding here. It seems to me that every time there is a noise you experience it as an intrusion into my mind, as if you fear that in that moment you lose my attention and interest in you to the other noisy patients out there. When this happens, you feel enraged and you want to walk out. This reminds me of how you said that you found it difficult to feel close to your first wife after your child was born and the way you now also resent your wife's interests, which you feel take her away from you. I think that you are perhaps letting me know that it feels unbearable when you cannot be sure that the other person has space in their mind for you".

THE CHALLENGES OF WORKING IN THE TRANSFERENCE

Not untypically, those new to the practice of psychoanalytic therapy are hesitant about making transference interpretations. When patients are encouraged to work directly with transference reactions, conflictual issues are identified and the patient's anxiety is heightened. The patient may perceive our behaviour as critical, attacking or intrusive. In these situations, we may find it difficult to be experienced as the bad, persecuting object. The interpersonal strain that is generated when working in the transference sometimes steers us away from taking up the transference implications in the patient's communications. If the patient is angry, it may feel easier to locate his anger elsewhere, for example, in the patient's past, rather than take it up in the transference, thereby allowing us to remain the helpful, caring therapist with whom the patient is not angry. We all like to be liked, especially when we feel we are doing our best to help another person. However, our job is not to be liked, but to be helpful. This often involves being unpopular with our patients given the common resistance to uncovering unconscious motives and desires and given their need to project into us a range of feelings.

Besides a wish to avoid drawing the patient's negative feelings towards ourselves, there are other commonly voiced concerns about working in the transference. Let us look at some of them:

- *The transference interpretation overemphasises the significance of the therapist to the patient.* Reducing everything the patient says to a "You *really* mean me..." type intervention is formulaic and unhelpful. Approached in this manner, working in the transference becomes a parody and may indeed reflect the therapist's need to be at the centre of her patient's affective life. However, used thoughtfully and guided by the overall formulation of the patient's conflicts and the treatment goals, a transference interpretation does not in itself overemphasise the significance of the therapist in the patient's life; it merely acknowledges the fact that the therapist invariably becomes an important figure in the patient's life because the intimacy recreated in psychotherapy elicits intense feelings and phantasies. The therapist avails herself to the patient's projections only so that the patient can work through his conflicts and can eventually re-own his projections.

- *By focusing on the patient's negative feelings towards the therapist (i.e. the negative transference), this will somehow preclude a positive experience that will disconfirm the patient's pathogenic assumptions in relationships.* Taking up the negative transference is challenging for both patient and therapist. Whether it is helpful to interpret the negative transference early on in the therapy is a moot point. In the absence of a solid enough therapeutic alliance, the exploration of negative feelings towards the therapist may be experienced as too threatening by the patient who may fear the therapist's retaliation for the expression of his hostile feelings. Timing is thus of the essence. A well-timed interpretation of the negative transference can be experienced as very helpful by the patient – the therapist who can bear to hear that the patient hates her is providing the patient with an experience that may implicitly serve to disconfirm negative expectations of others (e.g. "No one can bear my hatred"). It models a capacity to manage ambivalence without the need to retaliate when on the receiving end of hostile feelings.

In psychodynamically oriented supportive therapy, it is unlikely that the negative transference would be interpreted except where the patient's hostile feelings are undermining the course of therapy. In longer-term therapy, the absence of interpretations of the negative transference would be an indication, however, of avoidance by the therapist. This is because we all harbour ambivalent feelings and it would be unusual if the therapist did not become the focus of the patient's hostility at some stage in the therapy.

- *A focus on the transference can divert attention away from the present, conscious concerns of the patient, which also need to be addressed.* True enough, a few analytic practitioners are so intent on working in the transference that *everything* the patient says is reduced to a transference interpretation overshadowing the patient's present concerns. In my experience, this tendency is more prevalent amongst relatively inexperienced therapists than amongst experienced ones. An overemphasis on such interpretations is likely to be experienced by the patient as a failure to hear everything that he is saying, that is, both manifestly and in a displaced fashion. This can feel very alienating and is often counter-therapeutic.

Too great an emphasis on the transference may be associated with a negative outcome (see below) and a weakening of the alliance when the patient's immediate need is to verify and process actual historical events, for example, as with patients who have been traumatised. In such circumstances, it is important to firstly acknowledge what *has* happened and only then to elaborate the potential transference implications of the story if we consider that the patient will be helped by this.

- *Working in the transference encourages regression that is damaging for the more severely disturbed patient.* It is the case that transference interpretations are not indicated with all patient groups and may be more difficult to manage with particular patients. For example, those patients who are dominated by persecutory and sadistic phantasies cannot maintain an ongoing internal or external relationship with the therapist. Such patients may use extensive projection, denial or splitting to dilute and destroy evidence of an attachment, and they are often unaware of any feelings or thoughts about their relationship to the therapist. In such cases, working in the transference will involve holding in our minds, without interpreting out loud, the different unconscious phantasies in the matrix of the patient's self-to-object representations until the patient's own state of mind is receptive to taking some responsibility for his effect on us. These are instances when Steiner's distinction between patient-centred and therapist-centred interpretations is helpful (see Chapter 5). The therapist-centred interpretation allows for an exploration of the patient's view of the therapist's mind, for instance, *"You are concerned that I am sitting here in judgement of you today"*. A patient-centred interpretation would, on the other hand, suggest to the patient that he is projecting into us his own critical self.

With psychotic patients, it is not advisable to work in the transference unless under expert supervision. This is because the transference relies on the patient's capacity to appreciate the "as-if" quality of the transference, creating an "illusion that is experienced simultaneously as real and not real" (Ogden, 1986: 239). Psychotic patients lose this capacity in the grip of psychosis, though they may regain it at other points.

All of the above criticisms are worthy of note as they helpfully remind us that making a transference interpretation is a powerful intervention that needs to be carefully evaluated. Nevertheless, clinical experience repeatedly suggests that a well-timed and accurate transference interpretation can be very helpful in bringing to the fore core patterns of relationships that assist the patient towards change. Although transference analysis is at the very centre of psychoanalytic work, this should not lead us to neglect other types of interpretations. A transference interpretation is but one of several kinds of interventions at our disposal. Analytic sessions call upon us to make a variety of interventions, with a possible skewing towards transference interpretations, depending on our theoretical allegiances. However, as anyone who has had personal therapy will know, most therapists say far more that would be classified as "extra-transference" than the published case material suggests.

Approaching critically the use of transference interpretation is important since this intervention has become overvalued in some analytic circles as the main pathway to change. Although the most mutative transference interpretations are widely considered to be those related to the person of the therapist, there is no evidence that this is so since even supportive therapy, and other types of therapy that do not interpret the transference, have been shown to be effective. Indeed, Stewart (1990) also draws attention to the importance of transference interpretations towards other people in the patient's life. Although such interpretations, along with historical reconstruction, may be used defensively to avoid the present situation, this is by no means always the case. As Blum (1994) warns, a focus on the here-and-now can also function as a defence against the disturbing "there-and-then".

Reconstructive interpretations are an important part of technique. An interpretation based on historical reconstruction may help to bring coherence. For example, those patients who are insecurely attached may have a powerful phantasy of caregivers as unable to soothe and of themselves as somehow unmanageable. This experience is dominant in the transference relationship. For such patients, closeness may be, paradoxically, only experienced through an angry outburst. Such intensity is psychically vital because in its absence the anxiety is that those close to you might not respond. In therapy, the aim with such patients is to create structures that enable them to contain affect. Holmes (1998) refers to this as the process of "making stories", whereby the therapist helps the patient to make sense and meaning out of early experiences that have not been emotionally processed. With such patients, transference interpretation may not be the main focus of the therapeutic work, whereas reconstructive interpretations may be very helpful.

Having cautioned against an idealisation of transference interpretation over and above other kinds of interpretations, we can now consider the ways in which these interpretations are helpful, mutative interventions.

- *Transference dynamics are live and more immediate and hence verifiable in the here-and-now than the patient's report of past experiences or relationships outside of the therapy.* The material we work with in therapy is of two kinds: the actual stories and events recounted to us by the patient and the live experience with the patient in the consulting room. What the patient tells us has happened to him is subject to the distortions of memory. So, whilst this is a valuable source of information about what troubles the patient and how he manages his life, the information is of necessity once removed. By contrast, the relationship that develops with the therapist provides a more immediate experience of some of the conflicts that occur outside the therapeutic relationship. It allows us to make these conflicts explicit to the patient as they are happening in the room, thus providing raw material to reflect on with the patient.

- *The transference interpretation allows the therapist to make use of the emotional immediacy of the therapeutic relationship to counter intellectual resistances.* Some patients are very adept at telling stories, yet struggle with expressing affect. Working in the transference can help bypass intellectual resistances by seizing the emotional immediacy of the way the patient relates to the therapist. It is the live interaction with the therapist that facilitates the eventual reconstructions of primitive anxieties and defences (Roys, 1999). The immediacy of the interventions based on this more direct source of information can have a very profound, and often moving, effect on the patient.

- *The transference interpretation facilitates an increase in interpersonal intimacy by allowing the therapist to demonstrate attunement to the patient's current experience.* A well-timed and accurate transference interpretation is perhaps one of the most powerful expressions of the therapist's empathy as it shows the patient that he has been heard at various levels, not only in terms of what once happened, but also in terms of what *is* happening. For those patients who have not had the experience of being with another person who reflects back to them what is only indirectly implied in their communications, a transference interpretation can be experienced as containing and transformative.

- *The transference interpretation allows the therapist to address the patient's defences against intimacy as they emerge in the therapeutic relationship and so contributes to a strengthening of the alliance.* We all recognise that patients turn up for their sessions but this does not necessarily mean that they want to be there. The transference interpretation squarely focuses on the reasons why the patient may want to avoid the therapeutic relationship by trying to reflect on the anxieties it generates. At its best, this kind of interpretation helps the patient to move on from a resistance. However, a word of caution in this respect: it is precisely the patients who are most resistant who invite transference interpretations in the hope that this will resolve the therapeutic impasse. Such a focus may backfire as the patient may feel hounded by the transference focus on his resistance and may terminate treatment. In other words, too great a focus on the transference may compound resistance if the patient ends up feeling "got at". As Greenson (1967) helpfully noted, our interventions need to be sensitive to the fact that the patient may need to "run away" from insight. A transference interpretation should ideally further and/or deepen the patient's exploration of his conflicts. There will be times when the transference implications are evident to us, but it will not be timely to interpret them.

As I have repeatedly suggested, a transference interpretation is but one of several kinds of interpretations available to us. We thus always have to consider whether there may be particular reasons for *not* opting for a transference interpretation. If we do opt for this type of intervention, then we have another important consideration to make. As we saw in Chapter 5, an interpretation is only as good as its timing. Although Freud's early injunction to interpret only after the establishment of a positive early relationship is too rigid, as a transference interpretation with a very hostile patient in an initial session may contain the patient, we always have to be mindful of the current state of the therapeutic relationship before we interpret. Timing requires us to see things from the patient's point of view. Sometimes transference interpretations can acquire an unhelpful "return to sender" quality. To interpret prematurely that the patient is projecting something into us that he wishes to disavow in himself may simply leave the patient feeling that we cannot bear his projection (Mitriani, 2001). In this kind of situation we help the patient by allowing him to locate his bad objects in us for some time. This may be especially important for patients who would otherwise feel internally persecuted if they did not rid themselves of "bad" aspects of the self. Through bearing the split-off aspect of the patient's self and not returning it to the patient prematurely under pressure of our own need to be seen to be a "good" therapist, we may allow for a helpful transference of the bad internal objects. Sometimes we need to allow the transference to intensify, even if this feels uncomfortable and refrain from interpreting it as soon as we identify it.

- *Through a transference interpretation the therapist models a way of handling negative perceptions.* Many transference interpretations highlight the patient's negative perception and experience of the therapist. In making an interpretation that acknowledges such feelings and phantasies the therapist implicitly conveys to the patient that it is possible to reflect on such feelings without fearing being destroyed by them. The clarification of the distortions in the patient's experience of the therapist may contribute to a strengthening of the therapeutic alliance by allowing the patient to see the therapist as a potentially helpful person rather than the persecutory figure she may have come to represent in the transference.

THE AIMS OF WORKING IN THE TRANSFERENCE

Before we can approach how to make a transference interpretation we need to consider its most fundamental aspect, namely its function. If we subscribe to the view that we represent our interactions with others as procedures for how to be with others (see Chapter 2) and further, if as research indicates that these early procedures will be for the most part inaccessible as conscious memories, then all we can really work with in therapy is the patient's behaviour in the present relationship with us in the consulting room. Through what transpires between us and our patient, we can track shifting identifications, changing expectations of self and other and the accompanying affective states that may call into play particular defensive manoeuvres. Working in the transference helps us to bring to awareness the possible meanings of patterns of *current* relationships so that the patient can learn to modify patterns that have become automatic through the creation of a second-order representation of his inner experience.

The transference position of the patient at each moment in therapy is predominately coloured by a particular object relationship. The interpretation tracks these shifting configurations of self-and-other-in-interaction and, in so doing, has several, overlapping aims:

- *To help the patient recognise and own denied/spit-off aspects of the self.* This allows for a more integrated experience of the self, characterised by greater autonomy and flexibility.
- *To help the patient become aware of the discrepancy between how he perceives the therapist/other people and how they actually are.* This involves helping the patient understand how perception is coloured by internal states of mind and how this, in turn, gives rise to particular affective experiences and thus shapes behaviour. Insight into these distorting influences helps the patient separate old relationships from the new ones and is the starting point for the development of new models of relationships.
- *To help modify the force of the "bad" internal object.* This requires an exploration of the patient's bad or persecutory internal objects and the

associated matrix of anxieties and defences, with the aim of helping the patient internalise a more benign experience of the other.

- *The overall aim is to establish a link between internal and external figures* by helping the patient appreciate the dialectical nature of internal and external reality.

MAKING TRANSFERENCE INTERPRETATIONS: AN APPLIED EXAMPLE

In deconstructing a transference interpretation for the purposes of illustrating how to approach its formulation, I cannot recapture the immediacy of the therapeutic interaction, which is a key source of information that guides the intervention. Moreover, transference interpretations are not meant to be formulaic. These guidelines (see Table 7.1) are only intended to provide a possible framework to orient us as we approach making an interpretation. In this respect, Luborsky & Crits-Cristoph's (1998) "core conflictual relationship theme approach" (CCRT) is an alternative very helpful source. In this approach, the stories told by patients about their relationships are conceptualised as reflecting a wish (e.g. to be looked after), leading to a response from the other (e.g. rejection) that results in a particular response from the self (e.g. depressive withdrawal). The research carried out suggests that patients display the same CCRT patterns in the stories they recount about significant others as they do in their interactions with their therapist, thus supporting the notion of transference. Effective therapy has been found to be associated with accuracy in interpreting CCRT patterns (Crits-Cristoph et al., 1998).

Working in the transference requires that we attend to the patient's communications at different levels. As we approach a transference interpretation, we remind ourselves that the interpretation aims to link the patient's affect and behaviour with an internalised object relationship that has become actualised in the therapeutic situation. A transference interpretation makes explicit the patient's prototype of a relationship as it is actualised – whether negative or positive – at a given juncture in the session. It can only hope to capture a snapshot of the patient's way of relating at a particular moment. In other words, within a session, there will most probably be multiple transferences, depending on the patient's state of mind as it develops during the session and in response to our interventions.

Table 7.1   General considerations when constructing a transference interpretation

- Ask yourself what is the purpose of the interpretation? How does this relate to the aims of treatment?

- Ask yourself if there is a fit between the thematic content of the interpretation and the overall formulation of the patient's difficulties and the goals of treatment. This is especially important in brief work where it is essential that the interpretations are related to the focal area/conflict that has been agreed upon with the patient.

- Consider what evidence you have for the interpretation. Like any other type of interpretation, a transference interpretation is no more than a working hypothesis.

- Before sharing the interpretation, consider its timing: is the patient ready to hear it? How might it be experienced by him? Are you feeling a pressure to speak and give back a projection to the patient? If so, hold back from verbalising what you think may be going on until you have a clearer understanding of this.

- Especially with patients who are not well versed in psychoanalytic treatment, structure the interpretation by starting with what the patient has said or done (or not said or done) that suggests to you that he may be feeling in a particular way about you.

- Keep the interpretation relatively simple, without too many sub clauses! Including a reference to how you have arrived at the interpretation does not require you to cite chapter and verse.

- When you offer it, the interpretation needs to include clear references to the here-and-now. Especially in brief work, it is helpful to link more systematically the here-and-now experience to parallel relationship patterns in the patient's life.

- Where appropriate, it will be important to acknowledge that the stimulus for the patient's transference perception and reaction may partially come from something you have said or done (or not said or done).

- Too great an emphasis on transference interpretation may be associated with a negative outcome and weakening of the alliance when the patient's immediate need is to verify and process actual historical events (e.g. with patients who have been traumatised).

- If the intensity of the transference relationship is too strong and the patient cannot tolerate it (e.g. if the patient is in a psychotic state and cannot appreciate the as-if quality of the transference), reconstructive interpretations may be indicated as they de-escalate the intensity of the transference. Reconstructive interpretations can be supportive and are especially useful when working in once-weekly psychotherapy with patients with weak ego strength.

As we listen to our patients' narratives, we are listening out for the following:

- *Who does what to whom?* This involves identifying perceived intentions (benign and/or malign) towards the self and of the self towards others.
- *Who feels what towards whom?* This involves identifying the main affects present in the narrative.
- *How do we feel as we listen?* This involves identifying our countertransference (e.g. do we feel swamped, seduced or excited by the story?)

Once we have formulated a skeleton pattern of actions and affects, we can proceed to consider whether these have any relevance to the here-and-now situation. We rely on our capacity to sustain an internal process of supervision (Casement, 1985) and try to identify the ways in which we may have also contributed to the patient's experience. We thus aim to *identify the trigger* for the activation of a particular transference reaction – the trigger may be internal (e.g. a conscious or unconscious phantasy) as well as external, that is, an actual event.

A transference interpretation pulls together the above information. Often it does so piecemeal as we may not be able to capture the full picture all at once.[7] For example, we may have a clear sense of our countertransference but be less clear about the object relationship that is being played out in the transference. In practice, we build up to a full interpretation that eventually describes to the patient "What is going on and we explain why we think it is going on" (Riesenberg-Malcom, 1986: 75).

For the sake of illustration, let us imagine that we have bumped into one of our patients in the street. At that time, we were talking with a friend. We acknowledge the patient discretely but do not engage in any further exchanges with him. Later that same week, the patient arrives late for his session and begins the session voicing ambivalence about the therapy. He says that exercise helps to release his tension and that he thinks that if he made the effort to exercise regularly, that is all he needs. The patient then recounts a long story about a close friend he feels let down by because she has not phoned him for some weeks. As we listen to this, in our mind, we hypothesise that the lateness and the ambivalence about therapy are probably related to the chance encounter during the week and the feelings and phantasies this has stirred up. The eventual interpretation

---

[7]It is important to note this as the examples I have given throughout the book may give the misleading impression that we wait until we have formulated a full interpretation before interpreting it and that we arrive at such an interpretation within seconds. Nothing could be further from the painstakingly slow reality of what is involved in understanding another person's unconscious.

will typically contain a reference to the following [I have put in italics the thinking and hypotheses that gradually build up to a full interpretation]:

- *How we arrived at the formulation*   (e.g. *"Today you were late and you tell me that you could not see the point of coming. You then tell me that X has no time for you . . .I think that you are letting me know that. . ."*).
- *The patient's self-representation*   (e.g. "Today you were late and you tell me that you could not see the point of coming. You then tell me that X has no time for you. . .*I think that you are letting me know that when you met me in street the other day and saw me talking with another person you felt excluded, as if this was confirmation that I have another life separate from our relationship. Of course, you know that at some level, but at another level I think that my not stopping what I was doing and acknowledging you made you feel like a small child who isn't noticed"*).
- *An object representation*   (e.g. "Today you were late and you tell me that you could not see the point of coming. You then tell me that X has no time for you. . . I think that you are letting me know that when you met me in street the other day and saw me talking with another person you felt excluded, as if this was confirmation that I have another life separate from our relationship. I know you know that at some level, but at another level I think that my not stopping what I was doing and acknowledging you made you feel like a small child who isn't noticed, *as if I was neglecting you"*.)
- *A particular affect or anxiety linking the self and object representations*   (e.g. "Today you were late and you tell me that you could not see the point of coming. You then tell me that X has no time for you. . . I think that you are letting me know that when you met me in the street the other day and saw me talking with another person you felt excluded, as if this was confirmation that I have another life separate from our relationship. I know you know that at some level, but at another level I think that my not stopping what I was doing and acknowledging you made you feel like a small child who isn't noticed, as if I was neglecting you. *This has left you feeling very angry with me"*).
- The above interpretation would most probably then be further elaborated during the session by adding an account of the patient's possible conflicts in relation to internal objects along with the associated anxieties and defences put into action to avoid psychic pain (e.g. *"When you feel neglected in this way, it feels so painful that you say to yourself 'I don't need her. I can help myself by exercising more'"*).

We each develop a particular therapeutic style that influences how we present our interpretations to the patient. The "how" to convey our understanding of the transference to a patient – especially one who has not had exposure to psychoanalytic therapy before – is worth considering.

Given that a transference interpretation essentially involves describing a particular object relationship that is active in the patient's mind, I have found it helpful with some patients to present this dynamic as a kind of "internal conversation". For example, say we formulate that at a given point in a session the patient feels criticised by us and that his way of managing this is to become contemptuous of our interventions. In this scenario, we might share our formulation thus: *"I think that when you experience me as critical in your mind, you are no longer talking with someone who is on your side but with someone who is attacking you. The only way you feel you can protect yourself is by putting me down as if you are saying to me 'I don't need you anymore. What you have to offer me is worthless'"*.

Mark was a man in his late twenties who presented with longstanding interpersonal difficulties starting in adolescence. He had never successfully managed to sustain a long-term intimate relationship. He recounted a difficult family life as he was growing up: his father had suffered from manic depression and his mother appeared to have managed her unhappy marriage by working hard and having affairs. Mark was an only child and recalled spending most of his childhood either playing alone or in the care of other family members whom he felt resented the burden of having to care for him. He described his early experience of being cared for as a kind of "pass the parcel". Over time, we came to understand the instability of his early life as one of the sources of the obsessionality that was characteristic of his approach to life. Mark liked routines and reacted with anger when these were in any way altered. In therapy he related quite concretely to the physical environment. He liked it if the room was exactly as he had left it after his previous session and reacted anxiously and/or angrily if he noticed any changes, however minor.

After one Christmas break he returned to his session and lay on the couch very silently. This was unusual for him and I made a mental note of this. As the minutes ticked by, I began to feel ill at ease with the silence. After five minutes, Mark started to talk: "There is a new picture on your wall outside the room," he remarked. "It's an interesting one. I'm not sure what I think of it", he added. Mark then quickly moved on to telling me about his break. Everything had been fine except that his mother "as is her wont", he said acerbically, decided to stage what he had experienced as a very dramatic scene during the Christmas lunch. He berated her for always putting her needs first without a care for anyone else. He said: "The stupid cow made a quick exit after her performance, saying she was going to visit her elderly aunt". But Mark "knew", he emphasised, that she was only going to go a few houses down the street to the latest man in her life. He said that his father had by then fallen asleep in the armchair, snoring, and he had been left at the dinner table staring at an old print of his birthplace that his mother had given him as a present for Christmas. He concluded by telling me that she should know by now that he did not like coloured prints and that this disregard for his wishes was typical of her.

To arrive at an interpretation, I progressively work through a series of stages in my own mind:

- *Step 1: Identifying the themes:* Mark gives me a vivid picture of a desultory Christmas lunch. He relates a story in which he is left stranded at the dinner table staring at the present his mother gave him – a picture that Mark says his mother should have known he would not like – whilst he knows that she has gone off to see her lover. There are two dominant themes: one is the experience of his mother not keeping him in mind enough to know his preferences and a related theme of being supplanted by a rival, that is, mother's lover – another version of not being the most important one in his mother's mind.
- *Step 2: Identifying the trigger:* Internalised object relationships are triggered by the patient's idiosyncratic perception of an external event. Working in the transference involves approaching Mark's narrative not only as an expression of his feelings about what happened over Christmas but also as the manifestation, in the transference, of a very specific internalised object relationship. The activation of this object relationship is reinforced by two events associated specifically with the therapy. The story about the print that Mark had not liked and that his mother, according to him, should know that he would not like makes me think about the meaning of the new painting I have introduced since the break. I hypothesise that the vacation break and the change to the physical frame are fuelling a hostile transference towards me.
- *Step 3: Noting the countertransference:* I am aware of a number of emotional reactions as Mark speaks. I feel reprimanded for being a selfish mother/therapist who has not kept him in mind. This feeling helps me to connect with the possible meaning of the two triggers identified above. I speculate that the appearance of the new picture in my corridor is evidence to Mark that during the break I have been meeting my own needs, leaving him alone, whilst I engage with my interests and other people in my life as symbolically represented by the new picture. Mark's narrative suggests to me that I have become identified in his mind with a version of a mother who abandons him at the dinner table whilst she visits her lover, just as I left him for the break and engaged with my personal life, which excludes him.
- *Step 4: Identifying the patient's self-representation:* Mark seems to be positioning himself in the narrative as the neglected and rejected

little boy who is supplanted by a rival in his mother's affections. This hypothesis is informed not only by all the above considerations but it is also based on Marks' description of his father asleep, snoring. This description conjures up in me an image of an ineffectual man who does not represent in Mark's mind a potent man who can sustain his wife's interest. In light of this, I speculate that Mark is identified with a castrated father and he feels that he is not exciting enough to sustain my interest during the break.

- *Step 5: Identifying the object representation:* The focus of the narrative is on Mark's mother. She is depicted as selfish and insensitive to his needs and preferences. This suggests to me that Mark internally relates to an object that is selfish, who prioritises her needs over his and, importantly, who does not know his mind, that is, as Mark tells me, his mother should have known that he does not like coloured prints. I hear this as him saying to me in the transference that as his therapist I should have known that he does not like change in the physical environment of the consulting room and that he finds the break difficult. I hypothesise that my new print is evidence that I have a life separate from him, and more specifically, that it symbolises the existence of a rival – my partner – in his phantasy.

- *Step 6: Identifying the dominant affect:* Mark is giving voice to a number of affects. He is angry and contemptuous towards his mother (e.g. "She's a stupid cow"). I speculate that this is a defence against his feelings of abandonment and an experience of himself as not exciting or potent enough to sustain his mother's interest. Though this may be right, these affects are not the most immediate and therefore would only be interpreted at a later stage, depending on how Mark reacts to the first interpretation focusing on his anger.

- *Step 7: Formulating the interpretation:* This needs to take all of the above into account and might look something like this: "Christmas at home was difficult and I am aware that it was difficult for you to get going in the session today. I think you are also perhaps letting me know that you found the break difficult. It's as if the new picture in my hallway becomes painful evidence in your mind that I have other interests that invade your place in my mind. In my absence you quickly feel as if I am rushing off to see another man whom I prefer to you, leaving you alone with a print that I should know is not to your taste. I think that this makes you feel very angry with me."

In making this kind of interpretation, I am trying to help Mark identify how he positions himself in relation to his objects. Whether my interpretation is helpful will depend on whether Mark "runs with it", that is, whether it leads to an elaboration of the patterns I identify in the interpretation and their associated affects and whether it extends to helping him perceive his interactions with others in light of this pattern.

WORKING WITH COUNTERTRANSFERENCE

One of the most important sources of information that we can draw upon to formulate the transference is our own countertransference. Nowadays most therapists view their reactions and feelings towards the patient as countertransference, which allows for an understanding of the patient's as-yet unverbalised, and sometimes, pre-verbal, experience. When the patient projects an unwanted feeling into us, we understand this, in our countertransference, as an opportunity to feel and experience for ourselves what the patient may be feeling (Rosenfeld, 1987).

Like the transference, the major part of countertransference is unconscious. Our countertransference is the response to the patient's projective identification. Sandler (1976) speaks of "role responsiveness" to denote the way in which the patient may actualise an internal scenario with the therapist who is recruited to play a particular role scripted by the patient's internal world. Such unconscious communication is powerful and we may at times enact the role we are unconsciously recruited to. The majority of enactments are neither intrinsically good nor bad for the analytic process; their value or otherwise depends partly on the use made of them. Needless to say, this can never justify abusive actions by the therapist in the name of an unconscious pressure to respond in a particular way to the patient.

How do we recognise that we have become the recipient of a projective identification? Unfortunately, there isn't a formula for this. Usually we become aware of it when we discover, through our internal and external supervision, that we are participating in the patient's unconsciously scripted scenario. Mostly, we experience countertransference as a pull away from our analytic role that strives to be neutral towards enacting a particular role in relation to the patient:

> Most contemporary analysts would agree that at times the patient actualises an internal scenario within the analytic relationship that results in the analyst's being drawn into playing a role scripted by the patient's internal world. The exact dimensions of this role, however, will be coloured by the analyst's own subjectivity and goodness of fit between the patient's projected contents and the analyst's internal representational world (Gabbard, 1995: 481–2).

Gabbard draws attention to an important fact, namely that our own vulnerabilities or blind spots will sensitise us to particular projections. Supervision is an indispensable space that allows us to monitor these unconscious pulls. The countertransference becomes an obstacle if what the patient projects into us corresponds too closely with aspects of ourselves that we have not yet fully assimilated. We do well to remind ourselves that our own conflicts and transferences are never fully resolved. Through our own analysis, we may have reached a better understanding of ourselves but we are always potentially vulnerable to a revival of our conflicts in our every-day personal relationships and in our relationships with our patients. Our capacity for primitive feelings such as jealousy, fear or rage is always an inherent potential that we need to closely monitor in our work (Searles, 1979). Money-Kyrle elaborates the process of "working-through" which enables the therapist to disentangle what belongs to whom:

> . . .first, the analyst's emotional disturbance{is attended to], for he may have to deal with this silently in himself before he can disengage himself sufficiently to understand the other two; then the patient's part in bringing this about and finally its effect on the [patient] (1956: 361).

When a disruption in our analytic functioning occurs, Segal suggests that we must:

> . . .try to understand the nature of the disruption and the information it gives us about our interaction with the patient. When such disrup-tions occur, there is always an internal pressure to identify with our countertransference and it is very important to be aware that counter-transference is the best of servants but the worst of masters, and that the pressure to identify with it and act it out in ways either obvious or very subtle and hidden is always powerful (1993: 20).

Because the pressure to identify, as Segal suggests, is "always powerful", the most important skill we need to acquire in using countertransference constructively is to learn to be patient. An interpretation informed by countertransference is the end point of a long process of gradually testing out hypotheses. The process of interpretation when we have become identified with, and have acted on a projective identification involves identifying the following (see Table 7.2 for guidelines):

- What has been projected.
- What defensive purpose the projection serves, that is, what feeling or state of mind or part of the self is the patient wishing to rid himself of and why.
- Whether we have contributed to an enactment, that is, whether instead of thinking about what is happening in the therapeutic relationship we are pushed into some kind of action.

Assuming that we consider that the patient's state of mind is receptive to re-owning his projection, we pull together these various strands into an interpretation. This involves two stages:

Table 7.2   Guidelines for working with countertransference

- Get accustomed to noting your own emotional responses to the patient's verbal and non-verbal behaviour.
- Don't dismiss seemingly unconnected associations that may come to mind as you listen to your patient (e.g. a song or a character from a book).
- Are the feelings you experience (or that you think you should be experiencing but are not) accountable for in terms of issues in your own life at the time?
- Even if you think that the feelings are personally relevant to you, you may still be also responding to the patient's projection. It may simply be that you are especially sensitive to that particular projection at the time. Be careful to monitor what belongs to you so as to create enough mental space to reflect on what your emotional reaction may also be telling you about your patient.
- Refrain from intervening, especially if you experience an urge to do so. The need to interpret is often an indication of the power of the projection that you want to hand back to the patient because you feel intruded by it.
- Try to stay with the feeling(s) evoked in you. Note what it makes you feel like doing or what it makes you feel about yourself (e.g. incompetent, powerful, attractive). If you feel under pressure to say something, this may be a further indication that projective identification is operative.
- Typically, the process of internal reflection eases the psychological strain as you gain important emotional distance and hence perspective. When you have reached this stage internally, you are probably ready to begin to formulate a possible interpretation and to judge the patient's receptivity to it.

- We begin by exploring with the patient the phantasy component of the projective identification and establishing this as a separate construction from the reality of the situation. This may require a lot of work and time but is important since as long as we embody the projection, our interpretation will be meaningless to the patient.
- Once the patient is able to recognise that he has distorted an aspect of reality, the defensive function of the projective identification can be talked about.

Anne was a young woman with a sharp intellect. She was relatively successful in her work but very unhappy in her personal relationships. She had a highly ambivalent relationship with her mother from whom she sought advice only to then rebuff anything she might suggest. For a host of reasons she blamed her mother for her own low self-esteem and inability to establish an enduring relationship. She had felt that her mother always responded anxiously to any problem she presented her with.

During the course of our work together, Anne brought to the session the question of how she could meet a man. She said that she wanted a relationship but due to her heavy work schedule she did not have time to meet anyone. She also bemoaned the fact that she worked mostly with women so that the opportunities for meeting men were limited.

In the session in question, I thought to myself that a resourceful woman like Anne must have surely known that nowadays dating agencies were a possible way of meeting other men. However, rather than silently reflecting on why I was having these thoughts, I found myself deviating from my usual interpretative position and asked her why she did not consider a dating agency.

As soon as I spoke, I felt as if I had become her mother trying to fix her up with a man. By this stage it was, of course, too late. Anne seized on this, criticising me for making the suggestion. Dating agencies were unreliable, she told me, and she thought that only dysfunctional people joined them. She said that she felt I wanted her to find a partner at all costs so that I could discharge myself of my duties in relation to her.

Anne's response to my advice was very interesting. At one level she was, of course, right in criticising me for making a suggestion: it was not my role as her therapist to suggest how to meet a man. In that moment, quite accurately, Anne perceives me as a "dysfunctional" therapist as I have indeed acted rather than reflected on my wish to give advice. In making this suggestion, especially one about how to meet men, I shifted into acting like her mother to whom Anne often turned for help when a relationship failed. Between us, we thus appeared to have created a similar scenario to the one Anne had often described with her mother: she came to the session with a problem and I offered advice that she duly rebuffed. I became in her experience overeager to solve the problem as if I could not bear to stay with it. This mirrored Anne's own portrayal of her mother as someone who responded anxiously to her problems. There was no doubt in my mind that I had erred but Anne's response was worthy of exploration in its own right even if it was prompted by my enactment of a role familiar to her.

I described this pattern to Anne acknowledging that I had indeed given her advice. As we explored this together, we came to understand that Anne was heavily invested emotionally in proving her mother/me wrong. This was because if we were right or helpful in our advice, she could no longer blame her mother/me for her predicament. In other words, accepting her mother's help appeared to be equated with somehow letting her mother off the hook. By getting better, Anne recognised that she could no longer use her problems as a way of reminding her mother of her shortcomings. My enactment thus helped us to understand further some of the resistances to getting better that had been interfering with our work. The enactment was at one level an error, but one that we were able to use constructively to further the work.

TRANSFERENCE INTERPRETATION AND ITS RELATIONSHIP TO THE OUTCOME OF PSYCHOTHERAPY

The interpretation of the transference aided by a careful use of countertransference is one of the distinctive features of psychoanalytic work. In my personal experience of being in analysis, I have found that such interventions by my analyst have helped me to think about what kinds of relationships I set up in my own mind and how this profoundly affects how I then experience myself in relation to other people. The emotional immediacy of the transference makes such interpretations both challenging and often very moving, as I feel, in that moment, that my analyst has understood something profoundly important about what goes on in my mind and how that can distort what I then think is going on in other people's minds about me.

When an intervention such as the interpretation of transference can have such a powerful impact, it can be hard to approach it critically. There is indeed something almost "sacred" about the transference interpretation within some analytic circles such that it feels like heresy to even ask the question: "Does it make more of a difference than other interventions?". No doubt it will be apparent in reading this chapter that I believe that transference interpretations are powerful and often very helpful interventions. Nevertheless, it is important to balance what we feel "works" in our practice with what we can learn from research studies.

The therapeutic relationship broadly conceived has long been recognised as a potent vehicle for change. Research has consistently supported a robust association between the quality of the therapeutic alliance and the outcome overriding technical differences between the therapies studied (e.g. Krupnick et al., 1996). Influential reviews of this type of literature underscore the importance of interpersonal factors as prominent ingredients of change in all therapies (Horvath & Symonds, 1991; Roth & Fonagy, 1996).

The research supporting a robust relationship between the quality of the therapeutic alliance and the outcome stands in contrast to the comparatively scarce research on the association between transference interpretation and outcome. The available research provides contradictory results. Several of the studies concern themselves with quite a specific client group – borderline patients – with whom the question of whether the transference should or should not be interpreted liberally is the source of controversy amongst psychoanalytic practitioners. For example, the Menninger Foundation Psychotherapy Research Project (Kernberg *et al.*, 1972) found that borderline patients treated by skilled therapists who focused on the transference showed a significantly better outcome than those who interpreted the transference less. A later predictive study from the same research group, using both quantitative and qualitative measures, however, produced an unexpected result. Those patients treated by predominantly supportive therapists showed greater gain than had been anticipated by the previous findings (Horwitz, 1974). This mixed result may have been partly the function of the study's design. Firstly, the participants had not been assessed using the specific category of Borderline Personality Disorder (BPD). Secondly, no detailed process study was carried out precluding an analysis of treatment process over time. Lastly, the therapeutic alliance was not measured, and this may have accounted for a significant source of variance.

Process data is provided in a later study by Gabbard *et al.* (1994a) who undertook a detailed analysis of transcripts from six psychotherapy sessions with a borderline patient. They found that the transference focus increased this particular patient's collaboration. While the study is of note because of its detailed analysis of clinical material, it is not possible to draw any firm conclusions because it was a single case study. Nevertheless, the authors describe a potentially useful methodology that could be replicated with a bigger sample. The authors also draw attention to an important question, namely whether the clarification of distortions in the patient's experience of the therapist leads to the enhancement of the therapeutic alliance (defined as "collaboration" in this study) by allowing the patient to see the therapist as a potentially helpful person rather than the persecutory figure that they may have come to represent in the transference.

Ogrodniczuk *et al.* (1999) examined the frequency and proportion of transference interpretations along with the therapeutic alliance and treatment outcome in twenty sessions of individual psychodynamic psychotherapy. They found an inverse relationship between frequency of transference interpretation and both patient-related therapeutic alliance and favourable outcome among low quality of object-relationship patients. This study suggested that there may be limitations in the use of transference interpretations for certain types of patients.

A more recent study examined the relationship between transference interpretation and the therapeutic alliance in personality-disordered patients, using transcripts of psychotherapy sessions for five patients undergoing long-term psychotherapy. Bond *et al.* (1998) found that transference interpretations were followed by a deterioration in the therapeutic alliance when the alliance, as measured by a widely used scale (CAL-PAS), was weak, but by enhanced work when the alliance was rated as solid. However, whether the alliance was weak or strong, both interpretation of defence and supportive interventions enhanced therapeutic work without increasing defensiveness. This study suggests that transference interpretations are risky and should be carefully considered unless they occur in the context of an already well-established therapeutic alliance.

Piper *et al.* (1991) found that high rates of transference interpretations were associated with poor outcome for patients who had a history of high quality of object relationships. The best follow-up outcomes for patients with high quality of object relationships were associated with a low concentration of transference interpretations (a high level was defined as one in every five interventions) and high correspondence (i.e. accuracy of interpretation). It is, however, possible that the results of this study were skewed because some of the therapists made excessive use of transference interpretations. The results were also of a correlational nature and it neglected such confounding variables as the timing and accuracy of the interpretations.

The research studies available on transference interpretation are limited in number and by the methodological flaws encountered in many of them. Any conclusions we draw from them can only be tentative. The studies converge on the conclusion that the interpretation of transference can contribute both to a strengthening as well as to a deterioration in the therapeutic alliance. If this is the case, before we interpret the transference, it is incumbent on us to evaluate the strengths and weaknesses in the therapeutic alliance at different points in the therapy and to pay close attention to the basic elements of the relationship such as the patient's trust and his perceived support. Moreover, as Mollon reminds us:

> Too much attention to the transference can evoke inhibiting shame and can undermine the patient's own efforts at autonomous strivings for understanding. . . Sometimes patients may have valid insights into their own motivations and preoccupations and sometimes may be engaging in important analytic work through thinking and exploring their own thoughts. . . without the need for anything from the analyst other than his attention and reverie (2002: 135–136).

Whilst there is good reason to believe that transference interpretations are powerful agents of change, the research helpfully reminds us that change also occurs in the absence of such interpretations suggesting, at the very least, that they are very useful interventions but they need to be considered as part of a range of interventions available to us.

FURTHER READING

Alexandris, A. & Vaslamatzis, G. (Eds) (1993) *Countertransference: Theory, Technique and Teaching*. London: Karnac Books.

Esman, A. (Ed.) (1990) *Essential Papers on Transference*. New York: New York University Press.

8

WORKING WITH ENDINGS

We reach the end of the book, aptly, with an exploration of endings in psychotherapy. Perhaps even more than any other chapter, this one is slanted personally. How we end, that is, what modifications we allow for to the therapeutic relationship as we approach an ending and subsequent to it, probably reflects our personal therapeutic styles more than any particular theoretical allegiance. This means that we must be all the more vigilant about how we proceed with our patients as we work through the ending phase.

Endings bring sharply into relief the assumptions we make about the aims of therapy and hence of the criteria by which we evaluate the appropriateness of ending. In this chapter, we will focus on the nature of endings in therapy from both the patient's and the therapist's perspectives and on how to approach the task of ending and the management of post-therapy contact.

ENDINGS: THE PATIENT'S PERSPECTIVE

Melanie Klein likened the process of ending therapy to the process of weaning from the breast; others liken it to the emotional demands and pains of growing up. At the core of these descriptions is the assumption that endings restimulate other salient experiences of separation such as bereavements, transitions (e.g. leaving home) or the ending of other significant relationships. The way these experiences were negotiated will determine in part at least the way the patient approaches the end of therapy.

"The aim of psychoanalysis," writes Laplanche, "is to end it so new life can begin" (1998: 23). This is an ending loaded with anticipation and dread. Yet it is, paradoxically, the only certainty that therapist and patient can hold on to. Endings are a key part of the process of psychotherapy. Therapy is time limited and as Orgel put it, "Every analysis is a multidirectional journey towards a termination" (2000: 723). Even lengthy, open-ended therapies unfold in the knowledge that one day this relationship will come to an end. This unavoidable feature of the analytic frame is essential to the unfolding process. Longer-term therapy, of course, fosters the illusion of timelessness, but both therapist and patient still work within the strict confines of time even if both parties often do their best to try to avoid this fact:

> It is the lure of timelessness hovering all analytic psychotherapies that makes termination of therapy so hard. Timelessness takes away from our terror of finite time, our terror of endings and ultimately, our terror of death (Molnos, 1995: 1).

Time is the ultimate reality as it propels us unfailingly towards death. Of course, we don't all go about our daily lives keeping this fact at the forefront of our consciousness. We all find different ways of managing this reality. It is only when we are confronted with loss and endings that this primitive anxiety is awakened and floods consciousness. Because endings in therapy are usually clear-cut events, they can give rise to a feeling that what *is* will no longer be in a few weeks or months ahead. Hence, endings can be experienced by some patients as a head-on collision with an experience of finality.

The particular emotional colouring that the ending assumes will vary considerably between patients depending on their unique developmental histories and their relationship to time. We so take time for granted that we seldom stop to consider the emotional experience of time and what shapes our individual attitudes towards it. For example, time can be felt to be on our side or it can persecute us as it rapidly passes by. Psychotherapy offers a unique opportunity for an exploration of the subjective experience of time, especially around the negotiation of endings when "the illusory timelessness is transformed into a real temporality" (Grinberg, 1990).

For some patients, endings do not activate an anxiety about death as much as they force upon the patient the reality of separateness. Time is that gap between two people. Time is about separateness: the end of each session can feel like an unwelcome reminder that the therapist and patient are two separate beings. As the therapist calls time the patient, depending on his own experiences, hears and feels different things: he may feel rejected or abandoned. The final ending of therapy only serves to accentuate these feelings and the associated phantasies further.

Our individual experience of time is loaded with the quality of our early nurturing experiences and phantasies from the past (Molnos, 1995):

The first intuition of duration appears as an interval which stands between the child and the fulfilment of its desires (Whitrow, 1988: 5).

We learn about time, about waiting, in the encounter between our needs and their satisfaction or frustration or neglect. Delays in getting needs met awaken in the child a sense of time as well as a sense of reality. Neglect of the child's needs may, however, contribute to persecutory anxieties that lend to waiting, an intolerable quality in which time is experienced as a cruel other depriving the self.

Amanda had been in therapy for two and a half years when she had to end therapy because she had to relocate abroad due to work. We had known of this move six months before, so we had some time to explore the ending phase of our relationship.

When she first started therapy, Amanda was struggling with eating problems. She fluctuated between periods of restrictive dieting and bingeing. Her early life had been economically privileged but emotionally deprived. Her parents had remained together but both had extramarital affairs. Amanda was sent off to boarding school at the age of eight and by the age of fourteen she had become anorexic. Her brother was eight years older than her and she had only had a distant relationship with him.

Amanda's relationship to food and, more generally to the meeting of her needs, became a focus of the therapy. Just as she was very depriving towards herself, so could she be very withholding in the therapy. Many of our sessions were filled with a tense silence that I experienced as hostile. Amanda would lie on the couch, very still, barely uttering a few words. I was often left feeling as if I was craving for a few crumbs/words just as I imagined Amanda often felt when she deprived herself of food but determinately refused to eat more than a few pieces of fruit all day.

The work with Amanda was slow and often frustrating. When she discovered that she would have to relocate abroad, she both welcomed this as an opportunity to further her career and as a "legitimate" excuse for ending therapy. At first, she was excited and relieved to be finishing therapy. During this phase, her eating became more chaotic. She frequently binged and then subjected her body to vigorous and excessive exercise everyday. She seemed to be saying: "I am desperately hungry/needy" and would then manically deny any such need by reassuring herself that she could rid herself of food/need through three-hour-long exercise marathons. After such marathon sessions at the gym, Amanda would come to our sessions in a euphoric mood, speaking fast, leaving me with little opportunity for intervening.

It was apparent that the closer we got to our ending the more Amanda was using manic defences to manage it. When she spoke about the exercise she was undertaking, she described how whilst on the rowing or running machines she felt a surge of excitement about the move abroad. She angrily protested against any attempts on my part to metaphorically get off the running machine and slowdown the pace in the session and to reflect on what was happening between us. I often felt as if I was in the room with a very omnipotent Amanda telling me she did not need me or anything/anyone else.

At this point, I was reminded of Amanda's description early on in the therapy, of waiting for her parents to pick her up from boarding school and how distressed she was when they failed to turn up or arrived very late. Even prior to the boarding school experience, Amanda had described always having to "wait" for her parents as she experienced them as getting on with their lives, neglecting her in the process. She said that her mother occasionally jokingly recounted an incident when she had forgotten Amanda in her pram in a shop and had only realised this when she got home. By the time she had retrieved Amanda, her mother said that she had been inconsolable. Amanda had recounted this incident to me as further proof that her mother had neglected her.

In the last two months before Amanda eventually stopped therapy, we were able to make some inroads into her very rigid defensive structure. I was able to talk with her about how through her manic embrace of her new life abroad and her all-consuming exercise routines she had managed to obliterate any thoughts about our separation. It was as if she was giving me an experience of being the one who is forgotten in a pram and has to wait whilst she got on with her life. It was this connection that eventually enabled Amanda to stop the frantic talk in the sessions and she could then allow herself some space to reflect and connect with the baby part of her that so often felt abandoned but who had internally resolutely decided she would never feel like that again.

Ending therapy is about much more than the pain of saying goodbye. How the patient ends the therapeutic journey encapsulates his level of psychological functioning at the time and in many cases, is a good indicator of how the patient has progressed in therapy. This is because ending constructively involves a number of related processes:

- *Ending entails mourning.* The work of mourning requires of the patient that he can relate to the therapist as a whole object with imperfections that are frustrating without this overshadowing the strengths or qualities that will be missed. Ending requires accepting the separateness of the therapist and the pain that this can give rise to. Working through this loss promotes internalisation of the therapeutic relationship that allows the patient to establish the analytic process as a structure within his mind, that is, the patient becomes self-reflective. This internalisation can only occur once the patient has accepted the therapist's separateness and mourned the consequent loss.
- *Ending involves re-owning projections.* Over the course of therapy, we often become the container of the patient's projections – a repository for the split-off aspects of the self. Ending involves relinquishing this container as the patient has to re-own what belongs to him and learn to bear it within himself.
- *Ending involves coming to terms with phantasy of being replaced by the next patient.* This requires that the patient manages the feelings of envy and rivalry this arouses without recourse to destructive attacks that devalue the therapeutic experience in the patient's mind, thereby allowing him to defensively come to terms with the loss.
- *Ending involves gratitude.* The capacity to be grateful represents one of the most significant psychic achievements as it involves acknowledging our dependence on another, whilst recognising his separateness and autonomy. Only if the patient can do this can he take in and make his own what the therapist has given him. This allows the patient to internalise the analytic relationship such that at the end of the therapy he can experience the loss of the therapist, whilst also feeling that he has been enriched by the therapeutic relationship.

TERMINATION: THE THERAPIST'S PERSPECTIVE

Endings pose a challenge not only to the patient but also to the therapist. Milner (1950) rightly highlights that as therapists we often bypass the experience most of our patients have to go through since, by virtue of being in the profession, we seldom have to say a definitive goodbye to our own training therapists. As a result, Milner suggests that we may in fact be "... *handicapped in knowing about what endings feel like [since]... we have chosen to identify with our analyst's profession and to act out that identification*" (1950: 1950).

Just as our patients make an investment in us and develop an attachment to us, so do we have an emotional investment in the therapeutic process and in the patient's life. This investment is in many respects natural and assists the therapeutic enterprise, but it can tip into an investment that is about gratification of a narcissistic need within us to be central and indispensable to another person. When this is the case, endings can be very problematic.

The end of therapy represents a loss for us, just as it does for the patient. The loss can hold different meanings, for example, it may represent the loss of someone we genuinely like or the loss of a part of us that feels identified with the patient or the loss of an experience of ourselves as special and powerful or the loss of our therapeutic ambitions (Viorst, 1982). Just as each patient reacts differently to endings, so will there be a variation in our own responses. These will be partly determined by our own dynamics around separation and loss, as well as being coloured by the specific relationship we have with each patient.

There will be patients we will miss and find it hard to stop seeing, just as there will be a minority of patients we may feel relieved to stop working with. Both reactions are worthy of exploration. The patient we can't wait to stop seeing may be the one who taps into our own conflicts and reminds us of aspects of ourselves we would rather forget, just as the one whom we will miss may be the patient who has become a narcissistic extension of us. Basing a decision to end or not to end on such feelings is likely to be misguided and unhelpful. This is why our own dynamics with respect to separation require thoughtful monitoring as we approach ending as they may impinge on our capacity to help the patient to end. Supervision is a key part of this monitoring process: a supervisor can point out how we may unwittingly collude with a patient by not ending when it is indicated or when we agree to end, but what the patient needs is for us to understand his wish to end as a form of acting out.

Endings are a time when not only the patient reviews his progress but also when we assess our helpfulness or otherwise. If the patient has improved, we vicariously partake in his achievement and experience satisfaction in our work. Some patients will leave us feeling that we have done a good job, while others leave us feeling that we have failed and should start looking for an alternative career. Sometimes the sense of failure we experience can be understood as an attack by the patient that is actually his defence against loss: we become in the patient's mind a failed, useless therapist whose loss becomes trivial, thus easing the pain of separation. Under this kind of pressure, we may be left questioning our own competence.

In some cases we have to recognise that, unfortunately, we do fail our patients. This can be painful to bear, especially if we are at the beginning of our careers and our own professional identity is still taking shape and is fragile. Some so-called failures are avoidable, but I have in mind too the more ordinary failures that are unavoidable because no matter how good we are as a therapist, we can never be more than "good-enough". In minor, and sometimes more significant ways, we will fail our patients, just like the good enough parent will get it wrong some of the time. Moreover, therapy can never hope to "correct" the deprivations some of our patients have suffered. It can offer understanding of the past, it can never undo it. What we recognise rationally to be the limits of therapy can be experienced by some patients as our personal failure towards them. Likewise, the inevitable limitations of psychoanalytic treatments can represent for us a narcissistic injury that, if left unrecognised, can contribute to a wish to keep the patient in therapy in an attempt to omnipotently deny the fact that we cannot help him (Dewald, 1982). Irrespective of how much personal therapy we have had, our own infantile omnipotent phantasies are never completely renounced and can trip us up.

Working as a therapist is both deeply rewarding and emotionally taxing. Quite reasonably, we yearn for some recognition when we have done a good job. As we approach the end of a therapy, it helps, however, not to expect thanks or miracles. This is for two reasons. Firstly, endings awaken highly ambivalent feelings that may overshadow the patient's gratitude. Secondly, it is often only after the therapy has ended that its full value sinks in. In therapy, what happens once it is over is as important as what happens during it (Klauber, 1981). This is because all that ends is the analytic relationship but the process of psychoanalysis, which is hopefully internalised by the patient, is interminable (Grinberg, 1990). Keeping this fact in mind helps us to make sense of difficult endings that can otherwise leave us unnecessarily doubting our own competence.

Because endings are infused with ambivalence, I approach my patients' gratitude at the end of a therapy with curiosity to begin with, rather than take it at face value. Hopefully, most of our patients are genuinely grateful to us for the help they have received. Gratitude is rooted in a realistic appraisal that therapy has not been a magic cure and that we are not all-wonderful but the patient still feels that we have offered something helpful. With some patients, however, the conscious expression of gratitude is excessive: we are talked about as saviours or as the parent they never had. As we approach endings, we need to beware of the seduction of idealisation as much as the danger of denigration. Neither position will help our patients to deal with the infinitely more difficult psychic task of saying goodbye to a therapist who is both loved for what she has offered and hated for what she could not put right.

Gratitude comes in all shapes and sizes. There is the seemingly grateful patient who buys us an expensive present and the patient who is able to say thank you without needing to offer a gift. Gifts are sometimes a token of appreciation but they may also cover up considerable resentment that cannot be expressed. Although in the course of an ongoing therapy a gift usually needs interpreting, at the end of therapy it is often appropriate to accept it unless the gift itself is in some way inappropriate or it is offered in such a way that it suggests something is not being expressed directly.

Karl had been referred to me at the hospital for some "anger management". He was aware that his anger alienated people, especially his partner, Jane, who had left him, a few months prior to the referral. At the start he had not been keen on the idea of therapy, yet he had been worried about his own potential for destroying good things in his life. His relationships were subject to constant testing on his part and were based on an expectation that others simply did not care about him.

In the final session of a year-long therapy, Karl arrived with a gift. He handed it to me as he walked through the door in what I experienced as a very brusque manner. He sat down and asked provocatively: "Aren't you going to open it?". I paused and waited to see if Karl was going to say any more, but he remained silent, awaiting a response from me. I found myself feeling angry with him as well as hurt by the brusqueness of his gesture. I eventually said: "If I did open it I wonder what it is that you are really wanting me to see". Karl shuffled in the chair and then said: "It's all gone wrong". He placed his face in his hands and cried silently for a few minutes. He then said: "I woke up this morning and decided I wanted to make this a good ending, not like when Jane left and I chased her down the road, shouting. But when I saw you as I walked in I thought you looked like you didn't care and couldn't wait to see the back of me. And then I thought to myself: 'After all the trouble I've gone to, I bet you she won't even open it'".

Karl and I were able to understand how when he had gone shopping for my present he had been buying a present to a therapist/me to whom he had felt connected in a positive way. But as he arrived for his final session and handed me the gift, he was seized by what we had come to know as his expectation of others as disinterested in him, which had typically triggered angry outbursts. In our work together, we had recognised "separations" to be salient interpersonal events that activated this particular object relationship. When Karl had walked into the room for his final session, he was gripped internally by his familiar, internal separation scenario, in which he was no longer handing a gift to his helpful therapist/object but to a disinterested therapist/object.

Had I simply thanked him for the gift or agreed to open it, this would have deprived Karl of an opportunity to give voice to the anger about ending as he perceived me as wanting to get rid of him. In the event, once these feelings were aired and explored, it became possible for Karl to say that he did want me to keep his gift. In turn, it was possible for me to accept the gift from Karl, who was then able to relate to his experience of therapy as one that had helped him and that he was sorry to let go of.

Interpreting the Unconscious Meaning of Endings

The experience of loss often acts as a spur to seeking psychological help. The loss can be actual, as in somebody's death, but often it is a symbolic loss as, for example, when we feel we have lost a sense of who we are. The process of therapy itself can be construed from the outset as a process that activates loss and aims to facilitate a working through of various losses as the patient is faced with what he wishes had been and what may never be. Ending therapy recapitulates early losses and often mobilises intense anxieties about separation and the impossibility of being one with the object. As we reach the ending with our patients, we typically know them well enough to anticipate the emotional quality that the ending will acquire for them. We will be in a good position to guess, for example, that a particular patient will react with anger that usually masks anxiety about being abandoned.

The experience of ending will be affected at least in part by how the ending is negotiated. Time limited therapy that is dictated by service demands and/or the therapist's assessment of what the patient requires can arouse a range of phantasies in the patient who may become the passive recipient of someone else's decision, be it the therapist's or the anonymous organisation's. In long-term therapy, the ending is usually a matter of joint negotiation, though less frequently it may be imposed by external exigencies, as discussed above, which are beyond the control of either party. Even where endings are mutually agreed upon, the patient may nonetheless be prey to a host of phantasies about why we even agree with him to end.

In brief therapy, the fact that the patient knows of the ending from the outset does little to avert the phantasies that are often activated as the ending approaches. No matter how amenable or even positive the patient's conscious response to the ending, it is best not to be seduced by it. It will always be closer to the truth to anticipate a mixed response, even when the work has gone well and the patient has made gains. A key task in the termination phase is, therefore, to identify the unconscious phantasy that the patient has about why the therapy is coming to an end.[1] Such phantasies usually operate whether or not the ending has been planned. However, they are more likely when the therapist ends the therapy and the patient is presented with a situation he has no control over. These phantasies mostly concern the patient's view of the therapist's mind and her perceived intentions in relation to the patient. In other words, they reflect the patient's experience of himself in relation to his object. Broadly speaking, the phantasies are of two kinds, each typically, but not exclusively, linked to borderline/psychotic or neurotic levels of personality organisation:

Paranoid/manic phantasies

- *Paranoid phantasies* reveal how the therapist is experienced as malevolently or carelessly leaving the patient behind because she no longer wants to see the patient. In these cases, the patient's own hostility about ending is projected into the therapist, who is then experienced as the one who is harming him by leaving.
- *Manic phantasies* reflect the operation of primitive defensive manoeuvres to manage the ending by either attributing to the therapist a sense of failure and incompetence (e.g. the patient who views the ending as proof of the therapist's inability to manage him because he is too difficult) or by retreating into an omnipotent denial of the therapist's significance in the patient's life (e.g. the patient who denies any feelings of loss and diminishes or devalues the therapist's helpfulness in his own mind).

Neurotic phantasies

- *Depressed phantasies* reveal the patient's preoccupation about his impact on the therapist, for example, a phantasy that the therapist is ending the work – or at the very least not discouraging the patient from ending – because she finds the patient boring or too demanding. In such cases, there may be associated guilt for the phantasised damage the patient fears he has caused as a result of his own anger towards the therapist for ending and an anxiety about not having sufficient time before the therapy ends to make reparation.

---

[1] I am indebted to Heather Wood for this helpful way of formulating one of the therapeutic tasks as we work towards an ending with patients.

- *Oedipal phantasies* reveal the patient's preoccupation with who else occupies the therapist's mind and who is experienced as more loveable, interesting or exciting than the patient. Two qualitatively different phantasies have an oedipal flavour. In one version, the therapist is thought to be ending the therapy because she has a more special patient in mind. In the second version, the therapist is ending because there is another patient who needs her more (e.g. "I understand we have to stop. There are more needy people than me"). The latter reflects a defensive approach to the existence of the rival – it is a defensive "giving up" of one's space to an "other" that usually masks resentment.

Clinical Indicators for Ending

A commonly voiced criticism of psychoanalytic therapists is that they keep their patients on in interminable therapies and foster unnecessary dependency.[2] It is fair to say that in contrast to other therapeutic modalities, the question of how we know when an analytic therapy has come to an end has been explored less systematically than it deserves. On the whole, our patients are unlikely to arrive to a session one day exclaiming: "I've worked through the depressive position. I'm ready to go now". The majority of patients do not track their progress in this way but may yet have a sense that they are ready to end. Patients often raise the possibility of stopping therapy but feel uncertain about whether it would be the right thing to do. They tend to turn to us and ask for guidance. Mostly, we will take such a question as an invitation to explore further what lies behind it. In other words, we tend to take the lead from the patient with regards to ending on the basis of his associations to the idea of ending. But unless we are clear about the criteria we use to determine when it is time to end, we cannot formulate why we might agree or disagree with the patient's own feeling about the best time to end.[3]

When we respond to a patient's wish to end, we need to monitor our own needs as they may get in the way of not ending. Given that the analytic process is an ongoing one, that is, there is no way of concluding a therapy with the feeling that all has been covered, as therapists we need to be able to bear with our patients the imperfections of the process and the inevitability of living with conflict.

---

[2] It is of note that in one of the few available studies, Firestein (1982), looking at senior analysts, found contrary to his own expectations that in many cases the decision to end was instigated by the analyst.
[3] Working in public heath service settings where the end is often externally dictated through protocols for how long patients can be seen, relieves us of the task of having to think about how one assesses whether a patient is ready to end.

Criteria for ending are linked to the theoretical models that define our view of mental health. The decision to end is partly related to goals and initial contracts, though in many cases these are refined as therapy progresses and are sometimes quite different to the initial ones, especially over the course of a longer-term therapy. In brief therapy, however, both patient and therapist articulate focal areas of conflict at the outset and these can be used to track change and evaluate the therapy and hence the appropriateness of ending.

It is well recognised that the goals of psychoanalytic therapy are less specific, more broad ranging and developmental, such that clear-cut criteria for ending can appear redundant. Its primary goal to help the patient understand his own mind is difficult to evaluate in any simple manner. This might explain why some therapists have resorted to somewhat woolly criteria for ending such as Ferenczi's (1927) suggestion that a therapy should end "when it dies of exhaustion".

In a surprising number of cases, a long therapy ends reactive to some external event that acts as a trigger, for example, getting married, having children, moving house, changing jobs. Any one of these events can provide a nodal point for negotiating an ending stimulating a fruitful working through of key conflicts.

In *Analysis Terminable & Interminable*, Freud (1937) outlined two conditions for ending: when there is no longer suffering from symptoms and when what has been repressed has been made conscious and the internal resistances have been conquered. It is of note that Freud did not scorn symptomatic improvement. Indeed, it would be churlish to dismiss this kind of improvement as meaningless. However, most therapists would view symptomatic improvement as insufficient to warrant the ending of therapy. This is because, as Winnicott wisely warned; "*You may cure your patient and not know what it is that makes him or her go on living. . . absence of psychoneurotic illness may be health but it is not life*".

Klein (1950) outlined somewhat different, as well as overlapping, criteria for termination to Freud's, consistent with her model of the mind. She suggested that a patient is ready to end when he demonstrates a capacity for heterosexual relationships, for love and work, a diminution of persecutory and depressive anxieties, increased ego strength and stability. Some of these criteria are obviously valid; others, such as a capacity for heterosexuality might be viewed more suspiciously as implying normative values about sexual orientation and its relationship to pathology than as legitimate goals of treatment and hence a criterion for the appropriate time to end.

Some therapists take the position that the patient is ready to end when he can perceive the therapist as she really is rather than distorted through the lens of transference. This criterion, however, is unsatisfactory since it is well recognised that the transference continues once therapy is finished. The idea that the patient is ready to finish when he has resolved his transference can thus only be at best an approximate guide rather than an absolute criterion since, presumably, just like all relationships in our lives, the relationship to the therapist will continue to be based partly on phantasy, unless we are suggesting that it is possible to achieve a state in which our internal world ceases to have an impact on us.

It is generally acknowledged that a patient ending therapy is not exempt from conflicts. As Hartmann put it: *"A healthy person must have the capacity to suffer and to be depressed"* (1964: 6). If we take this one step further, we might suggest that a healthy person is one that has this capacity because he can reflect on his own mental states. Being able to reflect on our mental states allows us to think about ourselves as prey to conflicting emotions or states of mind in response to internal and external triggers. It gives us a perspective on our own mind that allows us to tolerate changing moods because we can think about why we may be feeling in a particular way. Such a perspective allows us to manage effectively the ups and downs of our affective experiences. Indeed, nowadays many contemporary therapists view a capacity for self-reflection, akin to an internalisation of the analytic function, as a very important criterion for termination.

In my own practice, there are several indicators that I consider to be helpful guides in thinking about the progress of an analytic therapy. I have in mind here how I evaluate work with patients who have engaged in a longer-term therapy and who have sought help with quite diffuse difficulties. In brief work goals are more specific and related to a circumscribed area of conflict, which is the focus of the work.

The criteria I use are broad and need to be considered together rather than in isolation. Moreover, they are all relative rather than absolute criteria that can only be meaningfully considered in relation to the specific patient whose ending is being explored:

- *Is the patient suffering?* Although symptomatic presentations are but the tip of the iceberg, as we approach ending we must not neglect whether the patient is still suffering from the symptoms that initially brought him to therapy. We are not looking for a complete eradication of symptoms: at times of stress we can all fall back on symptomatic compromises. However, a degree of modification in the intensity or frequency of the presenting symptoms or problems can be reasonably expected.

- *What is the overall quality of the patient's relationships?* A healthy relationship is not one free of conflict. Rather, it is one that can survive conflict and overcome it constructively without recourse to the institution of rigid defence mechanisms. We are therefore essentially interested in the patient's capacity to sustain whole object relationships. Whole object relating allows for an experience of others that acknowledges their autonomy from the self. This relies on the patient's capacity to own his aggression, and to demonstrate a capacity to experience guilt and remorse in his relationships, along with a wish for reparation.

- *Can the patient tolerate triadic relationships?* One of the most significant developmental challenges is the move from dyadic to triadic relationships. How the patient manages this is therefore an important consideration. The essence of the Oedipus complex, as we have seen in earlier chapters, is that it confronts us with a real difference between our actual place in the world and our wishes: the reality of our parents' relationship with each other is a prototype of a relationship in which we are observers, not participants, however much we may want to be in on the scene, as it were. The feelings of exclusion and rivalry this gives rise to have to be managed internally, otherwise they can cause havoc in relationships.

- *Can the patient face reality?* It is not just the psychotic patient who cannot face up to reality. Neurotic patients too find myriad ways to falsify or evade reality. Facing reality,[4] as I am using the expression here, denotes a capacity to tolerate internally our own imperfections and limitations – and those of others – and to manage life's givens, frustrations and disappointments. An essential part of development is the relinquishment of our omnipotence: it is through giving up this illusion, no matter how comforting, that we can be in contact with other people, that is, to relate to them realistically, with all of their imperfections and all their qualities that might arouse envy.

- *Can the patient reflect on his feelings?* It is never a question of whether there is conflict but of how much and how this is managed internally and externally. Here, we are looking for evidence that the patient can think about his internal affective states without acting on them impulsively to rid himself of anxiety.

---

[4]In a similar vein, Money-Kyrle (1971) talked about the importance of psychically tolerating the "facts of life". He believed that the aim of psychoanalysis was "the recognition of the breast as a supremely good object, the recognition of the parents' intercourse as a supremely creative act and the recognition of the inevitability of time and ultimately death".

- *What is the patient's relationship to work?* Given that we all spend so much of our waking lives at work, the patient's functioning in the work setting, where applicable, is an important consideration. We are interested in the patient's capacity to focus on the task in hand, to engage with colleagues, to be able to be part of a team and to manage the inevitable rivalry and competitiveness this may give rise to.

   It is also important to consider the patient's relationship to *not* working as work can also be used defensively. In other words, we are looking at the patient's capacity to tolerate his own thoughts and anxieties without immersing himself in work or over working as a way of avoiding intimacy with others.

- *What is the patient's relationship to play and fun?* According to Winnicott, health depends on the capacity to love, work *and* play. Playing, as Freud pointed out, may be fun, but it is also the means through which the child discovers what is real. Play is considered to be central to emotional development because it bridges unconscious phantasy and external reality. The patient's capacity to be playful is thus very important. It implicitly reflects the patient's appreciation of the dialectical interplay between internal and external reality such that he can allow himself to enter a transitional space where thoughts and feelings can be played with, without this arousing too much anxiety.

   An assessment of how free the patient is to be creative is a related criterion. The capacity to be creative rests on a capacity to entertain wishes and possibilities about the future in the context of an awareness of the limitations that are imposed upon us (Caper, 2000). Once again, this is linked to the capacity to relinquish omnipotence.

- *Does the patient have a sense of humour?* One of the most gratifying changes that can be observed over the course of a therapy is the development of the patient's sense of humour. The ability to recognise our own shortcomings and our capacity for forgiveness are intimately related to our ability to adopt a humorous attitude towards our own predicament. This, in turn, rests on the extent to which we can manage depressive anxieties.

NEGOTIATING ENDINGS

Planned Endings

In brief therapy, the ending date is agreed upon when the therapy begins and becomes a part of the work of therapy from the very outset. By contrast, in open-ended therapy, the ending is usually led by the progress in the therapy and the patient's goals. The termination date is eventually set together with the patient and worked towards. Preferably, a date is set some months away from the time the decision to end is taken, so as to give ample opportunity to work though the termination phase. Nevertheless, it is best if the date is not so far ahead into the future that it prevents the patient from actually connecting with the reality of an impending separation. For some patients, it is only when an end has been set that the work actually begins. The feelings that ending stirs up can be used very fruitfully to bring to the fore conflicts and anxieties that may have been hitherto difficult to analyse. Endings are thus not only a time of sadness and loss, but also a time of therapeutic opportunity.

Once an end date has been set this should be adhered to. Postponement of an agreed ending may occasionally be necessary if events in the patient's life lead to a marked deterioration in the patient's mental state or bring to the fore important issues the patient wishes to address. However, we need to be mindful of the fact that some patients will do all they can to avoid ending and can be very adept at finding compelling reasons for postponing an end. More often than not, the decision to postpone an agreed end reflects an attempt by one or both parties to avoid the pain of separation. It is thus important to explore the patient's wish to avoid ending and to monitor in ourselves the temptation to agree to postpone an end date.

Unplanned Endings

Unplanned endings are surprisingly common. Premature termination brought about by unexpected life events can feel very difficult for both parties. The therapist's or patient's illness or relocation abroad may curtail suddenly a process that both therapist and patient had anticipated to be a long-term, ongoing process. Such abrupt endings may leave behind a trail of unfinished business, but they may also be opportunities. In the psychoanalytic world, we are so accustomed to thinking long term that we forget that the majority of people often have little opportunity to engage in long-term therapy and yet derive significant benefits from brief therapeutic contracts that do not allow for months of working through. The pressure of real time may constructively challenge some patients into facing up to core anxieties and conflicts as they have to come to terms with an enforced separation.

Yasmin had been in therapy for four months, twice weekly. When we had started therapy, we agreed on an open-ended contract that reflected Yasmin's wish to take stock of her life. Having turned fifty, there were many aspects of her life that she wished to review: she had not been able to have a family and her husband had left her two years previously. In childhood, her mother had left the family home when she was aged six and she had not seen her since. She had developed a very close attachment to her father who had never remarried. She told me that as a child she had found it very difficult whenever he had brought female friends to the house as she worried he might re-marry. Her jealousy had also been a problem in her adult life throughout her marriage.

Yasmin was the ideal analytic patient. She free-associated spontaneously and assiduously reflected on my interpretations in between sessions. She made me feel like I was a very good therapist, often praising me. As far as Yasmin was concerned, the therapy had been progressing well. I increasingly grew to feel, however, that my interpretations led us nowhere. I had the feeling that in five months we had stood still, as if Yasmin was cosy in the knowledge that we were not going anywhere.

As we entered the fifth month of therapy, Yasmin left a message on my answer phone the day before the session to say she could not make the session the next day. Her voice sounded brittle, on the edge of tears. I was left feeling both concerned and somewhat perplexed by the absence of any explanation for the cancellation, especially since her tone of voice clearly conveyed distress. Whenever she had cancelled before, she had always left an explanation. Two days later, she left a second message cancelling the second session of that week. Once again she sounded distressed yet measured but left no explanation as to why she could not make it. This time I felt as if she was keeping me in suspended animation and I noted my irritation at this.

When Yasmin returned the following week, she announced that she could no longer continue with the therapy. She told me that her father had been diagnosed as terminally ill and had been given only a few months to live. As the only child, she felt that she needed to nurse him. Since he lived abroad, she had resigned from her job and she told me that she was set to fly out to be with her father two weeks later. She said that she was very upset about having to end therapy but that she had no choice under the circumstances. We thus only had four sessions to end. Although we had not been meeting for very long, four sessions seemed like a very short time to end.

The news of her father's ill health had shocked Yasmin, and for the first time, she seemed more connected with her feelings rather than trying, as she usually did, to say the right thing. In light of the deeply upsetting news about her father, I was surprised that I found myself reflecting once again on her two telephone messages that did not leave any reason for her absence rather than simply focussing on the impact of her father's ill health. A part of me felt that the messages were of little significance in the wider context of what had happened and yet I also felt that if I ignored my hunch I might be missing something that could be of help to Yasmin. In this context, I decided to explore further the manner in which Yasmin had managed the recent events with relation to me, that is, I began by taking up the tantalising quality of the messages she left on my answerphone. This seemed like an opportunity to explore another aspect to her that contrasted with the ideal patient she had strived to be up until that point.

After my intervention, Yasmin was at first angry and resistant to exploring my suggestion. Her angry response made me question my intervention. She said that she could not remember what she had said in her messages. She then added that in any case none of this was important anymore. Once again, as she spoke I found myself feeling shut out as if now there was only space in her mind for Yasmin and her father and no one else existed or should intrude into this special relationship, all the more so as she now so feared its loss. Although I felt more hesitant about my hunch, I nevertheless went ahead with a tentative interpretation informed by my countertransference and what I knew from our work together about Yasmin's relationship with her father.

As a starting point for my interpretation, I reflected within myself on the impact of the way Yasmin left the messages: I had felt like the excluded third who was not being told what was happening. I was kept waiting, not understanding yet feeling that something quite serious had happened to Yasmin. I was aware too from the work we had done to date that her mother's departure had been sudden and Yasmin had never really understood why she had left her. I used this to inform a very tentative intervention: I suggested to Yasmin that maybe there had been a part of her that had wanted me to know something about how it felt to not be "in the know". This, we were able to understand, closely matched her own experience of her mother's sudden departure. In response to my interpretation, Yasmin recounted to me for the first time how she had been asleep the evening before her mother left but had been woken up by a loud argument between her parents. She recalled getting up and going into their bedroom to see what was happening as she had felt very afraid. She said their voices were "so different to usual" as if she could not recognise them. When she opened the door, her mother had pushed her away saying, "This is nothing to do with you. Go to bed". Yasmin became very distressed as she told me this story.

Over the remaining three sessions we were able to explore these feelings further. The unexpected news of her father's ill health, coupled with the suddenness of the end of therapy, acted as catalysts for an emotional re-run of a very significant early scenario. Within our relationship, I became the little Yasmin who was left out of the picture, and had to work out alone the meaning of the distress I had detected in her voice, just as she had done when she heard her parents arguing the night before her mother left. In this case, the unexpected ending thus facilitated the exploration of a dynamic that had hitherto been inaccessible.

The decision to end can arise as a form of resistance. For example, the patient may feel that there are irreconcilable differences between himself and the therapist and expresses a wish to end. The patient's decision to leave therapy because he feels misunderstood by his therapist would incline most therapists – often justifiably – to consider such a decision in terms of the transference and to try to work with the patient to enable him to remain in therapy. In my experience, the majority of such cases are resolved through a sensitive understanding of the transference and its interpretation, thereby containing the patient and averting a premature ending. If the patient persists in wanting to end, and in our opinion this constitutes a form of acting out, it is important to share this understanding. It is not a question of coercing patients to stay in treatment but of remaining true to the analytic stance of understanding and leaving it up to the patient to make his decisions on the basis of the fullest understanding possible of the dynamics driving the decision. We have a professional duty to share with our patient what we think may be happening. Nevertheless, if the patient persists in his decision, even if we disagree with it, then we need to support him as best we can until he ends therapy.

Often the patient's experience of feeling misunderstood by his therapist is a manifestation of a negative transference and requires interpretation. Nevertheless, occasionally therapies come to an unexpected end as a result of an unhelpful "fit" between patient and therapist that should not be attributed either primarily or exclusively to the patient's pathology or to his particular transference. We all recognise that "fit" is an important variable in therapy, even if a poorly understood one. There is no reason to suppose that just because someone is a therapist she can reach all patients in equally helpful ways. In fact, most therapists would recognise that they work more effectively with some patients than others. It is therefore important to remain alert to the possibility that the patient's wish to end therapy with us is not always a form of resistance to be interpreted and ascribed to his psychopathology. This requires self-integrity and supervision as any rejection by a patient can feel wounding and may lead us to interpret in a defensive manner.

One ending that is impossible to ever prepare our patients for is that brought on by our own death. Anticipating our own death is difficult but when we choose to work as therapists, we undertake an important commitment that necessitates planning for our patients' welfare in the event of our death. Most training organisations now have policies about this and requires that we make arrangements for this. Usually the most helpful approach is to leave the names and contact details of the patients we are seeing with a colleague who is charged with the responsibility of contacting our patients in the event of our death or serious accident. Our elected colleague would also have responsibility for making alternative arrangements for the patients. They are, therefore, in a very important position in relation to our patients and the selection of this person is a decision that requires much thought. It is someone we need to trust.

RESISTANCES IN THE TERMINATION PHASE

Each patient reacts to termination in highly idiosyncratic ways but, generally speaking, for the vast majority, feelings of loss and separation anxiety are never too far away. These feelings are not always expressed directly. Since ending stirs a lot of ambivalence, it is unsurprising to find that as the therapy approaches termination, this phase is ripe for acting out. Strictly speaking, acting out refers to the bypassing of a secondary representation of a feeling (i.e. not being able to think about a feeling); instead it is expressed indirectly through action. The most common forms of acting out in the termination phase are as follows:

- *The patient misses sessions* (especially the last one). This is one way in which the patient turns what may feel like the passive experience of being left into an active one, whereby he is the one to do the leaving. With some patients in particular, it becomes important to actively help them to link their ambivalence about ending with their missed sessions as the ending approaches so as to pre-empt them from missing the final session.
- *The patient has nothing to talk about* in the last few sessions. This is often the patient's way of discharging aggression, leaving the therapist feeling impotent and redundant and the one who has to work hard to reach the patient.
- *The patient's symptoms reappear or deteriorate.* Patients often recapitulate old patterns in the termination phase and in doing so express a wish to begin treatment again. The return of symptoms may also be used to attack the therapist, showing her what a bad job she has done as the symptoms have not been "cured".

- *The patient rejects others in his life.* The wish to have a "good" ending can mitigate against the free expression of ambivalent feelings towards the therapist. This can give rise to a displacement of the hostility he may be feeling towards the therapist onto other people in his life.
- *The patient avoids ending by replacing the therapist* with another therapist or helping figure, thereby reversing the patient's own anticipated experience of being supplanted in the therapist's attentions once the therapy has come to an end. The seamless transition from one therapist to another is one way of denying the pain of separation and loss.

TECHNIQUE AND THERAPEUTIC STYLE IN THE TERMINATION PHASE

Ending therapy does not require any particular techniques. It simply requires of us that we remain attuned to the meaning termination has for the patient and for ourselves. An effort needs to be made to help the patient face the ending with all the attendant ambivalence and anxieties.

A common question about endings is whether the therapeutic relationship changes as we approach the end, for example, whether it becomes more gratifying or self-disclosing. Like any relationship, the therapeutic one slowly evolves over time as both therapist and patient find their own unique rhythm. Just as the patient reveals characteristic ways of relating, so do our ways of responding to his communications become more familiar to the patient over time. Both participants grow in confidence with each other: the patient dares to say more about what is on his mind and we too become less hesitant in our interventions. By the time the ending nears, we are familiar with one another's quirks and idiosyncrasies.

As the transference has been worked through over the course of a therapy, the patient hopefully relates to his "real" therapist more than to his phantasised one. One of the tasks of ending involves helping the patient to develop a more realistic relationship to us. This is a natural and desirable by-product of the patient's increasing awareness of his projections. As we near the end of therapy, we can support this more reality-attuned relationship by engaging in a review of the work,[5] allying ourselves with the patient's reflecting ego. The experience of two adults taking stock of the work of therapy and thinking about what has changed and may yet have to change is a form of collaborative activity that reinforces the adult, more realistic selves of both patient and therapist.

---

[5] I am not referring to a directed review of the work. Rather, I have in mind a receptive attitude to the patient's own attempts to review progress.

Some therapists, on the other hand, approach the task of helping the patient to develop a more realistic relationship to them by relaxing the therapeutic boundaries. This may take the form, for example, of varying degrees of self-disclosure. Any deviation from the analytic attitude and the boundaries of the therapeutic frame even as a therapy comes to a close requires careful consideration because we always need to keep in mind the possibility that the patient may well require our help in the future. In other words, we need to balance an acknowledgement that two real people are saying goodbye, which might involve a more direct expression of particular feelings and attitudes, along with retaining enough distance to allow the patient to return into therapy at a future stage without feeling that we have now somehow become "more like a friend". This is a very difficult balancing act.

There is no doubt in my mind that very real and deeply affecting attachments develop over the course of therapy between us and our patients. Although aspects of the therapeutic interaction are intrinsically gratifying for the patient, such as having one person's undivided attention for fifty minutes, therapy arouses other longings that we do not gratify either in the patient or in ourselves. This is why pain and frustration are an inevitable part of the therapeutic experience. This can arouse intense conflicts in both parties. I can think of several patients whom I have liked a great deal, and were it not for the circumstances in which we met, I would most probably have enjoyed developing a friendship with them. Yet, by becoming therapists, we make a choice that precludes such gratifications. Much as we like our patients, our warmth and affection towards them is more safely conveyed through our understanding of the pain of separation, our capacity to let go of them and to enjoy their achievements whilst renouncing the gratification of our own needs. Changing gear completely at the end of the therapy, for example, by being more self-disclosing may reinforce fantasies – conscious and unconscious – that the relationship is one that can become what one wishes it could be. If we allow this to happen we dilute the work of mourning its loss, substituting pain for an illusion.

Although we need to monitor our behaviour and guard against slipping into a non-analytic role, in my experience subtle changes do occur in the therapeutic relationship, often spontaneously and imperceptibly, as the ending approaches. For example, in my practice, although I would rarely give direct feedback to a patient during an ongoing therapy, as the end approaches I find it helpful to give some realistic appraisal of how the therapy has proceeded and to enjoy with the patient in his achievements, without shying away from what could not be achieved. Bearing the imperfections of the therapy together is an important part of ending and of helping the patient to develop a realistic relationship with us. In the last session, as we part, I make some more personal reference to the experience of our work together and warmly wish the patient well.

POST-THERAPY CONTACT

Post-termination contact can include a range of interactions: letters, phone calls, e-mails, face-to-face meetings and social meetings. Whether we have any such contact is most probably influenced by our own analytic experiences with our therapists. Indeed a recent study of analysts by Schachter & Brauer (2001) confirmed this: those analysts who made themselves available to their patients after termination had maintained strong feelings of attachment to their own analysts. In this study, the analysts who reported frequently, consciously thinking about their own analysts were also contacted more frequently by their patients, suggesting an effect of the therapist on post-termination rather than the contact being a function of the patient.

What kind of contact, if any, we should have with our patients once therapy has finished is a controversial topic. In one sense there is no rational justification for not having any kind of contact at all with the patient after the end of therapy. But if we do have contact, we need to think carefully about why we may be setting this up as it may reflect difficulties – on both sides – with letting go. The post-therapy period is rife with opportunities for acting out on both parts, as Kubie suggests:

> Even an entirely innocent informality creates an opportunity for the analyst to turn to the patient with his own needs. . . . Unconsciously he [the analyst] feels, 'I have been the giver. Now it's my turn to be given'. . . . I have seen more than one magnificent analytic job destroyed by the premature invasion of an intrinsically innocent and platonic social relationship into the post analytic period (1968: 345).

How we manage post-therapy contact is a very individual matter for each of us to consider. In my own work, in the last session, if the patient expresses a wish to write to me to let me have news of his life, I warmly indicate my pleasure at receiving some news. In my experience, a minority of patients do not ask if this is possible, fearing a rejection. Typically, these are patients who have been quite deprived or neglected and who have little hope that the object will be interested in them. This is why it is my practice to convey explicitly to these patients my interest in hearing news if they so wish to let me know how they get on.

Most patients want to leave the door open as they approach the end. Some request a follow-up and want to arrange it in the last session, whilst others find that they make contact eventually even though they might not have anticipated a need to do so when the therapy ended. If a patient asks for a pre-arranged follow-up, I am inclined to explore this quite extensively before agreeing to it since it usually denotes considerable anxiety about ending that is best worked through rather than assuaged by the false reassurance of a follow-up meeting. With more disturbed patients, however, follow-ups can be very valuable as they allow the patient to feel there is a safety net if things do not work out and indeed they might not. In these situations, I would more readily agree to seeing the patient a few months down the line to review progress.

During follow-ups, I strive to maintain a professional but more interactive manner. For example, if I have not seen the patient for some time and the patient comments on change in the room or in my appearance, I would acknowledge that things are different and that perhaps that might feel disorienting, but I would not approach such a comment or question with silence or an interpretation as would be my normal inclination if such a comment were made in the context of an ongoing therapy. This is because I am not wishing to encourage any kind of regression; rather, unless the patient has decompensated, the aim of the follow-up is to reinforce the patient's adult, reality-oriented self. Nevertheless, I would keep my answers brief and quickly shift the focus back onto the patient.

The follow-up meetings take place face-to-face. I generally let the patient take the lead and tell me whatever it is that he wishes me to know. I ask questions more liberally than I would do if it were an ongoing therapy. I do not interpret the patient's material, unless it becomes apparent that the patient is contemplating returning into therapy or if they are evidently anxious about something. My basic stance is one of interest in the developments in the patient's life since ending therapy: it is a broadly supportive stance rather than exploratory.

Even if no arrangements were made at the end of therapy to meet the patient, we may yet meet him by chance. Again, how this is managed varies. If I meet a patient outside the confines of the consulting room, whether during or after the end of therapy, I greet him discretely but warmly. If the therapy has ended and the patient clearly wants to approach me and exchange a few words, I will happily engage with this. It can feel very rejecting to the patient if we barely acknowledge him in a public place.

Other kinds of contact post-termination of therapy pose potentially significant problems, though they may be very tempting for both patient and therapist. The question of whether one should have any kind of social contact with a patient after the end of therapy is a challenging one. As with many aspects of the therapeutic frame, how and whether we have contact with patients can never be reduced to some simple guidelines. Being prescriptive in these matters seldom helps since each case deserves special consideration. Those of us who go on to train as therapists will most probably encounter our training therapists in professional and possibly even social situations. The transition from being a patient to becoming a colleague is likely to arouse a lot of intense feelings. Likewise for the patient who is not a therapist but who establishes a more social contact with his ex-therapist.[6] Although consciously this may feel very gratifying, at another level there is often a price to pay. The moment a more friendly, social rapport is established, it becomes impossible to rewind to the patient–therapist relationship. The boundaries of these two relationships are different: you can't exchange pleasantries over tea and then discuss your sexual fantasies.

Some therapists suggest that the patient who cannot manage the transition from therapy to social contact has not worked through his transference. To my mind, this represents a serious error of judgement. If the transference, as we generally understand it, is ubiquitous to the extent that all our relationships are filtered through varying degrees of projection, then the transference can never be fully worked through. Of course, by the end of the therapy we hope that the patient will have re-owned enough of his projections to allow him to relate to us more realistically. But being able to relate to us more realistically does not necessarily mean that the patient should feel comfortable having a social relationship with us. Indeed the patient's difficulty, as it were, to shift to a more social relationship may reflect his "realistic" appreciation that the analytic relationship does not end once therapy is over and that to pretend otherwise is a denial of the reality of that relationship as it lives on inside the patient. The goal of therapy is not to help the patient to reach a position where he can manage to feel relaxed about meeting his therapist socially; rather, it is to help the patient tolerate the limitations of this relationship without resorting to denigration or idealisation.

Once therapy is finished, no matter how much the transference has been worked through, we remain for our patients someone who has privileged knowledge about them. Being interested in our patients once therapy is over and meeting them for follow-ups can be a helpful way of allowing them to maintain a live connection with us. However, if we undertake to be therapists, even when we experience a particular resonance with some of our patients, we need to maintain the boundaries necessary to

---

[6] I am not referring here to anything other than social contact. Sexual contact with a former patient is, in my opinion, invariably damaging, no matter how many years have lapsed since the end of the therapy.

Table 8.1   Preparing for ending

- Make contracts clear and specific at the outset.
- In brief therapy, work with the ending from the start – keep referring to it in each session as a reminder from the middle phase onwards and explore the patient's reactions to this, systematically.
- In longer-term therapy, ensure that you have sufficient time to prepare for the ending (one year or several months rather than weeks depending on the overall length of the therapy).
- Think about whether there are particular features of the patient's background and experiences that might make him especially sensitive to endings and how these earlier experiences will colour his experience of the ending.
- Try to put into words the unspoken feelings/phantasies stimulated by the ending.
- Encourage the patient to express affect related to ending. Normalise the experience of anger, sadness and loss if the patient is struggling to express his feelings.

---

allow them to come back into therapy with us should they need to. The job of being a therapist requires that we renounce some of our wishes so as to remain available to the patient well after the therapeutic contract has ended.

FURTHER READING

Molnos, A. (1995) *A Question of Time*. London: Karnac Books.

REFERENCES

Ablon, J. & Jones, E. (1999) Psychotherapy process in the National Institute of Mental Health treatment of depression collaborative research programme. *Journal of Consulting and Clinical Psychology*, **67**(1): 64–75.

Adler, E. & Bachant, J. (1996) Free association and analytic neutrality: the basic structure of the psychoanalytic situation. *Journal of the American Psychoanalytic Association*, **44**: 1021–1046.

Ainsworth, M., Blehar, M., Waters, E. & Wall, S. (1978) *Patterns of Attachment: A Psychological Study of the Strange Situation*. Hillstain, NJ: Laurence Erlbaum Associates.

Akhtar, S. (2000) From schisms through synthesis to informed oscillation: an attempt at integrating some diverse aspects of psychoanalytic technique. *Psychoanalytic Quarterly*, **69**(2): 265–288.

Alexander, F. & French, T. (1946) *Psychoanalytic Therapy: Principles and Applications*. New York: Ronald Press.

Alvarez, A. (1992) *Live Company*. London: Routledge.

Baker, R. (2000) Finding the neutral position: patient and analyst perspectives. *Journal of the American Psychoanalytic Association* **48**(1): 129–153.

Balint, A. & Balint, M. (1939) On transference & countertransference. *International Journal of Psychoanalysis*, **20**: 225–230.

Balint, M. (1968) *The Basic Fault: Therapeutic Aspects of Regression*. London: Tavistock Publications.

Barber, J., Crits-Christoph, P. & Luborski, L. (1996) Effects of therapist adherence and competence on patient outcome in brief dynamic therapy. *Journal of Consulting and Clinical Psychology*, **64**: 619–622.

Bateman, A. (2000) Integration in psychotherapy: an evolving reality in personality disorder. *British Journal of Psychotherapy*, **17**(2): 147–156.

Beebe, B. & Lachmann, F. (1988) The contribution of mother/infant mutual influence to the origins of self and object representations. *Psychoanalytic Psychology*, **5**: 305–330.

Beebe, B. & Lachmann, F. (1994) Representation and internalisation in infancy: three principles of salience. *Psychoanalytic Psychology*, **11**: 127–165.

Berger, B. (1999) Deprivation and abstinence in psychoanalytic psychotherapy. *Israel Journal of Psychiatry and Related Sciences*, **36**(3): 164–173.

Bion, W. (1962a) A theory of thinking. *International Journal of Psychoanalysis*, **43**: 306–310.

Bion, W. (1962b) Learning from experience. In W.R. Bion (Ed.) *Seven Servants: Four Works*. New York: Jason Aronson.

Bion, W. (1967) *Second Thoughts*. London: Karnac Books.

Bion, W. (1970) *Cogitations*. London: Karnac Books.

Blagys, M. & Hilsenroth, M. (2000) Distinctive features of short term psychodynamic interpersonal psychotherapy: a review of the comparative psychotherapy process literature. *Clinical Psychology Science and Practice*, **7**: 167–188.

Blatt, S., Auerbach, J. & Levy, K. (1997) Mental representations in personality development, psychopathology and the therapeutic process. *Review of General Psychology*, **1**(4), 351–374.

Bloch, S., Browning, S. & McGrath, G. (1983) Humour in group psychotherapy. *British Journal of Medical Psychology*, **56**: 89–97.

Blum, H. (1985) *Defence and Resistance: Historical Perspective and Current Concepts.* New York: International Universities Press.

Blum, H. (1994) *Reconstruction in Psychoanalysis.* New York: International Universities Press.

Bollas, C. (1996) Figures and their function: on the oedipal structure of a psychoanalysis. *Psychoanalytic Quarterly*, **65**: 1–20.

Bollas, C. (1999a) The goals of psychoanalysis. *The Mystery of Things*. London: Routledge.

Bollas, C. (1999b) *The Mystery of Things*. London: Routledge.

Bond, M., Banon, E. & Grenier, M. (1998) Differential effects of interventions on the therapeutic alliance with patients with personality disorders. *Journal of Psychotherapy Practice and Research*, **7**: 301–318.

Bram, A. & Gabbard, G. (2001) Potential space and reflective functioning: towards conceptual clarification & preliminary clinical implications. *International Journal of Psychoanalysis*, **82**: 685–699.

Brazelton, B. & Cramer, B. (1991) *The Earliest Relationship*. London: Karnac Books.

Brennan, K. & Shaver, P. (1994) Dimensions of adult attachment, affect regulation and romantic relationship functioning. *Personality and Social Psychology Bulletin*, **21**: 267–283.

Brenneis, C.B. (1999) The Analytic present in psychoanalytic reconstructions of the historical past. *Journal of the American Psychoanalytic Association*, **47**(1): 187–201.

Brenner, C. (1982) *The Mind in Conflict*. New York: International Universities Press.

Brenner, C. (1994) The mind as conflict and compromise formation. *Journal of Clinical Psychoanalysis*, **3**: 473–488.

Brenner, C. (2000) Observations on some aspects of current psychoanalytic theories (In Process Citation). *Psychoanalytic Quarterly*, **69**(4): 587–632.

Brewin, C. (1997) Psychological defences and distortion of meaning. In M. Power & C. Brewin (Eds) *The Transformation of Meaning in Psychological Therapies*. Chichester: Wiley.

Brewin, C., Andrews, B. & Gotleib, I. (1993): Psychopathology and early experience: a reappraisal of retrospective patterns. *Psychological Bulletin*, **113**: 82–98.

Britton, R. (1989) The missing link: parental sexuality in the Oedipus complex. In R. Britton, M. Feldman & E. O'Shaughnessy (Eds) *The Oedipus Complex Today*. London: Karnac Books.

Britton, R. (1991) The Oedipus situation and the depressive position. In R. Anderson (Ed.) *Clinical Lectures on Klein & Bion*. London: Routledge.

Britton, R. (1998) *Belief and Imagination*. London: Routledge.

Britton, R. & Steiner, J. (1994) Interpretation: selected fact or overvalued idea? *International Journal of Psychoanalysis*, **75**: 1069–1078.

Busch, F. (2000) What is a deep interpretation? *Journal of the American Psychoanalytic Association*, **48**(1): 237–254.

Caper, R. (1999) *A Mind of Ones Own*. London: Routledge.

Caper, R. (2000) *Immaterial Facts: Freud's Discovery of Psychic Reality and Klein's Development of his Work*. London: Routledge.

Carlsson, E. & Sroufe, L. (1995) Contribution of attachment theory to developmental psychopathology. In D. Cicchetti & D. Cohen (Eds) *Developmental Psychopathology: Vol. 1: Theory & Methods*. New York: Wiley.

Casement, P. (1985) *On Learning from the Patient*. London: Routledge.

Chessick, R.D. (2000) Psychoanalysis at the millennium. *American Journal of Psychotherapy*, **54**(3): 277–290.

Clowther, J. (1968) *Difficulties in the Analytic Encounter*. London: Free Association Books & Maresfield Library.

Coles, R. (1992) *Anna Freud: The Dream of Psychoanalysis*. New York: Addison-Wesley.

Couch, A. (1979) *Therapeutic Functions of the Real Relationship in Psychoanalysis*. Unpublished paper. Revised version of a paper on The Role of the Real Relationship in Analysis given at a scientific meeting at the Boston Psychoanalytic Society on 10.01.79.

Crits-Christoph, P. & Connelly, M.B. (1999) Alliance and technique in short term dynamic therapy. *Clinical Psychology Review*, **19**(6): 587–704.

Crits-Christoph, P., Cooper, A. & Luborsky, L. (1998) The measurement of accuracy of interpretations. In L. Luborsky & P. Crits-Christoph (Eds) *Understanding Transference: The Core Conflictual Relationship Method*. Washington, DC: American Psychological Association.

Damasio, A. (1999) *The Feeling of What Happens*. London: Heinemann.

David, L. & Vaillant, G. (1998) Anonymity, neutrality and confidentiality in the actual methods of Sigmund Freud. *American Journal of Psychiatry*, **155**: 163–171.

Dewald, P. (1982) The clinical importance of the termination phase. *Psychoanalytic Enquiry*, **2**: 441–461.

Druck, A. (1998) Deficit & conflict: an attempt at integration. In S. Ellman, S. Grand, M. Silvan & S. Ellman (Eds) *The Modern Freudians: Contemporary Psychoanalytic Technique*. Northvale, NJ, NY: Jason Aronson.

Dunn, J. (1995) Intersubjectivity in psychoanalysis: a critical review. *International Journal of Psychoanalysis*, **76**: 723–738.

Edgecumbe, R. (2000) *Anna Freud*. London: Routledge.

Etchegoyen, R. (1991) *The Fundamentals of Psychoanalytic Technique*. London: Karnac Books.

Fairbairn, W. (1954) *An Object-Relations Theory of the Personality*. New York: Basic Books.

Fairbairn, W. (1958) On the nature and aims of psychoanalytical treatment. *International Journal of Psychoanalysis*, **39**: 374–385.

Ferenczi, S. (1919) On the technique of psychoanalysis. *Further Contributions to the Theory and Technique of Psychoanalysis*. New York: Basic Books.

Ferenczi, S., (1927) *Final Contributions*. London: Hogarth.

Ferris, P. (1997) *Dr. Freud: A Life*. London: Random House.

Firestein, S. (1982) Termination of psychoanalysis: theoretical, clinical and paedagogic considerations. *Psychoanalytic Enquiry*, **2**: 473–497.

Flax, J. (1981) Psychoanalysis and the philosophy of science. *Journal of Philosophy*, **78**: 561–569.

Fonagy, F., Gergely, G., Jurist, E. & Target, M. (2002) *Affect Regulation, Mentalisation and the Development of the Self*. London: Other Press.

Fonagy, I. & Fonagy, P. (1995) Communication with pretend actions in language, literature and psychoanalysis. *Psychoanalysis and Contemporary Thought*, **18**: 363–418.

Fonagy, P. (1982) Psychoanalysis and empirical science. *International Review of Psychoanalysis*, **9**: 125–145.

Fonagy, P. (1989) On the integration of psychoanalysis and cognitive-behaviour therapy. *British Journal of Psychotherapy*, **5**: 557–563.

Fonagy, P. (1996) The future of an empirical psychoanalysis. *British Journal of Psychotherapy*, **13**: 106–118.

Fonagy, P. (1999a) Relation of theory and practice in psychodynamic therapy. *Journal of Clinical Child Psychology*, **28**(4): 513–520.

Fonagy, P. (1999b) Memory and therapeutic action. *International Journal of Psychoanalysis*, **80**(2): 215–224.

Fonagy, P. (2001) *Attachment Theory and Psychoanalysis*. New York: Other Press.

Fonagy, P. & Target, M. (1996) Playing with reality, 1: theory of mind and a normal development of psychic reality. *International Journal of Psychoanalysis*, **77**: 217–233.

Fonagy, P. & Target, M. (2000) Playing with reality, 3: the persistence of dual psychic reality in borderline patients. *International Journal of Psychoanalysis*, **81**(5): 853–874.

Fonagy, P., Kachele, H., Krause, R., Jones, E., Perron, R. & Lopez, L. (1999) *An Open Door Review of Outcome Studies in Psychoanalysis*. London: International Psychoanalytical Association.

Fonagy, P., Steele, H., Moran, G., Steele, M. and Higgitt, A. (1991) The capacity for understanding mental states: the reflective self in parent and child and its significance for security of attachment. *Infant Mental Health Journal*, **12**: 201–218.

Fonagy, P., Target, M. & Gergely, G. (2000) Attachment and borderline personality disorder: a theory and some evidence. *Psychiatric Clinics of North America*, **23**(1): 103–122, vii–viii.

Forrester, J. (1997) *Truth Games*. Cambridge, MA: Harvard University Press.

Frayn, D. (1992) Assessment factors associated with premature psychotherapy termination. *American Journal of Psychotherapy*, **46**: 250–261.

Freedman, N., Hoffenberg, J.D., Vorus, N. & Frosch, A. (1999) The effectiveness of psychoanalytic psychotherapy: the role of treatment duration, frequency of sessions and the therapeutic relationship. *Journal of the American Psychoanalytic Association*, **47**(3): 741–772.

Freud, A. (1936) *The Ego and the Mechanisms of Defence*. London: Karnac Books.

Freud, A. (1954) The widening scope of indications for psychoanalysis. *Journal of the American Psychoanalytic Association*, **2**: 607–620.

Freud, A. (1965) *Normality and Pathology in Childhood: Assessments of Development*. London: Penguin Books.

Freud, S. (1899) *Screen Memories*. Standard Edition 3.

Freud, S. (1900) *The Interpretation of Dreams*. Standard Edition 4.

Freud, S. (1905) *Studies in Hysteria*.

Freud, S. (1910) *The Future Prospects of Psychoanalytic Therapy*. Standard Edition 11.

Freud, S. (1912) *The Dynamics of Transference*. Standard Edition 12.

Freud, S. (1913) *On Beginning the Treatment: Further Recommendations on the Technique of Psychoanalysis*. Standard Edition 12.

Freud, S. (1914) *Remembering, Repeating & Working Through*. Standard Edition 12.

Freud, S. (1915a) *Repression*. Standard Edition 14.

Freud, S. (1915b) *Observation on Transference Love*, Standard Edition 12.

Freud, S. (1919) *Lines of Advance in Psychoanalytic Therapy*. Standard Edition 17.

Freud, S. (1920) *Beyond the Pleasure Principle*, Standard Edition 18.

Freud, S. (1921) *Group Psychology and the Analysis of the Ego*. Standard Edition 18.

Freud, S. (1923a) *Two Encyclopaedia Articles*. Standard Edition 18.

Freud, S. (1923b) *The Ego and the Id*. Standard Edition 19.

Freud, S. (1926) *Inhibition, Symptoms and Anxiety*. Standard Edition 20.

Freud, S. (1930) *Civilization and its Discontents*. Standard Edition 21.

Freud, S. (1937) *Analysis: Terminable and Interminable*. Standard Edition 23.

Freud, S. & Breuer, J. (1895) *Studies on Hysteria*, Standard Edition 2.

Friedman, L. (1999) Why is reality a troubling concept? *Journal of the American Psychoanalytic Association*, **47**: 401–425.

Friedman, L. (2000) Modern hermeneutics and psychoanalysis. *Psychoanalytic Quarterly*, **69**(2): 225–264.

Frosh, S. (1997a) *For and Against Psychoanalysis*. London: Routledge.

Frosh, S. (1997b) Most modern narratives: or muddles in the mind. In R. Papadopoulos & J. Byng-Hall (Eds) *Multiple Voices: Narrative and Systemic Family Psychotherapy*. London: Routledge.

Gabbard, G. (1994) *Psychodynamic Psychiatry in Clinical Practice*. Washington, DC: American Psychiatric Press.

Gabbard, G. (1995) Countertransference: the emerging common ground. *International Journal of Psychoanalysis*, **76**: 475–485.

Gabbard, G., Horowitz, L., Allen, J., Frieswyk, S., Newsome, J., Colson, D. & Coyne, L. (1994a) Transference interpretation in the psychotherapy of borderline patients: a high risk high gain phenomenon. *Harvard Review of Psychiatry*, **2**: 59–69.

Gabbard, G., Horowitz, L., Allen, J., Frieswyk, S., Newsome, J., Colson, D. & Coyne, L. (1994b) The effect of therapist's interventions on the therapeutic alliance of borderline patients. *Journal of the American Psychoanalytic Association*, **36**: 697–727.

Gaston, L. (1990) The concept of the alliance and its role in psychotherapy: theoretical and empirical considerations. *Psychotherapy*, **27**: 143–153.

Gay, P. (1988) *Freud: A Life for Our Time*. New York: W.W. Norton & Co.

Gedo, J. (1986) *Conceptual Issues in Psychoanalysis: Essays in History and Method*. Hillsdale, NJ: The Analytic Press.

Gergely, G. (1991) Developmental reconstructions: infancy from the point of view of psychoanalysis and developmental psychology. *Psychoanalysis and Contemporary Thought*, **14**: 3–55.

Gergely, G. & Watson, J. (1996) The social bio-feedback model of parental affect mirroring. *International Journal of Psychoanalysis*, **77**: 1181–1212.

Gill, M. (1954) Comments on neutrality interpretation, therapeutic intent. Letter to the Editor. *Journal of the American Psychoanalytic Association*, **42**: 681–684.

Gill, M. (1979) The analysis of transference. *Journal of the American Psychoanalytic Association*, **27**(Suppl.): 263–288.

Gill, M. (1994) Comment on "Neutrality, Interpretation and Therapeutic Intent". Letter to the Editor. *Journal of the American Psychoanalytic Association*, **42**: 681–684.

Giovacchini, P. (1985) Introduction: counter-transference responses to adolescents. *Adolescent Psychiatry*, **12**: 447–467.

Gitelson, M. (1952) The emotional position of the therapist in the psychoanalytic situation. *International Journal of Psychoanalysis*, **33**: 1–10.

Glassman, N. & Andersen, S. (1999) Activating transference without consciousness: using significant-other representations to go beyond what is subliminally given. *Journal of Personality and Social Psychology*, **77**: 1146–1162.

Glenn, J. (1980) Notes on psychoanalytic concepts and style in Freud's case histories. In M. Kanzer & J. Glenn (Eds) *Freud and his Patients*. New York: Jason Aronson.

Glover, E. (1955) *The Technique of Psychoanalysis*. New York: International Universities Press.

Goldfried, M. & Weinberger, R. (1998) Towards a more clinically valid approach to therapy research. *Journal of Consulting and Clinical Psychology*, **66**: 143–150.

Good, M. (1998) Screen reconstructions, traumatic memories, communication and the problem of verification in psychoanalysis. *Journal of American Psychoanalytic Association*, **46**: 149–183.

Goodyer, I. (1990) *Life Experiences, Development and Childhood Psychopathology.* Chichester: John Wiley & Sons.

Green, A. (2000) What kind of research for psychoanalysis? In J. Sandler, A. Sandler & R. Davies (Eds) *Clinical & Observational Psychoanalytic Research: Roots of a Controversy.* London: Karnac Books.

Greenberg, J. (1996) Psychoanalytic words and psychoanalytic acts. *Contemporary Psychoanalysis*, **32**: 195–203.

Greenson, R. (1967) *The Technique and Practice of Psychoanalysis.* London: Karnac Books.

Greenson, R. & Wexler, M. (1969) The non transference relationship in the psychoanalytic situation. *International Journal of Psychoanalysis*, **50**: 27–39.

Greenspan, S. (1977) The oedipal-pre-oedipal dilemma: a reformulation in the light of object relations theory. *International Review of Psychoanalysis*, **4**: 381–391.

Grinberg, L. (1990) *The Goals of Psychoanalysis.* London: Karnac Books.

Hamilton, V. (1996) *The Analyst's Preconscious.* Hillsdale, NJ: The Analytic Press.

Hanly, C. (1999) On subjectivity and objectivity in psychoanalysis. *Journal of the American Psychoanalytic Association*, **47**: 427–444.

Hartmann, H. (1950) *Egopsychology and the Problem of Adaptation.* New York: International Universities Press.

Hartmann, H. (1964) *Essays on Egopsychology.* New York: International Universities Press.

Heimann, P. (1943) Some aspects of the role of introjection in early development. In P. King & R. Steiner (Eds) *The Freud–Klein Controversies 1941–1945.* London: Routledge.

Heimann, P. (1950) On countertransference. *International Journal of Psychoanalysis*, **31**: 81–84.

Heimann, P. (1960) Countertransference 2. *British Journal of Medical Psychology*, **33**: 9–15.

Hesse, E. & Main, M. (2000) Disorganised infant, child and adult attachment: collapse in behavioural and attentional strategies. *Journal of the American Psychoanalytic Association*, **48**: 1097–1127.

Hilliard, R.B., Henry, W.P. & Strupp, H.H. (2000) An interpersonal model of psychotherapy; linking patient and therapist developmental history, therapeutic process and types of outcome.. *Journal of Consulting and Clinical Psychology*, **68**(1): 125–33.

Hinshelwood, R. (1989) *A Dictionary of Kleinian Thought.* London: Free Association Books.

Hinshelwood, R. (1991) Psychodynamic formulation in assessment for psychotherapy. *British Journal of Psychotherapy*, **8**(2): 166–174.

Hinshelwood, R. (1995) Psychodynamic formulation in assessment for psychoanalytic psychotherapy. In C. Mace (Ed.) *The Art & Science of Assessment in Psychotherapy.* London: Routledge.

Hinshelwood, R. (1999) Countertransference. *International Journal of Psychoanalysis*, **80**: 797–818.

Hirshberg, L. (1993) Clinical interview with infants and their families. In C. Zeanah (Ed.) *Handbook of Infant Mental Health.* New York: Guildford Press.

Hobson, P. (2002) *The Cradle of Thought.* London: Macmillan.

Hoffman, I. (1992) Some practical implications of the social constructivist view of the psychoanalytic situation. *Psychoanalytic Dialogues*, **2**: 287–304.

Høglend, P. (1993) Suitability for brief dynamic psychotherapy. *Acta Psychiatrica Scandinavica*, **88**: 104–110.

Høglend, P. (1996) Long term effects of transference interpretations: comparing results from a quasi-experimental and a naturalistic long-term follow-up study of brief dynamic psychotherapy. *Acta Psychiatrica Scandinavica*, **93**(3): 205–211.

Hoglend, P., Fossum, A. & Sorbye, O. *et al* (1992) Selection criteria for brief dynamic psychotherapy. *Psychotherapy and Psychosomatics*, **57**: 67–74.

Holmes, J. (1998) Defensive and creative uses of narrative in psychotherapy: an attachment perspective. In G. Roberts & J. Holmes (Eds) *Narrative in Psychotherapy and Psychiatry*. Oxford: Oxford University Press.

Horvath, A. & Symonds, B. (1991) Relation between working alliance and outcome in psychotherapy: a meta-analysis. *Journal of Consulting and Clinical Psychology*, **38**: 139–149.

Horwitz, L. (1974) *Clinical Prediction in Psychotherapy*. New York: Aronson.

Hurvich, M. (1998) The influence of object relations theory on contemporary Freudian technique. In C. Ellman, S. Grand, M. Silven & S. Ellman (Eds) *The Modern Freudians: Contemporary Psychoanalytic Technique*. Northvale, NJ: Jason Aronson.

Inderbitzin, L.B. & Levy, S.T. (2000) Regression and psychoanalytic technique: the concretization of a concept. *Psychoanalytic Quarterly*, **69**(2): 195–233.

Jackson, M. & Williams, P. (1994) *An Imaginable Storm: A Search for Meaning in Psychosis*. London: Karnac Books.

Jacobs, T. (2001) On misreading and misleading patients: some reflections on communications, miscommunications and counter-transference enactments. *International Journal of Psychoanalysis*, **82**: 653–670.

Jones, A. (1997) Experiencing language: some thoughts on poetry and psychoanalysis. *Psychoanalytic Quarterly*, **66**: 683–700.

Jones, E. (1997) Modes of therapeutic action. *International Journal of Psychoanalysis*, **78**: 1135–1150.

Jones, E. & Pulos, F. (1993) Comparing the process in psychodynamic and cognitive behavioural therapies. *Journal of Consulting and Clinical Psychology*, **61**: 306–316.

Jones, E., Cumming, J. & Horowitz, M. (1988) Another look at the non specific hypothesis of therapeutic effectiveness. *Journal of Consulting and Clinical Psychology*, **56**: 48–55.

Joseph, B. (1981) Defence mechanisms and fantasy in the psychoanalytical process. In B. Joseph (Ed.) *Psychic Equilibrium and Psychic Change*. London: Routledge.

Joseph, B. (1983) On understanding and not understanding some technical issues. *International Journal of Psychoanalysis*, **64**: 291–298.

Joseph, B. (1985) Transference: the total situation. *International Journal of Psychoanalysis*, **66**: 447–454.

Joseph, B. (2000) Agreeableness as obstacle. *International Journal of Psychoanalysis*, **81**(4): 641–650.

Joyce, A. & Piper, W. (1993) The immediate impact of transference interpretation in short term individual psychotherapy. *American Journal of Psychotherapy*, **47**: 508–526.

Kandel, E. (1999) Biology and the future of psychoanalysis: a new intellectual framework for psychiatry revisited. *American Journal of Psychiatry*, **156**: 505–524.

Kaplan-Solms, K. & Solms, M. (2000) *Clinical Studies in Neuro-Psychoanalysis*. London: Karnac Books.

Katz, E. (1999) When is enough enough? The process of termination with an older patient. In S. Ruszczynski & S. Johnson (Eds) *Psychoanalytic Psychotherapy in the Kleinian Tradition*. London: Karnac Books.

Kernberg, O. (1965) *Countertransference in Borderline Conditions and Pathological Narcissism*. North Vale, NJ: Jason Aronson.

Kernberg, O. (1976) *Object Relations Theory and Clinical Psychoanalysis*. New York: Jason Aronson.

Kernberg, O. (1984) *Severe Personality Disorders: Psychotherapeutic Strategies*. Newhaven, CT: Yale University Press.

Kernberg, O. (1985) *Internal World and External Reality: Object Relations Theory Applied*. New York: Jason Aronson.

Kernberg, O. (1986) Institutional problems of psychoanalytic education. *Journal of the American Psychoanalytic Association*, **34**: 799–834.

Kernberg, O.F. (1997) The nature of interpretation: intersubjectivity and the third position. *American Journal of Psychoanalysis*, **57**(4): 297–312.

Kernberg, O. (1999) Psychoanalysis, psychoanalytic psychotherapy and supportive psychotherapy: contemporary controversies. *International Journal of Psychoanalysis*, **18**(6): 1075–1092.

Kernberg, O.F. (2000) The influence of the gender of patient and analyst in the psychoanalytic relationship (In Process Citation). *Journal of the American Psychoanalytic Association*, **48**(3): 859–883.

Kernberg, O. (2002) Present challenges to psychoanalysis. In M. Leuzinger-Bohleber & M. Target (Eds) *Out Comes the Psychoanalytic Treatment*. London: Whurr Publishers.

Kernberg, O., Burnstein, E., Coyne, L., Appelbaum, A., Horowitz, L. & Voth, H. (1972) Psychotherapy and psychoanalysis: final report of the Menninger Foundation's Psychotherapy Research Project. *Bulletin of the Menninger Clinic*, **36**: 1–275.

Kihlstrom, J. (1987) The cognitive and conscious. *Science*, **237**: 1445–1452.

King, P. (1977) Affective responses of the therapist to the patient's communication. *International Journal of Psychoanalysis*, **61**(4): 451–573.

Kirkpatrick, L. & Davis, K. (1994) Attachment style, gender and relationship stability: a longitudinal analysis. *Journal of Personality and Social Psychology*, **66**: 502–512.

Kirsner, D. (2000) *Unfree Associations: Inside Psychoanalytic Institutes*. London: Process Press.

Kirsner, D. (1990) Mystics and professionals in the culture of American psychoanalysis. *Free Associations*, **20**: 85–104.

Klauber, J. (1981) *Difficulties in the Analytic Encounter*. London: Jason Aronson.

Klauber, J. (1986) *Difficulties in the Analytic Encounter*. London: Free Association Books and Maresfield Library.

Klein, M. (1946) Notes on some schizoid mechanisms. In M. Klein, M. Heimann, S. Isaacs & J. Riviere (Eds) *Developments in Psychoanalysis*. London: Karnac Books.

Klein, M. (1950) On the criteria for the termination of a psychoanalysis. *International Journal of Psychoanalysis*, **31**: 78–80.

Klein, M. (1952) The origins of transference. *Envy and Gratitude and Other Works*. London: Virago.

Klein, M. (1957) *Envy and Gratitude*. London: Virago.

Kradin, R. (1999) Generosity: a psychological and interpersonal motivational factor of therapeutic relevance. *Journal of Analytical Psychology*, **44**(2): 221–236.

Kris, A. (1994) Freud's treatment of a narcissistic patient. *International Journal of Psychoanalysis*, **75**: 649–664.

Kris, E. (1956) The recovery of childhood memories in psychoanalysis. *Psychoanalytic Study of the Child*, **11**: 54–91.

Krupnick, J., Sotsky, S., Elkin, I., Watkins, J. & Pilkonis, P. (1996) The role of the therapeutic alliance in psychotherapy and pharmocotherapy outcome: findings in the National Institute of Mental Health treatment of depression collaborative research programme. *Journal of Consulting and Clinical Psychology*, **64**(3): 352–539.

Kubie, L. (1968) Unsolved problems in the resolution of the transference. *Psychoanalytic Quarterly*, **37**: 331–352.

Lachmann, F. & Beebe, B. (1996) Three principles of salience in the patient/analyst interaction. *Psychoanalytic Psychology*, **13**: 1–22.

Laplanche, J. (1998) Time and the other. In *Essays on Otherness*. London: Routledge.

LeDoux, J. (1994) Emotion, memory and the brain. *Scientific American*, **270**: 32–39.

LeDoux, J. (1995) Emotion: clues from the brain. *Annual Review of Psychology*, **46**: 209–235.

LeDoux, J., Romanski, L. & Xagorarise, A. (1989) Indelibility of subcortical emotional memories. *Journal of Cognitive Neuroscience*, **1**: 238–243.

Lemma, A. (1999) Starting from scratch: developing clinical psychology services in Bangladesh. *Psychodynamic Counselling*, **5**(2): 193–204.

Lemma, A. (2000) *Humour on the Couch*. London: Whurr Publishers.

Levine, H.B. & Friedman, R.J. (2000) Intersubjectivity and interaction in the analytic relationship: a mainstream view. *Psychoanalytic Quarterly*, **69**: 63–92.

Levy, S.T. & Inderbitzin, L.B. (2000) Suggestion and psychoanalytic technique (In Process Citation). *Journal of the American Psychoanalytic Association*, **48**(3): 739–758.

Lipton, S. (1977) The advantages of Freud's technique as shown in his psychoanalysis of the Ratman. *International Journal of Psychoanalysis*, **58**: 255–273.

Lipton, S. (1979) An addendum to the advantages of Freud's technique as shown in his analysis of the Ratman. *International Journal of Psychoanalysis*, **60**: 215, 216.

Little, M. (1951) Countertransference and the patient's responses to it. *International Journal of Psychoanalysis*, **32**: 32–40.

Loewenstein, R. (1958) Remarks on some variations in psychoanalytic technique. *International Journal of Psychoanalysis*, **38**: 202–210.

Lopez-Corvo, R.E. (2000) Self-envy and intrapsychic interpretation. *Psychoanalytic Quarterly*, **68**(2): 209–219.

Louw, F. & Pitman, M. (2001) Irreducible subjectivity and interactionism: a critique. *International Journal of Psychoanalysis*, **80**: 747–765.

Lowental, U. (2000) Defence and resistance in the psychoanalytic process. *Psychoanalytic Review*, **87**(1): 121–135.

Luborsky, L. & Crits-Cristoph, P. (1998) *Understanding Transference*. Washington, DC: American Psychological Association.

Lucas, R. (1992) The psychotic personality: a psychoanalytic theory and its applications in clinical practice. *Psychoanalytic Psychotherapy*, **6**: 73–79.

Lyons-Ruth, K. (1999) The two person unconscious: intersubjective dialogue, inactive relational representation and the emergence of new forms of relation organisation. *Psychoanalytic Enquiry*, **19**(4): 576–615.

Main, M. (1995) Adult attachment classification system. In M. Main (Ed.) *Behaviour and the Development of Representational Models of Attachment: Five Methods of Attachment*. Cambridge: Cambridge University Press.

Malan, D. (1976) *The Frontier of Brief Psychotherapy: An Example of the Convergence of Research & Clinical Practice*. New York: Plenum Press.

Malan, D. (1979) *Individual Psychotherapy and the Science of Psychodynamics*. London: Butterworth.

Malan, D. (1980) *Towards the Validation of Dynamic Psychotherapy*. New York: Plenum Press.

Mason, A. (2000) Bion and binocular vision. *International Journal of Psychoanalysis*, **81**: 983–989.

Meehl, P. (1994) Subjectivity in psychoanalytic inference: the nagging persistence of Wilhelm Fliess' Achensee Question. *Psychoanalysis Contemporary Thought*, **17**: 3–82.

Meissner, W.W. (2000) On analytic listening. *Psychoanalytic Quarterly*, **69**(2): 317–367.

Milner, B., Squire, L. & Candle, E. (1998) Cognitive neuroscience and the study of memory. *Neuron Review*, **20**: 445–468.

Milton, J. (1997) Why assess? Psychoanalytic assessment in the NHS. *Psychoanalytic Psychotherapy*, **11**(1): 47–58.

Mitchell, S. (1995) Interaction in the Kleinian and interpersonal tradition. *Contemporary Psychoanalysis*, **31**: 65–91.

Mitrani, J. (2001) Taking the transference: some technical implications in three papers by Bion. *International Journal of Psychoanalysis*, **82**(6): 1085–1104.

Mollon, P. (2002) *Shame & Jealousy*. London: Karnac Books.

Molnos, A. (1995) *A Question of Time*. London: Karnac Books.

Money-Kyrle, R. (1956) Normal countertransference and some of its deviations. *International Journal of Psychoanalysis*, **37**: 360–366.

Money-Kyrle, R. (1971) The aim of psychoanalysis. *International Journal of Psychoanalysis*, **52**: 103–106.

Moore, B. & Fine, B. (1990) *Psychoanalytic Terms and Concepts*. Newhaven, CT: Yale University Press.

Morehead, D. (1999) Oedipus, Darwin & Freud: one big happy family? *Psychoanalytic Quarterly*, **68**(3): 347–375.

Novick, J. & Novick, K.K. (2000) Love in the therapeutic alliance. *Journal of the American Psychoanalytic Association*, **48**(1): 189–218.

Ogden, T. (1986) *The Matrix of the Mind: Object Relations and the Psychoanalytic Dialogue*. North Vale, NJ: Jason Aronson.

Ogden, T. (1994) The analytic third: working with intersubjective clinical facts. *International Journal of Psychoanalysis*, **75**: 3–19.

Ogrodniczuk, J.S., Piper, W.E., Joyce, A.S. & McCallum, M. (1999) Transference interpretations in short-term dynamic psychotherapy. *Journal of Nervous Mental Disorders*, **187**(9): 571–578.

Ogrodniczuk, J.S., Piper, W.E., Joyce, A.S. & McCallum, M. (2000) Different perspectives of the therapeutic alliance and therapist technique in 2 forms of dynamically oriented psychotherapy. *Canadian Journal of Psychiatry*, **45**(5): 452–458.

Olivier, C. (1989) *Jocasta's Children*. London: Routledge.

Orgel, S. (2000) Letting go: some thoughts about termination. *Journal of the American Psychoanalytic Association*, **48**(3): 719–738.

Pally, R. (2000) *The Mind–Brain Relationship*. London: Karnac Books.

Paniagua, C. (1991) Patients surface, clinical surface and workable surface. *Journal of the American Psychoanalytic Association*, **39**: 669–685.

Pedder, J. (1988) Termination reconsidered. *International Journal of Psychoanalysis*, **69**: 495–505.

Perelberg, R. (1999) Psychoanalytic understanding of violence & suicide: a review of the literature and some new formulations. In R. Perelberg (Ed.) *Psychoanalytic Understanding of Violence & Suicide*. London: Routledge.

Phillips, A. (1997) *Foreword to Truth Games*. Cambridge, MA: Harvard University Press.

Phillips, A. (2001) Equalities. *Journal of the British Association of Psychotherapists*, **39**: 125–138.

Pine, F. (1981) In the beginning: contributions to a psychoanalytic developmental psychology. *International Review of Psychoanalysis*, **8**: 15–33.

Pine, F. (1998) *Diversity and Direction in Psychoanalytic Technique*. Newhaven, CT: Yale University Press.

Piper, W.E. & Duncan, S.C. (1999) Object relations theory and short-term dynamic psychotherapy; findings from the quality of object relations scale. *Clin Psychol Rev*, **19**(6): 669–685.

Piper, W.E., Azim, H.F., Joyce, A.S. & McCallum, M. (1991) Transfer interpretations, therapeutic alliance and outcome in short term individual psychotherapy. *Archive of General Psychiatry*, **48**: 946–953.

Piper, W.E., McCallum, M., Joyce, A.S., Azim, H.F. & Ogrodniczuk, J.S. (1999) Follow-up findings for interpretative and support forms of psychotherapy and patient personality variables. *Journal of Consulting and Clinical Psychology*, **67**(2): 267–273.

Pope, K., Keith-Spiegel, P. & Tabachnick, B. (1995) Sexual attraction to clients. In K. Pope, J. Sonne & J. Holroyd (Eds) *Sexual Feelings in Psychotherapy*. Washington: American Psychological Association.

Quinton, D. & Rutter, M. (1985a) Parenting behaviour of mothers raised in care. In A. Nicol (Ed.) *Longitudinal Studies in Child Psyhcology and Psychiatry*. Chichester: John Wiley & Sons.

Quinton, D. & Rutter, M. (1985b) Family pathology and child psychiatric disorders: a four year prospective study. In A. Nicol (Ed.) *Longitudinal Studies in Child Psyhcology and Psychiatry*. Chichester: John Wiley & Sons.

Rapheal-Leff (1991) *Psychological Processes of Childbearing*. London: Chapman & Hall.

Rayner, E. (1991) *The Independent Mind in British Psychoanalysis*. London: Free Association Books.

Reed, G.S. The analyst's interpretation as fetish. (1997) *Journal of the American Psychoanalytic Association*, **45**(4): 1153–1181.

Reich, W. (1928) On character analysis. In R. Fliess (Ed.) *The Psychoanalytic Reader*. London: Hogarth.

Reik, T. (1948) *Listening with the Third Ear: The Inner Experience of a Psychoanalyst*. New York: Farrar, Straus & Giroux.

Renik, O. (1993) Analytic interaction: conceptualising technique in light of the analyst's irreducible subjectivity. *Psychoanalytic Quarterly*, **62**: 553–571.

Renik, O. (1998a) The analyst's subjectivity and the analyst's objectivity. *International Journal of Psychoanalysis*, **79**: 487–497.

Renik, O. (1998b) Getting real in analysis. *Psychoanalytic Quarterly*, **67**: 566–593.

Reich, W. (1949) *Character Analysis*. New York: International Universities Press.

Rieff, P. (1961) *Freud: The Mind of the Moralist*. New York: Harper & Row.

Riesenberg-Malcolm, R. (1986) Interpretation: The past in the present. In E. Bott-Spillius (Ed.) *Melanie Klein Today (2)*. London: Routledge.

Riviere, J. (1936) On the genesis of psychical conflict in earliest infancy. *International Journal of Psychoanalysis*, **17**: 395–422.

Rorty, R. (1989) *Contingency, Irony and Solidarity*. Cambridge: Cambridge University Press.

Rosenberg, V. (1999) Erotic transference and its vicissitudes in the counter-transference. In S. Johnson & S. Ruszczynski (Eds) *Psychoanalytic Psychotherapy in the Independent Tradition*. London: Karnac Books.

Rosenfeld, H. (1987) *Impasse and Interpretation*. London: Routledge.

Ross, J.M. (1999) Once more onto the couch, consciousness and preconscious defences on psychoanalysis. *Journal of the American Psychoanalytic Association* 47(1): 91–111.

Roth, P. (2001) Mapping the landscape: levels of transference interpretation. *International Journal of Psychoanalysis*, **82**(3): 533–544.

Roth, A. & Fonagy, P. (1996) *What Works for Whom?* London: Guildford Press.

Roys, P. (1999) Recollection and historical reconstruction. In S. Ruszczynski & S. Johnson (Eds) *Psychoanalytic Psychotherapy in the Kleinian Tradition*. London: Karnac Books.

Sacret, J. (1999) Inter-relationships between internal and external factors in early development: current Kleinian thinking and implications for technique. In S. Ruszczynski & S. Johnson (Eds) *Psychoanalytic Psychotherapy in the Kleinian Tradition*. London: Karnac Books.

Sameroff, A. (1983) Developmental systems: context and evolution In: W. Massey. (Ed) *Massey's Handbook of Child Psychology*. Vol. 1. New York: Wiley.

Sandler, J. (1976) Countertransference and role responsiveness. *International Review of Psychoanalysis*, **3**: 43–47.

Sandler, J. (1983) Reflections on some relations between psychoanalytic concepts and psychoanalytic practice. *International Journal of Psychoanalysis*, **64**: 35–45.

Sandler, J. & Dreher, A. (1996) *What do Psychoanalysts Want?* London: Routledge.

Sandler, J. & Sandler, A.M. (1984) The past unconscious, the present unconscious and interpretation of the transference. *Psychoanalytic Enquiry*, **4**: 367–399.

Sandler, J. & Sandler, A. (1997) A psychoanalytic theory of repression and the unconscious. In J. Sandler & P. Fonagy (Eds) *Recovered Memories of Abuse: True or False?* London: Karnac Books.

Sandler, J., Dare, C. & Holder, A. (1973) *The Patient & the Analyst*. London: Maresfield Library.

Schachter, J. (1992) Concepts of termination and post-termination: patient/analyst contact. *International Journal of Psychoanalysis*, **73**: 137–154.

Schachter, J. & Brauer, L. (2001) The effect of the analyst's gender and other factors on post termination patient-analyst contact. *International Journal of Psychoanalysis*, 82(6): 1123–1132.

Schaffer, J.A. (1998) Transference and countertransference interpretations: harmful or helpful in short term dynamic therapy?. *American Journal of Psychotherapy*, **52**(1): 1–17.

Schore, A. (1994) *Affect Regulation and the Origin of the Self*. Hillsdale, NJ: Laurence Erlbaum Associates.

Searles, H. (1979) *Countertransference and Related Subjects*. Madison: International Universities Press.

Segal, H. (1957) Notes on symbol formation. In *The work of Hanna Segal*. London: Jason Aronson.

Segal, H. (1993) Countertransference. In A. Alexandris & G. Vaslamatzis (Eds) *Countertransference: Theory, Technique, Teaching*. London: Karnac Books.

Shapiro, D., Reiss, A., Barkham, M., Hardy, G., Reynolds, S. & Startup, M. (1995) Effects of treatment duration and severity of depression on the maintenance of gains following cognitive behavioural and psychodynamic interpersonal psychotherapy. *Journal of Consulting and Clinical Psychology*, **63**: 378–387.

Sinason, V. (Ed.) (2002) *Attachment Trauma and Multiplicity*. London: Routledge.

Slade, A. (2000) The development and organisation of attachment: implications for psychoanalysis (In Process Citation). *Journal of the American Psychoanalytic Association*, **48**(4): 1147–1174; discussion 1175–1187.

Smith, D. (1991) *Hidden Conversations*. London: Routledge.

Solms, M. & Turnbull, O. (2002) *The Brain and the Inner World*. New York: Other Press.

Spiegel, J., Severino, S.K. & Morrison, N.K. (2000) The role of attachment functions in psychotherapy. *Journal of Psychotherapy Practice and Research*, **9**(1): 25–32.

Spence, D. (1982) *Narrative Truth and Historical Truth*. New York: W.W. Norton & Co.

Spillius, E. (1988) *Melanie Klein Today*. Volume 1, Mainly Theory, Volume 2, Mainly Practice, London: Routledge.

Spillius, E. Bott (1994) Developments in Kleinian thought: overview and personal view. *Contemporary Kleinian Psychoanalysis. Psychoanalytic Inquiry*, **14**: 324–364.

Steiner, J. (1990) Pathological organisations as obstacles to mourning: the role of unbearable guilt. *International Journal of Psychoanalysis*, **71**: 87–94.

Steiner, J. (1992) The equilibrium between the paranoid schizoid and the depressive positions. In R. Anderson (Ed.) *Clinical Lectures on Klein and Bion*. London: Routledge.

Steiner, J. (1993) *Psychic Retreat*. London: Routledge.

Steiner, J. (1996) The aim of psychoanalysis in theory and practice. *International Journal of Psychoanalysis*, **77**: 1073–1083.

Stern, D. (1985) *The Interpersonal World of the Infant*. New York: Basic Books.

Stern, D. (2000) The relevance of empirical infant research to psychoanalytic theory and practice. In J. Sandler, A. Sandler & R. Davis (Eds) *Clinical & Observational Psychoanalytic Research: Roots of a Controversy*. London: Karnac Books.

Stern, D., Sander, L., Nahum, J. et al (1998) Non-interpretative mechanisms in psychoanalytic therapy: there's something more than interpretation. *International Journal of Psychoanalysis*, **79**(5): 903–922.

Stolorow, R. & Atwood, G. (1997) Deconstructing the myth of the neutral analyst: an alternative from intersubjective systems theory. *Psychoanalytic Quarterly*, **66**: 431–449.

Strachey, J. (1934) The nature of the therapeutic action of psychoanalysis. *International Journal of Psychoanalysis*, **15**: 127–159.

Strenger, C. (1989) The classic and romantic visions in psychoanalysis. *International Journal of Psychoanalysis*, **70**: 595–610.

Stewart, H. (1990) Psychic experience and problems of technique. *International Journal of Psychoanalysis*, **71**: 61–70.

Sullivan, H. (1953) *The Interpersonal Theory of Psychiatry*. New York: W.W. Norton & Co.

Svanborg, P., Gustavsson, P. & Weinryb, R.M. (1999) What patient characteristics make therapists recommend psychodynamic psychotherapy or other treatment forms? *Acta Psychiatrica Scandinavica*, **99**(2): 87–94.

Symington, J. & Symington, N. (1996) *The Clinical Thinking of Wilfred Bion*. London: Routledge.

Szasz, T. (1963) The concept of transference. *International Journal of Psychoanalysis*, **44**: 432–443.

Tarachow, S. (1963) *An Introduction to Psychotherapy*. New York: International Universities Press.

Target, M. & Fonagy, P. (1996) Playing with reality II: the development of psychic reality from a theoretical perspective. *International Journal of Psychoanalysis*, **77**: 459–479.

Ticho, E. (1972) Termination of psychoanalysis: treatment goals, life goals. *Psychoanalytic Quarterly*, **41**: 315–333.

Truant, G.S. (1999) Assessment of suitability for psychotherapy. II assessment based on basic process goals. *American Journal of Psychotherapy*, **52**(1): 17–34.

Tuckett, D. (2001) Towards a more facilitating peer environment. *International Journal of Psychoanalysis*, **82**: 643–651.

Tyndale, A. (1999) How far is transference interpretation essential to psychic change? In S. Johnson & S. Ruszczynski (Eds) *Psychoanalytic Psychotherapy in the Independent Tradition*. London: Karnac Books.

Tyrrell, C.L., Dozier, M., Teague, G.B. & Fallot, R.D. (1999) Effective treatment relationships for persons with serious psychiatric disorders: the importance of attachment states of mind. *Journal of Consulting and Clinical Psychology*, **67**(5): 725–733.

Ursano, R. & Hales, R. (1986) A review of brief individual psychotherapies. *American Journal of Psychiatry*, **143**: 1507–1517.

Vaillant, G. (1971) Theoretical hierarchy of adaptive ego-mechanisms. *Archives of General Psychiatry*, **24**: 107–118.

Vaslamatzis, G., Markidis, M. & Katsouyanni, K. (1989) Study of the patient's difficulties in ending brief psychoanalytic psychotherapy. *Psychotherapy and Psychosomatics*, **52**: 173–178.

Viederman, M. (1991) The real person of the therapist and his role in the process of psychoanalytic cure. *International Journal of Psychoanalysis*, **39**: 451–489.

Viorst, J. (1982) Experiences of loss at the end of analysis: the analyst's response to termination. *Psychoanalytic Enquiry*, **2**: 399–418.

Wallerstein, R. (1983) Self psychology and classical psychoanalytic psychology: the nature of their relationship. In A. Goldberg (Ed) *The Future of Psychoanalysis*. New York: International Universities Press.

Wallerstein, R. (1988) One psychoanalysis or many? *International Journal of Psychoanalysis*. **69**: 5–21.

Wallerstein, R. (Ed.) (1992) *The Common Ground of Psychoanalysis*. Northvale, NJ: Jason Aronson.

Waska, R.T. (2000) Intrapsychic momentum and the psychoanalytic process. *American Journal of Psychotherapy*, **54**(1): 26–42.

Whitrow, G. (1988) *Time in History: The Evolution of our General Awareness of Time and Temporal Perspective*. Oxford: Oxford University Press.

Winnicott, D. (1947) Hate in the countertransference. *Collected Papers*. London: Tavistock Publications.

Winnicott, D. (1958) *Collected Papers: Through Paediatrics to Psychoanalysis*. London: Karnac Books.

Winnicott, D. (1962) The aims of psycho-analytical treatment. In *The Maturational Processes and the Facilitating Environment*. London: Karnac Books.

Winnicott, D. (1971) *Playing and Reality*. London: Karnac Books.

Winnicott, D. (1975) *Through Paediatrics to Psychoanalysis: Collected Papers*. London Karnac Books.

Wiser, S. & Goldfried, M. (1996) Verbal interventions in significant psychodynamic interpersonal and cognitive behavioural therapy sessions. *Psychotherapy Research*, **6**: 308–319.

Wolff, P. (1996) The irrelevance of infant observation for psychoanalysis. *Journal of the American Psychoanalytic Association*, **44**: 369–473.

INDEX

Printed in Great Britain by
Amazon.co.uk, Ltd.,
Marston Gate.